DUE DATE			
OCT 1 0 1992			
OCT 2 4 1992			
			Printed in USA

G. H. LEWES

GEORGE HENRY LEWES.

Frontispiece: G. H. Lewes. Wood-engraving in the *Popular Science Monthly* (1876) from a photograph of 1858.

G. H. LEWES

A LIFE

———— ✖ ————

ROSEMARY ASHTON

CLARENDON PRESS · OXFORD

1991

Oxford University Press, Walton Street, Oxford OX2 6DP
Oxford New York Toronto
Delhi Bombay Calcutta Madras Karachi
Petaling Jaya Singapore Hong Kong Tokyo
Nairobi Dar es Salaam Cape Town
Melbourne Auckland
and associated companies in
Berlin Ibadan

Oxford is a trade mark of Oxford University Press

Published in the United States
by Oxford University Press, New York

British Library Cataloguing in Publication Data
(Data available)

Library of Congress Cataloging in Publication Data
Ashton, Rosemary, 1947–
G. H. Lewes : a life / Rosemary Ashton.
Includes bibliographical references (p.   ) and index.
1. Lewes, George Henry, 1817–1878—Biography.   2. Eliot, George
1819–1880—Relations with men.   3. Authors, English—19th century—
Biography.   I. Title.
PR4886.L4Z55 1991 828'.809—dc20 [B] 91–2995
ISBN 0–19–812827–4

Typeset by Cambridge Composing (UK) Ltd
Printed in Great Britain by
Butler & Tanner Ltd,
Frome and London

TO

MARY HAIGHT

PREFACE

G. H. LEWES (1817–78) is best known as the consort of George Eliot, the man who encouraged her genius and managed her publishing affairs, taking on the task in the years following 1853–4, when his relationship with Marian Evans, as she then was, began. His life, in this aspect, has been well documented in the scholarly edition of the George Eliot letters and the biography of her by the late Professor Gordon S. Haight. In the seven volumes of the *Letters* (1954–6), Professor Haight included all Lewes's letters written to publishers, admirers, and friends on George Eliot's behalf. In addition, he went on to print in two supplementary volumes (1978) all the Lewes letters from 1854 which he had found, whether they had to do with George Eliot or—as in the case of Lewes's correspondence with Darwin and Huxley—not. Professor Haight also collected, but did not publish, a large number of Lewes letters from the period before 1854. These he kindly passed on to me to add to my own collection of manuscript materials.

This biography of Lewes, while giving due weight to the most important relationship of Lewes's life—told for once from *his* point of view—also describes his multifarious career in the years before 1854. It seeks to throw light on his marriage to Agnes Jervis, his relationship with his sons, and his professional career as literary reviewer, novelist, actor, dramatist, editor of a radical newspaper, and author of a number of highly readable works on literature, philosophy, and science. His friendships with members of London's intellectual and artistic bohemia—especially Leigh Hunt and his young hangers-on—with the Victorian sage, Thomas Carlyle, with Dickens and his amateur acting company, with Thackeray and London clubland, are described in detail. Lewes was, both before and after the momentous meeting with Marian Evans, a man of remarkably versatile talent, always at the leading edge of Victorian culture, innovative, even shocking, in some aspects of his life and works, but nevertheless typical of the Victorian age at its progressive, energetic best. In short, Lewes deserves a biography of his own.

As with all attempts to write the life of a man long dead, there are some gaps in the available record as constituted by letters, diaries, and journals. In Lewes's case, because of the unusual aspects of his domestic life which raised protective feelings in his and George Eliot's relatives after their deaths, many materials have been lost or destroyed. Lewes himself may have destroyed his ten journals for the years before 1856 (the existing journals are numbered from xi); and John Cross destroyed all of George Eliot's up to 1854. No letters at all between Lewes and George Eliot survive. We do not know what happened to hers; she took his with her to the grave. Between Agnes Lewes and her husband only one letter exists—an undated note from him to her during the early, happy years of their marriage. Agnes remains, despite every effort to find out more about her, a shadowy figure, appearing only occasionally in the letters of others. Only two letters by her survive: one to Lewes's older brother Edward (himself a shadowy presence), and one to a female friend on the occasion of that friend's bereavement. A few letters from the three Lewes sons written to Agnes from school in Switzerland remain, but none from her to them.

As for Lewes's early life, that has long been shrouded in mystery. I have been able to discover some facts about his immediate family—his strange father and his two older brothers, both of whom died relatively young. Of his mother comparatively little is known, though she lived until 1870 and was close to her son. Only two letters from Lewes to her survive, and one from her to him.

Yet in places the record is full. Contemporaries commented on Lewes's relationships, and Lewes had correspondences with a wide range of friends in literary and scientific circles. His relationship with Thornton Hunt, his great friend by whom Agnes had four children, at first with Lewes's blessing, is documented early on, when they met at Leigh Hunt's house as very young men beginning their journalistic careers, and again in 1849–50 when they were planning the radical paper, the *Leader*, together, but at other times the record is irritatingly bare.

Thus, though some mysteries have been solved, others remain. Remembering Lewes's remark in an article on Auguste Comte (1866)— 'In Biography, as elsewhere, we should guard against the tendency to substitute a possible evolution for an actual evolution'—I have not attempted hypotheses at moments when nothing is known. On the other hand, I have sometimes allowed myself to speculate from existing evidence, as, for example, when the problem of dating the intimacy of Lewes and Marian Evans arises. The reader is given the available facts, with my interpretation, and is at liberty to disagree with the latter if he or she wishes. The story that emerges, despite the inevitable gaps, is, I think, as full, and as full of interest, as that of many others of whom a more constant written record exists.

In the course of researching and writing this book I have been indebted to many individuals and institutions, which I list below. I must, however, single out for special thanks Jonathan Ouvry, great-great-grandson of Lewes, who has been generous with permissions and with enthusiastic help. To the late Gordon S. Haight I owe a huge debt of gratitude, having been the beneficiary of his generosity in passing on to me the fruits of years of scholarly research. To his wife Mary Haight I dedicate the book in gratitude for her continued interest and help, and for her hospitality to me and my family.

Others who have helped me in various ways are: Mrs Kathleen Adams of the George Eliot Fellowship; Professor John de Bruyn; Professor K. K. Collins of the University of Southern Illinois at Carbondale; Dr Ceri Crossley of the University of Birmingham; Dr James A. Davies of the University of Wales at Swansea; Professor Angus Easson of Salford University; Vincent Giroud of the Beinecke Rare Book and Manuscript Library, Yale University; Mrs Sheila Sokolov Grant; Dr Emma Harris of the University of Warsaw; Dr Peter Helps ; Ms Sue Holland of the City University; Dr Philip Horne, Professor Dan Jacobson, Dr Daniel Karlin, Dr Charlotte Lennox-Boyd, and Professor Karl Miller, all of University College London; Mrs Enid Nixon of Westminster Abbey Library; Ms Kate Perry of Girton College, Cambridge; Professor Terry Pickett of the University of Alabama; Mrs Sandra Roiya of the Bermuda Archives; Dr Nicolaas Rupke of the Australian National University; Dr Andrew Sanders and Dr Michael Slater of Birkbeck College, London; Professor John Sutherland; Mrs Ann Thornton; Dr Peter Vernon; Dr Keith Walker of University College London; John Wells; Mrs Sarah Wintle of University College London; Gabriel Woolf; Professor Lewis Wolpert and Dr Henry Woudhuysen of University College London; and Professor G. Ziegengeist of the Akademie der Wissenschaften, East Berlin.

I wish to thank the archivists and trustees of the following libraries and institutions for permission to consult and quote from their manuscript holdings: in London, the Bishopsgate Institute; British Library; Census Room, Portugal Street; City University; Greater London Record Office; Guildhall Library; Imperial College Library; John Murray Archives; Keats Memorial House, Hampstead; London Library; *Punch* office; Public Record Office, Chancery Lane; Royal Institution; Royal Literary Fund; Somerset House; University College London Library; University of London Library and the Athenaeum; Victoria and Albert Museum; Wellcome Institute for the History of Medicine; Westminster Abbey Library; Westminster City Libraries; Dr Williams's Library.

Other British libraries to which I am indebted are: National Library of Scotland, Edinburgh; Girton College Library, Cambridge; Bodleian Library, Oxford; Hertford County Record Office; Liverpool Record Office; Brotherton Library, Leeds; and the Co-operative Union and John Rylands University Library, both in Manchester. The following libraries abroad have given help and permissions: Beinecke Rare Book and Manuscript Library and the Sterling Memorial Library, Yale University, and the Yale Medical Library; Houghton Library, Harvard University; Princeton University Library; the Carl H. Pforzheimer Collection and the Berg Collection at the New York Public Library; Pierpont Morgan Library, New York; Folger Shakespeare Library, Washington; Boston Public Library; University of Iowa Library; University of California at Los Angeles; Henry E. Huntington Library, San Marino, California; Harry Ransom Humanities Research Center, University of Texas at Austin; and the Armstrong Browning Library, Baylor University, Texas; Bermuda Archives, Hamilton, Bermuda; Jagiellonian University Library, Cracow, Poland; Kestner-Museum, Hanover; Bayerische Staatsbibliothek, Munich.

I am grateful to the British Academy for awarding me a Research Readership, held 1989–90, to enable me to write the book, and to Yale University for a Visiting Fellowship to the Beinecke Library, Easter 1989. Special thanks go to my husband, Gerry Ashton, for his practical support during the writing of the book.

CONTENTS

LIST OF PLATES

Frontispiece

G. H. Lewes. Wood-engraving in the *Popular Science Monthly* (1876) from a photograph of 1858.

A NOTE ON SPELLINGS

Victorian spelling is often irregular or unfamiliar. I have chosen neither to modernize original spellings nor to pepper the pages of the book with [sic]. Rather, when I quote from letters and journals, I follow the original spellings and punctuations without comment. Thus the reader can expect to see 'Shakespeare' spelt 'Shakspeare', 'don't' spelt 'dont', and so on, with, on one occasion, 'prophesy' spelt 'prophecy'. When Lewes uses foreign phrases, he usually gives them the correct spellings and accents, but occasionally his French words are without the proper accents.

PART I

BEGINNINGS

I

The Son of Somebody

(1817–1836)

'ONE is always the son of somebody', wrote Lewes in a whimsical piece under the pseudonym 'Vivian' in the radical newspaper the *Leader* in 1853. In his physiological and psychological researches during the 1860s, Lewes, one of Darwin's early supporters, studied the effects of the laws of heredity and environment in the development of plants, animals, and the human species. These laws may be observed operating—not without surprises, even mysteries—in Lewes's own life. Born into social and religious unorthodoxy, Lewes, whose life spanned the middle years of the nineteenth century, was himself from first to last unconventional. Yet by one of those quirks, whether we say of fate or of accident, his unorthodox life can be seen as in a sense characteristic of the age in which he lived.

'The Victorian Age' is a phrase which covers a multitude of meanings. It was an age of faith and of corrosive doubt; of stifling conventionality relieved by unconventional practices; of apparent conservatism yet equally of liberalism and radicalism in politics—the two great Reform Acts were, after all, passed in 1832 and 1867; of industrial wealth and imperial expansion, and of urban misery for the proletariat and, beneath even that, the new subclass, Marx's lumpenproletariat. The famous opening words of Dickens's *A Tale of Two Cities* (1859), describing the time of the French Revolution, are often remembered; not so often the continuation of the sentence, which draws a direct parallel with the mid-nineteenth century itself:

It was the best of times, it was the worst of times, it was the age of wisdom, it was the age of foolishness, it was the epoch of belief, it was the epoch of incredulity, it was the season of Light, it was the season of Darkness, it was the spring of hope, it was the winter of despair, we had everything before us, we had nothing before us, we were all going direct to Heaven, we were all going direct the other way—in short, the period was so far like the present period, that some of its noisiest authorities insisted on its being received, for good or for evil, in the superlative degree of comparison only.[1]

From this set of paradoxes about the period generally we may turn to the more particular paradoxes of Lewes's life, where they are to be seen most strikingly in his two most important personal relationships. His marriage to Agnes Jervis (1822–1902) was in its openness, its taking a triangular shape to include Lewes's friend Thornton Hunt, by whom Agnes had four children between 1850 and 1857, distinctly unconventional. By contrast, his irregular liaison with Marian Evans (1819–80), begun in 1853 and lasting until Lewes's death in 1878, was, as many contemporary observers declared, more monogamous, even 'sacred', than many a legal marriage. This fact was surprising to those who knew Lewes. For the man who set off for Germany in July 1854 with the 'strong-minded woman' of the *Westminster Review*[2] (not yet known as George Eliot) was, at 37, already a well-known figure in London's radical, literary, theatrical, and bohemian circles.

In 1854 Lewes was, above all, a consummate journalist, boasting that he had access to every periodical except, as he declared with glee, 'the damned old *Quarterly*'. Thomas Carlyle, whose acquaintance he had sought as a young student of German literature and the aspiring biographer of Goethe, called him 'the Prince of Journalists'.[3] By the time he began his relationship with Marian Evans, Lewes was also the author of a radical, popularizing history of philosophy, a book on the French positivist philosopher and father of sociology, Auguste Comte, a work on the Spanish drama of the Golden Age, and two bold, if mediocre, novels, *Ranthorpe* (1847) and *Rose, Blanche, and Violet* (1848). The latter work brought a whiff of French scandal in its very title—for George Sand had collaborated (with her lover) on a novel called *Rose et Blanche* in 1831—and in its sexually frank content.[4]

Lewes had also acted in Dickens's amateur theatre company, written a tragedy on a Spanish theme, *The Noble Heart*, and acted, both in his own play and in *The Merchant of Venice*. His friends observed with fascination the versatility of Lewes, who in February 1849 visited Manchester and Liverpool to give a lecture on the history of philosophy one evening and play Shylock—taking the then novel view that Shylock is not a sheer monster but a member of the human species—the next. Charlotte Brontë heard of her favourite critic's activities with admiring astonishment, and Jane Carlyle wrote to her cousin in Liverpool, alerting her to the imminent arrival of Lewes:

little Lewes—author of *Rose Blanche* &c., &c. is going to lecture in Liverpool—one of these days and I have given him my card for you . . . he is the most amusing little fellow in the whole world—if you only look over his unparalleled *impudence* which is not impudence at all but man-of-genius-*bonhomie*, . . . He is [the] best mimic in the world and full of famous stories, and no spleen or envy, or *bad* thing in him, so see that you receive him with open arms in spite of his immense ugliness.[5]

Lewes's ugliness was, like his wit, his unorthodoxy, and his versatility, legendary. But most of his contemporaries, when commenting on it, agreed that it was relieved by his bright expression, his talent for telling witty stories (many of them *risqué*), and his attractive honesty. They had fun comparing him to his best friend Thornton Hunt, Leigh Hunt's eldest son, also a man of notoriously plain looks, who shared Lewes's ability nevertheless to charm women. It was with Thornton Hunt that Lewes had the closest relationship of his youth. Worshippers of Shelley, they adopted the poet's advocacy of free love inside marriage. Stories went round London of a 'moral Agapemone' in Bayswater, a commune of young couples with some single female adherents, to which Hunt and Lewes were said to belong in the mid-1840s.

In March 1850, shortly before Agnes bore her first child by Hunt, the two progressive friends had begun co-editing their radical weekly newspaper, the *Leader*, devoted to free speech on all issues (particularly religion), the cause of political democracy, and social reform. Thornton Hunt was political editor, with Lewes in charge of the literary pages. Together they made the *Leader* the most intelligent voice of progress to be heard during the 1850s. Even Carlyle, who regretted its socialist tendencies, took it, telling his sister that it was a 'a very good paper'.[6] When Marian Evans left Coventry for London in January 1851 to lodge with the radical publisher John Chapman and edit the *Westminster Review* for him, she joined a set of progressive free-thinkers of whom Lewes was one of the most prominent.

In every sphere of his activity, Lewes was in the vanguard of contemporary thought. During his editorship of the *Leader* he gave frequent space to reviews of scientific progress; for his *Life of Goethe* (1855) he studied those branches of science which had interested Goethe; and by 1856, when he encouraged Marian Evans to begin writing fiction, he was himself engaged in the research for the first of several readable works on natural science, *Sea-Side Studies* (1858). Lewes was among the earliest critics to accept Darwin's hypothesis of natural selection as the mechanism of evolution, and Darwin was duly grateful for his praise.

After the union with Marian Evans, Lewes settled into a less bohemian way of life. Having discovered her literary genius, he gave generously of his time and energy on her behalf, encouraging her with her writing, protecting her sensitive feelings from adverse criticism both social and literary, and becoming a willing literary agent and negotiator with publishers. This was a role he can hardly have expected to fill when he began the relationship; he showed magnanimity in accepting the position of second fiddle to his great partner.

But Lewes continued in his own original path. Though his radical political views were toned down in later life, and though he and Marian rose socially—albeit in a most unusual way—until they were rubbing shoulders with nobility and even royalty in the 1870s, he never lost his instinct for novelty and controversy. In his late monumental work, *Problems of Life and Mind* (1874–9), he tried to evolve a metaphysics which would embrace the scientific method of verification, and to build the study of psychology on a physiological basis. His efforts met with much criticism, yet his research and writings formed part of the advance during the later nineteenth century which took the associational psychology of Locke, Hume, and Hartley to the point at which physiology and psychology became professional branches of science. Freud studied in this tradition; as a student, Pavlov was inspired by one of Lewes's works, *The Physiology of Common Life* (1859), to drop his theological interest and take up science.[7]

In his moving obituary of his friend in the *Fortnightly Review* (of which Lewes had been the first editor), Anthony Trollope gave expression to a view of Lewes shared by many. His was, wrote Trollope, a 'peculiarly valuable literary life', for Lewes had been 'carried up into a career of literature by the tide of [his] own fitness'.[8] Starting with no social advantages but his talent, he became adept in every kind of study. He had none of the insularity of many who had had a more conventional education. His knowledge of the French, German, Italian, and Spanish languages and cultures made him genuinely cosmopolitan. His was a mind, as another contemporary put it, 'peculiarly sensitive to the *Zeitgeist*', with 'a remarkable power of assimilating those floating thoughts which are to form the leading ideas of the immediate future'.[9]

What was the social and family background of the man thus characterized? His antecedents were unusual, but not obscure. His grandfather was Charles Lee Lewes (1740–1803), a celebrated harlequin and comic actor who had, like many members of the profession, a chequered career punctuated by periods of failure and debt but also by heights, as when he acted with success in Sheridan's *She Stoops to Conquer* and played Bobadil in *Every Man in his Humour* (see Plate 1).[10] As it happened,

Lewes's own acting career began with an appearance in the same Jonson play—though he acted the part of Old Knowell—when he joined Dickens's company in 1847. The social position of the actor in Lewes's day, as in his grandfather's, was dubious. Professional actors were not considered gentlemen. And Lewes's grandfather gave evidence also of being unorthodox, even irreverent, in religion. In 1794, during a run in Aberdeen of *The Hypocrite*, an adaptation of Molière's *Tartuffe* attacking the hypocrisy of some religious spokesmen, Charles Lee Lewes was himself assailed from the pulpit by a local Methodist minister, Alexander Kilham. Pamphlets were published on both sides; in his, Lewes robustly denied the charge of encouraging immorality from the stage. His knockabout essay, entitled 'The Stage and the Pulpit, The Player and the Preacher, Or, a Serio-Comic Answer to Mr. Kilham', begins with the promising address, 'Sanctified Sir'.[11]

Charles Lee Lewes's memoirs and anecdotes of the rough and tumble of theatrical life were published anonymously after his death as *Comic Sketches; or, The Comedian his own Manager* (1804). The following year his son John Lee Lewes edited more of Lewes's miscellaneous writings, some funny, some tedious, all unorthodox in religious and social tone, under the title *Memoirs of Charles Lee Lewes, containing Anecdotes, Historical and Biographical, of the English and Scottish Stages, during a Period of Forty Years*. Half a century later, in 1860, G. H. Lewes's son Thornie found in an Edinburgh bookshop another relic of his great-grandfather. This was *A Lecture on Heads, written by George Alexander Stevens and delivered by Charles Lee Lewes* (1785), a one-man programme of satire on various character types from 'poor Wit' to 'Lady Fashion', with many humorous references to topical political and social themes. Thornie 'instantly recollected it must be our Great grand-father', and bought the volume for sixpence.[12]

Charles Lee Lewes was married three times. By his second wife, Fanny Wrigley of Liverpool, he had two sons, John Lee Lewes, born in 1776 in London, and James Wrigley Lewes, born in 1781, also in London. The latter lived in Bermuda, where he was a Searcher in His Majesty's Customs until his death in 1819.[13] The former was G. H. Lewes's father and a somewhat mysterious figure. He was a minor literary man, who not only edited his father's memoirs in 1805 but also published two volumes of poetry. The first of these, *Poems*, appeared in 1811 at Liverpool, where he was then living.[14] It is a mercifully slim volume of mediocre verses on topics mainly public. There are poems expressing piety towards Liverpool

I turn where Mersey lifts its billowy tide

a patriotic poem addressed 'to the Memory of the Rt. Hon. Charles
James Fox'

> His heart's warm wish round Freedom's flag was bound;
> Where'er her banner waved, that heart was found

and several verses celebrating Nelson's victories over the French. The
only hint of something personal, even idiosyncratic, appears, not in the
poems, but in the Preface, in which John Lee Lewes confesses that 'these
Poems were produced under the particular restraints of a desponding
mind'.[15]

Lewes's second volume of poetry, *National Melodies and other Poems*,
was published by subscription in London in 1817, the year of G. H.
Lewes's birth. Again the poems are chiefly public and patriotic, many of
them celebrating the recent British success at Waterloo. But the opening
poem, 'Introductory Lines', though written in conventional form, is
unmistakably autobiographical, expressing a mood of depression in lines
not unlike those of Cowper at his most miserable and terrified:

> The Cloud which o'er my cradle hung,
>   Has spread its darkness round me;
> But though my heart's with anguish wrung
>   Though gathering ills surround me,
>
> Who, who is he that says I shrink;
>   And mocks my vain appealing?
> I care not what the Million think;
>   The Few, alone, have feeling.
>
>   •   •   •   •   •   •
>
> A Lottery's life; some rise, some fall;
>   In Fortune's wheel revolving:
> Though doomed to see the loss of all,—
>   My peace the wreck involving,
>
> From duty's post I'll never flee;
>   Whate'er reflections gall me;
>   Whatever ills I yet may see,
> What griefs soe'er befall me,—
>
>   •   •   •   •   •   •
>
> From friends, from home, from kindred hurl'd,
>   The bond of comfort broken,
> This Preface stands before the world,
>   Of all my pangs a token.[16]

This is interesting, for the man who wrote these partly conventional yet obviously personal lines and who had just fathered G. H. Lewes almost disappears from view after their publication. But though we cannot know the precise reasons for his despair or for the drastic step he seems to have taken soon after writing the poem, we do know a few details about his life. These are extraordinary, and must have a bearing on the early years of his remarkable son. Moreover, the facts show an uncanny resemblance in some respects to the details of Lewes's own domestic life half a century later.

John Lee Lewes lived in Liverpool from 1803 to 1811 with his wife Elizabeth Pownall, by whom he had four children, John (born in 1803), Frances (1804), Elizabeth (1806), and James (1808). In the baptism registers of these children John Lee Lewes's occupation is given as 'Gentleman', with the title 'Captain of the Third Lancashire Militia' added in 1803 and 1804.[17] (Presumably Lewes enlisted at the time of Britain's renewed declaration of war against Napoleonic France in May 1803.)

By 1811 John Lee Lewes had left his legitimate family to start a second, illegitimate one with Elizabeth Ashweek, a young woman born in 1787 of a Devonshire family. They had three sons, Edgar James, born probably between 1809 and 1811, Edward Charles, born in 1813 or 1814 in London, and George Henry, born on 18 April 1817, also in London.[18] Having fathered the three boys, John Lee Lewes vanished from their lives, emigrating to Bermuda to join his younger brother as a customs officer.

According to histories of Bermudan life, John Lee Lewes was well established in his HM Customs post in 1823, by which time he was also known as Bermuda's poet and the secretary of the Book Association in the island's capital, Hamilton. In 1827 the Governor of Bermuda conferred on this 'small, frail poetic gentleman' the office of Registrar of Slaves. Ill health and arguments with a powerful privateer, Hezekiah Frith, whom he tried to arrest on smuggling charges only to be answered by a pair of loaded pistols, caused him to retire in May 1829. He returned to his native Liverpool, where he died in February 1831. Lewes left no will and very little money. His legitimate daughter Frances Wrigley Lewes, who had, surprisingly perhaps, been with him in Bermuda, was granted administration of his estate of less than £100. In the announcement of his death in the Bermuda newspaper, he is described as 'John Lee Lewes, for many years a Customs officer here'. The notice continues, 'He was also a poet,' adding mysteriously, 'He had "a sad domestic history", and his losses and misfortunes are too sacred for public comment.'[19]

We can only guess at the reasons why Lewes abandoned his two families, the legitimate and the illegitimate. The more than gloomy tone of the 1817 introductory poem suggests he may have been unstable; a much later comment made in 1878 by George Eliot, to the effect that G. H. Lewes's gout was 'an anomaly in one so temperate—but we carry the penitential load of our forefathers', hints at a history of drunkenness of which Lewes may have been told by his mother.[20] Debt may also have been a factor. Whatever the reasons, John Lee Lewes escaped from his responsibilities soon after the birth of his youngest child, the George Henry Lewes who is the subject of this biography. Elizabeth Ashweek seems to have told her sons that their father died in 1819.[21]

It is not surprising, then, that we know nothing about G. H. Lewes's earliest years. They must have been precarious socially, and probably financially as well. Perhaps for this reason Elizabeth Ashweek, spinster, married Captain John Gurens Willim, bachelor, in St Pancras Old Church, London, on 29 November 1823. The husband who thereby took on a wife and three stepsons was a retired captain in the army of the East India Company. He was aged 46, ten years older than his wife.[22]

Whatever Lewes was told about his own father—whom he nowhere mentions in his surviving writings, except to tell one correspondent in 1873 that he died when Lewes was two—he certainly disliked his stepfather. All the Lewes boys hated him, and so, also, at least in later life, did his wife. In 1861 Lewes noted in his journal that his mother had given him a 'painful picture' of her life with the Captain, now in his eighties and exceedingly irritable.[23] When Captain Willim died in 1864, Lewes reported coolly to John Blackwood that he was 'unpleasantly tied by the leg by family affairs just now, having lost my stepfather—which though in no sense a loss to any one throws a great deal of my mother's business upon my shoulders'.[24] That the whole family viewed Willim as a nuisance in his old age is demonstrated by the response of the irrepressible Thornie, Lewes's second son and his heir in witty and irreverent expression. Writing from Natal, where he was farming, Thornie put it picturesquely: 'And so the Captain has "hopped the Living"? I thought he was going to live forever, and I half suspect somebody has been soaping the stairs.'[25]

The only glimpses we have of Lewes's childhood come from a few letters written between 1825 and 1830 to Mrs Willim by Lewes's oldest brother, Edgar, who was working for an English wine firm in Oporto. From these, we know that in 1825, when he was 8, Lewes lived near

Stroud in Gloucestershire with his mother, stepfather, and brother Edward. Edgar clearly took a proprietorial interest in his mother's welfare, giving a hint of his lack of faith in Captain Willim's common sense in the practical affairs of life. Writing to his mother in August 1825, Edgar offers advice:

You said in your last that your expenses exceeded your income in your present abode; why continue to live there? you also say that your health is not good, dear Mother would not Devonshire be better suited to both purse & pocket? perhaps Capt. Willim objects to it. I would not like to create discord between any man and his wife particularly if they were related to me but if the manner in which you are living is ill suited both to your health, which is so precious to my Brothers & myself & also to your means why not stop the evil in its growth.[26]

By the following summer, June 1826, Mrs Willim had moved to Southampton. During part of 1827 she was a visitor—possibly without the Captain, who gets scant mention in Edgar's letters—at her sister's house in Plymouth. By this time Edward and George were away at school in London. The family's finances were probably precarious, though Captain Willim had been able to retire on a half-pay pension; and when he died he left an estate of nearly £5,000.[27] However, Edgar's letter of 4 August 1828 suggests they were experiencing upheaval and difficulties at that time. Mrs Willim was now living in Jersey, having spent some time in Nantès:

You seem to have had your share of miseries, but having once made up your mind to leave your country upon *speculation*, repining is out of the question. Edward & George no doubt delight in a little bit of foreign travel and I hope that they will profit by their residence tho' I have some doubt of it; except that in the course of time they may learn to speak the *patois* of Jersey, which their admiring friends will call the French language.[28]

This was prescient in the case of George. Shifting and miscellaneous as his education was, the years spent in France and Jersey gave him a knowledge of French which he exploited as a young man trying to get articles accepted by periodicals. Much of his literary work was pioneering; he was one of the first to read and champion the philosophy of Comte, the historical works of Michelet, and the novels of George Sand. He also spoke French with no trace of an English accent for the rest of his life. With his 'witty, French, flippant' manner he alienated some, like the American author Margaret Fuller. Others were favourably impressed, including the cosmopolitan Henry James, who sat next to Lewes at a dinner party in the last year of Lewes's life, and reported to

his mother how 'clever & entertaining' Lewes was, telling 'lots of stories
. . . chiefly in French'.[29]

But Edgar also warned in his letters of the danger that his brothers
would not get a decent education at all; he remembered that he himself
'never learnt anything in Boulogne'. The remark suggests that the family
had lived there temporarily, probably before their mother's marriage.
She may well have been in financial trouble, for Boulogne was the
favourite retreat of the middle class in embarrassed circumstances. In
Vanity Fair Becky at such a crisis of her life 'perched upon the French
coast at Boulogne, that refuge of so much exiled English innocence'.
Thackeray himself (and Trollope too) knew such circumstances in his
own life; in 1867 Dante Gabriel Rossetti talked of fleeing to Boulogne, if
only his studio could flee with him.[30]

In his *Life of Goethe* Lewes himself offers us a rare glimpse of his life at
this time. Discussing Goethe's boyish enthusiasm for the French theatre
at Weimar, he confides:

Well do I remember, as a child of the same age [10 or 11], my intense delight at
the French theatre, although certainly no three consecutive phrases could have
been understood by me. Nay, so great was this delight, that although we
regarded the French custom, of opening theatres on Sunday, with the profound-
est sense of its 'wickedness', the attraction became irresistible: and one Sunday
night, at Nantes, my brother and I stole into the theatre with pricking
consciences. To this day I see the actors gesticulating, and hear the audience cry
bis! *bis*! redemanding a *couplet* (in which we joined with a stout British *encore*!);
and to this day I remember how we laughed at what we certainly understood
only in passing glimpses.[31]

The Lewes boys seem to have enjoyed their time in Jersey between
1828 and 1829. When G. H. Lewes returned in 1857 to study marine
life for his *Sea-Side Studies*, he noted in his journal the feelings aroused in
him by this visit, the first for 28 years, to the scene of his schooldays:

The first aspect of St. Helier's was quite novel to me. I had not seen it since
1829, & the place was of course much changed; except the Fort & Elizabeth
castle nothing wore a familiar aspect till I got to the Royal Square, & then the
old boyish feelings came back. The Square seemed so *much* smaller! Broad St.,
the theatre, the Market, and a few other places were revived; but for the rest the
place seemed as much changed as I.[32]

Prominent among his memories of Jersey, as he wrote in *Sea-Side
Studies* itself, was the beloved theatre, which had seemed 'the centre of
perfect bliss'. He recalled happy evenings when 'enchanting comedy and
tearful tragedy were ushered in by the overtures to "Tancredi", or

"Semiramide" (the only two which the orchestra ever played), and when ponderous light comedians in cashmere tights, or powerful tragedians "took the stage" with truly ideal strides'. Lewes noted a social change for the better since 1829. Of Royal Square, where he had lived with his mother in Kirby's Hotel, he wrote, 'No longer were criminals publicly whipped through the streets, as I once saw them with shuddering disgust.'[33]

Though Lewes's memories of Jersey were chiefly pleasant, his mother was unhappy there. Edgar encouraged her to return to England: 'and if you go to England no more of your Horse-stealing schools . . . Banish the Blue Devils dear mother and go back to England as soon as possible.' By February 1830 Mrs Willim and the boys were back on the mainland, though whether they were living with Captain Willim all this time is not clear. Edgar makes no further reference to him in his letters. To ease his mother's financial worries, Edgar sent £20 in February 1830, asking anxiously if an annuity being paid to her was to continue now that Mr Offley of the wine firm had died.[34]

In 1830 we lose all trace of Edgar, though a portrait of him was extant in 1880, when George Eliot invited Lewes's eldest son Charles to come and collect it, along with one of Mrs Willim as a young woman (see Plate 2). The family tradition passed down about him was that he died, still abroad, in 1836.[35] With the disappearance of Edgar, Lewes himself at the age of 13 almost eludes our grasp. However, one contemporary remembered attending the same school as Lewes in London. The dandyish poet and memoirist Frederick Locker-Lampson described his time at a 'huge unregenerate school' in Greenwich, run by Dr Burney. 'It was a bullying school', he wrote, where, though he cost his father £100 a year, he was 'ill looked after and poorly fed'. From Locker-Lampson's description, the school sounds similar to many others in the early nineteenth century, being spartan to the point of deprivation, though not quite so dreadful as great schools such as Charterhouse and Westminster. Lewes appears to have left the school at the end of 1832.[36] He never refers to it in his writings. In this, and in his reticence about fathers and stepfathers, he differs markedly from those Victorians— Samuel Butler, J. A. Froude, Edmund Gosse, for example—who documented in fact and fiction their struggle into adulthood against beatings and bullyings at school and a monstrous paterfamilias at home.

Lewes's movements from 1832, when he was 16, to 1837 are a little better known. All the obituaries of him, including that by James Sully, who had his article looked over at the proof stage by George Eliot, state that after school he entered a notary's office, then worked briefly for a

Russian merchant in the City, before trying the study of medicine. According to Sully—and George Eliot does not contradict him here, though she freely annotated and corrected his piece—Lewes 'actually began to walk the hospitals, and was only stopped in his course by an invincible repugnance at the sight of physical pain, a feeling which in his later life greatly narrowed his range of physiological experiment'.[37]

After his death, an effort was made to find out which college or medical school Lewes had attended. Richard Quain, a surgeon at University College, wrote to Sir James Paget, physician to the Queen and also to the Leweses in their later years, in response to Paget's 'wish to learn of Mr. G. H. Lewes's attendance on lectures at University College'. Because of the incomplete state of the early registers, he was unable to find Lewes's name, but remembered how 'Mr. Lewes spoke to me of Dr. Jones Quain who lectured on anatomy & physiology . . . at University College—Mr. Lewes distinctly said he had attended his lectures.'[38] It is quite possible that Lewes heard lectures without formally enrolling or taking examinations. His older brother Edward was a medical student in 1837, by which time Lewes himself had abandoned any similar ambitions, being now, according to his friend, the painter William Bell Scott, determined on a career as a 'philosopher and poet'.[39]

As well as his brother, some of Lewes's friends were medical students, among them Frederick Oldfield Ward of King's College, later an engineer and sanitary reformer. Lewes was undoubtedly drawing at least loosely on his own experience when he described his hero Ranthorpe, in the novel of that name, consorting with the hard-drinking, womanizing medical students Harry Cavendish, of St George's, and Oliver Thornton, of the Middlesex. These young men chase servant girls, are rowdy, and talk in the current bohemian slang:

'Oliver, are you going to the Cider Cellars [a dive also frequented by Thackeray's Pendennis] to-night?'
'Don't know. Short of *tin*. Spent a couple of sovereigns last night.'

The narrator knowingly asserts that 'the art of courting maidservants and milliners is an art much cultivated by medical students', even blaming their student status for their excesses. Of Harry Cavendish he says: 'His virtues were his own; his vices he owed to his position as a student.' This view of medical students as particularly prone to loose behaviour crops up often in the period. The printer Henry Vizetelly remembered the 'rowdy medical student days when probationary "saw-bones" made night hideous in quiet neighbourhoods with their inebriate shouts of "lul-ler-li-ety", the cant exclamation of the epoch'.[40]

Ranthorpe is at 19 a clerk with pretensions to authorship. Being hard up, he has to weigh with himself whether he can afford sixpence for a secondhand volume of Shelley's poems. Lewes later told Marian of his own 'diligent, hungry search in his days of youthful penury, when he dined on a sausage in order to buy a longed-for book'.[41] Ranthorpe gets his start, like Lewes himself, in journalism. The first of Lewes's surviving letters contains an appeal to Leigh Hunt, the ageing radical and bohemian, erstwhile friend of Byron and Shelley, and editor of a succession of radical journals, most of them short-lived for lack of cash. The 17-year-old Lewes wrote on 2 October 1834:

Sir

Some time back I sent you a tale called 'Mary Altonville' which you promised in your advice to correspondents should be 'considered'. This being some weeks ago & not having heard further from you I conclude you have overlooked or mislaid it.

I trouble you with this to know if it *is* worthy of insertion—or *not*—in the former case I shall commence a series of Tales (the plan of which I have already sketched out) for your journal, if acceptable to you—in the latter I should wish to have it returned to me, not having a copy, the one I condensed it from for you, being destroyed.

Should you think proper to insert it—may I trouble you to alter the name from '*Altonville*' to '*Alton*' the former being somewhat too Rosa-Matildaish.[42]

Hunt did not think proper to insert the story; in any case, his *Leigh Hunt's London Journal* came to an end a year later, in December 1835. But he did respond to Lewes's bold request by taking him up into the group of aspiring young Shelleys who already surrounded him in the early 1830s. For Leigh Hunt was the chief magnet which attracted young men with radical opinions in literature, politics, and religion, but with no fortune or prospects.

Lewes's most detailed description of his life at this time comes in an article on Spinoza written in 1866:

About thirty years ago a small club of students held weekly meetings in a parlour of a tavern in Red Lion Square, Holborn, where the vexed questions of philosophy were discussed with earnestness, if not with insight. The club was extremely simple in its rules, and quite informal in its proceedings. The members were men whose sole point of junction was the Saturday meeting, and whose sole object was the amicable collision of contending views, on subjects which, at one time or another, perplex and stimulate all reflecting minds. On every other day in the week their paths were widely divergent. One kept a second-hand bookstall, rich in free-thinking literature; another was a journeyman watchmaker; a third lived on a moderate income; a fourth was a boot-maker; a fifth 'penned a stanza when he should engross'; a sixth studied anatomy and many other things, with vast aspirations, and no very definite career before him.[43]

In 1836 young G. H. Lewes, with 'no very definite career before him', was a political radical, an atheist, a worshipper of Shelley, and an admirer of Spinoza, to whose pantheistic humanism he was introduced in the tavern in Red Lion Square. The watchmaker, a 'German Jew, named Cohn, or Kohn', lectured to the club on 'the great Hebrew thinker', inducing Lewes, as he said, to begin 'forthwith' a translation of Spinoza's *Ethics*. The effect of learning about Spinoza, both his philosophical system and his outlawed life, was to give Lewes a sense of kinship with the philosopher, at this time hardly known in England. Lewes recalled:

I happened to be hungering for some knowledge of this theological pariah—partly, no doubt, because he was an outcast, for as I was then suffering the social persecution which embitters all departure from accepted creeds, I had a rebellious sympathy with all outcasts—and partly because I had casually met with a passage, quoted for reprobation, in which Spinoza maintained the subjective nature of evil, a passage which, to my mind, lighted up that perplexed question.[44]

The suffering Lewes describes is very well documented in the case of so many of his contemporaries, among them J. A. Froude, whose autobiographical novel *The Nemesis of Faith* (1849) was burnt at his Oxford college and whose career as a university don was brusquely curtailed because of his self-proclaimed heterodoxy; and Marian Evans, whose doubts made her brave her father's wrath by refusing to go to church with him, with the result that she was nearly thrown out of his house at the age of 22.[45] For Lewes's own experience we have only these few remarks in his essay on Spinoza. *Ranthorpe*, though a valuable source of biographical material as regards Lewes's early literary and dramatic aspirations, offers no word on the hero's religious faith, or lack of it. Presumably the detested Captain Willim objected to his stepson's free-thinking. There is, however, no known story of persecution; still less do we have evidence of the kind of internal struggle to emerge from orthodoxy which perplexed the youth of so many Victorians.

It seems to me probable that Lewes was never orthodox; that his peripatetic childhood, the irregularities of his mother's life, and his irreverent theatrical antecedents would have made church-going and scripture-reading unlikely events in his early life. Later, when George Eliot in her novels showed tolerance, even warmth, towards the rejected evangelical Christianity of her childhood, Lewes was by contrast coolly and adamantly anti-Christian, shocking some believers, like Lord Acton, by the very decisiveness of his views. 'He was a boisterous iconoclast', wrote Acton, 'with little confidence in disinterested belief and a positive aversion for Christianity.'[46]

Nothing could have been more natural than that a young man with literary pretensions and without strong family or religious roots should have gravitated, as Lewes did, towards Leigh Hunt, the living relic of the literary, liberal, atheistic milieu of Byron and Shelley. Hunt was to set him on his miscellaneous and astonishing career and to cast a long shadow, through his son Thornton, on Lewes's future life.

Literary Bohemia

(1837–1841)

IN 1837 Leigh Hunt was 53 years old and living in Chelsea with his (alcoholic) wife and several children. Carlyle, his near neighbour, observed the chaotic Hunt family life at close quarters with feelings both severe and amused. Leigh Hunt, though pleasant, was 'a born fool' who 'had to prowl about, borrowing &c. &c.', and to whom the Carlyles found themselves doing rather too much '*lending of sovereigns*'. Carlyle caught Hunt's picturesque qualities, describing him as 'one of the ancient Mendicant Minstrels, strangely washed ashore into a century he should not have belonged to'.[1]

In the 1820s Hunt had 'borrowed' from Byron and Shelley, whom he had followed to Italy with his family. Later he borrowed from Mary Shelley, from the Carlyles, and from others. He alternately amused and irritated his acquaintances with his unique combination of innocence in matters practical and financial and knowingness in matters political, social, and literary. It was an open secret that Dickens caricatured him in *Bleak House* (1853) as Harold Skimpole, a 'romantic youth who had undergone some unique process of depreciation'.[2] But the feckless Skimpole is in fact no caricature. The real Leigh Hunt was at least his equal in coyness and a kind of harmless dandyism.

Much later, the sober publisher George Smith, not given to fancifulness on the whole (though he may have had Dickens's caricature in mind), remembered writing out a cheque to Hunt in 1845 for some literary manuscript. 'Well', said Hunt, apparently, 'what am I to do with this little bit of paper?' Smith told him to present it at the bank, where he would receive cash in return. Having done so, Leigh Hunt kept the banknotes in an envelope which his wife inadvertently burned. Hunt came to Smith in distress, but his agitation 'while on his way to bring this news had not prevented him from purchasing on the road a little statuette of Psyche, which he carried, without any paper round it, in his hand'. Smith found out the numbers of the banknotes and took Hunt to the Bank of England. As they waited in a room where three clerks were at work, Hunt got up and addressed one of them 'in wondering tones':

'And *this* is the Bank of England! And do you sit here all day and never see the green woods, and the trees and flowers and the charming country?' Then, in tones of remonstrance he demanded, 'Are you contented with such a life?' All this time he was holding the little naked Psyche in one hand and with his long hair and flashing eyes made a surprising figure.[3]

This kind of behaviour attracted much criticism and scorn; Hunt's 'Cockneyism', pilloried in the 1820s by the educated reviewers of the *Quarterly Review* and *Blackwood's Magazine*, was still an object of attack, especially in journals of a conservative tendency. In 1859, when Lewes read Hunt's *Autobiography*, he noticed it was 'unpleasantly apologetical' and 'intensely coxcombical & feeble'.[4] But for the young Lewes in 1834, seeking an entrée into literary London, having already formed unorthodox opinions and being himself a kind of semi-educated cosmopolitan 'Cockney', what could have been more natural than to turn to Hunt for help? The more so as Lewes soon conceived the idea of writing a life of Shelley, and Leigh Hunt was not only the repository of many memories of the poet but also the conduit to Mary Shelley.

Lewes first proposed the plan in June 1837, before he had met Hunt personally. In his letter, now lost, he must have asked Hunt to write down his reminiscences of Shelley, for Hunt replied on 12 July 1837 that he was unable to do so, partly on grounds of ill health. But he encouraged Lewes to visit him and talk over 'all the subjects in your letter'. Skimpole–Hunt continued, 'It is very few people I can admit into the humble abode of a battered patriot; but to love Shelley as heartily as you seem to do, argues a refinement from which I need have no fear on such a point.' He warned Lewes that his hopes of publishing a book on Shelley might be dashed by the fact that Mary Shelley was 'not so much at liberty to encourage publications respecting her husband, as you might suppose, owing to the opposition of his kindred'.[5] Presumably he explained to Lewes when they met that Mary Shelley was dependent for her livelihood and for the education of her son on the benevolence of Shelley's father, Sir Timothy, and that this benevolence was extended only on condition that she refuse to sanction or aid any publication relating to his reprobate son.

However, Lewes was not put off. His letters to Hunt during 1838 make frequent references to his progress on the Shelley biography; he even advertised it as forthcoming in one of the minor periodicals to which he was now contributing, the *National Magazine and Monthly Critic*. That the book actually took shape is made clear in Lewes's long letters to his mentor from Berlin and Vienna, where he lived from August 1838 to July 1839. By 15 November 1838 he was telling Hunt that the manuscript of the biographical part was complete, and that he intended to add a critical section.[6] He worried that someone else was being permitted to write on Shelley, but Hunt assured him in March 1839 that no biography was about to appear, only Mary Shelley's four-volume edition of Shelley's poems, with biographical notes appended by her, 'done under permission from Sir Timothy, and under *conditions*'. Hunt went on to tell Lewes that Mary Shelley still did not 'willingly hear of new lives' by young Shelley enthusiasts.

There follows in Hunt's letter a piece of pure Skimpoleism, which surely made even his enthusiastic and admiring young correspondent cringe:

I was also obliged to remonstrate a little with [Mary Shelley], entre nous, for saying that she had never known any one at all worth mentioning as an unworldly man by the side of Shelley (or some such phrase) which under the circumstances of his and my life I thought not quite considerate towards a certain person whom he deigned to call his 'Friend'; and she expresses great regret and says it was a mere piece of absence of mind, and that I am 'very unworldly' etc.

At the time he wrote this, Hunt was gently but persistently begging Mary Shelley for financial help, reminding her of promises Shelley had made to him of sharing his fortune with the Hunts.[7]

Lewes's Shelley plan was finally put to rest in December 1839, when he sent Hunt the completed manuscript, asking him to pass it on, with an enclosed letter, to Mary Shelley. He expressed the sanguine hope that 'she *cannot* refuse the smallest of my requests—the reading of the MS— if you can say a word for me to her I know you will'. Unfortunately for Lewes, Mary Shelley thought otherwise. She wrote to Hunt, who had clearly done his best for Lewes:

I am very much puzzled to know how to answer your friend. Of course I wish in every way to write *pleasingly* to a man of whom you have a good opinion—& who as you say worships Shelley. But I do think his request *indiscreet* . . .[8]

So ended the projected 'Life of Shelley'. In 1844 the irrepressible Lewes could write cheerfully about it to his German acquaintance Varnhagen von Ense, to whom he had shown the half-completed Shelley manuscript in Berlin in October 1838. Explaining that Mary Shelley 'was bound not to countenance any thing of the kind', and that he had therefore given it up, he added:

Very, very glad am I that it turned out so! For though I have not altered my opinion of Shelley, I have considerably altered my views of composition; and the m.s. of that Life makes me shudder when I look at it. I was so young when it was written; and though only six years older now these six years have been twelve in point of development.[9]

We know pretty well what Lewes would have written in the 'Life', for he did not let his efforts go to waste. He reviewed Mary Shelley's edition of the poetry in the *Westminster Review* in April 1841; some months later he undertook the Shelley entry in the *Penny Cyclopaedia*, a publication of the Society for the Diffusion of Useful Knowledge;[10] and in 1852 he wrote, again in the *Westminster Review*, on Shelley as a letter-writer.

The first *Westminster* essay, written in 1840 and printed the following year, is a good example of Lewes's early literary journalism. It is lively, wide-ranging, and ambitious. The writer is anxious to establish his credentials as a commentator on Shelley; he does so by revealing his acquaintance with Leigh Hunt, using manuscript letters of Shelley at his disposal, most of them flattering letters from the poet to his friend Leigh Hunt(!). Knowing that he is dealing with a controversial subject, Lewes resorts to rhetorical strategies to win his readers to his enthusiasm. One such strategy is to open the article with a litany of the sufferings of poets: 'The poet's life is often little but a record of blighted hopes, of unrealised aspirations after the beautiful, the good, and the happiness of man.' Shelley thus keeps good company: Dante, Tasso, Michelangelo, Alfieri, Milton, Cervantes, Cowper, Chatterton, Coleridge, and Byron are all invoked. A second strategy is to use Byron as a scapegoat, so that Shelley can shine by comparison. Both poets were sceptics and free livers, but how negative and cynical was Byron, how positive and idealistic, by contrast, was Shelley.

Thirdly, Lewes cleverly goes on the offensive by summing up all the arguments against Shelley in their most extreme form. A 'brief summary' of the *Quarterly Review* judgement of Shelley runs as follows:

'He was a black-hearted Atheist, a mad demagogue, uttering blasphemies and seditions for the purpose of corrupting the minds of men, and *to excuse his own detestable vices*; of meagre intellect, and of the flimsiest, dreamiest poetical power.'

It then falls to Lewes to question this view: 'But how, if on nearer inspection, it turn out quite otherwise?' Lewes's plan is to view 'the man and his actions, not from *our* central point of view, but rather from *his*'. Not quite having the courage to support Shelley's atheism publicly, but being unwilling to attempt a jesuitical denial of it, Lewes rather weakly allows his atheism to be seen as 'one speculative error', but not enough to 'sweep from out our minds the fervent admiration of a life of almost unparalleled goodness and self-sacrifice'. (Lewes may not have known the details of Shelley's often callous behaviour, particularly towards Mary, who herself had banished her husband's faults from her memory and now earnestly spoke of him as not only the ideal poet, but also the ideal husband.)

Lewes proceeds, in tones reminiscent of Carlyle at his most trenchant and disputatious, to 'speak some sincere words respecting this Shelley', declaring, 'If one quality might be supposed to distinguish him pre-eminently, it was that highest of all qualities—truthfulness, an unyielding worship of truth.' These claims being made, the review settles into an account of Shelley's works, with some criticism of the lack of 'light and shade' in the longer poems, despite Shelley's marvellous command of language, music, and imagery, and a bold statement of the claim of Shelley's notorious drama of incest and parricide, *The Cenci*, to be considered the 'most magnificent tragedy of modern times'.[11]

The essay is a clever one, with the faults one might expect of a young writer trying to impress on a controversial subject. John Stuart Mill, who befriended Lewes at this time, wrote shrewdly about the young-mannishness of the article. It was, he said, full of good things, but suffered from a vice of style he recognized in his own early writings—his 'Carlylism'. 'I think Carlyle's costume should be left to Carlyle whom alone it becomes.' Mill also pointed out an awkwardness in the plan of the essay. Did Lewes mean to vindicate Shelley before his detractors, to criticize the poems, or to give a 'biographic Carlylian *analysis* of him as a *man*'? Lewes had overstretched himself in trying to do all three. As for his half-hearted attempt to excuse Shelley's atheism, Mill felt he should have been bolder: '*we*, I think, should leave that to others, & should take for granted, boldly, all those premises respecting freedom of thought & the morality of acting on one's own *credo*, which to anyone who admits them, carry Shelley's vindication with them.'[12]

Lewes was not the only young man in London to worship Shelley and approach Leigh Hunt as a living link with him. Among the many youths of unorthodox views and unprivileged background who appealed to Hunt with flattering letters at the same time as Lewes were John Forster, Richard Henry (later Hengist) Horne, Charles Ollier, William Bell Scott, and Egerton Webbe.[13] Hunt welcomed them all, and set them writing to one another too. Thus Lewes addressed himself boldly to W. B. Scott in 1837:

Sir,

Leigh Hunt tells me that as 'cordial natures' & neighbours we ought to know each other. How far that be the case I know not but this much I do know—that we both agree in heartily loving Shelley—are fond of books—of poetry—tho' you are a poet and I am none—and I have no doubt there are many other points in which we so far assimilate as to enjoy each others society, which in spite of its not being selon les regles of this most artificial of worlds—and might by most people be looked on as impertinence (but which I feel assured will not by you)— is the shortest & easiest way I can think of for our better acquaintance. We are near neighbours. If we like each other we have only reached that liking per saltum—if we do not why no harm is done we can 'shrink into our conscious selves' once more.

The quotation is, appropriately, from *The Cenci*. Lewes describes himself to Scott as 'a student living a quiet life' but having 'a great gusto for intellectual acquaintance with which I am sorry to say that I am not overburdened'.[14] Scott responded warmly to this frank appeal for friendship, and the two young men began to meet in Scott's studio in Edward Street, off Hampstead Road, 'where we talked well into the night', Scott recalled, 'as youngsters do', on 'the wisest and most recondite subjects'.[15]

Scott later remembered his new friend, five or six years his junior and 'therefore just out of his nonage', as 'an exuberant but not very reliable or exact talker, a promising man of parts, a mixture of the man of the world and the boy'. This description agrees well with the impression we have on reading Lewes's early letters. He was keen to impress, ambitious, rather boastful, careless, and apparently carefree. Whether Scott is being equally accurate when he says that while he, Scott, practised 'high and pure ways of life and habits of body', Lewes 'ignored and repudiated them', we do not know.[16] The two friends planned to collaborate on a work illustrating 'the great typical events of life', for which Lewes would write the poetry and Scott would do the engravings. The plan fell through, partly because Lewes went abroad in the summer of 1838, partly because of rivalry between the poet and the artist.[17] In 1851 Scott published the work alone, under the title *Chorea Sancti Viti; or, Steps in the Journey of Prince Legion*. Lewes noted its appearance in his 'Vivian' column of the *Leader*, and indulged in some reminiscing: 'Some thirteen years were pushed aside, and once more I was sitting beside the grave and high-minded Scott, in his low-roofed study, crammed with books, casts, wood-blocks, sketches, and papers.'[18]

The friendship with Scott petered out. In 1844 Scott took up a post at

the Government School of Design in Newcastle, where he stayed until
1864. He and Lewes met again in London in 1868 and renewed their
acquaintance, but not their intimacy, though Scott did present Lewes
with a copy of his *Poems* (1875), inscribed 'G. H. Lewes from his ancient
friend W. B. Scott, April 1875'.[19]

Another of Leigh Hunt's young followers was Egerton Webbe, a
promising musician whose death in 1840 put an end to his budding
friendship with Lewes. Webbe and Lewes both did their first pieces of
journalism for Leigh Hunt's *Monthly Repository* in 1837–8. These consisted of some over-solemn essays in answer to one another—and also to
Thornton Hunt—with such titles as 'Hints towards an Essay on the
Sufferings of Truth' and 'Thoughts for the Thoughtful'. When Lewes
left for Berlin in August 1838, Webbe and Thornton Hunt wrote
cheerful letters to him, Webbe assuring Lewes in March 1839 that they
would all be very glad to see him back again, though he did not think it
would be possible 'to get a word in when we meet, for as you were such
an immense talker before you had started abroad, what must be your
nature now—with all the gossip of Berlin at your finger ends and a great
batch of Greek and German to boot?'[20]

These young men—Lewes, Scott, Webbe, and Thornton Hunt—ran
a minor magazine, the *National Magazine and Monthly Critic*, of which
Lewes appears to have been joint editor with one of the others, with
Leigh Hunt as the inspirer and 'dear friend' whom the young friends
quoted and puffed shamelessly in their critical articles. In his tongue-in-
cheek description of the magazine staff at a 'National' supper in October
1837, Lewes sends himself up as the first of two coxcombical editors,
'Vivian Latouche' and 'Erpingham Lorraine'.[21] In *Fraser's Magazine* in
1846 he wrote an article on the history of pantomine under the pen-name
'Vivian Latouche'; in 1850 he became famous as simply 'Vivian', the
witty bachelor, lady's man-cum-misogynist, and theatre critic of the
Leader.

The *National Magazine* was short-lived. In July 1838 Thornton Hunt
wrote to Lewes from Stockport, where he was briefly on the staff of a
local paper, commiserating on 'the death of your Mag'.[22] But one article
in it was of consequence to Lewes. This was his favourable review in
December 1837 of Dickens's early works, *Pickwick Papers*, *Oliver Twist*,
and *Sketches by Boz*. 'Boz' should be compared to no other writer, said
Lewes, because no one had written like him before: 'no one has ever
combined the nicety of observation, the fineness of tact, the exquisite
humour, the wit, heartiness, sympathy with all things good and beautiful
in human nature, the perception of character, and accuracy of descrip-

tion, with the same force that he has done.'²³ Dickens was grateful for this praise, and invited Lewes to call on him, which Lewes duly did, though the friendship between the two men was postponed by Lewes's departure for Germany.²⁴

This trip, begun in August 1838, may have been decided on in a hurry. Certainly Thornton Hunt makes no mention of it in his friendly letter dated 6 July from 'smoky, cottony, oily' Stockport. It is clear from his chat that all the friends were more or less at a loose end. Thornton mentions a 'speculation' of Lewes's, a new magazine of which he begs to be sent a specimen number 'when it knows the light'. But none of the circle had money; consequently no new magazine appeared. Lewes obviously intended to continue working on the Shelley biography, but he also wished to learn German, and while in Germany to study Greek too.²⁵

The one indispensable thing for any young Englishman about to visit Germany was a letter of introduction from Carlyle, the great champion of German literature in the periodical press during the 1820s and the undisputed guardian of Goethe's reputation in England.²⁶ Lewes duly met Carlyle through the ever-helpful Leigh Hunt, and was furnished with an introduction to Varnhagen von Ense, the grand old man of letters in Berlin, widower of the actress Rahel and former friend of Goethe himself.

Altogether Lewes spent almost a year away, living most of the time in Berlin, then moving on at the end of April 1839 to Vienna for about three months. We do not know how he supported himself; perhaps, like Percy Ranthorpe, he gave English lessons 'to the young ladies of the upper classes'.²⁷ He worked at his German and set about meeting as many literary notables as he could. In the first of his long letters home to Leigh Hunt, written on 3 October 1838, Lewes adopts the flattering tone so familiar in correspondents of Hunt, catching the infection from Hunt's own cloying style. Thus Lewes is careful to let his friend know how highly the really educated people in Berlin value the works of 'Lie Hoont', with one lady—'one of the most celebrated savantes in Berlin'—even making an 'idol' of him. He also boasts a little on his own account: 'I am intimate here with a great many of the first families and am considerably petted, especially by my best friends ever, the ladies.'

Lest Hunt think him idling his time away, however, Lewes assures him that he is also working hard. He has been borrowing books from Varnhagen, has had discussions on the philosophy of language and on Homer and his translators, and has even met 'the great Boeckh', Professor of Classical Philology at Berlin University. He sends regards to Carlyle, Dickens (to whom he has recently sent an article), and the rest of the Hunt circle. 'Is Thornton still Stockportising?' 'How wags the world with the "admirable Egerton"?—who out-Crichtons Crichton—puns he as ever? and laughs as joyously over his own and others' jokes?' The letter finishes with an account of an adventure which nearly ended 'in a manner too Romantic to be pleasant'. He and two companions had been cutting across country near Berlin when they got stuck in a swamp, floundering up to their necks in complete darkness.[28] Lewes later worked up the story into the burlesque 'Night in a German Swamp', which he published in *Douglas Jerrold's Shilling Magazine* in February 1847: 'To die in a bog! To be cut off in the commencement of my ambitious career, with all my dreams of glory unfulfilled, and to bury them in a swamp! I gnashed my teeth with rage.'[29]

Lewes attended some lectures at the University, where a fellow student was the young Turgenev; the two men met at the salon of Varnhagen's literary friend Henriette Solmar.[30] He gave Hunt an account of how he generally passed his time:

My days are spent in study—my evenings in society—at Concerts or Theatre. Touching the former I am reading 'Faust' in the original—no easy task—& translating Goethe's 'Torquato Tasso'—by the bye I wish you could tell me whether this has ever been translated, as I am here on the spot & can resolve a difficulty at once—it is susceptible of a very interesting preface & notes. I am ever working at the Shelley, and am more than ever delighted at having come to Germany were it only on this account, for my views have been much altered & developed. . . . Criticism here is a very different thing from criticism in England & believing it also to be immeasurably superior I shall not shun it.[31]

When the plan to write Shelley's life had to be abandoned, Lewes turned instead to researching his *Life of Goethe*, which, though more than ten years in the making, was to be an instant and lasting success, both in England and in Germany. As for German criticism, Lewes's enthusiasm for that was not destined to last, but under the influence of his discussions at Berlin, and with a copy of Hegel's lectures on aesthetics given to him by Varnhagen, he was to write a spirited article on the subject in the *British and Foreign Review* in October 1842. There is further evidence of the 'Germanizing' of Lewes in his request that Hunt ask John Stuart Mill, at this time editor of the *Westminster Review*, if an article on Carlyle would be acceptable. Lewes presented himself in these letters to Hunt as a hard-working student of German literature and philosophy, keen to follow in Carlyle's footsteps in that respect, while remaining the ever-grateful adherent of Leigh Hunt's Anglo-Saxon amateurism, the faithful disciple of Shelley, and the traditional 'gay young bachelor' enjoying his year abroad.[32]

On his return in June or July 1839 Lewes settled back into the Hunt circle, returning no doubt to those 'champagne evenings' in Hunt's study, where a group of initiates sat by the fire 'ransacking the worlds of Literature and Philosophy for food', as he put it rather fulsomely in one of his letters from Berlin.[33] Annie Gliddon, a member of the circle, drew a sketch of Lewes, in November 1840 (see Plate 3), dressed as a student with a German pipe in his hand, leaning on a volume of Leigh Hunt's works, with shelves of books behind him bearing the names of his favourite authors—Shakespeare, Dante, Calderón, Shelley, Spinoza, Goethe, and Hegel. For the time being, Lewes continued his work on Shelley, making yet another friendship with a fellow worshipper, the bizarre Richard Henry Horne.

Horne, born in 1802, was considerably older than the other members of Leigh Hunt's circle. But he was still only the aspiring author, who was to make a great but brief splash in 1843 when he published his epic poem *Orion* at the experimental price of a farthing. His background was unstable. The son of a gambling, drinking army officer, he was himself sent to Sandhurst, where he was bullied, and from which he was sent home after a year. Horne later claimed to have got himself expelled, like Shelley, for his atheism. In 1823 he dedicated himself to becoming a poet, identifying obsessively with Shelley. Having spent some time in Mexico fighting against the Spanish, he returned to England and took up the cause of Hazlitt, whose burial he arranged in 1830. Through his friendship with the reforming Unitarians of the *Monthly Repository*, among them W. J. Fox and Dr Thomas Southwood Smith, he took over the editorship of the periodical in 1836. A year later he sold it to Leigh Hunt, at the same time joining Hunt's group of friends. Horne dedicated his play *The Death of Marlowe* (1837) to Hunt, who gave his copy to Lewes, suggesting he might try to get it translated in Germany.

Horne was the author of several tragedies, but he could not get any of them published or produced. In 1852, having tried and failed at authorship, journalism, marriage, and commissionership—through Southwood Smith he was appointed in 1841 to the Royal Commission investigating the employment of children in mines and factories—Horne left England alone for Australia and gold-digging. There his fortunes rose and fell, and he returned to England in 1869, looking to old friends like Dickens and Lewes to get him magazine work. His life drew to a close with a trial for indecent assault on a pupil in 1875, at which written testimonies to his character from Lewes, Carlyle, and others were read out. He died, an oddity and nine days' wonder of 40 years before, in 1884.[34]

Lewes liked him. After returning from Vienna in the summer of 1839, he had settled down again with his mother in Hampstead Road and was busy trying to make a living in the periodicals. Rather as he had introduced himself to W. B. Scott two years before, he now wrote to Horne, professing himself an admirer of Horne's genius. Being a 'hater of conventionalities', he asked Horne if he might call on him.[35] Lewes looked up to his older friend, who seemed set for literary success. Horne had at least managed to get his latest play, *Gregory VII*, published, though it was at his own expense. Lewes, who was reviewing it for the *Monthly Chronicle*, wrote mock-threateningly to Horne in May 1840, saying he intended to 'slaughter' the play with 'all the envy, hatred & malice of the unread poet for a more fortunate & read one, & all the gall of light-pocketness, with all the unquestioned unquestionable superiority of the "We" Reviewer over the poor Reviewee!'[36] Of course Lewes praised the tragedy to the skies in his article, calling Horne 'one of the greatest dramatists of the day'.[37]

Lewes was faithful to his friend, praising his works whenever he could. But Horne's works had no success, and Lewes, too, was struggling. The only periodicals to which he had access were those run on a shoe-string and therefore in varying stages of collapse. The *Monthly Chronicle* itself, owned by Dionysius Lardner and Edward Bulwer, was wound up in 1841. Already in May 1840 Carlyle, planning to publish prospectuses in the periodicals of the founding of the London Library, told his colleague W. D. Christie that G. H. Lewes, a young man whom he knew 'slightly', would help by putting one in the *Monthly Chronicle*. 'But', Carlyle added, 'I understand the *Monthly Chronicle* is just about expiring.'[38]

Another such periodical for which Lewes wrote at this time was the *British Miscellany*, of which only one volume appeared, in 1841. It carried three articles by Lewes, the first fruits of his visit to Germany: an account of the career of Varnhagen von Ense, whom Lewes describes as 'a sort of German Leigh Hunt'(!), and two pieces by 'Professor Wolfgang von Bibundtücker', a German persona adopted in imitation of Carlyle's Teufelsdröckh in *Sartor Resartus*. One is a not very witty 'Ode Pindaric on the Princess Royal', the other an ironic piece of heavy German criticism, breaking the butterfly of 'Where are you going to, my pretty maid?' on the wheel of philosophical-aesthetic commentary. Like Carlyle, Lewes takes a double attitude towards German scholarship, partly respecting its seriousness and partly sceptical about its heaviness. As 'editor' he appends a note to his professor's analysis:

I have thought it right to give the public the remains of this great man uncorrupted; but I cannot let this pass without observing, that he seems to me to be here truly German, with his Aesthetic spectacles to see 'more than is set down in the book'.[39]

This was mere hack-work. Lewes's one more solid prospect at this time was writing for the *Westminster Review*, the great radical quarterly journal set up in 1824 by Bentham and James Mill to rival the *Edinburgh* and the *Quarterly* Reviews. Its writers had championed the cause of electoral reform in the years leading up to the 1832 Reform Act, and it was the chief organ of political, philosophical, and religious radicalism. The younger Mill, whom Lewes met about this time, edited it until 1840; Lewes himself was later to attempt to buy it; in 1851, when he first met Marian Evans, he was one of its chief contributors and she its editor.

In September 1840 Lewes's first article for the *Westminster* was published. Though written in Germany, it had for its subject the French drama.[40] Lewes mounts a spirited defence of the classical drama of Racine and Corneille against the criticisms not only of Francophobic English critics but also of the German 'philosophical' critic A. W. Schlegel, who in his celebrated *Dramatic Lectures* had praised Shakespeare at the expense of the 'unnatural' French drama. Lewes insists that 'in studying the poetry of another nation, or period, our first necessary step towards its appreciation is the going out of ourselves, and imaginatively identifying ourselves with the people of that nation or period.' He finds beauties in Racine in spite of his over-strict adherence to the Aristotelian unities. The classical drama is objective, the modern subjective.[41] Lewes's remarks here bear the signs of his having learnt this critical relativism from German critics such as Herder, and even A. W. Schlegel, whom he attacks, in effect, for not applying the generous principles of criticism he sets out in the first place.

Lewes finds room in the article for a puff for Horne's tragedies. Alerting Horne to this service in a letter of 8 May 1840, Lewes writes extravagantly of Horne as the true successor to the Shelley of *The Cenci*. He finishes his letter on a characteristically spirited note:

All this is written in a high state of excitement & sympathy with your genius but do not let it therefore appear mere froth—you know that I pique myself on

my criticism & dramatic knowledge—and as to criticism being a cold logical
thing 'I doot the fack' as the Scotch say—at any rate the very exuberance (if
there be such) is a proof of the impression made on yours very truly

G. H. Lewes.[42]

The infatuation with Horne lasted a few more years, but by 1850,
when Lewes was literary editor of the *Leader* and Horne at the age of 48
was still writing juvenile stuff, Lewes was rejecting, though kindly,
Horne's manuscripts. He sent back a novel, 'The Coming Man', as 'too
extravagant for effective satire & not sufficiently broad in its humour to
be enjoyable as an extravaganza'. 'Don't be disgusted with me', he added,
'but send something else.'[43] Perhaps this novel was the one George Smith
remembered Horne submitting to him:

It was wonderfully clever, but, from a publisher's point of view, was quite
impossible. It was written to sustain the proposition that every man, and every
woman, had a pre-ordained and natural affinity for some other particular man
or woman; and this theory was illustrated from a rather coarse and physical
point of view which certainly offended severe taste. The characters of the
novel were extraordinary; the most extraordinary was a philanthropist
impressed with the view that the world was over-populated, and anxious on
grounds of purest benevolence to remedy the mistake by murdering as many
people as he could.

The philanthropist achieves his aim by having one leg cut off at the knee
and a 'wooden leg' (really a rifle) attached instead. 'At last it occurred to
the magistrate that there was always a poor old man with a wooden leg
somewhere in the neighbourhood when one of these murders occurred.'
The method chosen was for the murderer to 'engage his intended victim
in conversation, cock his wooden leg in an apparently careless fashion
over his other knee, and suddenly shoot his unsuspecting interlocutor
dead!'[44] Smith rejected the novel, though not, one suspects, without
some regret.

Lewes had planned another trip to Germany in the summer of 1840,
but in the end he did not go.[45] We lose sight of him between 12 June
1840, when he wrote to Horne about the latter's enthusiastic work on
Napoleon and talked of 'whirling about in a vortex of visitings, dinings
out, concerts, operas &c.', and 3 January 1841, when he commenced his
correspondence with Varnhagen von Ense. He sent Varnhagen a copy
of Horne's *Gregory VII*, hoping he might review it in one of the Berlin
journals. Lewes promised Varnhagen another letter soon, pleading lack
of time to write more at present.[46]

An announcement in *The Times* of 23 February 1841 reveals what had kept Lewes too busy to write at length. Under 'Marriages' there appears the following:

On the 18th inst., at St. Margaret's Westminster, G. H. Lewes, Esq., of Kensington, to Agnes, eldest daughter of Swynfen Jervis, Esq., M.P.

3

First Years of Marriage: Making a Reputation

(1841–1845)

LEWES'S marriage seems to have been a surprise even to his friends. He made no mention of its imminence in his letter to Varnhagen of 3 January 1841, though in his subsequent correspondence he was to keep Varnhagen regularly informed about Agnes and their family. Even Horne had not met Agnes by the time of the wedding. Lewes wrote to him the day before, thanking him for his 'kind & overflowing congratulations':

Your wishes have every prospect of being realized as I think you will say when you come to know her. She is indeed a treasure! & her truthful elevated nature is to me like an incarnate poem—not however to make you *envious* with a lover's raptures. I hope you will learn to regard with favorable eyes one who quite shares my admiration of Pontius-Pilatus-Gregory-Cosmo-Horne—especially as my *first present* to her was a copy of *Gregory*—sent with my *regards* & duly treasured.[1]

Lewes had probably not known Agnes for long. It is likely that he met her during his busy season of dining out and visiting, probably through such friends of Leigh Hunt's as the sanitary reformers Neil Arnott and Southwood Smith, both of whom Lewes knew. The former, a doctor, inventor, and writer on physics, was a friend of Swynfen Jervis, Agnes's father.[2] He was to be a witness at the wedding.

Lewes met Agnes either at the Jervises' London home in Whitehall Place or at her father's country seat, Darlaston Hall, near Stone in Staffordshire, where the family generally spent the summer months. By 1841 Jervis had been radical MP for Bridport in Dorset for four years. He supported electoral reform, was a free trader, and voted for the suppression of church rates. Jervis—cousin of the more famous MP for

Chester, Sir John Jervis, who became Lord Chief Justice in 1850—was especially keen on education reform and on the removal of the newspaper tax, known by campaigners as 'taxes on knowledge'.[3] He had long been a subscriber to the Society for the Diffusion of Useful Knowledge. Carlyle met Jervis about this time, and gave his opinion in an amusing epistolary tirade to his brother:

I have had a host of foolish visitors. . . . A wonderful menagerie! . . . A wretched dud called Swinfen Jervis, Member I think for Chester, called one day with his wife. . .; a dirty little atheistic radical, living seemingly in a mere element of pretentious twaddle. . . . He has a kind of anxious-indeterminate circular twitch, attended with a snuff, in the lower part of his poor peaked meagre nose, a certain melancholy in his somnolent grey eyes; he writes verses in annuals;—and his bent back seems hardly eighteen inches broad across the shoulder blades! I will return the lady's call; but hardly visit any of her routs, which must be a mere sea of *blash* [heavy rain], the elixir of all the Triviality there is in England.[4]

For all Carlyle's rhetorical excess, Jervis, who gave up his seat at the July 1841 election and subsided into the life of a private gentleman with a literary turn of mind, seems indeed to have been rather a fussy eccentric. His letters to the Society for the Diffusion of Useful Knowledge show him punctilious, well-meaning, and vain.[5] Lewes himself thought him funny, and his son Thornie was to ask in 1861 how his father's visit to 'Mrs. Jervis, no.3' had turned out. 'Is the venerable gentleman still like Pantaloon?'[6] At the time of Lewes's marriage Jervis was married to the second of his three wives, having four daughters and two surviving sons by his first wife. Agnes, born on 24 May 1822, was the eldest of his children.

As Carlyle said, Jervis was in the habit of publishing poems in annuals; when Lewes was editor of the *Leader* he printed in 1850 an 8-line poem, 'A Thought in Spring', by his father-in-law.[7] Jervis also turned his attention to editing Shakespeare, publishing *Proposed Emendations of the Text of Shakspeare's Plays* in 1860, and preparing a *Dictionary of the Language of Shakspeare* (1868), which was brought out after his death by his friend Alexander Dyce. Dante Gabriel Rossetti also had a connection with Darlaston Hall: his father had been a tutor in the Jervis family when Agnes was a child and his sister Christina stayed with them in the summer of 1852, helping the younger daughters with their conversational Italian. In that year, Rossetti sketched a satirical portrait in pen-and-ink of Christina sitting at the feet of the scholar Jervis, with a bust of Shakespeare smiling down at his enthusiastic editor. The caption reads

'We ne'er shall look upon his like again', with the annotation 'Oh Ah!
S.J.' Dante Gabriel sent the sketch to Christina with a letter of 4 August
1852 explaining it:

On the opposite page is an attempt to record, though faintly, that privileged
period of your life during which you have sat at the feet of one for whom the
ages have probably been waiting. . . . On *his* countenance is a calm serenity,
unchangeable, unmistakeable. In yours I think I read awe, mingled however
with something of that noble pride which even the companionship of greatness
has been known to bestow. Are you here transcribing from his very lips the
title-deeds of his immortality, or rather perpetuating by a sister art the aspect of
that brow where poetry has set up her throne? I know not.[8]

Rossetti is also the source of the most often repeated account of how
Lewes met Agnes. The radical MP apparently invited the radical young
aspiring author into his house as a tutor to Agnes's younger brothers and
sisters. In a letter to Jane Morris in 1880, Rossetti described Agnes as 'a
reminiscence of my earliest years, when I (a boy of 10 or so) knew her (a
very handsome good-natured girl of some 17 or 18 I suppose) in the
house of her father, Swynfen Jervis MP, a radical member of those days
and a very cultivated scholar. I remember Lewes also as tutor in the
house.' Rossetti was thinking back to 1840, when he was 11 or 12 and
Agnes 18.[9] Lewes may, indeed, have become a tutor in the Jervis family
instead of going to Germany in the summer of 1840.[10] He was doubtless
short of money at the time.

There are two other accounts of the meeting, which differ in particulars from Rossetti's. George Smith recalled in his memoirs that Lewes
was appointed private secretary to Jervis. This is quite possible. But
Smith was embroidering a little when he added that the plot of *Rose,*
Blanche, and Violet holds the key to events. He says that there were three
Jervis sisters—actually there were four—and that Lewes married the
prettiest of them 'much against the wishes of the family', who tried to
stop the wedding.[11] The other story is told, at third hand, by the
daughter of Bessie Rayner Parkes, who became a close friend of Marian
Evans in 1852, and who had by then heard several rumours about
Lewes's life. According to Bessie's daughter, Lewes was not a tutor, but
was called in to help with some private theatricals at the Jervis home and
quickly eloped with Agnes. 'Her father went after them, but it was too
late—they had already married, the unfortunate bride being only
seventeen.'[12] Picturesque as these stories of elopement are, they are
disproved by the fact that Swynfen Jervis was one of the witnesses at the

wedding, giving his written consent to the marriage of his daughter, who was still a minor, though she was 18, not 17.[13]

Thus the more exciting accounts of Lewes's marriage appear to be fiction. But in his own fiction Lewes did use some characteristics of the Jervis household and his relations with its members. Mr Meredith Vyner, father of Rose, Blanche, and Violet, looks and sounds suspiciously like Swynfen Jervis as described by Carlyle and others. Lewes sketches him rather coarsely:

A book-worm and pedant, he had the follies of his tribe. . . . He looked like a dirty bishop. . . . A physiognomist would at once have pronounced him obstinate, but weak; loud in the assertion of his intentions, vacillating in their execution . . .

People laughed at Meredith Vyner for his dirty nails and his love of Horace. . .; but they respected him for his integrity and goodness, and for his great, though ill-assorted, erudition. In a word, he was laughed at, but there was no malice in the laughter.[14]

Of the daughters, Rose is both pretty and witty—and 'Rose' was the name by which both Lewes and Thornton Hunt knew Agnes in later years—and she eventually marries the most attractive of the three 'heroes', Julius St John. Lewes makes a great deal of the fact that St John, though learned (he discusses Leopardi, Dante, Byron, Bulwer, Scott, and Jane Austen with Rose, who is charmed by his knowledge), is 'remarkably plain' to look at:

A head of enormous size was set upon the miserable shoulders of a diminutive body. . . . This head was covered with a mass of black, crisp, curly hair, which fell carelessly over a massive but irregular forehead, ornamented with two thick eyebrows, which, meeting over the nose, formed but one dark line.[15]

Lewes is here having fun at his own expense, while also congratulating himself on his intellectual attainments and his ability to attract women despite his ugliness. George Smith remembered that Lewes 'was fond of boasting of his success with the fair sex'; when Smith asked him how this was, he 'fixed upon the only feature he possessed which was likely to excite admiration. He put his finger to his eye and said, "*It is my eye!*"'[16]

Ranthorpe, too, may hold an indirect clue to Lewes's and Agnes's early relationship. Here not the hero but his friend Wynton becomes a 'private tutor in a rich Gloucestershire family'. Being 'a wit, a scholar, and a gentleman', he is treated as an honoured guest. He soon falls in love with the 18-year old daughter of the house. 'It was a mad thought, in such a country as England, for a poor tutor to aspire to the only daughter of a wealthy gentleman.'[17] In this case, unlike Lewes's own, all does not end happily. The girl marries not the tutor, but a nobleman. Later, the narrator indulges in a strange rant about how the 'aristocracy of intellect', to which Ranthorpe (and Lewes) belongs, is now set to overturn the aristocracy of birth. He concludes robustly:

Either there is dignity in intellectual rank, or there is not: if there is, no other rank is needed; if there is not, no other rank can give it; for dignity is not an accident, but a quality.[18]

Whether or not Lewes was made to feel an equal in the Jervis household, his marriage was accepted by Swynfen Jervis, who not only gave his daughter away but helped her with money in 1842, and maintained cordial, if not particularly close, relations with Agnes and his son-in-law, whom he seems to have admired.[19]

And what of Agnes herself? She was 18, small, pretty, and had obviously been well educated by her eccentric father. In the early years of her marriage she helped Lewes with his articles, and in 1846–7 she herself submitted several translations from French to *Fraser's Magazine*.[20] W. B. Scott remembered meeting Agnes, Lewes's 'child-wife', and thinking her 'one of the loveliest creatures in the world'. George Jacob Holyoake, an associate of Lewes's on the *Leader*, spoke of her being known as Rose—'and she looked it, for she had a singularly bright complexion'; Jane Carlyle talked in 1849 of Lewes's 'charming little wife'.[21]

We have one published account of the wedding. Leigh Hunt made it the centrepiece of an article entitled 'Epithalamiums—Wedding-Days—Vivia Perpetua' in the *British Miscellany* in April 1841. Hunt's description is, as we might expect, amiable, with much sentimentality varied by a touch of sharpness:

On the occasion which gave rise to the present article, the parties assembled in the church were all of a nature which it was agreeable to contemplate. The father, a man of wealth and consequence, with a spirit above the ordinary notions on such points, was at the altar, to give his daughter away to a young man of letters, not poor, but not rich. The latter, no ordinary scholar, with a rare universality of apprehension, and destined, if we are not greatly mistaken, to make a distinguished figure in his career, if he can but subject a certain vehemence of will to the greatness of his heart and understanding, had fancied that this said will would carry him through any scene unshaken; and yet, here he was, trembling as the service began, through every masculine fibre, at the thought of the solemn responsibility he was taking upon him for the happiness of the person he loved. The young lady, than whom none could have been better qualified for his companion, both by good temper and by a like catholic tendency of brain, discernible through that very kind of child-like gaiety and ingenuousness, which is confounded with a simplicity of a different sort, was more collected than himself. . . .[22]

The young couple settled down at 3 Pembroke Square, Kensington, with Mrs Willim,[23] and soon Agnes began to bear children. Because of the absence of materials relating to her, we are afforded only passing glimpses in Lewes's letters, with their references to her pregnancies, the births of their sons, and their occasional house moves from one set of rented rooms in Kensington to another. Soon after they settled into their first home, a letter of congratulation came from Leigh Hunt, who wrote with 'tears in his eyes', sending suitable poems for a honeymooning couple, including Spenser's 'Epithalamium' and a volume of *Arabian Nights*, 'full of luxuriosifications not to be thought ill of by those who love books'.[24] John Stuart Mill also wrote warmly to Lewes, whom he was helping in his career. Mill had already arranged for Lewes's article on the French drama to be published in the *Westminster Review*, and through him also the Shelley article appeared there in April 1841. He was now reading another of Lewes's essays in manuscript, the one on Hegel's *Aesthetics* which had been contemplated since Lewes's visit to Berlin. Mill wrote briefly soon after the wedding, still addressing Lewes formally:

My dear Sir,
  Excuse my breaking in upon you at such a time as this, but I think it best to write while the impression is fresh. Of course I do not expect any answer. I have read your MS. which I think very well done, & likely when finished & finally revised to be quite suitable to the Edinburgh. You have not however yet convinced me that the line between poetry, & passionate writing of any kind, is best drawn where metre ends & prose begins. . . .
  And now without any more on these untimely matters let me conclude by wishing you as I do most cordially all possible prosperity & happiness in your new condition, which all I have heard of the lady inclines me to regard as an enviable one.[25]

Lewes took his long Hegel article very seriously, and seems to have hoped Mill would get it placed in the prestigious *Edinburgh Review*. Mill exerted himself generously on this, as on many occasions, for his young acquaintance. Obeying Lewes's request, he annotated the manuscript freely—'I have been, & intended to be, *hyper*critical'—but he was afraid the *Edinburgh*'s editor would find it 'too German', as Francis Jeffrey had found Carlyle's articles in the 1820s, though he had made an exception and let Carlyle enthuse ocasionally.[26] Mill advised Lewes to tone down his diatribes against English criticism, for 'if I were sending such matter to the editor of the Edinburgh I should feel as if I were civilly giving him a thump on the face.'[27]

No doubt Lewes took some of Mill's well-meant and shrewd advice. But the 'vehemence of will' noted by Leigh Hunt in the wedding article prevented him from tailoring the essay enough to suit the *Edinburgh*, whose editor, Macvey Napier, rejected it in the end. The article was accepted by John Mitchell Kemble of the *British and Foreign Review*, once again thanks to Mill, who wrote to Kemble in May 1841, describing Lewes as 'rather a good writer' who 'has ideas (even in the Coleridgean sense) & much reading'.[28]

The Hegel article as it was finally published, in October 1842, was long, detailed, showy, and impressive. No English critic had taken on Hegel before, and Lewes was still half-infected with enthusiasm for Hegel's attempt to deduce a critical method from his philosophy of mind. Whereas English criticism, apart from efforts by Coleridge, had avoided asking fundamental questions about the nature and origin of art, being on the whole content merely to praise isolated passages here and pick holes there, German critics had attempted a philosophy—even a science—of criticism. Before reaching the *Lectures on Aesthetics*, Lewes spends many pages discussing, in a rather loose and rambling way, the questions about poetry raised by Wordsworth, Coleridge, and Mill himself in his article 'What is Poetry?' (*Monthly Repository*, January 1833). But he finds even Coleridge wanting—'Coleridge is everywhere vague and unsatisfactory'.[29]

What Hegel in particular has to offer here is a definition of art, including literature, as the expression of a 'religious Idea'. Lest British readers baulk at this, Lewes hastens to inform them that this has nothing to do with formal religion, but means, '*more Germanico*', that every Idea can be thought religious which is 'the formula of any truth leading to new contemplations of the infinite, or to new forms in our social relations'. Aware that these two kinds of 'truth' might seem rather far apart to the English reader, he cautions us to guard against 'any narrow or exclusive interpretation' of the terms used.[30] Hegel's aesthetics are but a part of his whole system, in which intellectual and experiential contradictions are resolved, only to generate further contradictions; through this historical process the universal Ideal of Spirit becomes actualized.

Being both conscious of how strange such language sounds to Anglo-Saxon ears and less than wholly convinced himself by Hegel's argument—though he undoubtedly admired Hegel's wide learning and ambitious sweeping of all art at all times into his system—Lewes hovers on the brink of plunging into a full discussion of that system. Instead, he spends pages quoting from Carlyle, Shelley, and other favourite authors, coming round on page 41 to a brief biography of Hegel and leaving himself only a few pages for an exposition of Hegel's ideas on art. He is open about his difficulties:

We candidly admit that we neither *understand* every part of Hegel's 'Aesthetik', nor do we agree generally with German philosophy; but that, nevertheless, Hegel is the most delightful, thought-inciting and instructive work on the subject we have yet met with, and that four years' constant study of it has only served the more to impress us with its depth and usefulness.[31]

Lewes had studied the *Lectures* closely when in Germany, as his annotations to the copy given him by Varnhagen show, but his heart was not really in the Carlylean task of winning admirers for a German philosopher. He was candid enough for his purposes here; when he came a few years later to consider Hegel's place—and German philosophy's place—in the history of philosophy in general, his tone had become almost entirely negative. Though referring to the *Lectures on Aesthetics* as 'suggestive' and capable of throwing new light on the subject, Lewes pronounced anathema on the philosophical system of which they are part:

But the system itself we may leave to all readers to decide, whether it be worthy of any attention, except as an illustration of the devious errors of speculation. A system which begins with assuming that Being and Non-Being are the same, because Being in the abstract is the Unconditioned, and so also is Non-Being; therefore both, as unconditioned, are the same; a system which proceeds upon the identity of contraries as the method of Philosophy; a system in which Thought is the same as the Thing, and the Thing is the same as the Thought; a system in which the only real positive existence is that of simple Relation, the two terms of which are Mind and Matter; this system were it wholly true, leaves all the questions, for which science is useful as a light, just as much in the dark as ever; and is, therefore, unworthy the attention of earnest men working for the benefit of mankind.[32]

The 1842 essay ends with a few quotations from the *Lectures*, drawing from them the lesson that, to quote from A. W. Schlegel's *Dramatic Lectures*, a critic must 'possess an universality of mind; a flexibility, which, throwing aside all personal predilections and blind habits, enables him to transport himself into the peculiarities of other ages and nations, and *feel them, as it were, from their central point*'.[33] If any mental qualities particularly characterized Lewes as a literary critic over the next fifteen years or so, these were flexibility and universality of mind; but with Lewes they stopped well short of the 'absolute relativism' of Hegel.

In 1841 Lewes, with Agnes expecting their first child in December, needed a regular income. Still keen to benefit from Mill's introduction to the *Edinburgh Review*, he wrote to Napier in November, accepting with equanimity the editor's objections to 'German philosophy' but assuring him that the Hegel article had not been consigned to the waste paper basket:

From what you said before I am sure you will be glad to learn that the trouble I took with the Hegel article (& it was immense) has not been lost for Mr Kemble—innovating & German!—likes it & prints it in the forthcoming number of the British & Foreign—which tho' not exactly the *Edinburgh* has nevertheless a solid reputation of its kind—and it is not contradicted by the tone of the article. Indeed my reason for supposing that the *Edinburgh* would print such a paper was solely that it had printed far more *unusual* things of Carlyles—tho' to be sure *his* writing compensates for its excentricity.[34]

The tone is typical of Lewes at this time: he is the young man seeking to make a reputation (and money), and willing up to a point to flatter and petition those in a position to help him, but a strong streak of independence and devil-may-care insouciance finds utterance in some boasting and tactlessness.

Napier proved recalcitrant on two other subjects offered by Lewes in his letter: 'Recent Tragedies', which was subsequently accepted by the *Westminster Review* (April 1842) and 'The Spanish Drama', which appeared in the *Foreign Quarterly Review* (July 1843). Mill had to write to Napier in February 1842, protesting against the latter's impression that Lewes was a 'coxcomb'. Not at all, said Mill, though he was 'very likely to be thought so':

But what gives him that air is precisely the buoyancy of spirit which you have observed in him, & he is so prompt & apparently presumptuous in undertaking anything for which he feels the slightest vocation (however much it may be really beyond his strength) only because he does not care at all for failure, knowing & habitually feeling that he gets up stronger after every fall & believing as I do that the best way of improving one's faculties is to be continually trying what is above one's present strength. I should say he is confident but not at all conceited, for he will bear to be told anything however unflattering about what he writes . . .[35]

Though Mill and Lewes were so different in temperament, they became quite intimate in the first years of Lewes's married life. The rather dry Mill, living in a chaste relationship with Mrs Harriet Taylor, whom he was unable to marry until 1851, after her husband's death, wrote mildly flirtatious letters to Agnes. Egged on by Lewes to write to her while she was visiting her family in Staffordshire in July 1841, he talked elaborately of 'you princesses' and his desire to kiss her hand. He was also instructed to tell her that Lewes was 'perfectly miserable' without her, adding how envious he, an unmarried man, was of Lewes's married bliss. On 20 December 1841, two days before Agnes gave birth to a daughter—who died on 24 December—Mill wrote to her to thank her for some slippers she had sent him. He playfully indicated a change in the chemistry of his friendships, urging her to tell Lewes that 'the elective affinity for you and Beethoven is likely very much to disturb the attraction toward Carlyle'.[36] Mill was perhaps thinking here of how he had recently sat at the feet of Carlyle (and had to extricate himself from the increasingly unsuitable role of disciple), somewhat as Lewes now— though with less deference—sat at Mill's feet.[37]

Lewes also encouraged his other friends to come and meet Agnes. To Horne he wrote flippantly in July 1841 that Agnes was 'very anxious' to see Horne and had 'certain sinister intentions' of falling in love with him, whether he chose to come in the shape of his Cosmo, or Gregory, or with the 'more suitable, sustained, enviable, Homeric grandeur & gravity of A Commissioner!'[38] That Lewes was still seeing Leigh Hunt often is clear from the letter he wrote to Varnhagen on 5 December 1841. He thanks him for his good wishes about Agnes, adding, 'I am happier than I could ever have believed—expect to be a father the end of this month— and love my wife more every day—she knows German very well and our friend Leigh Hunt the poet, says She is his ideal of a German woman.'[39]

Of his intellectual efforts, Lewes writes that he has been 'doing a good deal' to 'bring about a healthy study of German Literature here'. Not only is there the Hegel article, but he is also beginning an article, also for the *British and Foreign Review*, on 'Göthe as Man and Artist' (not published until March 1843). He also claims to have written a tragedy and two comedies; the tragedy (possibly his translation of Goethe's *Tasso*) cannot be acted because Macready played in a similar part years ago— 'Can you conceive such a state of things?'—but one of the comedies has been accepted at Covent Garden. However, a problem has arisen here too, 'because the principal comic actor (Farren) would not play his part, alledging that another character in the piece would get "*more laughs*" than he should!! This is pleasant, eh?'[40]

Though some of this may have been exaggerated in order to impress Varnhagen, it is true that Lewes was sending manuscripts of plays to

Charles James Mathews, manager of Covent Garden, at this time. Falling easily into the ebullient, familiar, rather brash tone of many theatre people of the time, he sent Mathews in October 1841 a sketch of his comedy, swearing 'as God is my judge & short is my shirt' that the characters are '*new*' and that 'a rattling comedy in five acts' could be made of them—'*ten*, if *you* like, for with them I could write one as long as—as long as—my hair! or as short as the shirt, before mentioned'. He urges Mathews to decide before the end of the theatre season, signing himself: 'Yours "breathless" (not "*like a nun*" but like an "Unacted") G. H. Lewes.'[41]

Mathews seems to have declined, and Lewes's chances of getting a play put on at Covent Garden evaporated when Mathews left abruptly in May 1842, having declared himself bankrupt. Lewes wrote wryly in October of that year that he had almost had the opportunity of becoming 'minister' during Mathews's 'pleasant reign' at the theatre but that after Mathews's abdication he had 'prudently retired from the field; for though anxious to become a Dramatist I cannot afford to be an Unacted one'. A new plan, that of collaborating with Mathews on a comedy, is suggested, Lewes being sanguine that Mathews would command favourable and 'above all, *immediate attention*; which I might cool my heels & whistle for through two seasons'. But, alas for Lewes's hopes, Mathews was on the point of fleeing his creditors in the usual fashion, by bolting to France, which he did in November.[42] For the time being Lewes put aside his ambitions to follow in his theatrical grandfather's footsteps.

He was busy on several other fronts. Through Mill he had access to the *Westminster Review*, now edited by William Hickson; the *British and Foreign Review*; and the *Foreign Quarterly Review*, owned by Dr Worthington and edited in 1842–3 by John Forster. He was also contributing to the *Monthly Magazine*, which carried short articles of his on Balzac and George Sand in 1842, as well as his 'Bibundtücker' squibs, described in a letter to Varnhagen as 'setsoff against my *aesthetic* praises' in the Hegel essay.[43] Showing remarkable energy and versatility, Lewes published articles during 1842–3 on English drama, English criticism (its 'Errors and Abuses'), the poetry of the Roman Empire, A. W. Schlegel's dramatic criticism, Spanish drama, modern French philosophy, and Goethe. It must have been about this time that he decided to work on the biography of Goethe; he probably began his correspondence with Varnhagen partly with this aim in view, for Varnhagen was the chief source of Goethe material in Germany. On 2 March 1842 Lewes wrote to Varnhagen that he had just finished a 'long and laborious *étude* on *Göthe*'. Later in the letter he quotes Goethe, 'my revered Author', on the necessity for avoiding religion and politics.[44] The Goethe essay mentioned here is the most interesting of his many journalistic pieces at this time.

The article, like its predecessor on Hegel, is massive. It opens on a striking note, a pastiche of the kind of thing said and written by English critics and editors:

'Ah! now do you really think Göthe was not a *charlatan*?' asked a smart dogmatical critic, with that complacent smile, which, while it indicates a tender pity for the weakness of another, reflects so serenely on one's own superiority. The speaker was ignorant of German—'but that's not much!' The speaker was also quite incapable of seeing into the significance of such a man as Göthe, whatever knowledge he might have of the language—*n'importe*![45]

Lewes thus adopts the stance of a latter-day Carlyle; he will put benighted England right by attacking its absurd prejudices against a foreign author's claim to greatness. The essay is detailed, comprehensive, and attempts a balance of criticism and biography. Lewes spends too long, perhaps, arguing with German critics about whether Goethe was cold, indifferent to politics, and too much the willing servant of the Duke of Weimar. His reply, however, is interesting. Never mind if he *was* cold and selfish—'he has had no equal in poetry in these modern times; no one has caught his grace, beauty, irony, clearness, and above all *wisdom*.' Goethe was 'essentially an artist', and Lewes uses this argument against those critics, English and German, who complain of the immoral tendency of his works: 'ethics became subordinate in fact to aesthetics.'[46] Here is the germ of the thesis which was to inform the *Life of Goethe*.

Mill thought the essay Lewes's best to date, in spite of the Carlylism of the opening pages, not to mention 'something of the tranchant manner which makes people call you by various uncomplimentary names indicative of self-conceit'.[47] Kemble, too, though he accepted the article, criticized some points of style. Lewes answered his objections, insisting that where Kemble suspected carelessness of composition he had, in fact, had deliberate effects in mind. 'I am sensible of many deficiencies', writes the young critic, 'but, as Sir Positive Atall would say "if there is *one thing* in which I am *superlatively* endowed" it is carefulness!' He goes on to explain, in that half-mocking, forward manner understood by Mill but disliked by some others, how he always, 'as a matter of Art', begins an article with a joke, a paradox, or some startling proposition, to provoke the reader's attention. 'Knock a man down & he listens to an explanation.' The *Edinburgh Review* writers really did label Goethe a humbug, so such tactics are necessary in writing of Goethe. But if Kemble thinks certain words or phrases need to be changed, Lewes is not one to manifest a 'passionate attachment' to his own prose, being quite willing to have his articles improved.[48]

Lewes's tone with his different editors shows subtle variations. With Kemble he was polite but assertive. With Hickson of the *Westminster Review* he was more aggressive, since Hickson paid only £10. 10s. 0d. for each article, whereas for the Hegel Kemble gave him £50 and for the Goethe more than £60. 'I got more money by one single article in the British and Foreign than by all the articles I ever wrote in the Westminster', he told Hickson in June 1842. When Hickson criticized, Lewes kicked back.[49] But to Macvey Napier of the *Edinburgh* Lewes adopted a much more deferential tone. Sending his paper on dramatic reform in November 1842—a topical subject, since Parliament was considering a bill to remove the monopoly of Covent Garden and Drury Lane in the presentation of legitimate drama—he gave in willingly to Napier's criticisms. So eager was he to have a connection with the *Edinburgh* that he was happy to 'submit to its regulations'.[50]

In the event, Lewes wrote no more than six reviews for the *Edinburgh*, beginning with 'Dramatic Reform' (October 1843) and ending with his rather controversial review of Charlotte Brontë's *Shirley* (January 1850). His style never really suited Napier. Lewes was conscious that this had something to do with his lack of orthodox (i.e. university and classical) education. On two occasions he wrote quite humbly, apologizing for his 'tendency towards *abstractions*', which he blamed on his having spent, as he said, 'the greater part of my youth in France and Germany', with the result that he 'naturally became impregnated with Gallicisms & Germanicisms'.[51]

If he trod thus carefully with Napier, Lewes was more often inclined, rightly, to think of his miscellaneous education as an asset. Certainly it gave him a chance to write on subjects hardly touched on by his more insular contemporaries—subjects like the Italian poet Leopardi, the philosopher Spinoza, and the French novelist George Sand.[52]

The Spinoza essay, published in the *Westminster Review* in May 1843 and soon reprinted separately in pamphlet form, is a well-told narrative of Spinoza's life of excommunication and poverty, together with a clear exposition of Spinoza's position as a precursor of Strauss and Feuerbach in his historical treatment of the Bible, and an account of the *Ethics* of 'this wonderful man'. Spinoza's chief merit, according to Lewes, was to have given to the old doctrine of pantheism a 'systematic exposition and development'. Far from being the anathematized atheist of report,

Spinoza turns out 'on nearer acquaintance' to be rather the 'God-intoxicated man' of Novalis' description.[53] In thus introducing Spinoza to the English public, Lewes for the first time gives evidence of his powers of popularizing, of making difficult, even technical, arguments palatable to the layman. In deftly placing Spinoza in the history of philosophy, he anticipates the much larger task he was soon to undertake in the *Biographical History of Philosophy* (1845–6).

While Lewes was writing busily on the literature and philosophy of Germany and—increasingly—France, his domestic life was exceedingly happy. On 24 November 1842 Agnes had a boy, named Charles Lee Lewes after his famous ancestor. Lewes told Horne in January 1843 that Agnes was well, 'and the young Socrates also'. Giving Varnhagen all his news in July 1843, he described his life:

Young, ambitious, and ardent, you may easily imagine that I have not been idle the last two years, but I cannot enumerate the various outlets of my activity. My time has been pleasantly, profitably and happily employed. I am as happy in the marriage state as man can be—love my wife more and more the longer I know her—and have got a glorious little boy, the admiration of every one, and the pet of his parents.[54]

He also told Varnhagen (rather tactlessly) that he now found himself more and more sympathetic with French thought and less and less with German. In March 1842 he had already declared his leanings towards French philosophy, particularly Comte's *Cours de philosophie positive*, ' a wonderful book', especially in those parts where it dealt with social science.[55] The influence of Comte, via Mill, was at work on Lewes. In the spring of 1842 he visited Paris, first asking Hickson and Mill for introductions to 'all the Literary & Philos. or otherwise interesting people' there, and promising the former that the *Westminster* would taste the fruits of his trip.[56] Mill was particularly helpful, furnishing him with letters to Comte and Victor Cousin, as well as the historians Alexis de Tocqueville and Jules Michelet. To Cousin he wrote that Lewes was a young friend of wide knowledge and promising talent, who was beginning to become known by his writings. With the notoriously prickly Comte Mill was more cautious, thanking him fulsomely for agreeing to see Lewes, who, he said, proved his character and intelligence by his 'lively admiration' of Comte's work.[57] Comte graciously announced to Mill in a postcript to his letter of 29 May 1842 that he had enjoyed meeting Lewes, who seemed to him a 'loyal and interesting young man'.[58]

Lewes's visit to Paris was cut short, as he told Michelet on 26 May, by his hearing from home that Agnes was ill.[59] (She may have feared a miscarriage.) But, brief as the visit was, it did indeed bear fruit in several articles: 'The Modern Metaphysics and Moral Philosophy of France' (July 1843), 'The State of Historical Science in France' (October 1843), and 'The State of Criticism in France' (January 1844), all published in the *British and Foreign Review*. Showing his debt to Mill's thinking at this time, he seeks in the first of these articles to correct the erroneous impression current in England that French philosophy is entirely materialist, atheist, and sceptical, in the tradition of the eighteenth-century *philosophes*. On the contrary, writes Lewes, Comte in his great work *Cours de philosophie positive* (1830–42) has shown that 'a social science is possible and that it must be studied on the same method as the other sciences'. Thus Lewes declares himself a thorough disciple of the positivist philosophy.[60]

In a letter of July 1843 Mill told Comte that his 'jeune ami Lewes' had just eulogized him in the *British and Foreign Review* in such a way as to draw the attention of English readers to Comte's intellectual superiority. The great man replied calmly, professing himself happy to hear of Lewes's efforts, but excusing himself from actually reading Lewes's essay, not feeling he could suspend his 'regime of abstaining from serious reading' while he was working on his great system. He authorized Mill to thank Lewes for his article on his behalf.[61]

With Mill and another of Mill's disciples, Alexander Bain, Lewes was party to a plan to translate for the first time into English parts of Comte's voluminous work (six volumes so far). Mill addressed Comte on the subject in 1845, saying how honoured all three would be if Comte would allow it. Comte was also asked to help the venture by presenting his ideas in a form suitable for translation in English periodical articles. Mill was aware how much of a 'derangement' this would be to Comte's 'régime cérébral habituel'. This was Mill's tactful way of trying to help Comte financially at a difficult time for him—Comte having lost his teaching position at the École Polytechnique—as well as to proselytize for him in Britain.[62] Nothing came of it. But Lewes's interest in Comte found full expression in his exposition of the *Philosophie positive* in the *Leader* in 1852–3, reprinted as *Comte's Philosophy of the Sciences* in 1853, and, more immediately, in the *Biographical History of Philosophy*.

This work, Lewes's first published book, is entirely·characteristic. It consists of four small volumes (i and ii bound together and published in 1845, iii and iv published as one in 1846), in which Lewes takes Western philosophy from Thales, the 'father of Greek speculation', up to Comte, the master of modern philosophy. He prefaces the work with two quotations. One is from Goethe:

Man is not born to solve the mystery of Existence; but he must, nevertheless, attempt it, in order that he may learn how to keep within the limits of the Knowable.

The other is from Tennyson's 'Locksley Hall' (1842):

> Yet I doubt not thro' the ages, one increasing purpose runs,
> And the thoughts of men are widened by the process of the suns.

From these quotations it is clear that Lewes favours the empirical tradition of Aristotle, Bacon, Locke, and Hume over the idealist tradition of Plato, Descartes, and Leibnitz. He also declares himself an optimist, a follower of Comte's belief in the inevitable progress of human knowledge. The work is intended to be 'a contribution to the History of Humanity', despite its brevity, which Lewes vigorously defends: 'It is small: not because materials for a larger were deficient, but because only what was deemed essential has been selected.' Lewes boasts that he is no professional philosopher—'I make no pretensions to the character of a *savant*'—but he assures any reader inclined to be snooty that 'such as it is, the erudition is not "second-hand"'.[63]

What the book is, for all its ambitious scope and tiny size, is a bright, opinionated, informative contribution to the history of philosophy aimed unashamedly, but not condescendingly, at the layman. Its publisher, Charles Knight, was well known for his educational publications, intended to bring classical works of literature and philosophy within the financial reach of the increasing number of literate readers. Such readers found in the first two volumes, priced at a shilling each, accounts of the ancient philosophers, for whom philosophy was metaphysics, i.e. the study of phenomena beyond the physical, and therefore belonging under the protective wing of theology. Volume iii begins with 'modern philosophy', with two thinkers sharing the claim to be 'fathers': Descartes, representing 'the pure Deductive, *a priori*, movement' and claimed by all metaphysicians as their leader, and Bacon, 'head of the Inductive, *a posteriori*, movement' and claimed by 'men of science' as *their* leader.[64] Given Lewes's own proclivities, it is not surprising to find him praising Bacon in particular for his experimental method, by which all claims to knowledge are to be verified by appealing to experience. Descartes, on the other hand, argues from ideas to things, assuming the existence, and validity, of innate ideas; this, for Lewes, is his 'cardinal error', and one which is fundamental to the whole tradition of philosophy which holds ideas to be possible independently of experience.[65]

Descartes is followed by Spinoza—here Lewes incorporates his *Westminster Review* essay into the work. Then come the empirical philosophies of Locke, Hume, and Condillac. When he arrives at Kant, Lewes is not perplexed by the notorious difficulty of Kant's writing:

Kant called his system the *Critical* Philosophy. His object was to examine into the nature of this *Experience* which led to Scepticism [in Hume especially]. While men were agreed that Experience was the source of all Knowledge, Kant asked himself, what is this Experience? What are its Elements?[66]

In other words, Kant criticized the limitations of the empirical method without returning to the uncritical dogmas of the school of innate ideas. While Lewes may be accused of oversimplifying Kant in his brief exposition, he cannot be found guilty of underestimating or misrepresenting Kant's system and its contribution to the history of philosophy. Lewes's ability to see the wood as well as the trees here is admirable. His 43 pages on Kant are as good an introduction—and they claim to be no more than that—as could be wished for.

The little book ends on a high point—with Comte. 'Comte is the Bacon of the nineteenth century.' Lewes describes the three stages through which each branch of knowledge passes until it reaches the desired one—the positive stage:

In the *supernatural* stage, the mind seeks after *causes*; aspires to know the *essences* of things and their modes of operation. It regards all effects as the productions of supernatural agents, whose intervention is the *cause* of all the apparent anomalies and irregularities. Nature is animated by supernatural beings. Every unusual phenomenon is a sign of the pleasure or displeasure of some being adored and propitiated as a God. . . .

In the *metaphysical* stage, which is only a modification of the former, but which is important as a transitional stage, the supernatural agents give place to abstract forces (personified abstractions) supposed to inhere in the various substances, and capable themselves of engendering phenomena. The highest condition of this stage is when all these forces are brought under one general force named Nature.

In the *positive* stage, the mind, convinced of the futility of all inquiry into causes and essences, applies itself to the observation and classification of *laws* which regulate effects; that is to say, the invariable relations of succession and similitude which all things bear to each other. The highest condition of this stage would be, to be able to represent all phenomena as the various particulars of one general view.[67]

The attraction of the system for Lewes, as for Mill, Herbert Spencer, George Eliot, and many other Victorians, was its combination of the empirical method—the inclusion of science—and the exclusion of theology from philosophy. Moreover, as the pressing need in a rapidly industrialized age was to have a 'scientific' study of society, Comte's new science of 'sociology' (he coined the term) seemed timely.[68]

Lewes's book was a success. Of course there were those who sneered at its ambitious scope and superficiality. The reviewer in the *Classical Museum* said Lewes had 'undertaken a history of Greek Philosophy without knowing any thing of Greek, nor of Philosophy'; and someone, possibly J. A. Froude, wrote rather similarly in the *Oxford and Cambridge Review*.[69] It was the first time, but by no means the last, that Lewes came under attack as an upstart by members of the 'Establishment'.

But there were enough people who admired the work. By August 1845 Lewes could report to Varnhagen that the first two volumes had sold 7,000 copies. A year later he told W. B. Scott that 10,000 copies of all the volumes had gone. Lewes also had 'a most flattering letter' from Comte, as well he might.[70] Comte wrote to him in July 1846, thanking him for the present of volumes i and ii (the classical part) and expressing gratitude for Lewes's words of praise for him in the introduction. Indeed, Comte confessed that he had been so engrossed in reading these pages (about himself) that he had been carried on, 'almost involuntarily', past the passages on his own work, and had found himself reading the whole book. Happily, this 'premature infraction' of his usual abstinence from reading the works of others had given him no regrets. Lewes's reply to this shows him deferential—he signs himself 'your sincere and affectionate Pupil'—and able to boast of his success: 'My book is read at Oxford and Cambridge as well as by artisans and even women.'[71]

And so it was. In November 1857 John Sharpe of the *Leicester Advertiser* wrote to the publisher of the second edition, J. W. Parker, begging him to bring out a special cheap edition. 'I believe I am only expressing the opinion of many', he wrote, 'when I say that a cheap edition of this, the best work of its class, would be an invaluable boon to many to whom expensive books are inaccessible.' As for women, when Harriet Martineau read the account of Comte in Lewes's book in 1851, she immediately made plans first to read Comte's works and then to translate them.[72] Her abridged translation of the *Cours* was published by John Chapman in 1853, at the same time as Lewes's own reprint of his *Leader* articles. Herbert Spencer, too, recalled in his *Autobiography* that after meeting Lewes in 1850 he read the *Biographical History of Philosophy* in its shilling volumes. Before this he had ignored philosophy, giving up after reading the first few pages of Kant's *Critique of Pure Reason*. Spencer, who almost rivalled Comte in his self-confidence and habit of 'cerebral hygiene'—keeping the mind free of the clutter introduced by the reading of the works of others—claimed that on reading Lewes's book he became acquainted for the first time with 'the general course of philosophical thought'. This in turn stimulated his interest in psychology, which he was to make his subject of study over the next fifty years.[73]

For the second edition in 1857 Lewes revised and enlarged the book. A third edition, further revised and 'greatly altered', with the word 'Biographical' dropped from the title, appeared in 1867,[74] with more editions being published in 1871, 1880, and 1891. Opinion was divided as to whether Lewes's additions over the years represented an improvement on the original. Positivists were generally pleased with the book in all its versions, though in later reworkings Lewes added dissenting criticisms of Comte's late works. Frederic Harrison, one of the leading English Comtists, felt that in its original form the book had 'acted on the mind of this generation almost more than any other single book except Mr. Mill's *Logic*'.[75] Many non-Positivists, from Benjamin Jowett to Lord Acton, were sceptical. In 1885 Acton rudely pronounced the work a 'vacant record of incoherent error' which, he nevertheless admitted, was 'still read with pleasure', though not, presumably, by him. More temperately, Jowett expressed his bewildered opinion—one which is probably shared by most modern readers for whom Comte's is at best a name vaguely known to belong among the minor figures in the history of philosophy—that it was a poor thing to have studied all philosophies and to end up adopting that of Comte.[76]

As to whether Lewes's additions were improvements, it seems to me that Holyoake's assessment is the right one. The first edition, he recalled, 'fascinated all students who were beginning to turn their attention to philosophy':

To this day [1892], all who possess the original volumes value them highly. Mr. Lewes afterwards reproduced the work, with all the erudite illustrations and authorities with which he was so familiar. It is valued by scholars, but is beyond the appreciation of the far larger class whom he had first interested, instructed, and inspired.[77]

Over the years Lewes allowed himself to be piqued by academic critics into overloading the work with scholarly references, thus ensuring that it fell between two stools, being neither genuinely popular nor truly scholarly. In its original form the book deserved to be, as it was, in all its boldness and aggressiveness, the maker of its author's reputation.

4

---⬥---

A Man of Many Parts

(1846–1849)

DR ARNOTT, whom Lewes praised in the *Biographical History of Philosophy*, calling his *Elements of Physics* 'perhaps the most perfect specimen of positive philosophy this country has produced',[1] gave his middle name to the Leweses' second son, born on 14 April 1844. The boy was called Thornton Arnott Lewes, taking his first name from Thornton Hunt, Lewes's best friend and near neighbour in Kensington.[2] It was probably during her pregnancy with Thornie, as he was known, that Lewes wrote the only letter to Agnes which has survived. It is an undated note from Vernon Hill, the Hampshire home of Arthur Helps, miscellaneous writer and private secretary to Lord Morpeth. Helps moved in the Southwood Smith–Arnott circle of sanitary reformers, and he also knew Kemble of the *British and Foreign Review*. He admired Lewes's Goethe article in that journal, thinking it 'one of the best specimens of biography' he had ever read, and described other Lewes articles, particularly the one on dramatic reform (*Edinburgh Review*, October 1843), as 'really extraordinary productions'.[3] Helps therefore sought Lewes out, and the latter was soon visiting Vernon Hill regularly, one of a set of congenial talkers whom Helps gathered round him, usually between Christmas and New Year, and on whose conversation he based his dialogues, *Friends in Council* (1847). Lewes and Helps were to become very good friends, dedicating their books to one another and remaining close until Helps's death in 1875.

Lewes's letter to Agnes, probably written during the Christmas or New Year week of 1843–4, is a playful, affectionate piece of writing (and drawing), alluding to Agnes's being five months pregnant with Thornie. It is short, reading in its entirety:

Darling & Beautiful Fat!
As you have only one eye to read with I wont bother the other.

'Bother' is still the word. I have written to Mathews. I have grieved over your eye.
I have reread your letter.
I have pronounced it pretty.
I send you my portrait as it is painted on the hearts of Lionesses.

The letter ends with a sketch of a lion, with its tail—'Postscript'—on the reverse of the page.[4]

Lewes's literary earnings in 1845 were £288. 14s. od., not a large income for a man of 28 with a wife and two children to support. His earnings rose to £403. 1s. 6d. in 1846, when Knight gave him £160 for the third and fourth volumes of the *Biographical History of Philosophy*, and he was publishing articles in the *Westminster*, *Foreign Quarterly*, and *Edinburgh* Reviews, and *Fraser's Magazine*. Agnes, too, though expecting a third child, Herbert Arthur Lewes, born on 10 July 1846, contributed translations from French to *Fraser's Magazine* during 1846. Their income was further boosted that year by a legacy of £100 from Agnes's uncle.[5]

In February 1846 Lewes paid another visit to Paris. He called on Comte on 1 April, but could not see him. Comte was nursing Clotilde de Vaux, a married woman (separated from her criminal husband) with whom he had an intense, adoring, and chaste relationship. (Interestingly, his situation had a parallel in Mill's, who also adored a married woman, Mrs Taylor, though *her* husband was not an absconded forger and embezzler.) When Lewes next called, on 6 April, he found the philosopher mourning the death, the previous day, of the woman who later became the chief (secular) saint in his positivist calendar.[6] Much later Lewes recalled his pity for the grieving Comte.

While in Paris, Lewes saw for the first time another French writer whom he greatly admired. This was George Sand, at whose house he met, among others, Louis Blanc, socialist and later exile in London, and Chopin.[7] Lewes had already written several enthusiastic articles on George Sand; in the first of them (*Monthly Magazine*, May 1842) he had adopted the same defence-by-aggression tactics as in the Shelley and Goethe essays. First he stated the case often made against her: George Sand dressed as a man, smoked cigars, was separated from her husband, openly took lovers, and sometimes wrote 'with vehemence' against marriage. Then followed the defence: she had been the victim of an unhappy arranged marriage with an indifferent older man; and she did not write so much against marriage as against its legalized abuse and the unfairness of the marriage laws towards women. Lewes vigorously defended her right to do so. When he came to edit the *Leader* with Hunt in 1850, they ensured a frequent airing for the subject of the marriage laws, particularly in England, advocating a fairer and more affordable system of divorce. As for George Sand's merits as a writer, these were her habit of writing, like Goethe, naturally from her own experience, and having, also like Goethe, a 'magical' style.[8]

In his next article on George Sand, in the *Foreign Quarterly Review* of July 1844, Lewes praised her by comparing her to Balzac, rather as he had used Byron to show Shelley in a brighter light. Though professing to differ somewhat from her adherence to free love, social democracy, and the religion of humanity, Lewes paid tribute to her sincerity and her intensity, so different from Balzac's shrewd but prolix manner. Where Balzac 'cannot mention a single room in the house, but he must instantly make an inventory of the furniture, as if with an eye to distraining for rent', George Sand's writing is 'impassioned inspiration'.[9]

Lewes had first tried to see George Sand when he was in Paris in 1842. Having failed on that occasion—she was probably at her country home—he began a correspondence with her. She wrote pleasantly to her English admirer in May 1843, congratulating him on the birth of Charles and sending warm greetings to Agnes.[10] In Paris once more in March 1846, Lewes wrote to her again, sending her his 1844 article as 'a feeble expression of my admiration for your genius' and begging to be allowed to see her:

That you have no time for visits of curiosity I am aware; but you too well know my sentiments towards you, not to be assured that whatever curiosity I may have to see the femme célèbre, my great desire is to press the hand and hear the voice of one whom I have long considered as a friend.

My wife begged me, if I had the good fortune of seeing you, to say a thousand sweet things for her.[11]

She did receive him, several times, as he reported to Varnhagen on his return to London, and she seems to have been favourably impressed by her visitor. When her friend Charles Duvernet was about to visit London at the end of April, she gave him two letters of introduction, one to Harriet Grote and one to Lewes. Her comments about these two English acquaintances are most interesting.

With regard to Harriet Grote, wife of George Grote, the celebrated historian of Greece and Professor of History at University College London, George Sand tells Duvernet to spell out the fact that his wife *is* his wife and not his mistress. She explains that she has given Mrs Grote an account of Duvernet's family and fortune, such things being necessary 'dans ce pays-là, même avec les meilleures personnes'. But as to Lewes, he and his wife, whom George Sand has not met but from whom she has received 'des amitiés charmantes' in letters, will offer Duvernet perhaps the most relaxed, unstuffy welcome ('sans-gêne') he could hope to find in London. Lewes had clearly painted a picture of his family life as close and happy—'c'est une famille très unie'—but socially free and easy. George Sand's perceptiveness about the social difference between the Leweses and the Grotes is endorsed by a snobbish comment made at this time by Harriet Grote to another acquaintance she had in common with Lewes, Varnhagen von Ense. Though Lewes 'is known to Mr Grote as a very studious and accomplished young man', she wrote in May 1846,

he does not happen to belong to the social cluster in which our friends are comprised, and being a married man we have not wished to entice him from his home by inviting him to Burnham. You, living under a different social organization from ours, may not be aware how much English people are influenced in the choice of their associates by the similarity of *position* enjoyed by the individuals. It is true, that Mr Grote & myself have, during a large portion of our connubial lives, surmounted these trammels, and have perhaps selected our companions more according to individual quality than from their belonging to any given circle. Yet, since we are fortunately able to command very interesting society among the class who compose the élite of English lettered men, we have not cultivated that of men whose condition, as *working* men of letters, necessarily separates them from our section.[12]

Lewes impressed George Sand not only with his social avant-gardism, but also with his intellectual abilities, not to mention his astonishing knowledge of her own works. She told Duvernet that Lewes could be most helpful to him in London, since he knew many distinguished people and was indeed himself intellectually distinguished, having written a history of philosophy, 'qui a eu un grand succès', as well as some poetry and many critical articles. He seemed to have her works by heart, especially her *Lettres d'un voyageur*, which he knew 'beaucoup mieux que moi'. In addition to having a large, cosmopolitan group of acquaintances, including the Grotes, the actor Macready, and the Italian patriot Mazzini, Lewes was further to be recommended by the fact that he was 'fort aimable et plus français qu'anglais par le caractère'.[13] The sharp-eyed George Sand immediately recognized in Lewes a young man who had recently made his mark as an author, who was, unlike most of his countrymen, fluent in French, and who had, again unusually for an Englishman, a 'French' way of viewing social and sexual arrangements.

Though Lewes had written in the *Foreign Quarterly* article that he 'differed widely' from George Sand in her social, political, and religious views, this was a piece of piety adopted to suit the editor. In fact, he largely shared her opinions, and was soon known in England for his George Sandism. Disapproval of George Sand both as a sensual novelist and as a woman who took lovers—indeed these two roles were usually merged in people's perception of her—was widespread. Lewes was rebuked for his enthusiasm by Bulwer (somewhat hypocritically in view of Bulwer's own marital behaviour) in a letter of 1849:

I do think, if you wd. clear your bosom of the perilous stuff you have got into it, about G. Sand, & other compounders of sensual sentimentalism you might, more than most men, do much towards effecting a real, healthy young England of Criticism & Art.[14]

And Carlyle, though fond of Lewes, objected publicly to George Sandism in general and privately to Lewes's particular case of it. In 'Model Prisons', one of his *Latter-Day Pamphlets* (1850), he talked darkly of a 'strange new religion, named of Universal Love, with Sacraments mainly of *Divorce*, with Balzac, Sue and Company for Evangelists, and Madame Sand for Virgin . . . a *new* astonishing Phallus-Worship, with universal Balzac–Sand melodies and litanies in treble and in bass'.[15] His objections, we may note, did not deter Jane Carlyle from avidly reading George Sand's novels, though she took the precaution of borrowing them from the London Library under the name of their friend Erasmus Darwin.[16] Nor could he stop her reading Lewes's two novels; indeed, he read them himself, and clearly enjoyed the experience hugely, judging from his annotations with their meaningful exclamation marks and dissenting adjectives at points where feelings between the sexes are described. To Carlyle, Bulwer, and other English observers, the tendency of George Sand's novels, like her life, was towards sexual immorality. The same seemed to be true of her young English disciple Lewes.

Little evidence about the first ten years of the Leweses' marriage survives, so that we do not know the details of their arrangements. They were clearly happy, working together and increasing their family—by 1848 there were four boys: Charles, born 24 November 1842; Thornie, born 14 April 1844; Herbert, born 10 July 1846; and St Vincent Arthy, born 11 May 1848, who died of whooping cough and measles on 23 March 1850. The letters Lewes wrote to Varnhagen von Ense during the first six years of his marriage contain frequent references to his domestic happiness. The Leweses lived at Pembroke Square until June 1843, when they moved—perhaps without Mrs Willim, who some years later was living with the Captain and a female companion in St John's Wood—

to nearby 2 Campden Hill Terrace, then again in June 1846 to 26 Bedford Place, also in Kensington. Agnes remained at Bedford Place until 1855 or so, when she moved back to Campden Hill Terrace, living at Number 3 with her children by Hunt for most of the rest of her long life. Though Lewes was to leave Kensington when the marriage broke up, Agnes spent more than 50 years in one small area around Kensington High Street. That the marriage was happy in April 1847 seems clear from Lewes's remarks in a letter to Varnhagen reporting on the progress of the Goethe biography, and sending a copy of *Ranthorpe*:

So much for my Literary avocations. With respect to family affairs I can only reecho the famous 'Happy the nation whose annals are dull'. The calm happiness of my domestic life leaves no incident to record. My wife & children are dearer to me than ever![17]

As it happens, no letter to Varnhagen has survived between this one and a letter of 3 August 1853, in which, for the first time, Lewes omits to send Agnes's love, and which, though written as from their address, 26 Bedford Place, was almost certainly *not* written from there, for Lewes was no longer living with Agnes. However, in 1847 Lewes and Agnes were still happily together, though they may not have been entirely monogamous at this time.

It is impossible to know when Agnes first became sexually involved with Thornton Hunt. Her last child by Lewes, St Vincent, was born in May 1848, and her first by Hunt, Edmund, in April 1850. The lynx-eyed Jane Carlyle noticed a change in Agnes's demeanour towards Lewes in April 1849, when she seemed to be 'taking a somewhat critical view of her shaggy little mate!'[18] There may, however, have been extra-marital relationships on both sides before 1849. No firm evidence exists, but contemporary gossip abounds.

It is of necessity difficult to separate fact from fiction on the subject of the Leweses' marriage. Much was written, early and late, by interested observers or, more often, recipients of gossip at third hand, about a 'phalanstery' at Thornton Hunt's house in Queen's Road, Bayswater, where he lived from 1844 until 1846. It is known that Hunt and his wife Kate, née Gliddon, shared the house with Thornton's sister Mary, who was married to Kate's brother John Gliddon, and the painter Samuel Laurence, also married to a Gliddon. Some unmarried female relatives of the families also lived in the household, which was shared on economic grounds, though of course rumours of sexual irregularity circulated with regard to them too. Lewes and Agnes were supposed by some to have been part of the household, though it is likely that they were simply frequent visitors there.[19] The Leweses, at any rate, had their permanent home at 2 Campden Hill Terrace from June 1843 to June 1846, then at 26 Bedford Place. But the fact that they were close associates of the Hunt–Gliddon group and that they belonged to London's bohemia, coupled with the certainty from 1850 that their marriage *was* unconventional, drew much comment from acquaintances who were often hazy about the dates of the scandalous arrangements they later remembered to have observed.

These memories take two forms: autobiographical memoirs written years later, and fictionalized accounts, novels in which the Lewes–Hunt relationship features in a more or less caricatured fashion. Of the former, there are malicious reports by people who knew Lewes at a later date and either disliked him or had no particular reason to write pleasantly of him and therefore thought fit to add some spice to their memoirs with general gossip at his expense. Representative of these is the 'memory' of Frederick Locker-Lampson in *My Confidences* (1896). Dwelling on the casualness of Lewes's dress—'an unlovely compromise between morning and evening costume'—and the ugliness of his features, he resorts to low comedy about Lewes's being 'credited with having been a Lothario, who could have boasted "personne ne connaît la puissance de ma belle laideur"'.[20]

More reliable, because he knew Lewes and Agnes in the 1840s, is George Smith's largely unpublished account in his 'Recollections of a Long and Busy Life', written in the 1890s. Even Smith, though, writing 50 years on, was vague about dates and not wholly trustworthy as to details. His description of Lewes's and Agnes's life must therefore be taken as approximate. But then, when are the details of others' intimate affairs ever anything else, even to close friends?

Smith gives one of the very few pictures we have of Agnes as a young wife and mother:

She was a delightful little lady, lively and gay, devoted to her children and household duties: the kind of wife who might well have retained any husband's affections. It was a pretty sight to see her take her two boys [Charles and Thornie] to school every morning, walking with one on each hand.[21]

The gentlemanly Smith hints at Agnes's mild unorthodoxy in her own home—'she used to give us coffee, and allow us to smoke in the drawing-room'—and at her more extreme unorthodoxy in sometimes not remaining in that home—'I used also to meet her at a house in Bayswater where Thornton Hunt lived and where there was open house every Sunday evening.' Of her relationship with Hunt, Smith says:

How it came to pass that she left her husband, and for such a man as Thornton Hunt, is not easy to understand. Lewes, it must be said, always preached a kind of doctrine of 'free love'—a sort of 'we may each do as we like' morality; and, unless report maligned him, he certainly did very much as he liked.[22]

Smith, in talking of 'such a man as Thornton Hunt', was referring, no doubt, to his free ways, but probably also to his impecuniousness and his habit of begging loans with pious references to his ill luck and extreme sincerity: like father, like son, in this respect. He may also have been remarking on Thornton's legendary ugliness.

At the time of Lewes's setting up home with Marian Evans in 1854, stories about Lewes's free style of living naturally circulated throughout literary London. Marian's friends Bessie Rayner Parkes and Barbara Leigh Smith heard them, and struggled to like Lewes despite the rumours. Bessie wrote to Barbara as late as 1863 about Lewes's 'previous character': 'You remember what Mrs Noel said to you; & Mrs Gaskell said just the same thing to me, only much more strongly. I dont think Lewes deserves the whole of it . . .' The 'full' story seems to have been that Lewes had seduced a young woman 'who had been employed by him in some kind of literary work'. The woman had a child by him, for whom Mrs Gaskell found a foster-mother.[23]

To this piece of hearsay we may add another, oddly enough occurring in a novel written a full century later. This is the curious work by Halcott Glover, *Both Sides of the Blanket* (1945), which mingles fictionalized and real names and events. For example, Lewes is, with heavy topographical wit, George Henry Downland, and Thornton Hunt is Theo Field; but the Leweses' real address at Campden Hill Terrace is used, and events such as the European Revolutions of 1848 and the Great Exhibition at the Crystal Palace of 1851 form part of the background to the story. Downland is 'the ugliest man in London', and also one of the vainest. He is 'whiskered and unkempt', with a face 'pitted from smallpox'. Nevertheless, his general look is engaging, and he has a 'lively audacious eye'. Downland comes of a theatrical family and is a young literary man on the make. He shares a room in Red Lion Square with Theo Field, from whom he has no secrets: 'We have shared one bench and one wench before now.' On his marriage to the naïve girl Adela, he takes her on honeymoon to Boulogne, being seen off at London Bridge by Theo, 'one of the brats Byron took such exception to at Pisa. You must like him, and call him Theo', Downland tells Adela. Downland loses no time in initiating her into his Shelleyan views. While crossing the Channel he tells her they are both free to follow their inclinations:

It is the essential thing in a marriage like ours; it is the only kind of marriage I could possibly have entered into. I am a man of my time, or perhaps I should say future time. You are to be the wife of such a man, with every privilege accorded her which he must necessarily have for himself.

Having got that straight, Downland proceeds to seduce Adela's maid on the wedding night; in due course Adela and the maid give birth to a son each, born within 48 hours of one another. Meanwhile, the Downlands have visited Paris, where George introduces Adela to George Sand. The Frenchwoman advises Adela to trust her own heart and take lovers whenever she wants to. Downland, like Shelley before him, manœuvres his best friend into his wife's bed.[24]

It is a curious mish-mash of fact and fiction. But Halcott Glover claimed in a letter to the *New Statesman and Nation* two years after his novel was published that it was all based on fact. Revealing that he knew Agnes Lewes when she was an old woman and that he had been told her 'personal confessions' by his aunt, a niece of Mrs Thornton Hunt, he insisted that the wedding-night declaration of principles and the seduction of the maid really happened.[25]

If the 'story' of Lewes's marriage could be thought worthy of fictional treatment in 1945, it was also seized on by Lewes's contemporaries. Eliza Lynn gave it a similarly trenchant yet confused airing in her novel *Realities* (1851). Here Vasty Vaughan the theatre manager toys with an attractive but naïve young actress, leaving his wife free to take a lover too. But Eliza Lynn soon takes flight into total fiction. Mrs Vaughan becomes a prostitute; it is clear that the 'free love' household has been a convenient peg on which to hang a description of her descent into the underworld of Victorian London. The novel is a piece of opportunism, following Henry Mayhew's factual and shocking accounts in the *Monthly Chronicle* (1849) of 'London Labour and the London Poor', and peppering such accounts with bits of bohemian gossip from the world on whose fringes Eliza herself perched in shocked fascination.

This novel was not the last of Eliza Lynn's utterances on the Lewes–Hunt, and later the Lewes–George Eliot, relationship. Like Glover, she took Thornton Hunt's side, objecting to what she saw as a spurious sanctimoniousness on the part of Lewes and Marian when the latter had become a famous novelist. In *The Autobiography of Christopher Kirkland* (1885), another peculiar, unbalanced *roman-à-clef*, Eliza, now Eliza Lynn Linton, remembered her arrival in literary London in the late 1840s. Christopher Kirkland tells how he 'fell in' with the Hunt–Gliddon group, who 'were living in a kind of family communion that was very remarkable', an

'Agapemone which had its charm and its romance'. According to Kirkland–Lynn, Lewes was 'the most pronounced Free-lover of the group, and openly took for himself the liberty he expressly sanctioned in his wife'.[26]

The 'moral Agapemone' appears again in E. M. Whitty's set of satirical sketches, loosely attached to a melodramatic plot, *Friends of Bohemia: or, Phases of London Life* (1857). Whitty knew Lewes and Hunt from the *Leader*, on which they all worked, and made fun of their 'fraternity' and sharing of the same woman (Agnes): 'They went in for pure democracy, pure religion, pure human nature.'[27] Indeed, Lewes's and Hunt's domestic arrangements seem to have been common knowledge in literary London. In 1856 a minor poet, Caroline Gifford Phillipson, offended by a harsh review in the *Westminster* which she assumed to be Lewes's—actually it was by Marian Evans!—took her revenge in a pamphlet called *A Song in Prose to the Westminster Owl, on the Criticism of the 'Westminster Review' of July, 1856, on 'Lonely Hours', Poems by Caroline Giffard Phillipson*. Mrs Phillipson aimed her swipes broadly—at 'these present railway, degenerate, and infidel days'—but soon settled into sending shafts at Lewes in particular. Addressing his Muse, she wrote:

Now, Dark Mightiness! what this favourite son of thine may be, or who he may be, the Authoress of the Poems reviewed knows not; although she would give much for the information. But she thinks that probably he hath his 'brows bound with nightcap instead of bays', and that his swan-quill—swan scarcely singing, if his own previous poetic efforts are to be judged of—he flourisheth in the brick and mortar and white stucco deserts of the far Bayswater, or the farther and greener Kensington.

Lest this reference be too mysterious, she adds further details to identify her persecutor: 'You—Westminster Reviewer!—Bard!—Dramatist!—Actor! (that is, provincial actor), Biographer! Philosopher! Squire to 'Knight'! [Charles Knight the publisher] Windmill of the hundred arms', and so on, ending with placing Lewes, as Pope had placed the Goddess Dulness in the *Dunciad*, in 'literary Smithfield'.[28] Crude and vengeful as the attack is, it represents, with the other accounts, a view of Lewes's life as loose in the matter of sexual morality which we may take as correct in general, if not always in the scandalous particulars recorded by observers. Lewes himself, after all, was the last man to be hypocritical or secretive about his free opinions and actions.

Mrs Phillipson's description of Lewes as a windmill with a hundred arms is a useful reminder of his multifarious professional activities at this, the busiest period of his life. In June 1846 he wrote to his old friend W. B.

Scott, that he was 'buried full five fathoms deep in work', writing 'a Life of Göthe; finishing a book for Knight on the Spanish Dramatists; revising a novel to appear in Chapman & Hall's series [*Ranthorpe*, published in 1847]; & writing Review articles by way of variety'.[29] Knight published *The Spanish Drama. Lope de Vega and Calderon* later in 1846. It is an expanded version of an essay with the same title in the *Foreign Quarterly Review* (July 1843), and consists of a detailed account of the plays, with an attack on A. W. Schlegel's excessive praise of Calderón.[30] Lewes joked to Varnhagen in November, when he wrote summing up his activities during the past few months:

Since my last, my little wife has brought me another boy [Herbert] who follows in the flourishing path of his brothers; and my other wife—the Muse—has also been safely delivered of a small infant, a portrait of which I send herewith. You will observe that he is a somewhat polemical infant, and kicks and cuffs an old woman, named Schlegel, who had proclaimed the baby Calderon to be the finest of born babies 'just what the nurse herself was when she was young!'

Beyond this Mrs Muse has been steadily occupied with Göthe—an infant whose period of gestation seems as yet indefinite—and also with cleaning and adorning as well as she can a child now four or five years old [*Ranthorpe*], but which has not yet left the nursery, it not being considered strong enough to go out.[31]

Apart from publishing the book on Spanish drama, for which he was paid £70, Lewes was writing articles on a dozen topics in several magazines. Though the *British and Foreign Review* had come to an end in December 1844 (the last number carrying an article of Lewes's on *Faust*, later incorporated into the *Life of Goethe*), and the *Foreign Quarterly* ceased in April 1846, other periodicals welcomed Lewes's contributions. A new magazine, the *British Quarterly Review*, edited by Dr Robert Vaughan, printed several articles by Lewes soon after it was started in 1845. These include some of Lewes's best critical writings, starting with a favourable account in August 1847 of his friend Helps's essays, *Friends in Council*.

In his review of Helps's work Lewes confesses to 'a peculiar regard for Essayists'.[32] He was to manage a journalistic coup when he turned to the essayist Charles Lamb in 1848. In 'Charles Lamb—His Genius and his Writings' (May 1848), Lewes drew heavily on his privileged relationship with Leigh Hunt, who supplied him with personal anecdotes of Lamb for the article. Lewes took a bold step—telling readers for the first time about Mary Lamb's insanity, her killing of her mother, and Charles's self-sacrificing decision to look after his sister at home as much as possible, despite serious bouts of depression of his own.[33] It was thanks to Lewes's airing of the details that the editor of Lamb's letters, Sergeant Talfourd, decided to include letters about the family tragedy in his *Final Memorials of Charles Lamb* later in the same year. Lewes took the credit in a follow-up article, 'Charles Lamb and his Friends' (*British Quarterly Review*, November 1848): 'The public is indebted to us for a precious gift. The history of man is enriched by a new and curious contribution to psychological experience.'[34]

Lewes's impressive knowledge of French literature, usually displayed in favour of George Sand or Comte, issued in a comic negative review of the works of Alexandre Dumas père. The list of Dumas's works at the head of the article (*British Quarterly Review*, February 1848) includes 15 novels in a total of 79 volumes. And it appears in the course of the review that Lewes—probably alone in all England—is at least noddingly acquainted with all of them. He questions how 'any mortal's pen' can 'traverse the vast regions of space—these reams, not realms of fancy and invention which bear the signature of Alexandre Dumas':

We have had rapid writers before now, and prodigies; but whose rapidity ever approached that of *Alexandre le Grand*? what prodigy ever surpassed this friend of princes? Mr James has a pen which one can scarcely call slow; Mrs Gore is not a tortoise; Mr Warren has recently written a novel of five hundred pages in one-and-twenty days; and Lope de Vega, the personification of celerity, who took only three days to write a three-act comedy in verse, is credited by marvel-loving chroniclers with having accomplished twenty-one million three hundred thousand lines of printed verse in his not very long career. But Dumas distances them all. His rapidity is something so fabulous, that all sorts of suppositions are put forward to explain it; and one virulent pamphlet undertakes to prove that he has a regular manufactory where numbers of young men work, he only putting his name to their productions.

Lewes himself inclines to the belief that Dumas writes the works in conjunction with one another, Auguste Maquet, and that the younger Dumas copies them out.[35]

As to the merit of these works, that is negligible. Dumas writes 'not historical, but hysterical romance', becoming particularly absurd when he exercises the Frenchman's 'prescriptive right to blunder on the smallest detail' of English history. Dumas rewrites *Hamlet* for his 'Théâtre Historique', 'enriching' the scene in which Hamlet kills Laertes and Claudius by having the Ghost come on and command them to die. Nor is Lewes, the 'Frenchified' Englishman, blind to the ridiculousness of some French attitudes to Shakespeare:

Shakspeare has a great reputation in France, as may be seen by the frequent quotation of '*voilà la question, comme dit Hamlet*', as also by the exquisite apostrophe of Eugène Sue:

'O great Williams!'
in which a Frenchman's well-known accuracy is gracefully exhibited.[36]

These articles in the *British Quarterly Review* at the end of the 1840s
show Lewes's versatility and verve, particularly when he has a grand, or
grandiose, subject he can deflate with satire. There is a long, vehement
essay on Macaulay's *History of England*, volumes i and ii, in February
1849. Macaulay is found to be 'deficient in speculative power' and
'immune from doubt'. He is, moreover, too much the Whig to give other
than a 'lively, one-sided view' of things.[37]

Lewes had long been, in a general way, a radical. In 1848 he became,
like many others, more specifically so. This was the year of revolutions
in most of the capital cities of Europe; London escaped the general
infection, though fears were expressed in Parliament and the press about
the renewed efforts of the Chartists to rouse the population. The English
Chartists held a public meeting at Kennington Common on 10 April
1848, at which elaborate police procedures were put into effect. Nothing
much happened, but the calls for extension of the suffrage and parliamentary reform which had continued since the 1832 Reform Act gained
momentum from the more extreme events in Europe.[38] That Lewes, like
Dickens and others, was fired by the Paris revolution in particular, may
be seen from the increase in political statements in his letters and works.
'Glorious news of France!', he wrote to Hickson in March 1848. The
following year he published his *Life of Robespierre* and made plans to bring
out the distinctly radical paper, the *Leader*. Even in his lighthearted
attack on Dumas, published in February 1848, the very month of the
Paris uprising, Lewes was prescient about the political situation in
France. The French, he wrote, were much 'disposed to revolutions', and
Dumas's preposterous fictionalized histories readily made conspiracy to
overthrow government seem romantic.[39]

At home, politics seemed to Lewes to be in a poor way, since such a
man as Disraeli was able to occupy an important position. In his most
polemical article outside the pages of the *Leader*, Lewes subjected Disraeli
to an attack launched half on political grounds and half on literary—the
essay, in the *British Quarterly* for August 1849, purporting to be a review
of the fifth edition of Disraeli's novel *Coningsby*. Lewes trenchantly takes
the double view throughout: Disraeli is the disgrace of our literature and
the disgrace of our Parliament; he is an adventurer in politics and an
acrobat in literature. He masquerades as a radical when it suits his
designs on power. Lewes uncharacteristically attacks Disraeli's dress and
appearance—'radiant waistcoat, resplendent jewellery, and well-oiled

whiskers'—and asserts that 'he has not the "look of a gentleman".' (Lewes's use of inverted commas does not absolve him of a snobbishness not usual with him.) His novels are 'political manifestoes spiced with personalities' and his statesmanship consists in 'the perception of the incapacity of others'. Of his fiction, quite apart from its political special pleading, Lewes declares, in an expression of his literary credo which would be repeated many times in his writings and which sounds strikingly like that of Marian Evans when she began her literary reviewing for the *Westminster Review* a few years later:

Let him write a novel, and 'all the world' will read it, quote it, laugh over it, talk about it; and among its hundreds of readers not one will have felt his heart stirred, his soul expanded, his experience deepened, his hopes exalted, his moral nature strengthened, or his taste refined; for not one single passage will have gone direct to any serious purpose.[40]

Though these articles for the *British Quarterly Review* are long, often between thirty and forty pages, Lewes was paid much less for them— £12 for one on Browning, £15. 15s. od. for Dumas, rising to £26. 5s. od. for Macaulay—than he was by the *Edinburgh Review*. But Napier was still resistant to Lewes. In 1845 he had accepted 'Lessing', which Lewes assured him would be un-German, since Lessing, though the 'father of German Literature', had an un-German lucidity of expression. Lewes continued to woo the fastidious editor, sending him the *Biographical History of Philosophy*, which contained flattering references to an essay by Napier on Bacon. Napier remained aloof. He provoked Lewes into defending his view that religious problems are insoluble by metaphysics, and that therefore 'the human mind cannot get *beyond* certain limits, but must girate *within* them'.[41] This was not an opinion to suit the orthodox *Edinburgh Review*, though it did print Lewes's essay, suitably 'corrected', on Arabian philosophy in April 1847. Lewes was also allowed to write an impressively detailed account of 'Shakspeare's Critics: English and Foreign' (July 1849). Napier paid him £40 for this essay of nearly 40 pages, but the relationship between editor and contributor remained distant and uneasy.

However, Lewes now commanded attention elsewhere. *Blackwood's Magazine* accepted some pot-boiling stories, mostly translated from French, though at least one, 'The Great Tragedian' (September 1848), a hastily written piece borrowing from his own experiences in Berlin and from the plot of *Wilhelm Meister*, was his own composition. When the Blackwoods proposed in 1878 to include some of Lewes's stories in their 'Tales from Blackwood' series, Lewes could not refuse, but he wisely requested that they appear anonymously, as he had 'long seen that Fiction is not my Forte'.⁴² More ephemeral stories were accepted by the *Punch* writer Douglas Jerrold, with whom Lewes now became friendly. Jerrold's *Shilling Magazine* was unashamedly lowbrow, but even so Lewes's stories are embarrassingly bad. He needed money, and was spreading himself across the spectrum of the periodicals. Even with Agnes contributing eight translations to *Fraser's Magazine* during 1847, their total income for the year was £347.⁴³

In fact, Lewes was in debt about this time. He applied for help to Jerrold—himself no stranger to financial difficulties—and was advanced £20 for two months.⁴⁴ And he contributed some semi-radical essays to Jerrold's magazine. Called 'The Coming Reformation' (May–August 1847), written under the pseudonym Vivian, they hail democracy as the coming form of government throughout Europe, invoking Comte as the guru for the immediate future.

Lewes saw Jerrold often during 1847–8, joining his literary clubs, where good food and drink were conducive to good literary talk. It is impossible to say whether Lewes's bachelorish ways at this time—attending clubs with other journalists, theatre people, bohemians in general—can be taken as a sign that he and Agnes were already less happy together than formerly. Lewes was genuinely clubbable, and he may have thought it important to mix socially with those who could further his journalistic career at this financially insecure time. He was a member of Jerrold's Museum Club, founded in 1847, which met once a week for dinner in a pub off the Strand. George Smith recalled that 'the best talkers of the club were Douglas Jerrold, Father Prout [pseudonym of Francis Mahony, a journalist and ex-Jesuit priest] and G. H. Lewes'. Lewes 'had a wonderful gift for dramatic representation, and could tell a story, reproducing the dialect and gestures of each actor in it, with lifelike effect'. This particular club lasted only a year or two, there being 'a lack of funds to pay its tradesmen'.⁴⁵ It was still going in September 1848, when Jerrold wrote to Lewes: 'Come and give us a laugh here at the Club. . . . Charles Knight and others grace the mahogany. Dinner plain and cheap to suit revolutionary times.'⁴⁶

Other such clubs were founded, notably Thackeray's Fielding Club in 1852, of which Lewes was a prominent founder-member. Indeed, he was much sought after for these social gatherings with their all-male unbridled humour. A connected group, in which Jerrold was a fixture and Lewes a very occasional guest, was the *Punch* set, who also had regular dinners. One of the contributors, Henry Silver, kept a diary of

the conversations, which are characterized by sexual puns and scatolo-
gical stories.[47]

Lewes had first come into contact with Thackeray through his review
of *Vanity Fair* in the *Morning Chronicle* in March 1848. Lewes praised
Thackeray's satire, but found 'something terrible' in it: 'The people are
all scamps, scoundrels, or humbugs.' Thackeray wrote to his critic,
answering the charge: 'I am quite aware of the dismal roguery wh. goes
all through the Vanity Fair story—and God forbid that the world should
be like it altogether; though I fear it is more like it than we like to own.'
But he thanked Lewes for his 'sincere goodwill'.[48] The two became
friends, with Lewes reviewing Thackeray's other novels in the *Leader*
(*Pendennis* in December 1850 and *Henry Esmond* in November 1852).
Lewes generally praised Thackeray's wit, style, and truthfulness, while
finding his plots carelessly constructed and his work lacking in passion.[49]
Thackeray, for his part, sketched a drawing-room scene depicting Lewes,
Agnes, and Thornton Hunt making an intimate threesome round the
piano (see Plate 4).

Just as his acquaintance with Dickens had begun with a letter of
thanks for a favourable review, and now Thackeray acknowledged his
critic in the same way, so also did Charlotte Brontë. She was extremely
lucky to have Lewes review *Jane Eyre* on its appearance at the end of
1847. His review stood out among the others for its intelligence and
fairness. Their correspondence began even before the review appeared
(in *Fraser's Magazine*, December 1847). George Smith, the publisher of
Jane Eyre, got his reader, William Smith Williams, to send a copy to
Lewes. The latter was so struck by this first work by the unknown
Currer Bell that, as he told Mrs Gaskell in 1857 when she was preparing
her biography of Charlotte Brontë, he went straight to see Parker, the
editor of *Fraser's*. Parker 'would not consent to an unknown novel . . .
receiving such importance, but thought it might make one on "Recent
Novels: English and French"', the title duly adopted for the article.
Lewes also wrote to Currer Bell, 'to tell her the delight with which her
book filled me'.[50] Lewes's letter to Charlotte Brontë has been lost, as
have all his subsequent ones. But her replies take up his remarks point
by point, so that we know pretty well what he wrote. It is evident that
Lewes formulated to her his ideas of what a good novel should be; in
doing so, he induced her to enunciate her own theory and defend her
practice.

As Lewes told Mrs Gaskell, he seems to have 'sermonized' Charlotte
in his first letter, in spite of his genuine enthusiasm. She wrote to Smith
Williams on 6 November 1847, the day after she received Lewes's letter,

asking him who Lewes was. 'Upon the whole he seems favourably inclined to the work, though he hints disapprobation of the melodramatic portions.' Lewes had signed himself 'a fellow-novelist' (*Ranthorpe* having appeared earlier in the year). Charlotte Brontë was intrigued: 'There is something in the candid tone of his letter which inclines me to think well of him.'[51] To Lewes himself she wrote on the same day, thanking him for his 'cheering commendation and valuable advice'. Then she launched into self-defence against his criticisms:

You warn me to beware of Melodrama, and you exhort me to adhere to the real. . . .

You advise me too, not to stray far from the ground of experience as I become weak when I enter the region of fiction; and you say 'real experience is perennially interesting and to all men'.

I feel that this also is true, but, dear sir, is not the real experience of each individual very limited? . . . Then, too, Imagination is a strong, restless faculty which claims to be heard and exercised, are we to be quite deaf to her cry and insensate to her struggles? When she shows us bright pictures are we never to look at them and try to reproduce them? And when she is eloquent and speaks rapidly and urgently in our ear are we not to write to her dictation?[52]

The opposition which Charlotte Brontë here sets up is that between realism and romance, with Lewes calling for the former and Charlotte defending the latter. But Lewes's view was less narrow than this, as we have seen in his description of the qualities he thought to be lacking in Disraeli's novels. In his *Fraser's* article on *Jane Eyre* he shows that he appreciates Charlotte Brontë's particular gift of creating romance out of real experience. He comes to *Jane Eyre* after a dutiful tour of other, more ordinary new novels. Turning to Currer Bell's book, he declares:

This, indeed, is a book after our own heart. . . . The writer is evidently a woman, and, unless we are deceived, new in the world of literature. But, man or woman, young or old, be that as it may, no such book has gladdened our eyes for a long while. Almost all that we require in a novelist she has: perception of character, and power of delineating it; picturesqueness; passion; and knowledge of life.[53]

Charlotte Brontë could ask for no better understanding of her work, and she knew it. 'Mr Lewes is very lenient,' she wrote to Smith Williams on 11 December 1847. 'This notice differs from all the other notices. He must be a man of no ordinary mind; there is a strange sagacity evinced in some of his remarks.' She added ruefully that Lewes might be less enthusiastic if he knew how little 'knowledge of life' she really had, or how limited the scope of her reading was. In other words, where he saw truth to actual experience, she felt she had been writing out of 'intuition'.[54]

So grateful to Lewes was she, and so interested in finding out more about him, that she read *Ranthorpe* and wrote pleasantly to him about it. She also argued with him about the merits of Jane Austen, whose novels she now read for the first time, at Lewes's urging.[55] Her letters to Smith Williams are peppered with references to Lewes, who became a kind of critical standard for her. Her question was always: what would Lewes think? 'Agnes Grey [by Anne Brontë] should please such critics as Mr Lewes.' 'Is the forthcoming critique on Mr Thackeray's writings in the "Edinburgh Review" written by Mr Lewes? I hope it is. Mr Lewes, with his penetrating sagacity and fine acumen, ought to be able to do the author of "Vanity Fair" justice.' 'What makes you say that the notice [of *Jane Eyre*] in the "Westminster Review" is not by Mr Lewes?'[56] And so on.

To Charlotte Brontë, at the beginning of her career as a published novelist, living at Haworth, far away from literary society, Lewes was the very type of the clever London critic, a man of power and influence. She followed his career over the next few years, asking Smith Williams about him and occasionally writing to Lewes himself. He seemed to her rather a marvellous being: cosmopolitan, energetic, clever, bold, frank, sometimes careless, a man of whom anything might be expected. On hearing in February 1850 that Lewes's play *The Noble Heart* had had its first (successful) London performance, she observed that he fully deserved such 'triumphs public, brief and noisy'.[57] If she had seen it, she would have thought a certain sketch of Lewes good-naturedly thumbing his nose quite characteristic. It was done about this time by Thornton Hunt on a note from Agnes to Lewes's brother Edward—'Dear Ned'— saying she had no spare theatre ticket to give him (see Plate 6).[58]

Lewes, the 'windmill of the hundred arms', was expanding beyond the sphere of literary journalism, though his income still depended on his ready use of the pen in criticizing the works of others. Between 1847 and 1850 he made an energetic attempt to succeed as a novelist, an actor, and a dramatist.

5

Novelist, Actor, Dramatist
(1847–1849)

LEWES naturally hoped to achieve fame and money as the author of a novel of London literary life. But even he, sanguine as he was by nature, was doubtful about the probability of success with *Ranthorpe* (1847). Uncharacteristically, he published it anonymously; in the preface, he confessed that the novel had been written in first draft five years before, but had been much altered after being submitted to the criticism of 'two eminent friends'.[1]

One of these friends was the successful novelist Edward Bulwer (later Sir Edward Bulwer-Lytton), with whom Lewes had begun to correspond in 1842, when Bulwer asked for his help in the preparation of a translation of Schiller's poems. Though useful to one another for a time, the two men never became intimate, the one being a literary aristocrat, the other a working journalist. Privately, each thought poorly of the other. Lewes talked contemptuously of the vogue for Bulwer's novels in Berlin in 1838, and mocked Bulwer's pretensions to be a 'philosophical' novelist. 'Bulwer has just published a new work *Zanoni* which I have not seen but from which I do not expect much', he wrote to Varnhagen in March 1842; 'flimsy tinsel which he calls Ideality, and rounded periods which he calls Philosophy.'[2] For his part, Bulwer, though admiring Lewes's knowledge of German literature, noted that he was 'a self-taught Man of great energy & wide range' who was 'often original' but 'not profound'. When Bulwer had the young Swinburne to stay with him in 1866, he described him to his son Robert as pale and sickly, but with self-esteem as 'solid as a rock': 'He reminds me a little of what Lewes was in youth, except that he has no quackery and has genius.'[3]

Despite such mutually suspicious feelings, the men found each other helpful during the 1840s. They exchanged long, detailed letters on the minutiae of Bulwer's translations from Schiller, with Lewes upholding Goethe and George Sand for their 'transparency of thought', expressed with 'perfection of melody', against the obscurity of some of Schiller's poetry.[4] And when Lewes was revising *Ranthorpe* in December 1846 he turned to Bulwer for advice, perhaps thinking that he might thereby be helped towards success, if not excellence, in fiction. Bulwer responded kindly, taking great care over the novel, though he was hardly complimentary:

I will tell you *frankly* my impression. I think the greater proportion of the coincidental and episodical matter—the remarks, theories analyses &c—of a singularly high order; full of subtlety of thought & beauty of expression—very wise & very eloquent. I think next, pardon me for saying it, the story itself greatly inferior to the genius appended to it. The principal characters are not interesting—why, I cannot say.

In fact, he can, and does, say exactly why. Ranthorpe, the literary genius, 'does nothing to prove his genius'. With remorseless truthfulness, Bulwer explains that though Ranthorpe certainly exhibits 'some of the errors & frivolities of the Poetic Nature', most of these errors might be shown equally 'by a nature *not* poetic'. Bulwer makes a few suggestions about how to end the novel, it being too late to do much about the main problem; suggests that Lewes should *not* publish it; thinks, on the other hand, that if Lewes does decide to publish, he should do so anonymously. The ostensible reason for this advice, which Lewes eventually followed, was that the effect would be 'greater for some mystery as to the Author'.[5] More likely, Bulwer thought Lewes would be protected from the bad criticism he fully expected the novel to receive.

Poor Lewes. He was ambitious, had worked hard on the novel, and, above all, needed the money that even a moderate success with a work of fiction would bring. His total earnings for 1847 without the £100 Chapman and Hall gave him for *Ranthorpe* would have been only £247. He needed to publish it. On Bulwer's advice, he asked John Forster to read the manuscript, reporting to Bulwer on 22 December 1846 that Forster's opinion, though more favourable than Bulwer's, 'pretty much agrees with it'. Lewes says he has adopted some of Forster's and Bulwer's hints for improving the work, and hopes to 'turn out a readable story after all. It is now printing.'[6]

So *Ranthorpe* duly appeared in the spring of 1847. Reviews were few, and those at best lukewarm, like the well-meaning attempt by Robert Vaughan of the *British Quarterly Review* in May 1848 to bring both of Lewes's novels to the public's attention. On the strength of his contributions to *Blackwood's Magazine*, Lewes wrote to John Blackwood in May 1847, asking for the favour of a review, perhaps by Thackeray. He added frankly, 'I have a pecuniary as well as literary interest in the *sale*

of "Ranthorpe" and that is why I am anxious to get it noticed—
favourably or unfavourably—in as many good quarters as I can.'[7]
Blackwood's Magazine did not review the novel.

In the London literary circles to which Lewes belonged, *Ranthorpe*
'made some sensation', according to Arthur Helps, who urged his friend
John Anster to read it. Lewes sent copies to several other friends, among
them Varnhagen, whom he asked to find a German translator for it;
Dickens, whose amateur theatrical group he joined at this time; and Jane
Carlyle. Perhaps mindful of her illicit passion for the novels of George
Sand, he inscribed her copy 'To Madame Jane Carlyle, Souvenir d'une
vraie Amitié'.[8] Carlyle, annotating the novel, notes a sensual passage
quoted from George Sand with a dismissive 'eh puis?', exclaims 'Gott im
Himmel' when Lewes steps out of the fiction to praise his philanthropic
friend Neil Arnott for his wisdom and benevolence, and responds to one
of Lewes's tendentious authorial statements about the 'dalliance with
misery, which has its vuluptuous orgies, powerful as those of the senses'
with the remark, 'What beggarly nonsense is this!'[9]

Carlyle's comments, though intemperate, are no more than the novel
deserves. It is an uncertain modern tract about the pitfalls of fame and
romantic love, hung with quotations from Lewes's favourite authors,
especially Goethe, George Sand, and Shelley. As the friendly Robert
Vaughan remarked, many of the chapters are 'little else than short essays
on some topic arising out of [the] narrative'.[10] Politics, the make-up of
modern society, aristocratic London, literary London, medical-student
and bohemian London are all on view, but are not integrated with the
story of the rise, fall, and resurrection of the fortunes of Percy Ranthorpe. Charlotte Brontë noted, when she eagerly read her 'fellow
novelist' and favourable critic in December 1847, that the last part, with
its circulating-library plotting—murder, false accusation and imprison-
ment, deliverance, and exile for Ranthorpe—was particularly bad,
showing evidence of having been 'hastily and sketchily written'.[11]

Everywhere Lewes *tells* us what motivates his people, but he seldom
shows them acting according to their minutely dissected psychologies.
There is, surprisingly, little humour, but there is much novelistic cliché,
as when Lewes comments on Ranthorpe's falling into debt: 'the book of
life had lain open before him, and on its fair pages he had scrawled the
characters of folly and misery; were it not better at once to throw that
book into the flames, than tear those blotted pages out?'[12]

Lewes's friends squirmed in their efforts to find something nice to say
about *Ranthorpe*. Mill, who was corresponding much less frequently with
Lewes now, wrote in May 1847 claiming he needed to read it a second

time (!) before passing comment, but could say meanwhile that he liked the book 'on the whole decidedly *better* than I expected from your own account of it'—which was not to say very much. Dickens was equally vague. He belatedly reported his impressions, in November 1847, his conscience about the delay making him insist on how '*very much*' the novel had pleased him. But he was evasive: 'I would I saw more of such sense and philosophy in that kind of Literature—which would make it more of what it ought to be.' Realizing that this comment falls far short of what an eager author wants to hear, he concluded lamely, 'This may not seem much to read, but I mean a great deal by it in the writing.'[13]

Actually, Lewes was soon admitting the awfulness of *Ranthorpe* himself. When his old friend Richard Henry Horne was on the brink of leaving for Australia in 1852, Lewes wrote inviting him to visit before he left, and asking, 'Is there any scribblement of mine you have not, & would care to have? (short of Ranthorpe, which I disavow)—if so I will get it for you.'[14]

The best parts of *Ranthorpe* are the literary discussions which take place in London drawing-rooms, and the rather funny theatre scenes, taken from Lewes's own brief experience as well as from his acquaintance with Goethe's autobiography and the theatrical episodes in *Wilhelm Meister*. Lewes gives free rein to his sense of irony at the conflicting interests of those involved in putting on a play. Ranthorpe has written a Roman play, but between them his literary friends, untrustworthy theatre managers, and egotistical actors ensure that when it reaches the stage it is hardly recognizable. The piece is subjected to a 'chorus of carpings'. Roman costume is 'in very bad odour at the theatre'; the censor will object to the epithet 'pregnant' (as in 'pregnant danger') as indelicate; the tragedy is lacking in action; it needs comic characters to enliven it; it is too long. Remembering his own bad luck with Mathews in 1842, Lewes has Ranthorpe offer the play to the manager of Covent Garden. He gets no response. The theatre closes for the summer recess without Ranthorpe having had a yes or no. When he is finally called to discuss it, the manager wishes to make fundamental alterations to the text. Financial considerations are uppermost in his mind:

'What you say is perfectly just', replied Mr ——, 'respecting the play as a literary production; but for the stage, other necessities are to be attended to. Now you have three Roman soldiers, who only come on in one scene, but that scene is important. Nevertheless it cannot be played, because I should have to put three understrappers, at a shilling a night, into those parts, and their very appearance would d – – n them.'

'But could you not have three good actors?'

'Impossible: they would not play the parts; *not their line*! Believe me, you have too many subordinate characters.'

In a suitably corrected form the play reaches the rehearsal stage. This represents more torture for the sensitive author:

Now came on the harassment of rehearsals. He was forced to attend them all for his own sake, as he had to instruct some of the actors in the right pronunciation of the Roman names, and some few English words. There was one most desperate cockney who could not be induced to call 'Fulvia' any thing but 'Fulv*iar*'; another had got irrev*ò*cable in his head, and couldn't get it out. Whenever Ranthorpe quietly suggested a correction, the invariable reply was:
'Oh, yes! I'll be sure to remember it.'[15]

When the tragedy is finally performed before an audience, a combination of unintelligent acting and a jealous *claque* in the audience ensures its dismal failure. Ranthorpe retires hurt from the scene.

There is at least some life—if broadly drawn—about these theatre episodes. Lewes himself had recently had another attempt at getting a play accepted by a London theatre. Forster had interceded on his behalf with Samuel Phelps, manager of Sadler's Wells, in November 1846, but Phelps rejected the unnamed play.[16] For the time being, Lewes had to make do with acting, unpaid, with Forster and Dickens, though he was finally to get a play of his own accepted in 1849–50. Otherwise, *Ranthorpe* has little to recommend it, being, in the words of a modern critic, 'a collapsed *Wilhelm Meister*'.[17] Lewes was unable to put into practice in his own novel his eminently sensible critical criteria, so shrewdly expressed in his writings on Charlotte Brontë and Jane Austen.

However, Lewes was still lured by the prospect of success as a novelist. He managed to get *Rose, Blanche, and Violet* accepted by George Smith in 1848, though he was paid only £50 for it. It shows little, if any, improvement on its predecessor. More conventional in a sense, being a story of multiple courtships, it is even less lively. Lewes presumed to send a copy to the literary Lady Blessington, who replied graciously about the 'intellectual treat' it afforded her. She even invited Lewes to call at her house.[18] Another fan was Geraldine Jewsbury, like Lewes the author of second-rate, bold, English 'George Sand' novels. She rashly told her friend Jane Carlyle in 1849 that she did not care for *Jane Eyre*, much preferring Lewes's novels.[19] Her correspondent took a different view. 'Execrable', she wrote to Carlyle in April 1848; 'I could not have suspected even the ape [the Carlyles' term of endearment for Lewes] of writing anything so silly.' Indeed, Carlyle's marginal notes—for he once again read the novel right through—'are the only real amusement I have got out of it hitherto'.[20]

Carlyle commented fluently enough in his marginalia. As the improbable multiple plot, including adultery, prostitution, separation, gambling, and suicide among its elements, gets thicker, Carlyle becomes witty at its expense. When he reaches the end of volume iii, he writes: 'Exeunt, different ways!' Elsewhere he is moved to ask 'Did you ever? No, I never—?' The wonder is that he persevered to the end, but that he did is proved by his comment on the last page: 'A book of some talent and much folly—je suis plus fou que toi!'[21]

Lewes was trying an experiment in this novel. As he explains in his preface, he is uneasy about novels in which 'a distinct Moral presides over the composition', because in these cases there is a danger that the story will be 'shaped to suit a purpose' and human nature will be falsified. He has therefore decided to leave the moral to 'shift for itself'.[22] Unfortunately, this does not in itself guarantee that the characters' actions will appear natural. In the case of Rose, Blanche, Violet, and their many suitors, mere confusion results from Lewes's rather interesting idea that people (in novels, as in life) act impulsively, contrarily, out of a complex of motives, so that even a shrewd analysis of their characters is not proof against surprise at their actions. All that happens, however, is that with such a large cast of leading characters we are bewildered by the turns and twists, without being engaged by the particular embodiments of the theory. The novel evokes social and emotional mess, but does not avoid narrative mess.

Once again, Lewes's friends were muted in their response. They all seized on the scenes in which Cecil Chamberlayne, married to Blanche, becomes addicted to gambling. Dickens thought this part 'admirably done'. For the rest, he pleaded the 'botherations' of the rehearsals he was conducting which had 'swallowed up' the great many other 'striking things' he had meant to note.[23] Charlotte Brontë, writing not to Lewes but to Smith Williams, was free to admit that she found Lewes's emotional scenes 'somewhat too uniformly vehement' in a 'French' way. For her, the most interesting character in the book was G. H. Lewes himself, with his 'sincerity, energy, and talent'. But while he can astonish with his display of knowledge through quotations from Latin, Greek, French, Spanish, and German authors, she concludes that if one is looking for the 'elevating charm of imagination', Mr Lewes 'must necessarily inform you that he does not deal in the article'.[24]

Bulwer, too, received a copy with the instruction that he was 'incontinently to fall in love' with Rose, Blanche, and Violet. Bulwer replied pleasantly, thinking the novel an improvement on *Ranthorpe*, but complaining of the disparateness of the plot. He added: 'You have not yet written a Book as clever as the Author. I can prophecy when you will do so. It will be, when instead of playing with your characters, you will hit upon one who will overmaster yourself, in whose life you will live, in whose heart your own heart will beat.'[25]

It was not to be, though a decade later Lewes was to live vicariously with just such characters as they were spun from the imagination of George Eliot. Lewes gave up novel-writing (though he did begin a serialized fiction in the *Leader* in 1850—'The Apprenticeship of Life'— which he had not the heart to carry beyond eleven uneven chapters). For some reason, he reread *Rose, Blanche, and Violet* in 1875, noting in his diary that it produced in him a *'very* unpleasant sensation!'[26]

Perhaps his forte would turn out to be acting. With a distinguished comedian among his forebears and his own admired talent for telling stories, putting on accents, and imitating gestures, Lewes might well feel that acting was in his blood. He had a chance to try out the theory when Dickens approached him in 1847 to join his celebrated amateur company for a tour of the provinces in aid of Leigh Hunt, who was in a worse way financially than ever. Dickens planned to get together a company of friends to put on *The Merry Wives of Windsor* and *Every Man in his Humour*, doing benefit performances during the month of July in Manchester and Liverpool, and finishing off with a performance at Covent Garden. Lewes, as a friend of Hunt's, was an obvious choice to add to the colleagues Dickens had acted with on previous occasions, among them Forster, Jerrold, Mark Lemon and John Leech of *Punch*, and Dickens's brother Fred.

Dickens wrote to Lewes on 15 June 1847:

You know what we are going to do for Leigh Hunt. . . . You have a hearty sympathy for Hunt, and are, I am told, an excellent Actor. The characters to let, are, the Host in the Merry Wives of Windsor (a very good part), and Old Knowell in Every Man in his Humour. . . .

If you will take these characters you will find yourself in excellent good company, and received with open arms. It is a point of honor among us that no expence whatever, is imposed on any one for anything; the plan providing dresses, travelling expences, &c &c. I should be delighted to hear that you are with us, and that you will attend the next Rehearsal of the Merry Wives next Friday Evening. Place, Miss Kelly's little Theatre 73 Dean Street Soho, where we rehearse at present, though we shall act on a very large stage. Time, a quarter before 6, for 6 to the moment.

My dear Lewes,
Faithfully Yours
Charles Dickens.[27]

Lewes's letters to Dickens have disappeared, being destroyed by Dickens with those of all his other private correspondents, but he obviously agreed to take the parts offered. Rehearsals duly began, and Dickens busied himself with writing to theatre managers and civic bigwigs in Manchester and Liverpool, arranging dates and advertisements. The indigent playwright John Poole was added to Hunt as a beneficiary. Late in June it was discovered that the Government had decided to give Leigh Hunt a pension, so the Covent Garden performance was cancelled. *The Merry Wives of Windsor* was shelved, leaving the company to do *Every Man in his Humour*, with a one-act farce as afterpiece, in Manchester and Liverpool, the intention now being to give most of the proceeds to Poole.

Dickens wrote to Mark Lemon on 4 July, asking him to find professional actresses for the female parts and arrange for wigs and costumes. As to the short farce to be played as an after-piece, he could find nothing suitable except Poole's *Turning the Tables*. 'Now', he asked Lemon, 'do you think it would be safe to give Jack Humphries [a cunning exciseman] to Lewes, and Jeremiah Bumps to Cruikshank, who is good at disguise? Lewes has nothing but Old Knowell, and certainly has a claim upon us.' A few days later he addressed Lewes: 'Invest six pence in the purchase of Poole's Turning the Tables . . . get up Jack Humphries (an admirable part) and come prepared on the 17th. Cordially CD.'[28]

Writing to Alexander Ireland, the head of the Manchester theatrical committee, Dickens gave descriptions of his actors for the posters to be put up. Of Lewes he wrote, 'Mr Lewes is . . . a man of great attainments in polite literature, and the author of a Novel published not long since, called Ranthorpe.'[29] He was having trouble with the jealousies, egotism, and incompetence of some of his troupe—though not, it is a fair bet, with Lewes. He exploded to Forster, who unfortunately removed the names when he published the letter in his biography of Dickens, replacing them with A, B, C etc. A, it seems, 'hasn't twelve words, and I am in hourly expectation of rebellion'; B needs his nerves quieting; C knows he cannot manage his part, but has 'clutched' it tenaciously; 'that infernal E forgets everything'; F will lose his memory when nervous; and G is 'not born for it at all'.[30] And this with only a week or so to go.

Some of the company, including Lewes, took their wives with them; in all, 24 people turned up at Euston Station on 25 July to travel to Manchester. The performance was given on Monday 26 July at the Theatre Royal, after which, according to one actor's wife, 46 bottles of champagne were drunk and some of the group did not get to bed at all that night.[31] After a day of rest the company acted in Liverpool on 28

July, returning home on Friday 30th. Dickens was elated at the success of the trip, the box office receipts showing that takings in Manchester were £440. 12s. 0d. and in Liverpool £463. 8s. 6d., with local newspapers reviewing the productions enthusiastically, especially Dickens's perform-ance as Bobadil.[32] It was undoubtedly an exciting trip for Lewes and Agnes and the others, but it was not a way of making money. Lewes soon received a bill from Dickens for Agnes's train fare, their hotel expenses, and Lewes's wine subscription—£11. 9s. 6d in all.[33]

After the tour the group separated, each to carry on with his own professional activities. Lewes was working at *Rose, Blanche, and Violet*, reviewing for *Fraser's* and the *British Quarterly*, and still looking for ways of acquiring a more substantial reputation and a more secure income. Never a man to put all his eggs in one basket, he was planning, even as he struggled to become a successful novelist, a new career in journalism. He and Thornton Hunt conceived the plan of raising enough capital to buy the *Westminster Review*, which its present owner-editor, Hickson, was ready to sell. It was rather a madcap scheme in view of Lewes's precarious financial position, and Hunt was a chip of the old block in matters of financial management. He was, as Holyoake recalled, 'incap-able of making provision for himself', let alone his growing family and a number of improvident relations whom he also generously tried to support.[34] Clearly Lewes placed his faith in his ability to persuade Swynfen Jervis to give the necessary financial backing. To this end he visited his father-in-law at Darlaston Hall in September 1847. It seems that Dickens was invited there too, for he told Lewes in August that he was unable to accept 'Giles Homespun's' invitation to Staffordshire. (Lewes had probably been doing imitations of his eccentric father-in-law during the theatrical tour.)[35] From Jervis's house Lewes wrote to Hickson on 12 September, announcing that Jervis was 'willing to give you his note of hand for such sum or sums as we may not find it convenient to pay down'.[36]

Jervis's offer was not enough to make the project viable (though he seems to have enjoyed offering hospitality to Lewes's famous friends—Jerrold, too, was invited to stay in September).[37] Early in December Lewes admitted to Hickson that he and Thornton could not raise the money:

Thornton & I having thoroughly & minutely considered the prospects of the review have come to the conclusion that although it might be a profitable speculation for a bookseller, it would be impossible for us to do anything like what we proposed with it without the total sacrifice of our own unremunerated

labour. . . . Your price by no means enters into the calculation—we both agree
that the review is well worth that sum; but the review itself is not practicable in
our hands with our means.

I should have written before since this conclusion has been more or less
evident to us from our first calculation of expenses but the desire not to give up
the idea if it could in any way be realized has led to fresh calculations & hence
the delay.[38]

It was not long before Dickens was in touch with Lewes again about
another acting scheme, this time to benefit the literary profession as a
whole. Dickens wanted to raise money for the Guild of Literature and
Art, an organization designed to help authors and artists with life
insurance. Lewes was called to a meeting in February 1848 with Dickens
and Lemon at the National Provident Office in the City. They planned
to put on Bulwer's play *Money* and Jerrold's *The Rent Day* at the St
James's Theatre.[39] But Dickens abandoned the idea because of the lack
of enthusiasm and reliability of some of his colleagues. He apologized to
Lewes, and cancelled orders for costumes and playbills.[40]

By April 1848 Dickens was again bringing up the subject in letters.
Rehearsals for *The Merry Wives of Windsor* began on 15 April; *Every Man
in his Humour* was also revived, and new farces were found for the after-
pieces. The good cause this time was the endowment of a 'perpetual
curatorship' of Shakespeare's birthplace at Stratford.[41] The company,
much the same as before, acted for two nights at the Haymarket Theatre
in London on 15 and 17 May 1848. The press reviews were not
particularly enthusiastic.[42] Hopes were high that the provincial performances would attract more attention. The company began its extended
tour, opening in *Merry Wives* at Manchester on 3 June, doing it in
Liverpool on 5 June, and moving to Birmingham on 6 June with *Every
Man in his Humour*. Wives did not go with them this time. The Leweses
must have found the expenses of 1847 alarming, and in any case Agnes
had a new baby, St Vincent Arthy, born on 11 May, to look after.

After returning to London briefly, the group set off for Scotland,
where they put on *Merry Wives* in Edinburgh on 17 July and in Glasgow
the next night, with Lewes taking the part of Wellbred in *Every Man in
his Humour* and of Sir Hugh Evans, the comic Welsh parson, in *Merry
Wives*, as well as acting in some of the after-pieces.[43] Lewes could be well
pleased with the reception of his performancs. Even the London reviews
were favourable, if rather grudgingly so. There was, said one, 'something
between the amateur and the professionally histrionic' in his acting of
the part of Sir Hugh Evans. 'In conception and manner, this gentleman
had well seized the character; but he was somewhat too unwearied in his

efforts to support it.' According to another review, cut out and kept by John Forster, Lewes was one of the best hits in the show, despite 'a trifling tendency towards exaggeration'. Other critics mentioned Lewes's physique as an asset for the part:

he skipped about the stage and snapped his fingers, and contorted his little wizzened figure in the grotesquest way. A good deal of laughter greeted the 'biographer of philosophy' as he led his troop of little sham devils in their dance around Falstaff and Herne's Oak.

It was as if Lewes was trying out—and reviewers recognized it—whether he could be taken for a professional actor, and might even aspire to the profession in earnest. He seemed, said one notice, 'most anxious to look like a real actor', avoiding the usual tendency of the amateur to act only when speaking.[44] The Manchester reviews were wholly enthusiastic. The one in which Lewes is described as 'the popular author of that admirable novel *Ranthorpe*, and the more recent and equally successful *Rose, Blanche, and Violet*' was very probably by his admirer Geraldine Jewsbury.[45]

Lewes did indeed have ambitions to act professionally. He also wanted to write for the theatre, as he had tried to, intermittently, since 1841. During the latter part of 1848, while he finished his *Life of Robespierre* and prepared a set of lectures based on the *Biographical History of Philosophy* which he intended, as he told Comte, to give in the provinces with a view to extending the knowledge of positivism in Britain,[46] he also wrote (or rewrote) his tragedy *The Noble Heart*.

The play, an original, longer version of which had been submitted in March 1848 to the Lord Chamberlain's Office,[47] has a Spanish theme and a pseudo-Elizabethan manner. A father and his son, Don Gomez and Leon de la Vega, love the same girl, Juanna, a merchant's daughter far beneath them in rank. The son has wooed her under an incognito. When the King needs help against the invading Moors, Leon goes to fight for him, while Don Gomez refuses out of disapproval of the King's susceptibility to flattering courtiers. Meanwhile, the merchant Reinaldos faces financial ruin, and orders his daughter to marry Don Gomez to save him from bankruptcy and dishonour. Leon returns from the wars, hears his father is about to marry a girl of low rank, and hopes this will mean he himself will be allowed to marry Juanna. He soon hears that it is she who has become his father's wife and accuses her of treachery. When Don Gomez discovers that his son and Juanna love one another, he sacrifices his own feelings for the sake of the 'natural' affection between the two young people. He petitions the Pope for an annulment of his marriage and goes off to a life of retirement and contemplation. His last words to Leon and Juanna are:

> Come to my arms
> Be happy! . . . That is the last wish of this broken heart
> Heaven's benediction rest on both!
> Now, to the Desert! On!

To which Juanna replies, before the curtain falls:

> O noble Heart![48]

The play, though not distinguished, is quite well crafted, and manages its 'Elizabethan' blank verse well enough. It certainly compares reasonably well with many other plays which passed through the censorship of the Lord Chamberlain's Office at the time. But more interesting even than the merits and faults of the play itself is the spectacle of Lewes breaking into the notoriously cliqueish theatre world as an *actor*. He not only acted in Manchester and Liverpool as Don Gomez in *The Noble Heart*, giving four performances in the former city during April 1849 and three in the latter during May, but he also played Shylock with a professional company in Manchester, Liverpool, and, later in the year, Edinburgh.

In fact, Lewes was scarcely ever at home between 7 February and 18 May 1849. Relations with Agnes may already have been strained, though whether this was a result or a contributory cause of his absences we cannot tell. On the one hand, Francis Espinasse remembered being in Lewes's company in Manchester, in February or March, when Lewes 'gave us most sympathetically—for with all his faults he was then an affectionate husband and always an affectionate father—nursery stories of his children, sent him from London by his wife, who, he said, wrote to him unfailingly every day'. On the other hand, it was in the middle of his toing and froing, early in April, that Jane Carlyle thought she saw a change in the Leweses' demeanour towards one another, from that of 'a perfect pair of love-birds always cuddling together on the same perch' to a critical stance, at least on Agnes's part. As Jane commented in a letter to her cousin, Lewes was in the habit of raving about other women, including Julia Paulet, a friend of Jane's whom he met while lecturing in Liverpool in February. Agnes, Jane noted, seemed 'rather *contemptuous* of his raptures about the women he has fallen in love with on this journey which is the best way of taking the thing—when one can'. Jane Carlyle well knew what marital jealousy was; she was even then in the throes of it over her husband's infatuation with Lady Ashburton, from whose house Jane—a reluctant guest— wrote this letter.[49]

Whatever the reasons—and among them were his pressing need for money, his desire for fame, and his extraordinary, perhaps even neurotic, capacity for multifarious activity—Lewes was constantly on the move during the spring of 1849. (Dickens's restlessness and energy, as well as his unhappiness in his marriage, make an interesting parallel with Lewes's here.) This period marks the beginning of the end of his happy marriage. It also shows him bidding for a career in the theatre, an ambition which George Eliot later said only finally died down in 1853, that is, when he became intimate with her.[50]

But Lewes's first appearance in the north was as a lecturer. He gave six lectures on the history of philosophy at the Manchester Athenaeum and the Liverpool Mechanics' Institute from 7 to 27 February. The lectures were sparsely attended, according to the *Manchester Guardian*, which reported them quite fully. Mrs Gaskell heard them, and put the reason for the small audience as 'the quantity of evening engagements there are in Manr. at this time of the year'. Espinasse, who had first met Lewes the previous year at Carlyle's house, remembered the lectures as successful, for an interesting reason:

Lewes's expositions were lucid and lively, his manner was animated, and his audiences, though not large, were distinctly appreciative. His contemptuous treatment of metaphysics and his exaltation of science were not unsuited to the inquiring intellects of that utilitarian city. It was pleasant to be told that though you had never troubled yourself about 'the problems of life and mind', you were just as wise as any of the long series of sages who had wended their toilsome way on the 'high *priori* road', which, according to Lewes, led nowhere. A new era, he proclaimed, had dawned on mankind with Comte's promulgation of the Positive philosophy. Of Lewes's hearers, among whom I was one, many, I doubt not, went home content to know nothing which could not be 'verified by experience', since beyond that, the clever and erudite gentleman from London assured us, there was really nothing to be known.[51]

Espinasse was again in the audience when Lewes returned to Manchester in March to act. The Theatre Royal playbills announced that 'Mr G. H. Lewes, the popular author' would 'make his début in the character of Shylock' on 10 March, with the professional actor Barry Sullivan playing Bassanio. We do not know how Lewes persuaded the theatre manager, Henry Wallack, to take him on; it was unusual for an amateur to have the leading role in a professional production. According to the *Manchester Courier*, a large audience turned up to see how the 'philosopher and author of some popular works' would treat the character of Shylock, and he was 'greeted with several distinct rounds of applause' before the audience settled down into the 'attitude of attentive listeners and judges'.[52] In fact, Lewes departed from convention by seeking to portray Shylock part-sympathetically. Espinasse thought it a misconception:

There was originality in Lewes's conception of Shylock, whom he endeavoured to represent as the champion and avenger of a persecuted race, and his gabardine and three-pointed beard were praised as accurate reproductions of old reality. Sooth to say, however, Lewes's presentation of the Jew that Shakespeare drew was palpably ineffective, and his best friends were obliged to admit that Nature had not intended him to be an actor.[53]

Lewes's idea of the character of Shylock was highly intelligent. When writing as Vivian in the *Leader* in 1850 he accused Macready of 'a radical misconception of the character' in his performance of the part. Lewes insisted: 'I say if Shylock be not represented as having the feelings of our kind, *The Merchant of Venice* becomes a brutal melodrama.'[54] But the idea was unconventional. In any case, it seems that he had not the strength of voice or physical presence to persuade an audience to accept his interpretation. His colleague Barry Sullivan thought him 'a poor weak creature'. Apparently there was a row at the theatre because Lewes was boastful of his own talent, announcing his intention of 'taking to the stage permanently' and supposedly speaking contemptuously of Sullivan. Thereupon, Sullivan told Wallack he would not appear again with Lewes.[55] Though this account, by Sullivan's biographer, is not wholly reliable, a version of the same tale was already current in 1849. It was known that Macready was soon to retire, and John Forster wrote to him in May 1849 (Macready being in America at the time): 'But oh when you return! Such stories about your old acquaintances. Lewes (who has become an actor, and talking familiarly of the time when your retirement will leave him undisputed lord of the scene . . .'[56]

Opinions differed about Lewes's performance in his own play. The critic in the *Manchester Guardian* of 18 April 1849 thought it an improvement on his Shylock, and cautiously encouraged him to adopt the 'arduous profession' of acting on the strength of it.[57] Geraldine Jewsbury extravagantly praised his acting as both Shylock and Don Gomez in the *Manchester Examiner and Times*; but Espinasse thought him no more successful as the 'elderly Spanish hidalgo' than he was as the 'Venetian Jew'.[58] Dickens, though fond of Lewes and happy with his acting as an amateur, was characteristically sharp when he heard of Lewes's preten-

1. Charles Lee Lewes senior as
Bobadil. Oil painting by Samuel
de Wilde.

2. G. H. Lewes's mother,
Elizabeth Ashweek, 1822.

3. G. H. Lewes, November 1840.

4. Agnes Lewes, G. H. Lewes, and Thornton Hunt, *c.*1848.

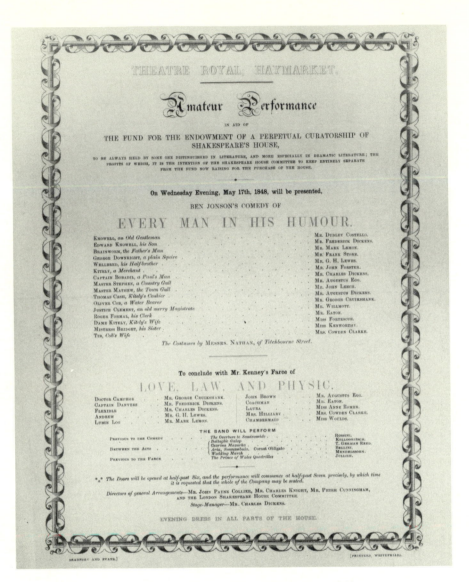

5. Playbill for *Every Man in his Humour*, 1848.

G. H. Lewes, Dux Ducum,
to
Edward Ditto, Esq.,
[in reply to a request for a ticket on Friday

Dear Ned.
The Princess order is given
away to Mrs Thornton Hunt,
& there is no other order to be
had. The Lyceum is closed &
Drury Lane several benefit nights.
Agnes Lewes

6. G. H. Lewes, *c.*1849.

7. Thornton Hunt. Drawing by Samuel Laurence.

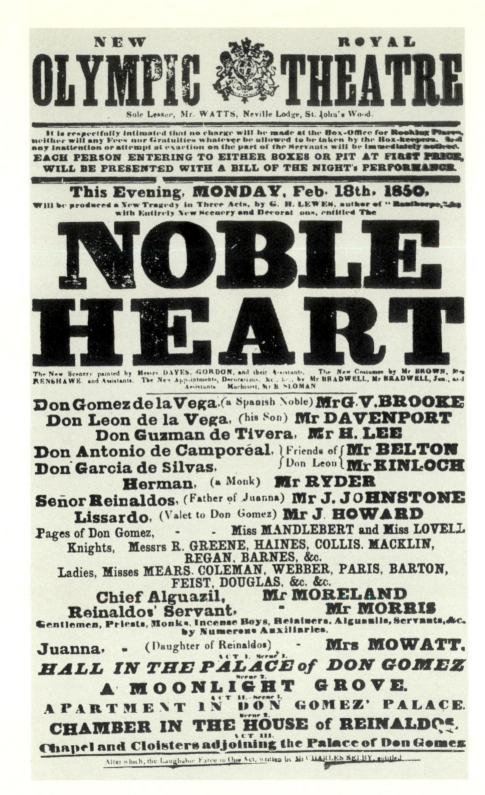

8. Playbill for *The Noble Heart*, 1850.

9. Hofwyl School: (*a*) photograph, *c.*1857; (*b*) lithograph, undated.

COUR ET FAÇADE DU GRAND INSTITUT DU CÔTÉ DU NORD

Geo. Eliot - 1858 - from photograph

MAYALL. PHOTO.   LONDON & BRIGHTON

10. George Eliot, 1858.
Etching by P. A. Rajon (1884)
from a photograph by Mayall.

11. G. H. Lewes, 1858.
Photograph by Mayall.

sions: 'I understand the Noble Heart says that "nothing has been seen like it, since the days of Kean". I should think not.'[59]

Two more performances as Shylock were given when Lewes visited Edinburgh in November 1849 to lecture and to drum up support for the projected *Leader*. The writer in the *Edinburgh News and Literary Chronicle* thought the performance 'extraordinary in an amateur', but found Lewes lacking in the physical energy necessary to give 'a vigorous rendering' of Shylock; the *Scotsman*'s reviewer added a complaint about 'the inherent weakness of Mr Lewes's voice'.[60] The acting experiment was not an unqualified failure, but it was not a success either.

Lewes now gave up the idea of making acting his profession. When he wrote a series of articles for the *Pall Mall Gazette* fifteen years later, subsequently published in book form as *On Actors and the Art of Acting* (1875), he talked of the successes and failures of others in a way which throws light on his own aborted acting career. Of the professional actor Farren he wrote: 'Like all comic actors, Farren had a secret belief in his tragic powers.' But his physical limitations and his lack of emotional power ensured failure: 'I saw him play the Hunchback . . . and never saw a fine actor so utterly feeble. Once or twice, I believe, he tried the experiment of Shylock upon provincial audiences; but he was not sufficiently encouraged to try it in London.'[61] This could easily be a self-portrait. And when he comes to Mathews, with whom he collaborated on adaptations of French plays at the Lyceum between 1851 and 1854, Lewes describes a comic actor who sounds like a more successful version of the Lewes who cavorted as Sir Hugh Evans in 1848:

Charles Mathews was eminently vivacious: a nimble spirit of mirth sparkled in his eye, and gave airiness to every gesture. He was in incessant movement without ever becoming obtrusive or fidgety. A certain grace tempered his vivacity; an innate sense of elegance rescued him from the exaggerations of animal spirits.[62]

Lewes's own craving to act seems to have been revived in March 1851, for Vivian confesses in an article prompted by Macready's final retirement from the stage that not only has he always loved the art of acting, but he still has a 'personal ambition' to act himself.[63] He had to settle instead for some success as a collaborator with Mathews on *A Game of Speculation* in September of the same year.

But this was not quite the end of his own play, *The Noble Heart*. Busy as he was at the end of 1849 visiting Manchester, Liverpool, and Edinburgh yet again in search of subscribers for the *Leader*, and staying with his co-founder and the financial backer of the paper, the Reverend

Edmund Larken, at his Lincolnshire rectory, Lewes also sought between times to get his play put on in London with professional actors. He approached various managers he knew, including Benjamin Webster of the Haymarket, who undertook to ask the great Charles Kean and his wife, proprietors of the Princess's Theatre, if they wanted it.[64] They didn't. Eventually Lewes's play was put on by Walter Watts at the Olympic, having its first performance on 18 February 1850. Lewes told his Edinburgh correspondent Robert Chambers on 8 February: 'They are in high spirits at the theatre about it & predict great success.'[65] The Irish actor Gustavus Brooke took the part of Don Gomez.

The first night was indeed a success. Some of Lewes's friends attended. Holyoake, his collaborator on the *Leader*, was there. Dickens intended to go, but wrote to Frank Stone at the last moment: 'I forgot.— I am engaged to dinner to day. The Noble Heart will have to beat without me.'[66] After the performance Lewes was called for and 'passed smiling across the stage'. Reviews were polite, though several noticed, not unreasonably, that the play contained too much 'talk'.[67] Lewes himself complained, in the preface to the printed version in March 1850, that his text had been interfered with by the censor, William Bodham Donne.[68] Addressing his preface to Arthur Helps, he spoke out, like his grandfather before him, for freedom of expression on the stage, particularly in religious matters, a topic much on his mind with the first number of the *Leader*, dedicated to such freedom, due to appear in a few weeks' time:

What think you, my dear Helps, of the established conviction among 'experienced' men, that English audiences will not tolerate the name of the Deity pronounced upon the stage! You may say '*Him*' and point upwards, but you may not say '*God*'. I am dull enough not to see the merits of this distinction; and moreover, I am curious to know where this prudery will stop. I write
'The heart hath but one resting place—in God.'
But I am not allowed the expression:—it is 'softened' into 'Heaven'. Very well: but how long may I say 'Heaven'?—will they not force me to *soften* that into 'sky', and then again 'sky' into 'that place'?—Must I not banish 'bosom' from my verse, and soften it to 'neck'?[69]

The play, even as censored, was successful enough to run for eight nights, and who knows how much longer it might have lasted if an unfortunate accident had not happened. The theatre manager, Walter Watts, whom Lewes praised in his preface for his promptitude in making arrangements for the production—'On the 7th January I took the Play to Mr Watts, and on the 28th all our arrangements were finally settled'—

was arrested for debt early in March. The theatre was closed, and *The Noble Heart* ceased to beat, as Dickens would say. Watts was not only bankrupt, but was convicted of embezzling about £70,000 from a City insurance office where he was employed as a clerk. Sentenced to 10 years' transportation, he hanged himself in his cell in Newgate prison on 13 July 1850.[70] After this mishap, *The Noble Heart* was not revived in England, though it was put on in New York in 1851 and 1858 and in Boston in 1855.[71]

At least Lewes was paid generously for the play. Watts gave him £100 in February 1850 for the rights for two years. It was his highest earning of the year. In March 1850 he made only £14, his salary for the first two weeks' editorship of the *Leader*, the paper he had been working so hard to bring into existence. It made its début on the same day that Dickens's weekly paper, *Household Words*, first appeared—Saturday 30 March 1850. Both papers were to be distinguished agitators for reform in the political, social, and religious life of mid-century England.

6

Founding the *Leader*
(1849–1850)

THE *Leader*, though it lasted for less than a decade, was a weekly newspaper of great distinction. It was radical in politics, espousing the causes of parliamentary reform, free trade, secular education, an advanced political economy, greater freedom of expression, particularly on religious subjects, and wider tolerance in social mores. In its early years it championed the liberalizing of the divorce laws and the case for Roman Catholics to have an established archbishopric in England. Radical members of Parliament were supported, international republicanism, with Mazzini at its head, was given enthusiastic attention, and Chartist meetings were fully reported.

Thornton Hunt was the originator and upholder of the political tone of the paper. He became an active Chartist in 1850, and his articles reflected his allegiance. Not only was the *Leader* largely his brainchild, but he was its political editor and chief writer. Lewes, his co-founder and co-editor, was responsible for the literary part. The two men had cherished ambitions to own and edit a radical journal since at least 1847, when they tried to buy the *Westminster Review*. By 1849 their sense of mission was intensified by the recent European revolutions which had been followed by a disappointing reinstatement of conservative governments throughout continental Europe. Hunt and Lewes met several European refugees, including the French socialist Louis Blanc (who helped Lewes with materials for his *Life of Robespierre*), Mazzini himself, and assorted radicals, liberals, and republicans, who naturally associated with the Chartists.[1]

The draft prospectus which Lewes drew up in December 1849 stressed the need to endorse 'the Sacred Right of Opinion and the Right to its *Free Utterance*'. The paper's title at this stage was 'The Free Speaker', and the first number was planned for 4 February 1850. Lewes's prospectus is interesting for its breadth, its insistence on tolerance, and its motto, borrowed from Comte, 'Order and Progress':

No journal hitherto has stood upon this broad dignified & liberal basis; no journal has given *free* utterance to the opinions of thinking men without respect to their agreement with the opinions advocated by the journal; and the reason has been less perhaps a want of tolerance, than a sense of the *difficulty* of executing such a volume: for a journal open to *all* opinions would obviously want the force & coherence which readers desire. But *The Free Speaker* without in any way lessening the force of its own doctrines—without in any way swerving from its distinct path will by a peculiarity of its construction be enabled to give publicity to any opinions however extreme.[2]

This 'peculiarity' was a regular column of letters to the editor, called 'Open Council', which represented, as Lewes said, a significant departure from the practice of other newspapers. All kinds of opinions were expressed in it, as Charlotte Brontë noticed in May 1850. 'Some of the communications in the "Open Council" department are odd productions; but it seems to me very fair and right to admit them. Is not the system of the paper altogether a novel one?' she asked a correspondent. Nevertheless, she was horrified to be asked by Lewes to contribute to the column herself in November 1850, when the *Leader* was defending the setting up of a Roman Catholic hierarchy in England against hysterical anti-Popery, which she rather vehemently shared.[3]

Other factors which spurred Lewes and Hunt on to found their newspaper were the worsening state of the economy and the influx of Irish beggars and unemployed labourers, a lumpenproletariat arriving to swell the already desperate ranks of the urban poor. The plight of those at the bottom of the industrial heap was nakedly exposed by Henry Mayhew in his *Morning Chronicle* articles of 1849, which consisted of interviews with impoverished tailors and other sweated labourers. In 1843 Carlyle had written *Past and Present*, in which he eloquently berated the evils of capitalism with its alternating periods of over-production and under-production, resulting in such 'novelties' as the phenomenon of 'too many shirts' in a world with 'nine-hundred millions of bare backs'.[4] He now followed this with his six intemperate but righteously angry *Latter-Day Pamphlets*, which appeared monthly from February 1850. In these he spoke of 'the Irish Giant named of Despair'; he also scorned Palmerston's heavy-handed and interfering foreign policy—'Hercules-Harlequin, waving, with big bully-voice' his sword over 'field-mice'. Though he diagnosed the same ills as did the writers on the *Leader*, he took the opposite view of the required cure. Not for Carlyle the bowing down before 'big black Democracy'; not for him the 'universal syllabub of philanthropic twaddle' offered by the liberals and radicals whom Lewes and Hunt were courting.[5]

Both the *Leader* and *Household Words* took up the call for universal education, and both attended to the efforts being made by Edwin Chadwick at the Board of Health to introduce sanitary reforms in the wake of the serious outbreak of cholera in London in 1849. Old friends like Southwood Smith and Arnott were frequently praised in the new papers for their philanthropic work in sanitary engineering and medical practice. Dickens, like Carlyle, wrote richly rhetorical essays on society's ills. In January 1851 he makes the old year 1850 speak out on its deathbed:

Do I, who have witnessed the opening of the Britannia Bridge across the Menai Straits, and who claim the man who made that bridge for one of my distinguished children, see through the Tube, as through a mighty telescope, the Education of the people coming nearer? Is Ireland in any better a state than it was a year ago? Are not children still starving despite the grandiose plans for the Crystal Palace? Is the Court of Chancery in any less of a fog than before?[6]

But Dickens had no very clear programme of reform to offer. By contrast, the *Leader* advocated specific reforms, such as the extension of the franchise, universal state education, and an enlightened economic policy to finance the reforms. Equal opportunities for all was the rallying cry of the amended Prospectus, published with the first number of the paper on 30 March 1850.[7] The motto finally adopted to head each issue was not in the end Comte's phrase, but a passage in much the same humanist spirit from Alexander von Humboldt's scientific work, *Cosmos*:

The one Idea which History exhibits as evermore developing itself into greater distinctness is the Idea of Humanity—the noble endeavour to throw down all the barriers erected between men by prejudice and one-sided views; and by setting aside the distinctions of Religion, Country, and Colour, to treat the whole Human race as one brotherhood, having one great object—the free development of our spiritual nature.

As neither Lewes nor Hunt had any money, the project needed a financial backer. They were lucky to find one—improbably—in the wealthy incumbent of a Lincolnshire parish, Edmund Larken. According to Holyoake, one of the early recruits, Larken was looking for an organ which would promulgate 'a larger Christian liberalism than then existed'. He was remarkably open-minded, as his letters to Thornton Hunt show. In common with European refugees and a very few other bold individuals at the time, he sported a beard, being, it seems, the first clergyman in England to do so. Holyoake, himself notorious as an atheist radical who had gone to prison for the offence of blasphemy—and who wrote about it in 1850 in his book *The History of the Last Trial by Jury for Atheism in England*—recorded that Larken was very careful when in the pulpit: 'Hearing him preach at his rectory on two occasions, I was very watchful, but no one by the use of a theological microscope could have discovered any departure from the tenets of the Church.'[8] Nevertheless, Larken was known to have funded the plan to translate all George Sand's works into English, a plan which was partly put into action by a friend of Geraldine Jewsbury's, Matilda Hays, but abandoned half-way through for lack of support.[9] That Larken was also an enthusiast for extended families and perhaps even Fourierist communal living is suggested by the open expressions of brotherly love he wrote to both Lewes and Hunt, whom he knew to be 'sharing' Agnes in 1849.

We are fortunate in having a rich store of letters from Lewes and Larken to Hunt (though none from Hunt) during the planning of the *Leader* from November 1849 to February 1850, as well as letters between them and some of their collaborators, such as Holyoake and the radical printer (and later husband of Eliza Lynn) W. J. Linton. Thornton Hunt was the leading spirit. The others deferred to him, though Lewes lost patience with him on one occasion. Hunt was the most experienced working journalist among them, having been employed by newspapers in Glasgow and Stockport, and being on the staff in 1849 of the daily paper, the *Spectator*. He was to spend the rest of his life writing leaders for several papers (not all of a liberal persuasion), and was acting editor of the *Daily Telegraph* from 1855 to 1872. Always overworked, often ill, surrounded by dependents, he became a kind of journalistic machine. Holyoake saw him late in life 'prostrated by the continuity of overwork' and unable to relax: 'You could see leading articles in his corrugated expression.'[10]

As Thornton Hunt was required by his *Spectator* post to remain in London, it fell to Lewes to travel the country late in 1849 in search of subscribers to the new paper. When acting and lecturing in Edinburgh in November, he spoke to leading liberals there. One was his friend Robert Chambers, co-editor of *Chambers's Encyclopaedia* and author of *Vestiges of the Natural History of Creation* (1844). This work, which Chambers published anonymously and never admitted to having written, but which was known in free-thinking and scientific circles to be his, was a popularizing account of biological evolution by means of natural law. Lewes described *Vestiges* in a *Leader* article of October 1851 as a 'delightful work', though 'imperfect and too metaphysical'.[11] Certainly it was not sound scientifically, and was superseded by the work of Richard Owen, Darwin, and Huxley, but it was an early attempt to bring together observable facts in the natural world and to draw conclusions about their history.

Chambers duly became a subscriber, and was also one of those whom Lewes approached in February 1850 to join a conversational society, closely related to the *Leader* in its aims. This would meet in London, where Chambers usually spent two or three months a year, and would consist of 'eminent men expressing their real opinions with all the frankness which security can give'. Lewes was sure that, in the wake of 1848, with the English Government listening to the complaints of foreign governments about the harbouring of political exiles, many of whom were—or were thought to be—plotting the next revolution in Paris, Frankfurt, or Rome, a 'tyranny' existed in 'free' England. This tyranny, 'though less *dangerous* than it has been in times past, is more domesticated, more searching and constraining'. Moreover, men felt unable to speak their minds on matters of religious belief. The society would keep no records and would be, in effect, secret.[12]

Lest Lewes appear to be romancing here, we might remember that John Stuart Mill wrote his famous essay *On Liberty* in 1854 to remind complacent 'free-born Englishmen' that there operated an insidious repression, more subtle than that employed by undemocratic governments abroad, namely the repression achieved by 'social intolerance' towards those with opinions differing from the majority view.[13] On the political front, the British Government did consider enforcing the Aliens Bill, which would deprive foreigners of the right of asylum, several times in the years immediately following 1848. Public opinion and Parliament always ensured that the Bill was not enacted, out of repugnance to foreign interference, on the one hand, and pride in Britain's reputation as a haven for all, on the other. The *Leader* spoke up against enactment too.[14] As for the *Leader's* bold bespeaking of causes like divorce, the abolition of hanging, and universal suffrage, Lewes reported with delight in June 1850: 'We have been burnt at Oxford! . . . We have spoken plainly, fearlessly; but we have also allowed those who oppose us to speak their differences as plainly. Our object is Truth, and quite naturally we are burnt at Oxford.'[15]

Another Edinburgh citizen invited to subscribe to the *Leader* and to join the conversational society—to which he objected on the grounds that it seemed too hugger-mugger—was George Combe. Like Chambers, he was an unbeliever but—bearing out Lewes's point—not inclined to make the fact public. He was Britain's foremost writer on phrenology, the semi-discredited 'science' of assessing psychological characteristics by means of measuring and interpreting the physiological contours of the head, or, in popular parlance, feeling the bumps. A more sober and respectable follower of the animal magnetism craze earlier in the century, promulgated by the Germans Gall and Spurzheim, Combe was the author of the extremely popular *Constitution of Man*, first published in 1828.[16] Lewes, though sceptical about phrenology, shared Combe's view of the material basis of mental processes. He worked hard to get Combe's help with the *Leader*. Combe wrote to him on 24 November 1849, suggesting he visit Glasgow to look for subscribers there. But Lewes thought he would have better luck in non-Scottish, Unitarian, free-trade Manchester. He addressed Thornton from Edinburgh, where he had given a lecture on *Hamlet* in addition to acting Shylock and lecturing on the history of philosophy:

My dear Thornton

I go to Manchester on Tuesday [27 November] in the belief that I may work the *Paper* there to some purpose, personally. My other plan also is to deliver my Dramatic Lectures there, & so perhaps gain some money. Hamlet was *most* successful, & people regret much that I dont continue; but I have no faith in Edinburgh shillings pouring in, & have done all I can with the Paper here—i.e. Nothing but got information! Espérons que le public de Manches*terre* saura mieux reconnaitre et mieux recompenser un talent aux abois! ['Let's hope the public of Manchester will better be able to recognize and repay a hard-pressed talent!'][17]

Lewes asks Thornton to send him programmes for the 'Free Speaker' to Manchester, care of Geraldine Jewsbury, as he does not yet know where he will lodge. The letter continues enthusiastically:

D– – n it Thornton the paper *must* be started! It is necessary for England (& what is more) indispensable to us! I am so sanguine of it—that I would risk any money (would that I had it to risk!) on its success.

Like all Lewes's letters to Hunt at this time, the letter ends, 'God bless you dear Thornton, Your ever true Brother George.'[18]

Once in Manchester at the end of November, Lewes set about speaking to old friends like Geraldine Jewsbury, who introduced him to like-minded people and also to 'several capitalists' from whom he hoped to get the promise of money. J. A. Froude, who had published earlier in the year his notorious novel of a clergyman's loss of faith, *The Nemesis of Faith*, for which he had been cut off by his family and had to resign his fellowship at Exeter College (where his book was, Oxford-fashion, burnt), gave a promise to contribute. However, Froude, though 'most friendly', had no money.[19] Lewes met all the influential people he could, and found it useful, as he told Thornton, to be able to tell them that they had a clergyman—Larken—with them.[20] He was successful in interesting two businessmen: W. E. Forster, a young manufacturer, later a liberal MP and author of the Education Act of 1870, and the philanthropic German factory-owner Salis-Schwabe, who made a point of improving the working and living conditions of his workers and who also supported German refugees in England. These men seemed prepared to put some much-needed capital into the business, though Larken was still the chief financial contributor.

Though Lewes generally looked to Thornton for guidance in these matters, he was aware of something volatile and unsafe in his friend. Thornton seems to have written suggesting that Larken help to edit the paper. Lewes's response was firm:

How *you* could think of urging him to such a thing is a wonder to me with your experience. Why you know very well that as an editor he *must* have everything to *learn*. Let him write as much as he pleases, but for his sake & our sakes dont let him bother himself with what he cannot do. Why even *I* would shrink from it. No; no; Thornton dear; it wont do.[21]

Meanwhile, others with no money but with some experience of running a newspaper offered themselves. Thomas Ballantyne, an experienced radical journalist, took shares and joined the team. Holyoake agreed to run the office, and became an occasional contributor, often under the pseudonym 'Ion'. Lewes had become friendly with Holyoake earlier in the year, when the latter had reviewed the *Life of Robespierre* enthusiastically in his secularist paper, *The Reasoner*. 'Your review of my "Robespierre" gratified me exceedingly by its tone & talent', Lewes wrote in August 1849, 'however I may dissent from most of its conclusions'—Holyoake being a more unequivocal admirer of the French revolutionary than Lewes, as his naming his infant son Robespierre Holyoake in May 1848 illustrates. Lewes invited Holyoake to come and 'smoke a cigar with me' the following week, when he would meet Thornton Hunt, who also wanted to get to know him.[22] Thereafter Holyoake was a firm friend of Lewes's, coming over the years to admire him as 'intellectually the bravest man I have known'. After Lewes's death he remembered that Lewes was his 'first friend in opinion'.[23] His enthusiasm even led him to buy the plot in Highgate Cemetery next to Lewes's and George Eliot's graves; he was duly buried beside them in 1906.[24] In his memoirs he recalled that as he was a notorious atheist, some on the *Leader* team were reluctant to include his name in the published list of shareholders. It was, he said, Lewes who insisted that it appear, an honourable but rash act, according to

Holyoake, who proudly estimated that his name 'probably cost the *Leader* £1000 or more' in lost support.[25]

Despite his oddities, Holyoake was useful as an office manager, and his contributions on the co-operative movement of which he was a leading member—usually in the 'Open Council' section and therefore kept at a distance from editorial policy—have their interest. Also eccentric, and much more difficult to manage, was Linton, who bombarded Hunt with suggestions and offers, most of them not wholly welcome. Already in October 1849 Linton was writing daily letters to Hunt from his home in the Lake District, urging Hunt to run the paper according to his republican but Christian principles rather than Hunt's communist, Chartist, and atheistic ones. An inveterate mystifier, Linton wrote tantalizingly about the funds he might raise from unnamed contacts, and promised to get 'my most important friend', otherwise known as 'M', to contribute. 'I want', he wrote on 11 October, as if the paper were *his* idea, 'to regenerate a new spirit among Englishmen . . . strong as Cromwell's Ironsides, with such faith in God, widened and humanised to a lovelier but no less heroic type.'[26]

He also wanted to promote international republicanism. His friend 'M' was Mazzini, the great conspirator, whom Linton visited in Lausanne in January 1850 to ask for his support. Not surprisingly, he represented the paper as his own project, and led Mazzini to believe it would be a mouthpiece for him. Mazzini wrote to his English friend James Stansfeld: 'The paper projected now by Linton can prove—if it succeeds— extremely useful not only as an organ, a vehicle for our opinions, but as the cradle of other things, as the nucleus of a sort of European club and association.'[27] It did not turn out quite like that, though Hunt and Lewes were keen to let refugee groups of all political aims and all nationalities have their say in the *Leader*. Mazzini's Italian and international associations were well advertised during 1850–1, as were those of the French, German, Polish, and Hungarian exiles.

However, Linton had to give way on several points. While he was abroad, his demand that Mazzini be mentioned in the Prospectus was ignored, and he was furious. He told Larken in February 1850 that he would not take a single prospectus or sign his name to what 'I utterly repudiate'; but later in the same letter he conceded defeat: 'Be sure I have no thought of rebellion against our worthy, our trusted & beloved chief.' He also objected to Lewes's position on the paper, being suspicious about his 'want of political ideas'.[28] The suspicion was mutual. Lewes asked Hunt in December 1849: 'Is Linton to be the Assistant [editor] & is he *quite* up to the mark?'[29] Hunt was sensible enough to keep Linton at bay;

he was made Paris correspondent. In 1851 he got into trouble over £25 of the paper's money which he was accused of spending without authority, and his connection with the paper soon ceased.[30]

After his successful visit to Manchester in November 1849, Lewes had gone to stay with Larken at Burton Rectory, from where the two men sent brotherly letters to Hunt. Lewes had not been at home with Agnes and the four boys since the middle of November. He spent Christmas with Larken, returning home on 2 or 3 January 1850. Agnes was now five months pregnant by Hunt, but there was no rancour between the friends; on the contrary, Lewes expressed fraternity with Hunt in every letter. Larken clearly knew about the relationship. He told Hunt on 24 December how delighted he was to have Lewes with him:

In spite of you and la bella Santa Agnes, to whom my love, I shall keep George here as long as I can. With ours to thee, amice dilectissime,—Thine in the bonds of brotherhood

Edmund.[31]

(His letter does not mention Hunt's wife Kate, nor do Lewes's letters mention Agnes—perhaps he wrote to her separately.)

Before leaving Lincolnshire, Lewes sent off prospectuses to Jervis, Combe, some Manchester supporters, and Charles Bray, the Coventry ribbon manufacturer, amateur phrenologist, and friend of Marian Evans.[32] He also had to keep Thornton's courage to the sticking point, responding strongly to his unwelcome suggestion that, because of the difficulties of getting started, they should postpone the launch for a few months or even a year. Lewes wrote angrily on 29 December 1849:

My dear Thornton
You had better say distinctly at once that you are not prepared to go on with the paper if *that* is your feeling, so that no more time bother & expence may be wasted on it. Your letter is altogether discouraging. . . . Not to mention the thousand accidents which may occur in 12 months, the very fact that upwards of 300 people now know all about the paper is sufficient to assure me that if we do not start somebody else *will* & so spoil our scheme by anticipation—I throw it up altogether if it does not come out in 1850. . . .
    I *want* to start in Feby 1850, but if that be not practicable then I say March.

Not unreasonably, Lewes stresses the amount of effort he has already put into the venture:

We have set to work in various towns an active machinery of sympathy &c—the people are expecting our paper & talking to their friends about it . . .
    I had written to Dawson [another radical parson] to say that I should go once

to Birmingham but now I doubt whether it is of any use taking further steps in the matter. I have wasted a month on it already.[33]

What he does not say, but what his literary receipts for 1849 show, is that he had published no articles since the *British Quarterly Review* essay on Disraeli in August (for which he was paid £13. 17s.0d.), and that his only earnings for September to December were the £31 he received for his Edinburgh lectures. His total income for 1849 was £257, nearly £100 down on the previous year, and hardly enough to support his family.[34]

Lewes seems to have been strangely in thrall to Hunt at this time. Angry though he was, he finished his letter with a defusing paragraph:

Edmund will write tomorrow. Kath is at present busy with E's sermon (I should like to be a parson & have such a clerk) but she sends sweet messages in lieu of writing. I am *growling* & feel like a *demnition hipped Bear*! God bless you.

> Ever your own loving
> Brother.[35]

During the next year or so Lewes veered between prostrating himself before his friend and expressing, indirectly in his articles in the *Leader*, a sense of betrayal and discontent with his lot. The pages of the *Leader* are dotted with odd remarks which may, though with caution, be seen as clues to Lewes's feelings about his domestic situation. But on the eve of launching the paper, his sense of brotherhood was uppermost. (So also was Larken's vis-à-vis Lewes himself. He told Thornton on 4 January 1850 that he was 'grieved to lose George'; 'he is a glorious fellow.'[36])

One cannot help wondering what the qualities were in Thornton Hunt which so attracted Lewes. He was, in a special sense, the type of the spoilt child, having been the favourite of poets in childhood, with Shelley petting him and Charles Lamb writing verses about him. He had been in prison with Leigh Hunt when only three or four years old, and was the subject of his father's cloying pride. In his *Autobiography* (1850), Leigh Hunt wrote in a tone not unlike that of Dickens's William Dorrit, the 'Father of the Marshalsea' (largely based on Dickens's own embarrassingly grandiose father):

My eldest little boy, to whom Lamb addressed some charming verses on the occasion, was my constant companion, and we used to play all sorts of juvenile games together. It was, probably, in dreaming of one of these games (but the words had a more troubling effect on my ear) that he exclaimed one night in his sleep, 'No: I'm not lost; I'm found.' Neither he nor I were very strong at the time; but I have lived to see him a man of forty; and wherever he is found, a generous hand and a great understanding will be found together.[37]

The Carlyles are the best source of information about Thornton, having observed their noisy neighbours in Chelsea in the early 1830s with amusement; they noted, among other things, the 'high-flown talk' in which the Hunt children were trained.[38] They were fond of Thornton, who was invited to spend some time with them in Scotland in the summer of 1833. Thornton, aged 23, got to Edinburgh where he was to to stay for two nights before setting off for Carlyle's house at Craigenputtoch in Dumfriesshire. But he never did set off. He was overwhelmed by homesickness as well as the poor health for which this journey was supposed to hold the cure, and returned to London straight away. Leigh Hunt wrote to Carlyle to apologize, combining as always naïvety with self-knowledge:

I was astonished one day, on returning home, to find him sitting, not at Craigenputtoch, but in one of the drawing-room chairs, impudently smiling in my face, as if nothing had happened. I was alarmed at first, but not long; & though he has been very ill since, he has not been as ill as at Edinburgh, & upon the whole is better than when he left us.

Leigh Hunt confessed to a fear that Thornton had inherited from him a tendency to depression (adding, however, that he himself had plenty of 'animal spirits' to compensate). 'At the same age with himself', he wrote, 'I fell into a hypochondriacal illness, which stirred up sources of thought in me frightful as if I had seen the gulfs of time & place opened.' Thornton suffered later in life, and perhaps at this time too, from epileptic fits.[39]

Needless to say, Carlyle cast a jaundiced eye on the plan for the *Leader*, writing to his brother on 5 March 1850, 'Thornton with Lewes, etc., are thinking of the *Socialist* line, I grieve to observe, in that Newspaper of theirs.' And, 'Thornton, a clever little creature, deliberately contemplates "revolution", *dangerous* upbreak of the Lower Classes, as the one thing that will make the Governing Classes serious, or do any good!' By the end of April, when Carlyle had read the first few numbers, he characterized the paper and its two editors for the benefit of his sister in Scotland:

The *Leader* is a very good Paper hitherto; indeed I take it out as the best I can get here for my own use. . . . The Paper has a *Socialist* tendency (it is understood) but they keep that under hatches pretty well. Leigh Hunt's eldest Son, a really clever, little brown-skinned man, and true as steel in his way, is Editor; he and a certain *dramatic* G. H. Lewes, an *airy* loose-tongued merry-hearted being with more sail than ballast,— they, on the funds of a certain heterodox Lincolnshire Parson whom I have seen, 'carry on the work of the day'.[40]

Even more than Lewes, Thornton was wedded to the principle of individual freedom in every sphere, regardless of convention. Holyoake remembered that he had 'two passions'—for political freedom and social improvement—but also 'a third, stronger than either, in favour of liberty of opinion and the right to translate it into action'.[41] All three passions merged in 1849–50 during his collaboration with Lewes on the *Leader* and his relationship, sanctioned by Lewes, with Agnes.

Meetings of shareholders and contributors took place throughout February 1850, mostly at Hunt's house in Hammersmith. Holyoake's diary noted the day-to-day arrangements. On 17 February he wrote: 'At Hammersmith to dinner with Hunt, Gliddon & Family. Lewes there at night. Arrangs. re paper.' The next day he met Hunt during the day and saw *The Noble Heart* at the Olympic in the evening. Holyoake's job included sending out prospectuses, meeting the printers, distributing advertisements in Brighton (28 February), and signing the share deed on 19 March.[42] The deed shows that the capital was raised chiefly through group shareholding, with Larken buying 35 shares, the printers Robert Palmer and Joseph Clayton ten, Thornton Hunt nine, and various others—manufacturers, radical clergymen, Ballantyne, and Holyoake—buying between one and five shares each. In addition, Larken, Hunt, Lewes, and Linton were each to hold ten shares gratis, in return for their work in setting up the paper.[43]

The first number appeared on Saturday 30 March. The front half was devoted to politics and public affairs. Under the heading 'News of the Week' the immediate news is given, followed by two pages reporting on the 1850 Parliamentary session so far; accounts of meetings protesting against free trade and of meetings in favour of parliamentary reform; and items on the Leeds Redemption Society, the tailors' sweating system, the German Parliament at Erfurt, 'ecclesiastical agitation' in the form of the Gorham Case (about a minister who questioned the Church of England's article on the spiritual regeneration achieved by baptism), 'the Bridgenorth murder' and other miscellaneous events. On page 12 comes the new column, 'Open Council', adorned with an engraving of the Griffin, the fabulous beast which guarded Scythia's gold in Greek mythology. The first letters are about land rights, the need for working men to associate, and—from Holyoake—the agitation to repeal the so-called 'Taxes on Knowledge' in the form of the Newspaper Stamp.

The back half of the paper, Lewes's responsibility, for which he was paid £28 a month, is given over to literature and the arts. Each week in the column 'Literature' Lewes gave a summary of the literary news. In number one he graciously noticed the simultaneous appearance of

Household Words. Then followed a review of Carlyle's third 'Latter-Day Pamphlet', called 'Downing Street'. Though nothing more than a 'jeremiad' offering no solution to the ills of government, Carlyle's pamphlet at least, says Lewes, 'makes us so supereminently conscious, so stingingly, so newly alive to what we know already' that we may be goaded by it into doing something.[44]

Apart from reviewing the latest books, Lewes also began the serial 'The Apprenticeship of Life', a halting and derivative fiction which he dragged on until 8 June, when he abandoned it abruptly, with a vague promise of continuing it on a future occasion. Instead, the fiction slot was filled first by a story by the minor novelist Catherine Crowe, then later in 1850 by Harriet Martineau's gloomy and melodramatic 'Sketches from Life', a kind of minimally fictionalized Mayhew.

Lewes's work borrowed, as its title suggests, from *Wilhelm Meister* the notion of seeing an innocent young man through his early mistakes in life and love. Novelty is attempted by having the hero, Armand, a convert *from* scepticism *to* Christian faith. Politics form the background; the story is set in Paris at the time of the 1830 revolution. Armand marries Hortense, who at 33 (Lewes's age) is many years older than he. The marriage turns sour; he falls in love with a younger girl; Hortense, an adherent of St Simon and free love, makes way for her rival by writing to tell Armand she is committing suicide in order 'to break a bond which, while it was a bond of affection, was one of exquisite bliss, but which now has become a load of wretchedness'.[45] Lewes's heart was not in the fiction—or perhaps it was, on the contrary, too much in it—for he never finished 'The Apprenticeship of Life'.

But he did try one more piece of fiction in the *Leader*. On 7 September 1850 a strange story began in its pages. Again the subject is marriage and the tone negative. The 'hero' is a vain but shy young man who is so afraid of being rejected that he cannot bring himself to propose to his beloved, and so remains a reluctant bachelor. Called 'Confessions of a Timid Lover', it is set in the country of Lewes's boyhood—near Stroud in Gloucestershire—and begins in a rather *risqué* fashion with a boy of 13 falling in love with a married woman who teases him, calling him 'the Lovelace of the nineteenth century'.[46] After some unpleasant experiences with a group of milliners (a byword for loose sexuality in women) who cheat him, he follows his chosen one around the country, but, hesitating once too often, loses the chance of marrying her and remains supersensitively and miserably single.

The oddly negative tone of these fictions and their obsession with marriage may betoken no more than the fact that Lewes was a journeyman writer in a hurry, filling copy with work for which he had little talent. The much better essays he wrote under the revived pseudonym Vivian may also have little private or personal significance. Vivian, like Thackeray's man-about-town *personae* in his journalism, is a confirmed bachelor who likes to boast about his social successes with women while being an outrageous but charming misogynist. Yet it is tempting to see some genuine bitterness rising to the surface in some of Lewes's *Leader* work in 1850, and again in 1853, when he was living apart from Agnes and working up to his full relationship with Marian Evans. Several of Vivian's remarks, always written in throwaway fashion, seem to bear directly on events in Lewes's domestic life.

On 13 April 1850, three days before Agnes gave birth to Thornton's child Edmund, appeared an odd little piece (his first as Vivian) on the Swedish novelist Frederika Bremer:

I like Frederika Bremer, but I must remonstrate against the miserable sophism which she puts forth in her *Easter Offering* on the superior attractiveness of married men. I am a bachelor myself, and mean to remain so. . . .

Shall I tell you the peculiar attraction? It is simply that Frederika is a daughter of Eve and longs for the forbidden fruit. While clusters of perfect apples glitter on every tree around her, ready to drop into her mouth if she will but open it, she fixes a longing gaze at the insipid fruit, made piquant to her imagination by being forbidden. While Bachelors with well-oiled whiskers and radiant waistcoats smile at her side, she fixes her gaze on some imbecile Benedict who sleeps after dinner, wears easy boots, talks nonsense to babies about their *tootsy pootsies*, and smiles dotingly on those dirty-faced 'citoyens dont il croit être le père'. . . . If bachelors are not the targets for assassinating glances, do you know what will come of it? Why, this: every woman will be loving somebody else's husband; and then I leave you to guess what Mrs Grundy will say![47]

By this piece of boldness, with its French phrase and its sexual innuendo about apples (Victorian slang for testicles), Vivian springs to life, establishing his 'naughty' bachelor credentials. But what if Lewes is also expressing some pain on behalf of husbands who love the children they *think* they have fathered? The last child Lewes had fathered (or indeed was to father), St Vincent Arthy, had died, an infant of 22 months, less than three weeks previously, on 23 March; the announcement of his death was included in the 'Births, Marriages, and Deaths' column of the first number of the *Leader*. Edmund, the child of 'somebody else's husband', was born on 16 April. Lewes registered Edmund as his own child; when he met and fell in love with Marian Evans, he was debarred from seeking a divorce on the grounds—not changed under the partially liberating Divorce Act of 1857—that he had thereby condoned his wife's adultery.

Lewes seems to have loved Agnes still, and to have loved his 'brother' Thornton too. On 15 June 1850, in an amusing piece about a clairvoyant he has unmasked, 'GHL' recounts how he found her out by asking her for details of his family. She told him it consisted of 'two girls and a tall, pale, dark, thin woman', whereas of course, he writes, the family comprises 'four boys [including two-month old Edmund] and a human Rose in the shape of their mother'.[48] (Lewes also refers in the article to the sketch of him in the attitude of 'a German student' with a meer-schaum pipe (see Plate 3) done in 1840 by Annie Gliddon, one of the Hunts' relatives by marriage.)

Three weeks later, on 6 July, Lewes pauses during the second of two reviews of his old mentor Leigh Hunt's *Autobiography*. He quotes Hunt's memory of the child Thornton's dream in prison and his tribute to his now grown-up son. To this Lewes adds an extraordinary tribute of his own:

A father may be excused from saying more than that, parental eulogies not being received with unlimited confidence, but the present writer cannot resist saying that, in that 'man of forty', there is more love, more benevolence, more unaffected sympathy with suffering and error wherever it may be found, more of the great stoical virtue of endurance combined with a gentleness and generosity the Stoics never thought of, more of the chivalrous spirit, more of the true *gentleman* according to the highest ideal we can frame, and consequently a greater power of inspiring unbounded attachment than in any man we ever met with. There are but few persons who will understand to whom this allusion is made; nor is it made for their peculiar information; it is rather the irrepressible utterance of a feeling which has animated the writer for many years. Some few will shake hands with us over the passage, and exclaim, 'That's true!' The others may read on and wonder, as they would in some old palimpsest, where, between the lines of a monkish homily, appear the faint traces of an ancient hymn to friendship.[49]

Reading this paragraph now, with no contemporary letters between the two men and no other records which would fill in the details, we may well wonder at this outburst. Almost the next we hear of Thornton in Lewes's surviving papers is that he was sending Lewes a challenge to a duel in 1856, his honour as a gentleman having been impugned, as he felt, by Lewes's complaint that he was not paying his share in the upkeep of his and Agnes's children. Lewes's adoring words remain one of those mysteries which we confront in other people's lives. There is no knowing for sure whether they are an expression of true devotion or of satirical bitterness or of some odd compound of both induced by the stress of his busy inner and outer life in 1850.

Throughout 1850 Lewes conducted the Literature section of the *Leader* with energy and intelligence. Charlotte Brontë was an avid follower of his articles, despite having been hurt by his unusually curt review of *Shirley* in January 1850. This article was Lewes's last in the *Edinburgh Review*; it must have been written swiftly while he was going round the country on *Leader* business at the end of 1849. 'Currer Bell' had written to him on 1 November, asking him to be honest in his review, not to flatter her, but also wishing he would not measure her 'by some standard of what you deem becoming to my sex'.[50] Lewes was not, in general, one of those who wrote patronizingly about women writers; when he praised Jane Austen, he praised her art as a novelist first and last. However, when discussing *Shirley*, a work which confronts with spirit the question of woman's lot, Lewes fails to discuss the subject with his usual intelligence. Instead, he opens his review with some conservative remarks about woman's sphere and woman's function. 'The grand function of woman, it must always be recollected, is, and ever must be, *Maternity*'— Agnes was pregnant, of course—and Lewes warms to his theme with an odd question:

What should we do with a leader of opposition in the seventh month of her pregnancy? or a general in chief who at the opening of a campaign was 'doing as well as could be expected'? or a chief justice with twins?

Lewes was a Comtist, and Comte placed woman squarely in the centre of the home and family, but it is peculiar to find this vehemence, particularly since Lewes is supposed to be reviewing a *novel*, not observing a female politician or general at work. It was obvious, and something of a commonplace, that writing was almost the only profession or pastime a woman could easily combine with wifehood and mother-hood. Then, as Lewes knew well enough, Charlotte Brontë herself was at this time neither a wife nor a mother, so that the question of pregnancy seems a complete red herring. Lewes himself admits two pages further on that he has 'wandered away' from his brief. The review which follows is not, in the main, unfair. Most readers would agree that *Shirley* is inferior to *Jane Eyre*. But, amazingly for Lewes, he remarks in exactly the tone Charlotte had asked him not to adopt—a tone not usual with him—on the 'Yorkshire roughness' of her language, which as a female writer she ought to sacrifice to 'the demands of good taste'.[51] It is an uncharacteristic piece, written on a topic perhaps too close to his heart, about which his feelings seem to have been strong, but by no means unambivalent.

Charlotte was hurt and angry. Feeling particularly depressed since the deaths during the previous year of Branwell, Emily, and Anne, she shot Lewes a one-sentence letter:

I can be on my guard against my enemies, but God preserve me from my friends![52]

This she followed up with a more conciliatory one, in which she shrewdly anatomized the man she had admired from afar and whose life fascinated her, as if he were a prominent actor on a stage and she a mere spectator. Her analysis is apt:

I know what your nature is; it is not a bad or an unkind one, though you would often jar terribly on some feelings with whose recoil and quiver you could not possibly sympathise. I imagine you are both enthusiastic and implacable, as you are at once sagacious and careless. You know much and discover much, but you are in such a hurry to tell it all, you never give yourself time to think how your reckless eloquence may affect others, and what is more, if you knew how it did affect them you would not much care.[53]

In fairness to Lewes, the recipient of this frank criticism, it must be assumed that he wrote the article in a hurry, that he was anxious about money, and that he was perhaps in two minds about the happy event expected in his own household in April. It is also possible—and Lewes claimed this in 1857 when he generously gave Mrs Gaskell permission to quote Charlotte's letters to him, including such unflattering ones as this, in her biography—that the *Edinburgh Review* management tampered with the article before publication. He was sure he had never intended to insult women in general or Charlotte Brontë in particular.[54]

Still Charlotte followed his career with interest, noting the arrival of *The Noble Heart* on the London stage in February. As to that, Lewes mentioned in his first review of the drama in the *Leader* on 30 March that the Olympic had closed, after producing 'Mrs Mowatt's comedy of "Fashion", Oxenford's adaptation of Corneille's "Ariane", and Lewes's tragedy of "The Noble Heart"'. He took the opportunity to scotch the rumour in Paris that his play was copied from Dumas's 'Le Comte Hermann', pointing out that the English play had been performed at Manchester and Liverpool nearly a year before. As for the Olympic, Lewes announced with honourable restraint that 'the career of the theatre was suddenly brought to a close, and the manager had to appear upon another scene, where a painful interest surrounds him'—a delicate reference to Watts's prosecution for embezzlement.[55]

Lewes's literary reviewing in the *Leader* is of a generally high standard, despite the demands of weekly journalism. His response to the publication of *The Prelude* soon after Wordsworth's death is a strong one. Reviewing the work on 17 August, he finds it picturesque and prosaic by turns. It does not, Lewes says—anticipating Arnold's famous judgement later in the century—fulfil the claims often made for Wordsworth as a great philosophical poet. There is little in the poem which is 'universally true'. But 'inasmuch as Nature appeals to all minds, and his diffusive egotism meets with responsive feelings, Wordsworth takes possession of us.' 'He is the greatest descriptive poet that ever lived. He is the greatest egotist that ever lived.' The review, though brief, is full of sharp insights and apt phrases, like that about Wordsworth's 'diffusive egotism'.[56]

Wordsworth's death in April 1850 led Lewes to speculate in his column about a suitable successor to him as Poet Laureate. While acknowledging the claims of Tennyson (who was eventually chosen), Lewes demonstrated his continued loyalty to the Hunt family by putting forward the claims of Leigh Hunt.[57] When considering Hunt's *Autobiography*, Lewes not only allowed his warm feelings for Thornton to spill out, but he also tried to explain the personal and intellectual attractions of his father. Knowing full well that the usual view of Leigh Hunt was that he was vain, improvident, and a hypocrite, Lewes aimed to analyse psychologically the man to whom he felt he owed a debt of gratitude:

A rebel in opinion, he has not placed himself at the barricades. In the very movement of his audacity you see a saving clause. Some men intimate audacities parenthetically. Leigh Hunt has such a parenthesis of propriety even in his most insurgent moods.

This temperament is, says Lewes, not affected, but constitutional. He *is* like that, uniting 'a child-like simplicity and trustingness' with 'a certain knowingness, which seems to throw a doubt on his simplicity'.[58] Though it is noticeable that Lewes forebears to gush about his fondness for the mentor of his youth, it seems from his remarks in the second of his two articles that something of that feeling has been transferred from Hunt senior to Hunt junior.

When Tennyson's *In Memoriam* appeared in June—what a year 1850 was for the English long poem!—Lewes acclaimed its author immediately as 'our greatest living poet'. Lewes gives examples rather than analysis, bidding the reader notice 'how exquisitely adapted the music of the poem is to its burden'.[59] Of the other Victorian poets, both Robert Browning and Elizabeth Barrett Browning published poems in 1850, and

Lewes reviewed them both, enjoying the boldness of Browning's *Christmas Eve and Easter Day*, though missing in it 'the element of Beauty'. His wife, says Lewes, has that quality in abundance; unlike her husband, she is a 'born singer'. However, she deals too much in reverie, not enough in the 'thoughts and sufferings of our work-day world'.[60] In *her* essays of the mid-1850s Marian Evans was to use variations on the phrase 'workaday world' as a litmus test for literature; in her first attempts at fiction she made a conscious effort to give imaginative colour to 'grey' people like Amos Barton and to show ordinary workmen like Adam Bede actually at work.[61] The last important literary work to come under Lewes's sharp eye in 1850 was Emily Brontë's *Wuthering Heights*, published by Charlotte along with Anne's *Agnes Grey*. Lewes finds these works by the two deceased sisters wild, 'painted as if by lurid torchlight, though painted with unmistakable power'. Not really able to be enthusiastic, Lewes nevertheless marvels that these novels were the work of 'two retiring, consumptive girls'.[62]

Lewes's notice scarcely amounts to a review. No doubt it did not endear him further to Charlotte Brontë, if she read it. But without knowing it, Lewes had partly regained her affection, and for the strangest reason. When she made a reluctant visit to London in June 1850 to be fêted by her publisher and to meet her favourite author, Thackeray, she also met Lewes. As she reported to her friend Ellen Nussey:

I have seen Lewes too—he is a man with both weaknesses and sins; but unless I err greatly the foundation of his nature is not bad—and were he a fiend in character—I could not feel otherwise to him than half sadly, half tenderly—a queer word the last—but I use it because the aspect of Lewes' face almost moves me to tears—it is so wonderfully like Emily—her eyes, her features—the very nose, the somewhat prominent mouth, the forehead—even at moments the expression: whatever Lewes does or says I believe I cannot hate him.[63]

Lewes is as a rule reticent in his journal; when he read this letter in Mrs Gaskell's *Life of Charlotte Brontë* in April 1857, he was maddeningly so. He made no mention of it.

Under 'Literature' in the *Leader* Lewes included reviews, by Vivian, of the London theatre. In October 1850 he praised Charles Kean's *Hamlet*, though disagreeing with Kean's interpretation of Hamlet's madness as entirely feigned. In November he reviewed Macready's Shylock adversely for his portrayal of a mere monster.[64] When the theatres closed for the annual recess, Lewes established an alternative column for Vivian, a kind of diary of his evenings, social and solitary (reading the Greek fathers during the latter kind), or of occasional journeys away from London to take walking tours—based on real ones Lewes took with Herbert Spencer—or water cures, also based on Lewes's attempts to recover from illnesses. Vivian was a highly success-ful invention, making Lewes one of the most feared and most courted of theatre reviewers.

Indeed Lewes's papers on drama were thought so good, so full of 'sparkling common sense', that William Archer reprinted the best of them in 1896.[65] George Bernard Shaw reviewed the reprint in the *Saturday Review* and confessed that Lewes's persona had suggested his own irreverent, witty tone in his theatre reviews: 'I consider that Lewes in some respects anticipated me, especially in his free use of vulgarity and impudence whenever they happened to be the proper tools for the job.' In 1897 Shaw paid Lewes the finest compliment of all; Lewes was 'the most able and brilliant critic between Hazlitt and our own contem-poraries' (in particular Shaw himself).[66]

Not all the pages of the literary section were written by Lewes, though most were. There was the occasional poem—by Swynfen Jervis, the ageing Walter Savage Landor, the young George Meredith, the Chartist poet George Hooper. And Froude, true to his promise, contributed some beast fables bearing on topical social and political events. But Froude was not a whole-hearted radical or socialist. He went with the *Leader* because it was anti-establishment. His hatred of the Church of England he had left after writing *The Nemesis of Faith* made him encourage the *Leader*'s attacks on the Church's intolerance on the Catholic question. Froude wrote most vehemently to Lewes in February 1851:

If the Roman Catholics are bullied I hope to see them resist, keep their titles & take the consequences. It would utterly checkmate good John Bull, who has so long gone without Religion himself, that the notion of suffering for it except in Novels or History has become entirely inconceivable to him. Cant you stir them up to it? The Church of England is the great lie which we must get burnt up; and I would help the Catholics to fire & faggot if I could.[67]

Yet Froude did not like Lewes; he wrote to his brother-in-law Charles Kingsley in November 1849 that he had met 'a great specimen of the blackguard'. 'He is agitating for assistants in the great work of the destruction of prejudices of all sorts by a weekly paper (this is strictly confidential), a pious crusade in which my help is wished for, and in which yours too will be thankfully accepted.'[68] Froude lets Kingsley think he may not write for the paper, not having enough respect for some of its 'clever writers' in London. There is undoubtedly some snobbery about working journalists and non-university men here, as well as a fear of making himself even more notorious than he already had with his novel. Froude settled in the country to begin his great history of England (in which he was hardly supportive of the Roman Catholics *historically*); in 1858 he rejoined the Church of England, signed the 39 Articles, and became once again a member of his old college. When he later reprinted his *Leader* pieces, this rehabilitated prodigal son took care not to mention that they were first published in that organ of advanced liberalism.[69]

The issue of the setting up of the Roman Catholic hierarchy in England late in 1850 received comprehensive coverage in the *Leader*. And it did so not only in the political half but also in Lewes's part of the paper. Thornton Hunt's 'Public Affairs' column spoke strongly on 26 October, welcoming 'the bull from Rome, reestablishing Catholic bishoprics throughout England'. Though the *Leader* itself adhered to no faith, it insisted on the right of all citizens to practise theirs. On 9 November Hunt reported with glee the panic among churchmen from John o' Groats to Land's End at the 'inroads of Catholicism'.[70] In the same issue, Lewes discussed the general alarm in his section: 'There is no alternative from absolute Authority other than absolute Freedom'; and he took the lofty Comtist view that religion is a 'progressive science'. As man has moved from polytheism to monotheism, so also he will move into a post-monotheistic phase, in which the religion of humanity will prevail.[71]

These comments brought Lewes the most astonishing letter from Charlotte Brontë, whom he had asked to contribute to the 'Open Council'. She wrote bitterly, sarcastically, almost hysterically—as she was also to do in the anti-Catholic passages in *Villette* in 1853:

I have one pleasant duty to perform which I must not forget ere I conclude this letter—that is to congratulate you and all others whom it may concern on the pious disposition evinced by 'The Leader' to walk bodily back to the True Fold. There is something promising and touching in the tone you have lately assumed—a something which will kindle the glow of holy expectation in the heart of Cardinal Archbishop Wiseman when his chaplain reads to him your lucubrations. . . .

Wishing you and Mr Thornton Hunt and all of you much facility of speech in your first experiment in auricular confession, and a very full absolution from your awful heresies together with no heavier penance than the gravity of the case (which will be pretty stringent) shall seem absolutely to demand,—I am, Yours sincerely, C. Bronte.[72]

What Lewes and Hunt, the notorious free-thinkers, made of this we can only guess. Lewes obviously mentioned it to Harriet Martineau, who was contributing her 'Sketches from Life' at this time, for she wrote in December: 'About Currer Bell's letter & the Catholics, I don't exactly understand. Do you mean she thinks you favour the Catholics? That is not like her.'[73] When Lewes reviewed *Villette* favourably in the *Westminster Review* in April 1853 he exercised great restraint in not mentioning its anti-Catholicism.

The literature section showed solidarity with the political not only on the question of religion, but also on social issues. The subject of the marriage and divorce laws was frequently aired, with Lewes and Hunt advocating easier divorce on humanitarian grounds and printing some rather daring letters in 'Open Council' about the unfairness of the law against a man marrying his deceased wife's sister.[74] Lewes, in one of his own signed letters under the heading 'Social Reform', spoke up for a kind of communism, based on Comtism, calling for the abolition of 'our present laws which give a man a *right* over his wife, and deny her that equality as a wife, which she has in virtue of her humanity'.[75] Thornton, feeling no doubt that his and Lewes's free arrangements were so enlightened as not to fall into the category of social ills, wrote eloquently about the evils of 'the present indissolubility of marriage' which produces an 'excessive amount of bigamy—especially among the working classes. And we here allude, not only to the bigamy in *law*, but the bigamy in *fact*—the double family which leads to so much misery and to so much crime.'[76]

Chartism, in which Hunt soon became a prominent figure, and the European Democracy movement of Mazzini, Louis Blanc, and other refugees, were given a great deal of attention from November 1850. Lewes, as well as Hunt, became involved in their committees. He joined Mazzini's Friends of Italy in 1851 and spoke at a banquet in Freemason's Hall in March 1851, held to commemorate the German revolution of 1848 and to agitate for democracy in Germany.[77] Lewes also attended, with Holyoake, Cobden, Hickson of the *Westminster Review*, and other liberals, a meeting in St Martin's Hall on 5 March 1851 of the Association for Promoting the Repeal of the Taxes on Knowledge.[78]

So Lewes was in 1850 at his busiest and most radical. His column covered not only literature, with forays into current affairs, but also, increasingly reflecting his own restless and omnivorous curiosity, science. From April 1850 a fairly regular slot was given over to 'the progress of science'. Here Lewes dealt with the development hypothesis (the doctrine, associated before Darwin with the French biologist Lamarck of the evolution of species, as opposed to their fixity at the Creation); mocked magnetic evenings and other pseudo-scientific phenomena; gave space to Charles Bray's work on the physical organization of character; and noticed George Combe's writings on phrenology.

Indeed, Lewes must have chuckled over Combe's letter of 10 April 1850, in which he asked for a review of his forthcoming biography of his brother:

If any of your people who have a large development of Comparison & Causality & of the organs of the moral sentiments will take the trouble to read this book, I am hopeful that it will interest him; & I shall submissively abide whatever criticism he may be disposed to bestow on it. But if you give it to a reviewer deficient in the coronal region of the brain, I predicate before hand that he will find it tedious & uninteresting, and I do *not* desiderate *his* censorship. There are men distinguished for intellect, who are not equally gifted in the moral region, & they do not sympathize with a writer like Dr Combe.[79]

This was indeed a novel way of demanding a favourable review.

Lewes, mindful of Combe's influence, kept a straight face, telling Combe that the book interested him 'exceedingly' and that he was to review it himself. He did so, carefully, on 18 May, and was able to praise the work for its powerful picture of a Calvinist family made miserable by its strict adherence to 'that unloving and unlovely creed', without upsetting the sensitive phrenologist by any references—which could only have been negative—to the 'scientific' creed with which he had replaced the religious beliefs of his childhood.[80]

At the end of the first year, the *Leader*'s editors and shareholders could be proud of the independence, intelligence, and progressive stance of their paper. It had attracted much attention, and could be considered a success. However, though it sold a respectable number of copies, nearly 3,000 copies a week in the first year, it was a victim of those 'taxes on knowledge' which Lewes and the others opposed. These were the duties levied on papers which carried news. In the case of radical newspapers and those, like the Chartists', which were aimed particularly at the working class, the tax could not be paid without raising the price, but to raise the price was to make the paper unsaleable among the audience it sought. Such papers usually collapsed within a few weeks or, if they defied the law and carried news without a licence, the proprietors were prosecuted and the papers were stopped by that means. Agitation for abolition of the duties continued throughout 1850 and beyond, with Dickens winning a significant victory in December 1851, when he courted prosecution by adding a supplement to *Household Words*, entitled *The Household Narrative of Current Events*. The jury acquitted him. In June 1855 the Stamp Act was finally repealed.[81]

In an effort to manage the finances of the paper better, ten of the original 12 partners in the *Leader* company gave up their shares in March 1851; the company was dissolved by mutual consent, and Larken and Holyoake took over the joint responsibility.[82] Nothing else changed. But by the end of 1851 the paper had a new owner, Edward Pigott, who became a lifelong friend of Lewes's. Pigott was a quiet, mild radical, as philanthropic as he was wealthy, and he was prepared to keep the paper going at a loss. Lewes, Hunt, and Holyoake made sacrifices too; from November 1850 they took reduced salaries, Lewes's being £20 a month. A further cut, to £16, was made in August 1852.[83]

From the middle of 1853 Hunt ceased to be political editor. Pigott brought in Edward Whitty, who had already become a popular contributor with his parliamentary sketches, 'The Stranger in Parliament'. Though Hunt and Lewes were still the chief writers until mid-1854, when Lewes left for Weimar and a few months later Hunt moved to the *Daily Telegraph*, the character of the paper changed. Whitty was whimsical, not radical or free-thinking—in fact he was a Roman Catholic. Holyoake soldiered on in the now uncongenial medium. But the paper, partly because it was no longer novel, partly through the loss of Lewes and Hunt, and partly because of the founding in 1855 of a rival weekly, the *Saturday Review*, was in decline. In 1857 subscriptions to a new shareholders' company were sought, the commercial section was much enlarged, and the paper struggled on until November 1860, when it finally became defunct.[84]

In 1857 Whitty wrote a parodic account of the history of the *Leader* to that date in his odd novel, *Friends of Bohemia*. He gives an amusedly hostile view of the paper in its radical heyday. The members of a dining club called 'Friends of Bohemia' gather for dinner. They include Fassell, the mild-mannered editor of *The Teaser*, which soon becomes the subject of after-dinner discussion. One of the company, Bellars, volunteers to tell the story of its founding: '*The Teaser*, as first started, was the result of two eminent men—one political, the other literary—being so reduced in circumstances that they had but one hat between them.' To the question 'How the deuce was that?' Bellars answers slyly, 'Intense as was their fraternity, they could not both wear the same hat at once. They therefore resolved to send it round':

'Round where?'
'For subscriptions. They projected a journal, devoted to the exposure of the hideous practicality of the country; its gross common-sense. They went in for pure democracy, pure religion, pure human nature. Old maids, who had heard

of the fraternity of the two eminent men, how they lived in the same house in a moral Agapemone, with several neighbours and country clergymen—always eager for a speculation, and always getting their fingers burnt, as a foretaste— But I am hurting your theological feelings, Roper.'

Bellars continues with a caricature of the paper's aims: 'Letters from divorcées, against that monstrous anomaly—Marriage. There was 'speaking out' in every page. Why should we kill animals for food—and so on.' As to the 'eminent literary man', he 'reviewed Holywell Street, and wrote poems on the Loves of the Flies'. Holywell Street, off the Strand, and not far from the *Leader*'s offices in Wellington Street, was known for its pornographic bookshops and publishing houses. Lewes did not, of course, review pornography. Nor did he write poems on the loves of the flies. But he did—like Whitty himself with his reference to Agnes as the hat shared by Lewes and Hunt ('hat' being slang for female pudenda)—sail close to the wind sometimes with language bearing sexual meanings. Vivian's very first essay plays with the notion of apples being ready in abundance for Frederika Bremer to pluck, in the shape of bachelors to woo her. In another of Vivian's pieces, in November 1853, by which time Lewes was disillusioned by the free love experiment in his own home, there is a quotation from *Romeo and Juliet*, in which Romeo describes love as 'a choking gall and a preserving sweet', to which Lewes adds a remark about love and jampots, 'jam' being slang for a mistress or, again, female pudenda.[85]

Meanwhile, according to Whitty: 'the eminent political man wrote up William the Conqueror, Pizarro, and the Corsair, and said that Property was a fiction.' His picturesque account of the rise and rapid decline of the paper's fortunes between 1850 and 1851 runs:

Well, it made a sensation: it was fresh. London would like to be a City of the Plain for a day or so—as a novelty. But it got tired of the rant. The first number or two had exhausted the indecency, and there were no funds left for illustration. The two eminent men, again reduced to community in shoes for visiting days, sent a circular round that they must stop. One of the clergymen [Larken], who had not half finished his series on the 'Naked Church', came up to town, pledged the church plate, joined with Mr Laburnumash, the atheist lecturer [the incongruously named Holyoake], and they kept the thing going. But they were dull; nothing but Theology, and that in opposition on opposite pages.

Soon Fassell found another editor for *The Teaser*. 'This was a young Irishman [Whitty himself], of an undisciplined sense of humour, who won Fassell by caricaturing the former set, and proposed to save the paper by turning its battery upon all its former supporters.' Even this

failed to make *The Teaser* a going concern, and Fassell now—in 1857—
did not lose 'more than £10 a week on it'. 'And that', finishes Bellars in
triumph, 'is the career of *The Teaser*.'[86]

Throughout 1850 Lewes devoted his energies almost entirely to his
editorial and reviewing work on the *Leader*. For the next three years he
continued at his post, developing his Vivian persona and noticing new
books in all spheres of learning. But he was widening his circle too.
Having to visit theatres so often as a critic, he found himself once again
bitten by the stage bug. His collaboration on adaptations of French plays
with Charles Mathews and Madame Vestris at the Lyceum Theatre
began in September 1851 with a hugely successful comedy, *The Game of
Speculation*. He also began writing again in the *Westminster Review*, which
was taken over by John Chapman at the end of 1851. It was edited for
him by Marian Evans, newly arrived in London to pursue her career in
radical journalism, and it attracted many of the most intelligent writers
in London—Spencer and Huxley among them—to its columns. It was
natural that Lewes, too, should be one of them.

PART II

NEW BEGINNINGS

7

The *Westminster* Circle
(1851–1854)

In 1851 Lewes was one of a group of clever progressive writers who often met at evening parties in John Chapman's house. Chapman had his bookselling business at 142 Strand, where he also lived with his wife, two children, Elisabeth Tilley, who was both the children's governess and his mistress, and several lodgers. Some of the latter were literary visitors passing through London, such as Ralph Waldo Emerson, who stayed with Chapman for a while in 1848. Others were more permanent guests, including Eliza Lynn and later Marian Evans, who had a room at Chapman's for two years from September 1851.[1] At this time Chapman was negotiating to buy the *Westminster Review* from Hickson; the first number under his owner-editorship came out in January 1852. Marian Evans was his assistant, but in effect she edited the journal for him.

Marian, born Mary Ann Evans, the daughter of an estate manager, in Warwickshire in 1819, had come to London following the death of her father in 1849. Her mother had died in 1836; and when her brother Isaac married and left home in 1841, she stayed to keep house for Robert Evans. Though he was proud of his daughter's prodigious appetite for learning, allowing her to have private tuition in German and Italian after she left school, he disapproved of her relationship with a group of politically progressive and free-thinking friends in Coventry—the philanthropic ribbon manufacturer Charles Bray and his wife Cara, Cara's sister Sara Hennell, and their brother Charles Hennell, author of *An Inquiry Concerning the Origin of Christianity* (1838). Under their influence, and under that of her reading of works of Biblical criticism by Strauss and Feuerbach—works which she soon translated from German—Mary Ann stopped going to church in 1842. For the next seven years she lived in a state of uneasy truce with her strict evangelical father—Isaac disapproving too—while she read widely and translated Strauss's *Life of*

Jesus (1846). After her father's death, she went abroad with the Brays, staying on in Geneva for five months as a paying guest of the painter François D'Albert-Durade and his wife.

When she returned to England early in 1851, Marian, as she now called herself, went to lodge with John Chapman, who had published the Strauss. She had decided to make her living as a journalist in London, and Chapman made good use of her talents and willingness to help with the *Westminster Review*. He also made love to her, causing his wife and mistress to join forces against her. On one occasion in 1851 they sent her—literally—to Coventry, where she stayed with the Brays until the row died down.[2]

In spite of Chapman's reckless and occasionally not quite honest use of others' money, he had the good luck to be supported by a series of wealthy radicals during his proprietorship of the *Westminster* and was able to attract some of the best Victorian writers to the journal. Some were, like Lewes and Chapman himself, free-thinking and socially daring. But there were also those who, though politically and theologically unorthodox, were socially 'respectable' men and women. These included Harriet Martineau and her brother James, Francis William Newman, Professor of Latin at University College London and brother of John Henry Newman, Froude, and Combe. William Hale White, a fellow-lodger at 142 Strand in the early 1850s, remembered Chapman in his autobiographical novel, *The Autobiography of Mark Rutherford* (1881) as a man with liberal notions about the relationship between the sexes. He 'disbelieved in marriage, excepting for so long as husband and wife are a necessity to one another. If one should find the other uninteresting, or somebody else more interesting, he thought there ought to be a separation.'[3]

Yet Chapman, though similar to Lewes in social beliefs and practice, was capable of grovelling to Mrs Grundy in a way Lewes never did. There is something disgraceful about his remarks to Robert Chambers in October 1854, when he discussed Lewes's and Marian's relationship during their absence in Germany:

I felt that Lewes was not as you imagined almost alone to blame. Still I think him much the most blameworthy in the matter. Now, I can only pray, against hope, that he may prove constant to her; otherwise she is *utterly* lost. She has a noble nature, which in good circumstances and under good influences would have shone out.[4]

At the time of writing this letter, Chapman not only still had his wife and mistress living with him, but was beginning an affair with Marian's friend Barbara Leigh Smith, whom he urged to live with him in a separate establishment, where she could 'look forward with joyous anticipation to becoming a Mother'. 'Rely upon it', he told her in September 1855, 'we shall be happy yet. Lewes and M. E. seemed to be perfectly so.'⁵ (After much heart-searching and consultation with her friends and broad-minded family, Barbara declined the offer.)

Chapman was, however, not a hypocrite in the simple sense of avowing one code of behaviour while practising another. Rather he seems genuinely to have believed he was acting as well as his nature permitted, while holding a higher standard by which to measure the behaviour of others. Rather comically, he refused to publish Eliza Lynn's *Realities* in 1851 because of its frank dealings with sexual matters. In his diary for 11 January he solemnly noted that the three women in his life at this time shared his view:

Received and read through one of Miss L's 'proofs' of a love scene which is warmly and vividly depicted, with a tone and tendency which I entirely disapprove. Miss Evans concurred with me, and Elisabeth and Susanna are most anxious I should not publish the work.

When he met Eliza Lynn on 12 January to ask her to change the passage, she refused, whereupon he told her, not without shrewdness, that 'as I am the publisher of works notable for their intellectual freedom it behoves me to be exceedingly careful of the *moral* tendency of all I issue.'⁶ The comedy of the episode is completed by the fact that Eliza was urged to 'submit to the censorship of Thornton Hunt'—of all people—and that Lewes, who was, did he but know it, so unflatteringly represented in the novel, called on Chapman on 21 January 'to effect a reconciliation between [Chapman] and Miss Lynn'.⁷ Chapman stood firmly by his principles, and Eliza took her novel to the firm of Saunders and Otley, who published it in April 1851.

Chapman was, as Hale White described him, 'a curious compound, materialistic yet impulsive'.⁸ He was a genuine radical in political and religious matters, publishing unorthodox works such as Marian Evans's translations of Strauss's *Life of Jesus* in 1846 and Feuerbach's *Essence of Christianity* in 1854. He charmed women and irritated men; Lewes came to dislike him cordially. His correspondence with contributors to, and supporters of, the *Westminster Review* reveals his intellectual shallowness and personal unreliability. George Combe, in particular, lectured him on his disqualifications to edit an intellectual review. Yet he was strangely successful. Lurching from one financial crisis to another, berated on all sides, he nevertheless ran the best quarterly journal of the period. This was partly because those with radical or unorthodox views saw that it was in their interest to keep such an organ of liberalism alive, and so it never lacked for intelligent contributors and philanthropic financial backers. Moreover, his unsung editorial assistant did sterling work, mediating between him and irascible contributors and getting the best out of them all. As Combe, the most touchy of them, told Chapman during the weeks running up to the publication of his first number as editor:

I would again very respectfully recommend to you to use Miss Evans's tact and judgment as an aid to your own. She has certain organs large in her brain which are not so fully developed in yours, and she will judge more correctly of the influence upon other persons of what you write and do, than you will do yourself.[9]

During the summer of 1851, when Chapman was negotiating to take over the management of the *Westminster*, he sought Marian's advice about contributors for his first number. She wrote to him from Coventry in August: 'I agree with you that Lewes would be likely to do an article on Modern Novelists very well. I advise you to ask him, as I should not like to engage myself to write anything not *ex officio* for the first number.'[10] She knew of Lewes as an experienced reviewer; they met for the first time soon after she moved permanently to London. It was Chapman who introduced them, on 6 October 1851, at Jeff's bookshop in the Burlington Arcade.[11]

Marian Evans was not the only new friend Lewes made at this time. Chapman had also introduced him to Herbert Spencer in the spring of 1850. Spencer was a sub-editor of the *Economist*, which had its office just across the Strand from Chapman's premises, and he was working on the first of his books on social and political progress, *Social Statics, or the Conditions Essential to Human Happiness Specified, and the First of Them Developed*, which Chapman published at the end of 1850. Spencer had trained as an engineer and was an amateur inventor. His view of the history and direction of society was not unlike Comte's, though he would not have liked the comparison, for, like Comte, he hated to be thought to owe anything to, or share any idea with, other thinkers, pursuing only slightly less fanatically than his French contemporary a course of 'cerebral hygiene'. He was confident, even boastful, earnest, fussy, and valetudinarian; naturally, he lived to be 83, outlasting most of his friends by twenty or thirty years. For all that, he was a loyal friend and not ungenerous towards others' achievements (though Lewes thought him jealous of the success of *Adam Bede*). In his *Autobiography*, written in the

1870s and 1880s but only published in 1904, the year after his death, he distinctly remembered his first meeting with Lewes at Chapman's house:

We happened to leave the house at the same time; and, discovering that we were going in the same direction, we walked together, and talked—I doubt not in an animated way enough. One of our topics was the development hypothesis; and I remember surprising Mr Lewes by rejecting the interpretation set forth in the *Vestiges of the Natural History of Creation*: he having supposed that that was the only interpretation. From this walk dated an acquaintance which a year later was renewed, and presently became an intimacy.[12]

Lewes reviewed *Social Statics* favourably in the *Leader* in March 1851, describing it as a fine blend of the scientific spirit with popular execution, and praising Spencer's 'clear epigrammatic style', his richness of illustration, and his careful avoidance of pedantry—all features which Spencer brought to his series of articles under the title 'The Haythorne Papers' in the *Leader* from January 1852. Spencer was pleased with Lewes's praise, and 'a further step was taken towards intimacy'. In the summer of 1851 they began to go on country excursions together, starting with Sunday rambles in Wimbledon and Richmond, sometimes in company with Pigott.[13]

On one of these rambles later that summer, Lewes and Spencer both benefited so much from their conversation that each later recorded its impression on him. Spencer recalled that 'observation on the forms of leaves set going a train of thought which ended in my writing an essay on "The Laws of Organic Form"; an extended exposition of which occupies some space in *The Principles of Biology*.' Now that he knew Lewes personally, he was stimulated to read his books. Lewes discouraged him from trying *Ranthorpe*, but thought better of *Rose, Blanche, and Violet*. So Spencer read it, finding, as he tactfully put it, that 'it did not make upon me any decided impression one way or the other'. But he also read the *Biographical History of Philosophy* and was excited by it into a study of philosophy which changed the direction of his own work.[14] As for the impression Lewes made on him as a person, that was wholly positive:

As a companion Lewes was extremely attractive. Interested in, and well informed upon, a variety of subjects; full of various anecdote; and an admirable mimic; it was impossible to be dull in his company.[15]

Lewes's cheerfulness in 1851 was, by his own account, hard won. In one of the few confessional remarks entrusted to his journal, he wrote in January 1859:

Walked along the Thames towards Kew to meet Herbert Spencer who was to spend the day with us; and we chatted with him on matters personal & philosophical. I owe him a debt of gratitude. My acquaintance with him was the brightest ray in a very dreary *wasted* period of my life. I had given up all ambition whatever, lived from hand to mouth, & thought the evil of each day sufficient. The stimulus of his intellect, especially during our long walks, roused my energy once more, and revived my dormant love of science. His intense theorizing tendency was contagious, & it was only the stimulus of a *theory* which could then have induced me to work.[16]

This passage suggests that the change in Lewes's feelings towards Agnes and Thornton Hunt took place during 1851, when Agnes was again pregnant by Hunt. If we look at the pages of the *Leader* in 1851, we find a less active G. H. Lewes and a less ebullient Vivian than in the previous year. Lewes began at this time to succumb to ill health brought on by overwork. Readers of the *Leader* on 19 and 26 July found Vivian's column headed 'Vivian Aegrotat' and written by Pigott under the pseudonym 'Le Chat huant' (the screech owl, with an allusion to the meaning of 'huer'—to boo in the theatre). Vivian, they were told, had been ordered to the country by his doctor. This was to happen often during 1851–4; usually when he returned Vivian would write up in his column his experiences of the country and the cures, including Dr Balbirnie's water cure at Malvern.

In January 1851 he promised a series of explanations of Comte's philosophy. By September he had still not begun it, though in announcing Harriet Martineau's forthcoming abridged translation of the positivist philosophy he claimed not to have forgotten the promise.[17] The series did not begin until April 1852. Perhaps his ill-health caused the delay; perhaps also the 'dreary, wasted' feeling came between him and his erstwhile enthusiasm for Comte, associated as it was with his optimism in the early years of his marriage. 1851 certainly presents a contrast with the previous two years of hectic activity, when he lectured, acted, wrote *Robespierre* and *The Noble Heart*, and planned and started the *Leader* with 'brother' Thornton.

During the year Vivian, when he was not ill, visited the theatre as usual. Perhaps surprisingly, in view of his amateur acting experiences with Dickens, he reviewed a production of *The Merry Wives of Windsor* negatively in November. Charles Kean was the director and chief actor; though Lewes was soon to get into a long and vicious row with him, he here praised his performance as Ford, as well as Mrs Kean's as one of the merry wives. But the play itself, he wrote, is 'one of the worst plays, if not altogether the worst, that Shakspeare has left us', the wit being dreary and foolish.[18] Lewes, though bored with the production, clearly enlivened the evening for others. Marian Evans went along on the same night with Chapman and Spencer, and found that they were sharing a box with Lewes. She reported to Cara Bray that he 'helped to carry off the dolorousness of the play by such remarks as "There's the swan [Shakespeare] preening", "The swan comes out now and then", and "The play is a farce in five acts. If it were in one act and one didn't see it, it would be very well" etc., etc.'[19]

Lewes reviewed Macready's whole career in February 1851, and in March he discussed the acting career in general, mentioning his own ambition, not yet quite given up, to act professionally.[20] The 'gay bachelor' Vivian also made some mock-miserable remarks during the year about his favourite topics: marriage, fatherhood, and the ultimate preferableness of remaining unmarried. In April he noted that 'Anderson the Wizard' was about to 'give his Royal Entertainment at the St James's Theatre, precisely as he gave it before the Queen (she is *such* a connoisseur in legerdemain! she sees so much of it with her Ministers!)'. His piece ends with the wistful comment:

This is an announcement to make me 'wish I were a boy again'—or, at any rate, that I were the father of a family, that I might take my noisy children to see this wondrous man. Decidedly one *ought* to be the father of a family! I shall make arrangements to become such.[21]

At this time Vivian's creator and *alter ego* was the father of three boys, aged eight, six, and four, the 'adoptive' father of a boy aged one, and the expectant adoptive father of another child fathered by Hunt—this would be Rose, born in October 1851.

Vivian's column on 25 October, four days after Rose's birth, is a plea for sympathy by the bachelor who has nothing to do in the evenings while the theatres are closed:

I very often don't know where to pass my evenings. The study? Oh yes, the study! What, after a whole day spent with the Fathers, or in prosecuting researches into the Coptic Drama, you propose that I should regale myself with books! Now, if I had but a *Partner* of my life (and copyrights), there would be a quiet, cosy fireside at which to gracefully unbend my mind, and unbutton my straps. If I did but know what Tertullian, with savage sagacity, calls 'the very bitter pleasure of children—*Liberorum amarissimâ voluptate!*' (those fathers had such discernment!), what evenings would be filled with enlightening their young minds and setting them copies in round text! If! ah if![22]

As far as we know, Lewes was still living with Agnes and the family at 26 Bedford Place. Rose's birth, like Edmund's, was registered by

Lewes, whose name appears on the birth certificate as the father. Though
he was also named as the father on the certificates of Agnes's future
children by Hunt—Ethel (1853) and Mildred (1857)—it was not he who
registered their births, but Agnes. He appears to have kept the unhappiness of his marriage to himself in 1851. Even Spencer was not taken into
Lewes's confidence. 'I knew nothing in those days of his domestic life',
Spencer wrote, adding however, 'alike then and afterwards, I was
impressed by his forgiving temper and his generosity.'[23]

Two things seem to have kept Lewes from despair. One was the
friendship with Spencer and its consequence—his renewed interest in
science. It was late in 1851 that he began corresponding with Britain's
leading comparative anatomist, Richard Owen. Owen was Professor of
Physiology at the Royal College of Surgeons and an expert on, among
other species alive and extinct, dinosaurs. It was he who coined the term,
and he who designed the model dinosaurs for the Crystal Palace,
monsters which are still to be seen in Crystal Palace Park. He was also
the founder and designer, later in the century, of the Natural History
Museum. Owen was the obvious person for Lewes to turn to with
questions about natural history; no doubt he was prepared to help
because of Lewes's position on the *Leader*. Lewes wrote an article in
October 1851 on 'Lyell and Owen on Development' in which he took
Owen's side in favour of the doctrine of the gradual development of
species over millions of years.[24] He told Owen about the review, and
asked for help on a question of the relative size of animals at different
stages in their history:

Can one as a generalization from known facts say that paleontologically all
species are *larger* in the earlier epochs than their correspondents in our epoch?—
and is there anything like a *serial* diminution? I dont of course mean are all
prehistoric animals larger than ours, but are prehistoric crustacea larger than
ours, are pachydermata uniformly larger than their descendants? My belief
inclines towards an affirmation, but I want better authority than my own
superficial knowledge.[25]

Lewes's specific reason for taking up science seriously at this time—
apart from the stimulus of Spencer's friendship and his exposure to the
latest scientific books as the *Leader*'s chief reviewer—seems to have been
his resumption of work on the Goethe biography which he had dropped
late in 1849 when the *Leader* occupied all his time. In a letter to Owen in
1852 he asks for help about Goethe's 'position in the history of comp.
anat.', as well as advice on an anatomical discovery he thinks he has
made— 'as Touchstone says of Audrey, "An ill favored thing, your

honor, but *my own*"'. [26] The immediate result of this work was an article in the *Westminster Review* in October 1852—later incorporated into the *Life of Goethe*—'Goethe as a Man of Science'.

The other cheerful spot in Lewes's life during 1851 was his renewed connection with the theatre. Charles Mathews took him on to the payroll of the Lyceum Theatre, situated on the Strand near Chapman's house and the *Leader* office. Lewes needed the money, since he and the family were living on his £20 a month from the *Leader* and very little else. His task was to translate and adapt, sometimes in collaboration with Mathews, French comedies and farces. Most of the London theatres were dependent for their economic survival on such adaptations, which were cheaper—there being no copyright to be paid—than commissioning original plays. [27] Lewes threw himself into the work, easy for him, of translation. His first venture was also his most celebrated. Adopting the pseudonym 'Slingsby Lawrence', he loosely translated *Mercadet*, an already much changed version for the Paris theatre of Balzac's *Le Faiseur*. The English play, *The Game of Speculation*, was one of Mathews's greatest successes at the Lyceum. It opened on 2 October 1851, and enjoyed 94 performances in its first season, which ended on 27 March 1852. [28]

Naturally the play was reviewed in the *Leader*, but not by Vivian. Instead, Thornton Hunt described the first night:

Seldom has a more unequivocal success attended the production of a new piece. . . . The play may be called an original translation. De Balzac wrote the comedy of *Mercadet*, a satire on the bourgeois trading spirit of Louis Philippe's regime; Mr 'Slingsby Lawrence', as the English writer pleases to call himself, has written a comedy with the same number of acts and the same plot, a satire on the trading speculative spirit of England. . . .

A ruined commercial gentleman has degenerated into the mere scheming adventurer, whose creditors approach him in numbers and in rage, melt under the influence of his winning ways, and become anew his *money-lenders*—with their eyes open! . . . The adventurer is almost, but not quite, a heartless schemer: he has still in him enough stuff o' the conscience for you to sympathize with him, and you relish his successes. [29]

The likeable swindler, Affable Hawk, became one of Mathews's most famous characterizations. Both the character and the play were singled out by critics and memoirists as his best during his eight years at the Lyceum. [30] Lewes himself, in *On Actors and the Art of Acting*, praised Mathews's performance, while modestly omitting to mention his own connection with the play:

It is needless to speak of his performance in 'The Game of Speculation', the artistic merit of which was so great that it almost became an offence against morality, by investing a swindler with irresistible charms, and making the very audacity of deceit a source of pleasurable sympathy.[31]

No wonder the play was such a hit. It is full of verbal and dramatic wit, like a Ben Jonson comedy updated to the nineteenth century. Affable Hawk, a more lovable Volpone, takes advantage of his creditors' greed and gullibility. The craze for speculation is shrewdly allied to political events; Hawk spins a yarn about having invented a 'Conservative pavement' on which it would be impossible for a revolutionary crowd to erect barricades:

'You see at once all the Governments interested in the maintenance of order become our first shareholders—Kings, Princes, Ministers form our Committee supported by the Banker Lords and Cotton Lords and all the commercial world. Even the very Republicans themselves finding this chance ruined will be forced to take my shares in order to live!'

After a dazzling display of presence of mind in the face of mounting problems, Hawk ends the play with a general dispensing of largesse; he is now no longer a debtor but a creditor: 'Look at me! I am one of you! I, too, am a Creditor, Magnificent development of human faculty!'[32]

Not only did the play become an instant and lasting success, but the speed with which 'Slingsby Lawrence' translated it became a legend. In the advertisement to the printed version he claimed that the play was 'written in thirteen hours and produced after only two rehearsals'.[33] This account, though perhaps exaggerated, was current years afterwards when theatre-goers remembered the sensation created by *The Game of Speculation*. A rival actor-manager, John Hollingshead, recalled the event interestingly in his autobiography in 1895. Hollingshead gives a good sense both of Lewes's reputation in 1851 and of the practice in London theatres at the time:

He was a many-sided and clever man—rather satisfied with his personal appearance, and as stock author at the Lyceum Theatre, under the management of Charles Mathews and Madame Vestris, he did yeoman's service for his employers. When Balzac's *Mercadet* was produced in Paris, and there was a rush of the few London managers, who were largely dependent on the French stage for the comedy, Lewes was first in the field. He got the play on a Saturday morning from France. He went up to a room at the top of the theatre with half-a-dozen shorthand writers. He dictated, *à la* Masaniello, to each and all in turn; the plan of the Parliamentary gallery of the House of Commons was adopted; the 'flimsy' was copied from shorthand into slips of English; the slips were sent down to the stage every half-hour to the actors, who were there, learning these fragments with one eye, while they were rehearsing, so to speak, with the other. This work went on through Saturday and Saturday night, a part of Sunday and Sunday night, and a greater part of Monday, and the result, the three-act comedy of the 'Game of Speculation' was produced at the Lyceum on the same Monday night [the opening night was actually a Thursday], spoken and acted to perfection. I was in the front row of the gallery—a place that suited my pocket. Was the dialogue slip-shod? No. Take 'what are creditors created for but to give credit' as a sample. Charles Mathews played the chief part, and no one, not even the French creator, could have played it better or so well. Was it badly adapted? No. Years afterwards, when I had the Gaiety Theatre, and Mr Alfred Wigan was my chief actor, the necessity of finding him a good play and part presented itself to my managerial mind. I turned to *Mercadet*, and Mr Alfred Wigan turned to 'Affable Hawk', the chief character. The next morning when we met we shook our heads. It was no good. Mr George-Henry-Lewes-Slingsby-Lawrence had cut the ground from under us with his forty-eight hours' adaptation, his phonographic echo of Balzac.[34]

Vivian himself went to see *The Game of Speculation* in December, reporting in the *Leader* that 'the comedy of my lucky, but over-estimated friend, Slingsby Lawrence, was played with great *verve* and finish' and that Mathews was cheered when he first came on stage.[35] Lewes was delighted with his success. In the spring of 1852 he wrote to his friend W. M. W. Call (a clergyman soon to resign his ministry because of religious doubts and to marry a friend of Marian Evans, Rufa Hennell):

I am in capital health in spite of the undue amount of work I have had to do. The Game of Speculation—'the success of which is unexampled in the annals of modern drama'—quoth the *Times*—has thrown me into a theatrical vortex which has greatly interfered with my physiological researches, but after Easter week I shall be calm again—comparatively.[36]

In the same letter Lewes talks of being in the midst of rehearsals for his next dramatization for Mathews. This was a collaborative effort, *A Chain of Events*, adapted from a French original in eight acts, which opened on Easter Monday, 12 April 1852, and ran for 52 performances.[37] Mathews obviously wanted to follow up the success of the previous season with another sensational production. This time the novelty lay in the extreme length of the play—rather a risky way of trying to woo audiences—and in the spectacular staging of a shipwreck. The play's success was founded on the latter feature. Lewes wrote to a theatre acquaintance, J. Stirling Coyne, while rehearsals were going on: 'As to the outline of the plot I am so bound to secrecy by the management that I havent told my most intimate friend—all I can say is that it is a drame comedie of people's life before the French revolution with "stunning" effects.'[38]

According to John Coleman, the actor and playwright, the 'stage management and mounting of this drama as nearly approached perfection' as anything he had seen, setting a precedent for rival lavish productions.[39] But the length of the play was a problem. Douglas Jerrold, discussing it at one of the clubs, thought that the manager would find it 'a door-chain strong enough to keep everybody out of his house'; and Marian Evans, who saw it with Spencer, also employed the obvious metaphor: 'It is a very long chain and drags rather heavily. No sparkle, but a sort of Dickens-like sentimentality all through.'[40] Lewes adapted one more French play for Mathews during 1852, the one-act farce *Taking by Storm*, which was first put on in June. For this he adopted another pseudonym, that of the man from London in Jane Austen's *Emma*, Frank Churchill.

Lewes's close connections with London theatre circles at this time were not entirely pleasant. As Vivian he occupied a position of influence, even power, *vis-à-vis* theatre managers. One of them, Charles Kean, was notoriously sensitive about his reputation both as manager of the Princess's Theatre in Oxford Street and as its chief tragic actor. He and Douglas Jerrold of *Punch* were already involved in a running battle of words, and he soon took offence at Vivian's mocking criticisms of his melodramatic style. Lewes, looking back in *On Actors*, gave a more impartial view of Kean's talents, but still believed that he was better in melodrama than in tragedy, where 'the inflexible nature of his talent' placed him at a disadvantage.[41] Kean's short temper was common knowledge; he was said to have locked up a critic for several hours for calling one of Mrs Kean's performances vulgar.[42] He took a different course of action with Lewes—withdrawing Lewes's right to a free seat as dramatic critic of the *Leader*.

It was a foolish action. On 7 February 1852 the *Leader*'s theatre column was headed 'Vivian in Tears! (All along of Mr Kean)'. Vivian complains:

Hear it, ye winds—Charles Kean has cut me off the Free List!

No more! never never more, am I to enjoy the exquisite privilege of seeing that poetic eye 'in a fine frenzy rolling!' . . . Oh, *why* didn't I write more glowingly about his genius; *why* did I not, by some critical alchemy, convert his peculiarities into talents; *why* did I not discover eloquence in his pauses, variety and expression in his gestures, and intelligence in his conceptions?

After more of this mock misery and witty insult, Vivian ends with the promise (or threat) that he will not be put off, but will continue to criticize Kean frankly, henceforth paying for his seat.[43]

The following week offered Vivian another chance to annoy Kean. 'On Monday *King John* was revived at the Princess's', he wrote, 'and I, like a sort of Oxford-street Tantalus, gazed at the bill, but could not feed my hungry eyes with the performance.' However, on Wednesday 'I would *not* be longer kept from that theatre, and I went.' There follows some cruel jesting about Kean mistaking his vocation; with such a 'prodigality of heraldic science' shown in the *mise-en-scène*, says Vivian, it is a pity Kean did not apply for a job in the Heralds' Office. As for Kean's performance as King John: 'I will not quarrel with him for the permanent stolidity of his face and bearing; he cannot help that—it is his misfortune, not his fault, as the man said of his blind horse.'[44] This kind of blithe insult was the feature of Lewes's theatre reviewing which so amused and attracted Shaw.

But Lewes was on the verge of going too far. What would he write the next week? Robert Chambers, spending some months in London on publishing business, during which time he frequently dined with Lewes, intervened to try to make peace. Lewes half relented:

My dear Chambers
   You have found out the défaut de ma cuirasse, and disarmed me by appealing to my generosity in the matter of Kean. He has behaved very ill, and my revenge was to laugh at him. But your frank and noble letter made me destroy the quizzing paper I had written for this week, and I promise you that, short of fresh provocation, I will cease plaguing him—except in so far as criticism plagues him.

He added that he hoped to see Chambers the following day (20 February), though 'I am the most overhead and ears engaged man of my acquaintance; what with manifold work and love of society I live in a whirl.'[45]

In fact, Lewes did go on sniping at Kean, avoiding direct insults but often including parenthetical thrusts in the course of his reviewing.[46] In October the two men exchanged angry letters over Kean's production of a play, *Mont St. Michel*, in the adaptation of which Lewes had had a hand. The details of the row are not important, but Lewes's long letter to Kean shows his peculiar ability to be frank and friendly and yet not in the least conciliatory. He professes to have felt, and to feel, no personal animosity towards Kean. When Kean 'commenced open hostilities' against him, Lewes insisted to a third party that Kean be told of his involvement in the adaptation, which Kean was considering for the Princess's. 'Whatever personal quarrel there might be between us (contemptible enough by the way!) this piece had nothing to do with it,

& I did not wish that you should consider yourself unfairly dealt with.'
Finally, Lewes calls upon Kean to verify his version of events, because,
'knowing as I do, how "statements" circulate, I shall hold you responsible
for any misrepresentations on this point, should they reach me.' Kean
responded not to the profession of friendly feelings at the beginning of
the letter but to the aggression at the end. In his reply he describes
Lewes's tone as 'gratuitously offensive' and he declines to have any more
correspondence with Lewes.[47]

Another confrontation in which Lewes became involved in 1852—
though this time not a personal one—was the war waged by a distinguished group of writers and publishers against the Booksellers'
Association. The association was controlled by a cartel of London
publishers who fixed the price of books, allowing members to offer
discounts of no more than 10 per cent to customers. It was Chapman
who started the battle in favour of free trade in books. He wrote a much-
discussed article in the April number of the *Westminster Review*. Dickens,
whose publishers Bradbury and Evans also disliked the Association's
rules, became involved. He took the chair at a meeting in Chapman's
house on 4 May 1852. Everyone was there: Spencer, Richard Owen,
Wilkie Collins, R. H. Horne, Lewes, Charles Babbage the inventor,
F. W. Newman, and—the only woman—Marian Evans. Letters of
support were read out from Chambers, Combe, Cobden and others. In
short, it was a gathering of *Westminster Review* writers, with the addition
of Dickens and some other great men.

Marian Evans described the proceedings in an excited letter to the
Brays in Coventry. She praised Dickens's way of 'preserving a courteous
neutrality of eyebrow, and speaking with clearness and decision' from
the chair; she was also pleased with Chapman's statement, which he read
'very well', looking 'distinguished and refined even in that assemblage of
intellectuals'. Lewes did not speak, but his friend Owen did. He 'has a
tremendous head', wrote Marian for the benefit of Bray the amateur
phrenologist, 'and looked, as he was, the greatest celebrity of the
meeting'.[48]

Apart from his theatrical activities and his editorial work on the *Leader*,
Lewes found time to squeeze in a few reviews for Chapman's and
Marian's new *Westminster Review*. His article on Browning's edition of
Shelley's letters for the April number has the air of having been written
hastily. It is a rather general meditation on the letters of poets, set off by
his wish to defend Browning from the 'unseemly merriment' of critics at
the discovery that the letters for which Browning had written his
introduction were forgeries. For the July number Lewes wrote another

breathless article, 'The Lady Novelists'. He adopted a more sensible stance than in the *Edinburgh Review* article on *Shirley*, finding women well adapted, by nature and circumstances, to write novels. Charlotte Brontë is praised, with Mrs Gaskell, for uniting deep feeling with keen observation. Jane Austen is held up as 'the greatest artist that has ever written, using the term to signify the most perfect mastery over the means to her end'. 'To read one of her books is like an actual experience of life.' The essay is full of insights, and Lewes touches interestingly on the distinction between 'the legitimate and illegitimate employment of experience' in novels. But, as he says himself at the end of the article, it has been merely a 'rapid flight over the large field of female literature'.[49]

While all these activities might be thought enough to fill the time of most men, they represent a relatively lean achievement for the energetic Lewes. It is likely that most of his efforts were being put into writing the long-promised and mysteriously delayed series of expositions of Comte, which finally appeared between April and August 1852. In addition to ill health and depression, a contributory cause of the delay may have been the awkward fact that Lewes, like Mill before him, found himself moving further away from discipleship just at the moment he had undertaken to introduce Comte's system to English readers.

Comte certainly expected great things of Lewes. Already in 1847 he sensed that he had lost Mill's allegiance and he wrote to Lewes, asking him to make discreet inquiries as to why Mill had stopped corresponding with him. Comte had heard that Mill was 'naturellement disposé a l'inconstance'—an accusation not without some foundation—and asked Lewes to investigate. He also flattered Lewes's own pretensions to take Mill's place as the chief English Comtist. Lewes replied in February 1847, cautiously confirming Comte's suspicions about Mill's defection, but adding the extenuating circumstance that Mill's beloved Mrs Taylor was very ill. Lewes expressed his own willingness to serve Comte, but characteristically preserved his independence with a bold statement criticizing the master's style and advising him to delete 'the *majority* of the adverbs and epithets and remove without scruple all those sentences of *anticipation* and *retrospection* which are practically of no use whatever'.[50]

Unwelcome as such criticism was to Comte, he kept up the correspondence, giving up Mill as a lost cause and encouraging Lewes's efforts on his behalf. In October 1848 he asked Lewes to find English subscribers to help him continue his studies and publications.[51] No doubt Lewes was too busy trying to make ends meet at home; in 1849–50 he was himself performing the difficult task of raising funds for the *Leader*, so that it is unlikely that he was able to do anything for Comte then. No letters survive between the two men from October 1848 to August 1852. By that time Lewes had finished his *Leader* articles on Comte, and had indeed tried to help financially by opening a Comte fund which was advertised alongside the essays. But the money had not poured in; Comte was angry; he soon lost interest in Lewes, even after being sent a copy of the book based on the series in 1853. Lewes was consigned to the discard pile of ex-supporters of the founder of positivism.[52]

Nothing less than rapturous evangelizing would have pleased Comte, and Lewes could not offer that. But in his articles he did give as clear an idea of what the system was as was then available to English readers; and where he evaluated, which was not often, he was generally favourable. Nevertheless, Lewes felt distinctly less warm about Comte's more recently published work, *Système de la politique positive* (appearing volume by volume from 1851 to 1854), in which Comte displays dogmatism, conservatism, and pseudo-religiosity, than he had about the *Cours de philosophie positive* (1830–42) with its survey of intellectual progress and its genuine interest in science and empirical method. Even as he began his attempt at popularizing Comte's work in the *Leader*, honesty obliged him to declare his heresy on some issues. Nevertheless, Lewes's intro-duction to the series contains a generous and sincere tribute:

For my part, I owe too much to the influence of Auguste Comte guiding me through the toilsome active years, and giving me the sustaining faith which previous speculation had scattered, not to desire that others should likewise participate in it. . . . If, after this recognition, I shall be found dissenting from some opinions energetically maintained by Comte and his unhesitating disciples, it is only necessary to call to mind that Reverence is not incompatible with Independence.[53]

The exposition continued from April to August, with a break due to 'sudden indisposition' in July. On 14 August Lewes brings to an abrupt end the 'difficult task' of expounding positivism from the more abstract point of view. He promises to return with a new series explaining Comte's view on 'the great moral, intellectual, and social questions'.[54] It never appeared. We can only speculate on the reasons for this. Lewes was unwell, going off to the country on doctor's orders some time in July. Possibly the *Leader* management was not keen on continuing the Comte series. Perhaps Thornton Hunt made difficulties. It is probable that life in the *Leader* office was less pleasant than before, with the two editors no longer sharing feelings of brotherly love. In any case, Lewes had lost his desire to be a proselytizer for Comte.

However, he seems to have defended Comte and his own series on him against one of Carlyle's typical onslaughts. According to Thomas Baynes, who knew Lewes from his lecturing days in Edinburgh, the two men crossed swords conversationally in Baynes's presence in July 1852. Carlyle asked if the papers on Comte were finished yet, to which Lewes replied no:

'Ah!' said Carlyle, 'in the mean time they are so much lost space to me. I generally look through most of the *Leader*, but I never read a line of those papers. Do you think anybody reads them?' On this Lewes bridled up a little, and replied in decisive tones, 'Oh, yes, they are exciting great interest in the English universities, and especially at Oxford. I have letters from Oxford that show they are attracting a good deal of attention there.' 'Ah!' retorted Carlyle, 'I looked into Comte some years ago, and soon found he was one of those creatures that bind the universe up into bundles, and set them all in a row like stooks in a field—one of those fellows who go up in a balloon with a lantern to examine the stars. I was soon done with him.'

Baynes's recollection of that hot July evening is interesting also for the explicit comparison he draws between the two so different friends: Lewes 'with his light badinage', 'lounging back in an easy chair, his frock coat thrown open, and revealing the greater amplitude of shirt front from the fact that he had no waistcoat', while Carlyle sat upright on a chair 'with his deep stock and high waistcoat'—in record summer temperatures—showing 'the set, almost rigid air of reflective intensity and self-centred strength'.[55] The reminiscence is useful, too, for its evidence that in July 1852 Lewes was still living more or less permanently at 26 Bedford Place. Baynes talks of visiting him there in the afternoon and finding Lewes writing his *Leader* copy in his shirt sleeves. It must have been about July, too, that Lewes wrote to his old friend R. H. Horne, inviting him to call before leaving for Australia. Horne, despairing of success in England, was joining the gold rush, which made Lewes, though no longer his intimate friend, sorry; perhaps he remembered when times were happier for both of them:

I am grieved indeed to think of your leaving . . . & it is immensely discreditable to England that a man of your genius shd be forced to quit it. Do contrive to come & see us one day, if possible. . . . I cant bear the thought of your going away without my seeing you. It is now something like twelve years I have known you, and through those years, in spite of all the differences which our different organic tendencies have necessarily forced into occasional collision [probably a reference to Lewes having rejected Horne's offerings for the *Leader*] there has been on my side an abiding sense of your genius & a constant affection for you. . . .

Agnes begs me to express her regrets, and to assure you how pleased she would be to see you once more.[56]

This letter, from a man with a near-broken marriage to another with a completely broken one, contains the last reference to Agnes as his wife in Lewes's surviving correspondence.

Exactly when Lewes stopped living with Agnes we cannot know for sure. There is a dearth of letters at this time; Lewes is thought to have destroyed his journals and other personal papers dating from before 1854.[57] He used the Bedford Place address for correspondence until his departure for Weimar in July 1854; and he visited often, for his children's sake, continuing to do so after he had returned from Germany and was living with Marian from 1855. To add to our uncertainty about the date of his final breach with Agnes is the further question of when his intimacy with Marian began. The two 'events' were not simultaneous. Contemporaries who knew the details were few, and those few agreed in stating that Lewes's marriage had been long broken up before he began his relationship with Marian. John Cross, widower of Marian Evans Lewes (the marriage took place only six months before her death in 1880), says in his *Life of George Eliot* (1885) that Lewes's home had 'been wholly broken up for nearly two years' before the flight to Weimar.[58] This would suggest that Lewes left home some time in the summer or autumn of 1852. Though to take Cross's word for it would be naïve, since in the first place he did not know Lewes and Marian in the 1850s and in the second he would naturally be keen to exonerate his adored wife from the charge of breaking up Lewes's marriage, it seems to me on other grounds that Cross's statement is correct.

Lewes and Marian came across one another frequently at Chapman's parties, in discussions over the *Westminster Review* and the *Leader*, and in the company of their mutual friend Herbert Spencer. Indeed, it is Spencer who holds the key to the progress of their relationship. But he gives only the vaguest account in his published *Autobiography*, and a rather less vague one in a letter of 1881 to his American friend E. L. Youmans. The issue is complicated. What Spencer knew, but could hardly publicize, was that Marian, whom he admired as 'the most admirable woman, mentally, I ever met' and whom he escorted to theatres and parties during most of 1852, fell in love with him, while he did not fall in love with her.[59] Spencer also knew that whereas one rumour in 1852 had him and Marian 'set down as engaged', as she herself told the Brays in June, another subsequently suggested that he was quickly jilted for Lewes.[60]. In later life Spencer objected to being thought to have loved Marian and been refused by her; equally, he felt obliged not to be discourteous enough to say outright that he had rejected her.

So when Spencer explained the whole thing to Youmans in 1881, he was deliberately unspecific about the course of his relationship with Marian and the timetable of events as they unfolded in Lewes's relationship with her. This is Spencer's account:

My friendship with Miss Evans began in 1851 and soon became very intimate. Having at that time free admission for two, to the Opera, the Theatres, Concerts, etc. and liking her society very much, I was in the habit of frequently taking her; and we were also thrown together in matters concerning the *Westminster Review*. After a while I began to have qualms as to what might result from this constant companionship. Great as was my admiration for her, considered both morally and intellectually, and decided as was my feeling of friendship, I could not perceive in myself any indications of a warmer feeling, and it occurred to me that mischief would possibly follow if our relations continued.

He goes on to tell Youmans that he wrote to Marian saying that while he was in no danger of falling in love with her, he feared she might fall in love with him. Thinking she might be insulted, he wrote again apologizing. 'She took it all smilingly', but 'by and by' his fears were justified. 'Her feelings became involved and mine did not. The lack of physical attraction was fatal. Strongly as my judgment prompted, my instincts would not respond.' Spencer remembered this 'painful affair' as lasting through the summer of 1852, 'on through the autumn, and, I think, into the beginning of 1853':

At length it happened that being with Lewes one afternoon when I was on my way to see her, I invited him to go with me (they were already slightly known). He did so. This happened two or three times; and then, on the third or fourth time, when I rose to leave, he said he should stay. From that time he commenced to go alone, and so the relation began—(his estrangement from his wife being then of long standing). When I saw the turn matters were taking it was, of course, an immense relief to me.[61]

Spencer's memory is in general corroborated by the only contemporary evidence we have—Marian's own letters in 1852–3 to him and to the Brays. (Her journals for the period were destroyed by Cross.)[62] She was certainly depressed during February and March 1852; she told the Brays in April that she and Spencer had 'agreed that we are not in love with each other'; to Spencer she had replied a few days earlier that she was not, as he thought, inclined to imagine he was in love with her.[63] She did, however, as Spencer said, fall in love with him a few months later. While on holiday alone in Broadstairs she wrote him some dignified but passionate letters, asking him to love her or at least be with her as much as he could—'or I must die'.[64] She accepted his rejection stoically, being well aware that her lack of physical beauty repelled him, as it had Chapman. In the midst of her appeal for his love, she joked learnedly about her plainness, putting herself on a par with 'the star-fish and the sea-egg—perhaps you will wickedly say, I certainly want little of being a *Medusa*' (a jelly fish, and also the legendary monster which was so hideous that it turned to stone those who looked on it).[65]

I think Marian's affections, so centred on Spencer until July 1852, were won by Lewes sooner than early 1853, the date suggested, though not firmly stated, by Spencer. Indeed, I think she was already attracted to Lewes while she was still 'in love' with Spencer. The heroines of George Eliot's novels are often in a state of doubt about their feelings. Maggie Tulliver, the most obviously autobiographical of them, certainly loves two men at once—or three, when one considers her deepest love, that for her brother. George Eliot knew from her own experience that it is possible, indeed not particularly unusual, to be confused and complicated in one's emotional life. Who knows with any precision the state of his own feelings at any given moment? We resort to myth-making when reviewing the course of our emotions, not only later, when memory elides and excludes difficulties, but also at the time.

In a sense, of course, it does not matter how or when exactly Lewes and Marian became lovers. The important thing for the rest of their lives is the fact that they did. On the other hand, the biographer is obliged to peer into their lives, albeit as through a glass darkly, trying to 'record the atoms as they fall',[66] as well as taking the easier large view offered by hindsight, the overview, as it were, of whole lives and whole careers.

It seems, then, worth recording from the limited sources available what we can observe about their relationship from 1852 until the journey to Weimar. It is striking that in Marian's letters of 1852, when telling her friends of her doings with Spencer, she often at the same time, or in adjacent passages, mentions Lewes. Thus the sentence immediately preceding the one in which she tells the Brays on 27 April 1852 that she and Spencer are not in love runs: 'I went to the opera on Saturday—I Martiri, at Covent Garden—with "my excellent friend Herbert Spencer", as Lewes calls him.'[67] In June the Brays were obviously trying to bring Marian and Spencer together in the hope of bringing about an engagement between them. They invited Spencer to visit them in

Coventry later in the summer, when she would also be staying with them. Marian connived at the match-making:

I told Herbert Spencer of your invitation, Mr. Bray, not mentioning that you asked him *with me*. . . . We certainly could not go together, for all the world is setting us down as engaged—a most disagreeable thing if one chose to make oneself uncomfortable. 'Tell it not in Gath' however—that is to say, please to avoid mentioning our names together, and pray burn this note, that it may not lie on the chimney piece for general inspection.[68]

This was written on 14 June. On 23 June Lewes enters the discussion; it seems that Bray had sent his invitation to Spencer via Lewes, whom he had also invited to stay, though not at the same time as Spencer. Marian was evidently excited and unsettled by the prospect:

I have assured Herbert Spencer that you will think it a sufficiently formal answer to the invitation you sent him through Mr Lewes if I tell you that he will prefer waiting for the pleasure of a visit to you until I am with you—if you will have him then. *Entre nous*, if Mr Lewes should not accept your invitation now, pray don't ask him when I am with you—not that I don't like him—*au contraire*—but I want nothing so Londonish when I go to enjoy the fields and hedgerows and yet more, friends of ten years' growth.[69]

In the end, Marian was to visit the Brays alone at the end of October, after a journey to Edinburgh to stay with the Combes and another to Ambleside to pay a brief visit to Harriet Martineau. Spencer also visited the Brays, but by this time he and Marian had definitely no intention of getting engaged. Lewes seems not to have visited Coventry.

Meanwhile, during July and August Marian spent her lonely holiday in Broadstairs, writing anxious letters to Chapman about the dire financial state of the *Westminster Review* and petitioning Spencer. The first of her letters to him is a wonderful amalgam of business—her opinion of Froude's recent article on Spinoza and her resolution to plunge into serious reading for her planned work on the 'Idea of a Future Life'— and emotional outburst fenced in by irony:

Dear Friend

No credit to me for my virtues as a refrigerant. I owe them all to a few lumps of ice which I carried away with me from that tremendous glacier of yours. I am glad that Nemesis, lame as she is, has already made you feel a little uneasy in my absence, whether from the state of the thermometer [a reference to the very high temperatures that July] or aught else. We will not inquire too curiously whether you long most for my society or for the sea-breezes. If you decided that I was not worth coming to see, it would only be of a piece with that generally exasperating perspicacity of yours which will not allow one to humbug you. (An agreeable quality, let me tell you, that capacity of being humbugged. Don't pique yourself on not possessing it.)

She mentions that she is reading Harriet Martineau's novel *Deerbrook* (1839), presumably in preparation for her visit in October. One wonders if she also had a special reason for reading another novel, none other than *Rose, Blanche, and Violet*. Of this she says she has read the first two volumes: 'the third I left behind and (damaging fact, either for me or the novel!) I don't care to have it.'[70]

Lewes was one of those who rallied round the ailing *Westminster Review* at this time, while Chapman was trying to raise a loan to keep it going. He praised the July number in his *Leader* column as 'brilliant'. Marian told Chapman to ask him to do an article on Lamarck for October. 'Defective as his articles are,' she wrote severely, 'they are the best we can get *of the kind*.'[71] But she was soon defending Lewes fiercely against criticism; her letters to the Brays and Cara's sister Sara Hennell during 1852 and 1853 contain carefully placed remarks designed to soften their dislike of him. She told Sara in September 1852 that Harriet Martineau had 'jeered at Lewes for "introducing *Psychology* as a science in his Comte papers". Why Comte himself holds Psychology to be a necessary link in the chain of science—Lewes only suggests a change in its relations. *Entre nous*, she writes very sillily on the subject.' There follows an odd passage, suggesting a fascinated coyness in her feelings towards Lewes:

But I am frightened to have told you this, for everything I say to any one at Rosehill [the Brays' house in Coventry] gets around by some incomprehensible means to Lewes—Lewes can tell you the whole state of your domestic affairs, if you like, of course with additions, if not emendations, by the editor or editors.[72]

A friend of her later years, Tom Trollope (brother of Anthony), was undoubtedly right when he speculated about the attraction Lewes held for the plain young woman of 32 with her provincial puritan background, whose arrival on the radical scene in London was unusual. It happened partly by accident—the death of her father in 1849 releasing her from her household duties and depriving her of her family home—and partly because her progressive views in religion and politics made the provincial environment seem stifling to her. Trollope believed that even in her later years

the touch of Bohemianism about Lewes had a special charm for her. It must have offered so piquant a contrast with the middle-class surroundings of her early life. I observed that she listened with great complacency to his talk of theatrical things and people. Lewes was fond of talking about acting and actors, and in telling stories of celebrated theatrical personages, would imitate—half involuntarily perhaps—their voice and manner.[73]

In 1852 Marian was rapidly getting to know the Lewes who could dash off a translation of *Mercadet* in 13 (or 48) hours, who could tell anecdotes in colloquial French and had a good stock of theatrical stories, with all the accents and gestures of the green-room. Given certain obvious differences in situation, she was as fascinated as Charlotte Brontë had been by his talents, and would have agreed with their mutual acquaintance David Masson, who described Lewes in May 1852 as a 'miracle'. Writing to Robert Vaughan of the *British and Foreign Review*, Masson declared:

Theatrical matters occupy Lewes so much at present; & I think his activity will go in that vein for a good while to come. I am glad to find that *you* like Lewes: he is, indeed, a most kindly, genial, guileless person, & with versatility & accomplishment that make him a miracle. All who really know him, like him, & appreciate him highly. The notice of him in Margaret Fuller's life is a specimen of the wretched unfairness that may be committed when a person, with a pre-established notion of what is required, meets something totally different.[74]

Margaret Fuller had met Lewes at Carlyle's house in November 1846 and described him to Emerson as witty, French, and flippant, engaged in writing a life of Goethe, 'a task for which he must have been as unfit as irreligion and sparkling shallowness can make him'. (Her *Life* was published in 1852. Lewes, of course, reviewed it in the *Leader*, quoting without comment the passage in which her attack on him occurs.)[75]

Marian put a lot of effort into trying to convince the Brays that there was more to Lewes than the flippant bohemian with the irregular marriage which they took him to be. From November 1852 her letters steadily include news of him, with frequent assertions of the kind 'he has quite won my liking, in spite of myself' and 'he is a man of heart and conscience wearing a mask of flippancy'. These passing remarks seem designed to initiate her friends gradually—and always a step or two behind the actual progress of her relationship with Lewes. Her tone on 22 November 1852, her thirty-third birthday, suggests that they were already enjoying an easy friendship. She tells the Brays how her work after lunch was just getting under way, 'with two clear hours before dinner', when 'rap at the door—Mr Lewes—who of course sits talking till the second bell rings'.[76] Marian and Lewes were very good friends indeed by the end of 1852. Soon she was visiting the theatre with Lewes rather than Spencer. By October 1853 she was helping him correct his *Leader* proofs; it was also in October that she finally moved out of

Chapman's house into lodgings in Cambridge Street, Hyde Park Square, a move she had been contemplating for many months.[77]

It has been thought by George Eliot's biographers that she and Lewes became lovers when she moved to the privacy of these lodgings.[78] No doubt she was able to receive him there without arousing too much interest. But it must be remembered that Chapman's house was known to be free in the comings and goings of its lodgers and visitors. Marian was visited there by Spencer, and though people talked of an engagement between them, they do not seem to have been shocked by the free companionship between the man and the woman. She already stood out in London literary society—with perhaps only Eliza Lynn cutting a similar figure (and Geraldine Jewsbury in Manchester)—as an unmarried woman living in a man's world and moving in all-male society. When Bessie Rayner Parkes got to know her early in 1852, she admired her new friend's independence, while noticing its unusualness. Writing her memoirs, *In a Walled Garden*, in 1895, she recalled dinner parties given by her father Joseph Parkes, a radical MP. 'On these occasions', she wrote, 'she used to wear black velvet, then seldom adopted by unmarried ladies':

I can see her descending the great staircase of our house in Savile Row (afterwards the Stafford Club), on my father's arm, the only lady, except for my mother, among the group of remarkable men, politicians, and authors of the first literary rank.[79]

William Hale White, on reading Cross's biography of George Eliot in 1885, was moved to complain in the *Athenaeum* that Cross had obscured the Marian Evans he knew in Chapman's house in 1852:

To put it very briefly, I think he has made her too 'respectable'. She was really one of the most sceptical, unusual creatures I ever knew, and it was this side of her character which to me was most attractive. . . . I can see her now, with her hair over her shoulders, the easy chair half sideways to the fire, her feet over the arms, and a proof in her hands, in that dark room at the back of No. 142, and I confess I hardly recognize her in the pages of Mr Cross's—on many accounts— most interesting volumes.

Hale White hopes that in the future some of the 'salt and spice' will be restored and that George Eliot will be seen in her proper 'class', that of 'the Insurgents'.[80]

This was the woman who became intimate with Lewes. He, too, visited her alone at Chapman's house. But Lewes, unlike Spencer, was married. The relationship may therefore have taken longer to mature, and discretion was much more a necessity once it had matured, than was the case with Spencer. It is probable that Lewes himself found lodgings some time after July 1852, and he may have received her there. There is a strong possibility, in fact, that he borrowed the quarters of a friend, F. O. Ward, who was abroad from September 1852 to the summer of 1853. It is therefore quite likely that Lewes and Marian became lovers during the winter of 1852–3.

Among the handful of Lewes letters surviving from this time is a most interesting one to Ward, a colleague of Edwin Chadwick's in the work to reform London's sanitary arrangements. FOW, as he was known, was a handsome bachelor, a member with Lewes of Thackeray's Fielding Club, the sanitary affairs writer of the *Times*, and well known for his fearless investigation of the state of London's sewerage and his invention of a new hygienic type of water closet. Marian described him to Bray in 1851 as 'the man of the Sewers'.[81] Only one letter from Lewes to Ward survives, but its intimate, allusive tone suggests they were very good friends indeed.

Like many of Lewes's letters, this one is undated and gives no address. It may well have been written from Ward's own address, 12 Cork Street, off Piccadilly, while Ward was in Brussels as a delegate, with Lewes's old friend Neil Arnott, to the International Hygiene Congress. This took place in September 1852, but Ward stayed on, studying the water and sewage systems of Brussels and publishing the results of his work in a pamphlet, *Moyen de créer des sources artificielles d'eau pure pour Bruxelles et pour d'autres grandes villes d'après le nouveau procédé anglais* (Brussels, 1853). As to the letter's date, it must have been after February 1853, for Lewes plays on Ward's being in 'Labassecour', Charlotte Brontë's invented name for Belgium in *Villette*, which was published in February.

The letter is extremely allusive, inviting some detective work on the part of the reader anxious to know what Lewes was doing around the spring of 1853. It is addressed to 'My dear FOW', and reads in part:

I was so glad to hear from you & I know how pleasant it is even to see handwriting when one is away, that I cant resist. Of all your public doings in Labassecour I have heard. Your private adventures I hope to hear over snug cigarettes in Cork St. Profitez en, mon ami!

Pigott & I laughed 'hugely' over your coronetted mystery and the suspicions of washerwomen. It would be an incident for a novel!

Dear FOW its no use—I *shall* praise you for brilliancy as long as you deserve it! Why, que diable! is there no brilliancy but in tinsel; what say you to Diamond—and to me!!! As to your bread—bake it & let us eat forthwith—but even the loaves may have des formes gracieuses as well as our solid quarterns, hein?

Of news I dont know that there is any—at least not *writable*. . . . May one ask when is Ward coming back? & Brussels answers When?

For myself I have been furiously occupied dissecting Fishes and carrying a torch into unexplored regions of Biology tant bien que mal. I must now set to work & write a play to get some money. L'amour va son train.

Thornton is in delicate health. Pourquoi Monsieur Pigott dort-il toujours? may still be asked, if fair countesses were here to ask it. Spencer calm & philos. as usual.

A postscript adds, in large writing, 'Come Back! Come Back! Cork St. gasps for you!'[82]

Not all the allusions are recoverable, but the general tone of the letter is a nudging, bachelorish one. The Anglo-French phrases seem to hint at indecency—'quartern' had acquired the ulterior meaning 'attractive woman' by the 1880s, and in the context of Ward's 'private adventures' it seems likely to have had some such meaning for Lewes here.[83] Lewes's research on fish was probably in preparation for an article for Chapman on the Development Hypothesis, over which the two men fell out in July 1853, with Lewes then planning a book on the principles of physiology which he offered to J. W. Parker later in the year.[84] The reference to writing a play for money refers either to *A Strange History*, which Lewes adapted for Mathews to stage in March 1853, or to *The Lawyers*, performed in May.[85] The isolated sentence 'L'amour va son train' may allude to Lewes's relationship, perhaps known to close friends like Ward, with Marian. And the odd remark about Thornton being 'in delicate health'—odd not in the fact, for Hunt was frequently ill, but in the euphemistic expression—might carry the meaning for one in the know that Agnes was again pregnant with a child by Hunt. (Ethel was born on 9 October 1853.) We can date the letter between February 1853, when *Villette* was published, and July 1853, when Ward returned to Cork Street, with March or April likely, given the references to writing a play.

Villette took on great significance for Lewes and Marian. She wrote to the Brays in March, 'Villette—Villette—have you read it?' and reported to them that Lewes had told her about his meeting with Charlotte Brontë three years before, when he found her 'a little, plain, provincial, sickly-looking old maid'. Yet, Marian adds on her own account, 'what passion, what fire in her! Quite as much as in George Sand, only the clothing is less voluptuous.'[86] It is easy to see why the novel took such a grip on her imagination. Its diffident heroine Lucy Snowe falls in love with an unlikely man (the original of whom was the married M. Heger of Brussels with whom Charlotte had fallen in love), and the novel ends unusually, with the reader being left to decide whether a happy marriage will, or can, ensue. Even without special knowledge of Charlotte's own experience, a sensitive reader could feel the taboo placed on Lucy's love and would know that it must end unhappily. Only ten days before departing to Weimar with *her* M. Heger, Marian wrote cryptically to Sara Hennell: 'I shall soon send you a good bye, for I am preparing to go to "Labassecour".'[87]

As for Lewes, he reviewed *Villette* in both the *Leader* and the *Westminster Review*. In both articles he praises Charlotte Brontë's power and passion, and he is in no doubt that the authoress has felt such passion herself. Like Marian in her letter, he compares her in this respect to George Sand. In the *Westminster* article in April he marvels at her 'contempt of conventions in all things' from ordinary morality to ordinary literary style. He ends by describing her characters in a striking metaphor:

They outrage good taste, yet they fascinate. You dislike them at first, yet you learn to love them. The power that is in them makes its vehement way right to your heart. 'Propriety', ideal outline, good features, good manners, ordinary thought, ordinary speech, are not to be demanded of them. They are the 'Mirabeaus of Romance'.[88]

No doubt Lewes had in mind Carlyle's famous sketch in *The French Revolution* (1837) of Mirabeau with his 'shaggy beetle-brows, and rough-hewn, seamed, carbuncled face', his 'natural ugliness, smallpox, incontinence, bankruptcy,—and burning fire of genius', and above all his honesty and lack of *sham*. Carlyle might almost—except for the bankruptcy—have been describing Lewes himself. Did Marian confide to Lewes at this time that she had used the very phrase 'a miniature Mirabeau' to describe Lewes on first meeting him in Jeff's bookshop in 1851?[89]

Lewes reviewed Mrs Gaskell's *Ruth* along with *Villette* in the *Westminster Review*. While praising her sympathetic treatment of the theme of the 'fallen woman', he finds her too conventional in her view of what constitutes 'guilt' or 'sin' in sexual relations. Interestingly, in view of his own family life (as well as his own illegitimate status, though this seems to have been unknown to him), he objects to the hysterical outburst of Ruth's 11-year-old son when he discovers his illegitimacy: 'in our day no such brand affects the illegitimate child.'[90] These are brave words. Despite this statement, Lewes and Marian seem to have decided not to have children together because of the lack of legal status of their 'marriage'.

Lewes continued his Vivian pieces in the *Leader*. A few weeks after the birth of Ethel, he again vented some bitterness about the Agnes–Hunt relationship under cover of his cynical but merry bachelor. Reviewing the Lyceum farce *How to Make Home Happy* on 9 November, he plays on the title with an ostentatious *non sequitur*: 'As I have *no* home, and that home is not happy, I really stand in need of [the author's] secret.' A week later Vivian contributes an unpleasant beast-fable, 'Two Old Owls', in which the male owl is tempted away from his faithful mate, returning from an unsuccessful attempt to live the life of a dandy to find his old wife murdered. In the same issue of the *Leader* Lewes makes his *doubles entendres* about love and jampots with reference to 'matrimony (right and left-handed)'. On the facing page, in that week's announcements appears the birth of a daughter on 16 November to Thornton and Kate Hunt, only a month after the birth of Ethel. On 10 December 1853 Vivian reviewed a play by Stirling Coyne, *The Hope of the Family*, digressing to talk in riddles about sons, fathers, and the hazards of paternity:

When I was on the Gold Coast I met a boy so very like me in general appearance, that had not considerations of geography (and my own strict morals) rendered the belief absurd, I should have believed that there before me stood a son of mine—an indirect heir—an 'accident'—an 'Oat', in short (that is, on the supposition of my having sown any wild oats!). On interrogating this boy I found he was what Mrs. Slipslop calls a 'fondling': a party without parents. He seemed to grieve somewhat over this obscurity, but I quoted the remark of the French sage—'One is always the son of somebody—*on est toujours le fils de quelqu'un: cela console*': which remark seemed to him profound.[91]

These sallies were no doubt directed at Thornton Hunt. But by the end of 1853 Lewes was no longer unhappy. He had found someone to love. Though we have no letters to tell us when he was first attracted to Marian or why, we know that though he was unhappy in his marriage, often ill, and inclined to overwork, he was still full of energy, including, presumably, emotional and sexual energy. We know, too, how unusual Marian was—the intellectual partner in the management of the *Westminster Review*, a single woman but one capable of passion and liable to unconventional behaviour; after all, her living at 142 Strand must have raised many eyebrows, if not within the immediate Chapman circle. And her relationship with Spencer, her going everywhere with him during 1852 as if they were engaged, though not exactly improper, would have been thought imprudent, at the very least, by conventional arbiters of social behaviour. But then, Marian had chosen to move in unconventional society, as had Lewes before her. He was as struck by her intelligence and independence as were all those who knew her. Bray, Chapman, Spencer—they all treated her as special. When Lewes got to know her, he found her intellect stimulating, as they did, but he also responded to her physically and emotionally. Chapman had done so up to a point, and Spencer not at all. For Lewes, whose marriage to a pretty woman had gone sour, her lack of handsomeness did not matter. Added to the journal entry of January 1859 recording his debt to Spencer for saving him from despair in 1851, by reviving his 'dormant love of science', is this testimony to his love for her:

I owe Spencer another, and a deeper debt. It was through him that I learned to know Marian—to know her was to love her—and since then my life has been a new birth. To her I owe all my prosperity & all my happiness. God bless her![92]

Already in August 1853 Lewes was thinking of going to Germany to research the life of Goethe and possibly to lecture on Shakespeare to make money. He asked Varnhagen if he thought it feasible for him to lecture in Berlin, sending him, for the first time, no greetings from Agnes. Marian was doubtless already included in the plan to visit Berlin, but money was a problem for them both. Lewes needed his regular income from the *Leader*, and he had Agnes and the children to think about; Marian earned very little, having done her *Westminster Review* work in return for board and lodging at Chapman's. Her annual income from her father's bequest was about £90. They may well have put off going abroad until she was sure of earning well from her reviews from the *Westminster* now that she was no longer living in the Strand. She also hoped, at first, that Chapman would be able to pay her something for the translation of Feuerbach's *Essence of Christianity*, which she undertook in September 1853; by November she realized he would not be able to pay anything. Finally, it was decided that she should write the Belles Lettres section of the *Review* at a regular salary of £16. 16s. od. a quarter. This, together with Lewes's income, would be enough for them to live on in Germany, where the cost of living was low, as well as allowing Lewes to continue supporting Agnes and the children, the amount given to them being, according to Marian's calculations in 1878, never less than £250 a year from 1854 until his death.[93]

Most of Lewes's reviewing work in the months leading up to the journey to Weimar was on scientific subjects. He began 1853 with a controversy on the pseudo-scientific hypothesis of spontaneous combustion, continued it with regular attacks on the serious pretensions of those who fostered the table-rapping craze, and finished it with an argument in print with the up-and-coming T. H. Huxley.

Spontaneous combustion was the topic when Lewes tackled Dickens over the death of Mr Krook in *Bleak House*, which was appearing in monthly parts during 1852 and 1853. In December 1852 Dickens had killed off the drunken rag-and-bottle man by the symbolically appropriate method of having him spontaneously combust. Had he signalled the death as merely symbolic of the rottenness of the Court of Chancery of which Krook was a vicious hanger-on, Lewes would not have objected. But Dickens gave a 'naturalistic' description of the death and suggested it was a scientific possibility. Lewes, angered by all the pseudo-science which was gaining adherents in the 1850s—phrenology, mesmerism, spirit-calling—felt obliged to rap his old friend over the knuckles. He did so in the *Leader* of 11 December, saying that Dickens was guilty of giving currency to 'a vulgar error'. Meaning to excuse Dickens in part, he finished his review with the tactless and condescending remark: 'As a novelist he is not to be called to the bar of science; he has doubtless picked up the idea among the curiosities of his reading from some credulous adherent to the old hypothesis, and has accepted it as not improbable.'[94]

Dickens was piqued into retorting; unfortunately he did so in the very next number of the novel, which appeared in January 1853. Describing the inquest on Krook, he writes in his most sarcastic (but also most uneasy) manner, airily referring to medical reports and authorities which support the hypothesis:

Out of the court, and a long way out of it, there is considerable excitement too; for men of science and philosophy come to look, and carriages set down doctors at the corner who arrive with the same intent, and there is more learned talk about inflammable gases and phosphuretted hydrogen than the court has ever imagined. Some of these authorities (of course the wisest) hold with indignation that the deceased had no business to die in the alleged manner . . .

Dickens follows up with some references to medical cases, mainly from nearly 100 years before, refusing to accept Lewes's argument that these have largely been discredited by modern science.[95]

Lewes did not let the matter drop. He returned to the topic in February, citing recent authorities against Dickens's old ones, and calling on him to add a qualifying statement in the preface to the book later in the year. Dickens's 'magnificent popularity', he maintained, not unreasonably but rather irritatingly for Dickens, carried with it 'a serious responsibility' to get things right.[96] Lewes's tone is friendly but also aggressive. Dickens was worried into seeking corroboration of his views from Dr John Elliotson, a mesmerist, and he wrote privately to Lewes, trying to keep his tone light but showing annoyance at Lewes's too ready assumption that he knew nothing about the subject and had not discriminated between 'truth and falsehood'. When *Bleak House* appeared in book form in September 1853, Dickens, far from printing a retraction, actually addressed the arguments of 'my good friend Mr. Lewes', refusing to accept Lewes's authorities. Lewes made one more half-hearted reply in the *Leader* on 3 September, then dropped the subject with relief.[97]

It is a pity Lewes became involved in such a row. Here he was, a man of generosity, attacking a friend just where it hurt most. Beneath his attack, and beneath Dickens's high-pitched response to it, lies an insecurity in both men arising from their lack of formal education. In compensation for his lack of a classical education, Lewes piqued himself on his extensive self-education, particularly in modern languages and in science. He was already aware of what it was like to be cold-shouldered by scholars and experts. He was not, on the whole, particularly sensitive about this. Part of his generally radical stance towards the establishment related to his sure sense that the learning of living languages and science was more important in the modern world than the learning of the classics. The establishment itself even showed signs of beginning to agree with him, for in the mid-nineteenth century both Oxford and Cambridge came under official scrutiny; their syllabuses began to change to include these subjects. But Lewes was just a little sensitive about his standing on scientific matters, and was to become increasingly so as the years went on.

As if anticipating the course of his own future career, he wrote in his long *Westminster* article, 'Goethe as a Man of Science' (October 1852) about the unfairness of the experts' response to Goethe's efforts in their fields. Goethe, being a poet, 'was somewhat superciliously regarded' as merely dabbling in science. Lewes defends Goethe's reputation, bolstered by the support of his friend Richard Owen, who admired Goethe's work, in the fields of botany and biology. Much of Lewes's article is taken up with exposing the vanity, hypocrisy, and jealousy of men like Oken who refused Goethe his fair share of praise. As he says, it is almost impossible to say with certainty which investigator may claim precedence in the discoveries of science. He could see in his own day how cheating and rivalry soured the pursuit of pure science. His own mentor Owen was found plagiarizing fossil descriptions from Gideon Mantell in 1852; and the gentlemanly Darwin was only enabled to enjoy his reputation as the discoverer of the mechanism of natural selection through the unusual modesty and generosity of his colleague Alfred Russel Wallace, who reached the same conclusions and was on the point of publishing them in 1858, a fact which pushed Darwin into finally publishing his findings of twenty years before in *Origin of Species*.[98] Huxley appeared on the scene in the 1850s, and was prepared not only to be 'Darwin's bulldog' but also to attack established scientists, like Owen, for their mistakes and sometimes dishonesty, and to ridicule those amateurs, like Lewes, who sought to be authoritative.

It was with Huxley that Lewes tangled at the end of 1853. This time Lewes was on the receiving end of condescending criticism. In October 1853 Huxley, described by Marian as 'a scientific man who is becoming celebrated in London', accepted Chapman's offer to write the regular science column of the *Westminster Review*.[99] One of the first things he wrote on taking up the post was a fierce denunciation of Lewes's scientific pretensions as demonstrated in *Comte's Philosophy of the Sciences*.

Marian saw it coming. Her sense of fair play was stiffened by her now intimate relationship with Lewes. Faced with the manuscript of the article in December, she did battle, without success, to have Chapman refuse or radically modify it. She sent him agitated letters, headed 'private', arguing that it would be unjust to allow such a *purely* contemptuous notice' to appear. Unusually, she refers specifically to her right of veto as co-editor. If the review goes in unchanged, the editors will disgrace themselves by printing this 'utterly worthless unworthy notice of a work by one of their own writers—a man of much longer & higher standing than Mr. Huxley & whom Mr. H's seniors in science & superiors both in intellect & fame [i.e. Richard Owen] treat with respect'. Finally, she points to the indelicacy of the publishing situation. Harriet Martineau's translation of Comte, which Huxley praises above Lewes's book, was published by Chapman himself. 'Do you really think that if you had been the publisher of Mr. Lewes's book and Bohn the publisher of Miss Martineau's, Mr. Huxley would have written just so? "Tell that to the Marines."'[100]

Her shrewdness and sharpness on behalf of her lover were employed to no avail. Either it was already too late to change the article, or Chapman hesitated, or Huxley refused. The wounding article was printed. In it, Lewes was taken to task for scientific mistakes which Huxley ascribed to his being 'without the discipline and knowledge which result from being a worker' rather than having 'mere book-knowledge'.[101] All Lewes could do was to use the pages of the *Leader* on 14 January to protest that 'it is eighteen years since I first began to occupy myself—practically and theoretically—with Biology', and to accuse Huxley, not unjustly, of disingenuousness and sneering.[102] To Chapman Lewes wrote in a dignified tone on 1 February, offering an article on development but referring to Huxley's attack and assuring Chapman that he required no favours from him.[103]

The affair blew over. Lewes continued to write for the *Westminster*, though only after his return from Germany in 1855. He and Huxley became friends some years later, when Lewes was working more and more at his scientific experiments. Spencer, their mutual friend, probably helped to reconcile them. For that matter, Dickens and Lewes came together again too in the late 1850s. But Lewes, though his scientific work was popular and sometimes well received even by experts, always felt anxious about his credentials. It was the one sore spot in a man otherwise remarkable for his lack of sensitivity about his reputation.

During the early months of 1854 Lewes and Marian were preparing to take the step which would affect both their reputations. In April Lewes was ill with headaches and singing in the ears; he was ordered not to work for a month. Marian did his *Leader* reviewing for him, as well as finishing her Feuerbach translation, while he went off to stay with Arthur Helps in Hampshire. On 19 May she reported to the Brays— surely they were beginning to guess at the nature of her relationship with Lewes—that Lewes was still ill. 'His poor head—his only fortune— is not well yet.' In the same letter she confessed to having her own 'purely psychical' troubles, though she was anxious not to mislead the Brays into thinking loneliness was the cause. 'When I spoke of myself as an island, I did not mean that I was so exceptionally. We are all islands . . . and this seclusion is sometimes the more intensely felt at the very moment your friend is caressing you or consoling you.'[104] She was, not unnaturally, afraid of the effect on her oldest and best friends of her imminent departure. And she was uneasy at half-deceiving them, even as she dropped passing hints—'it is quite possible that I may wish to go to the continent or twenty other things' (27 May 1854). At the last minute she told Bray and Chapman of her plans, but not Cara or Sara. They received a short note, dated 19 July 1854:

Dear Friends—all three

I have only time to say good bye and God bless you. Poste Restante, Weimar for the next six weeks, and afterwards Berlin.[105]

Lewes arranged for Agnes's financial security while he and Marian were abroad. On 20 July he set off, armed with references from Carlyle to friends in Weimar, in the company of the woman who was to be his wife—though not in law—for the next twenty-four years.

Weimar, Berlin, and Goethe

(1854–1855)

LEWES and Marian arrived in Weimar in the early hours of 2 August 1854, after a journey with stops for rest and sightseeing in Antwerp, Brussels—Villette to them—Liège, Cologne, Mainz, and Frankfurt, where they visited Goethe's birthplace. Weimar, famous because of its connection with Goethe and his enlightened patron Duke Karl August, was a surprise to them. Marian recorded in her journal that it was at first sight a 'dull, lifeless village'.[1] Lewes, describing the town in the *Life of Goethe*, admits that Weimar eventually grows on the visitor:

On a first acquaintance, Weimar seems more like a village bordering a park, than a capital with a Court, having all courtly environments. It is so quiet, so simple; and although ancient in its architecture, has none of the picturesqueness which delights the eye in most old German cities. . . . One learns to love its quiet simple streets, and pleasant paths, fit theatre for the simple actors moving across the scene; but one must live there some time to discover its charm.[2]

The Leweses enjoyed their time there. Carlyle had given Lewes a letter of introduction to his fellow-Scot, James Marshall, who was private secretary to the Duchess of Weimar. In it, Carlyle described Lewes as 'ingenious, brilliant, entertaining, highly gifted and accomplished'.[3] Through Marshall they soon met the academics, artists, and assorted nobility who made up the court and surrounding life of Weimar. Among these was Gustav Adolf Schöll, Director of the Art Institute and something of a Goethe scholar. He had edited some of Goethe's letters and was able to help Lewes with his research, for which Lewes thanked him in the *Life*, praising his 'careful, accurate editing'.[4] They met Eckermann, who had been Goethe's secretary and was thus one of the last living links with the poet, though he was now in mental and physical decline, and died later in the year. The other chief link was the society hostess Ottilie von Goethe, widow of Goethe's son, who lost no time in inviting the aspiring biographer to her salon.[5]

Most important of all, in terms of the couple's anomalous social position, was the friendship they struck up with Liszt, Kapellmeister and director of the Court Theatre. Not only was it exciting for them to hear Liszt play the piano—Marian wrote that for the first time in her life she 'beheld real inspiration'—but they took comfort from the fact that Liszt's relationship with the unhappily married Princess Carolyne von Sayn-Wittgenstein was tolerated in Weimar. Lewes and Marian, the latter in particular, used the example of Liszt several times when justifying their own relationship. Marian was careful to tell Charles Bray in her first letter to him from Germany that Liszt 'lives with a Russian Princess, who is in fact his wife, and he is a Grand Seigneur in this place'.[6]

They themselves found easy acceptance in the drawing rooms of Weimar. Lewes interested the inhabitants as the intending biographer of their greatest man, the more so as he was an Englishman, and as he meant to publish a full account of Goethe's life and works. So monumental was Goethe's output, and his reputation, that German scholars had on the whole confined themselves to writing about aspects of his life in partial biographies, studies of one or other of his fields of activity, or selections of his letters. There was awe, as well as some suspicion and envy, at Lewes's ambitious plan to discuss in detail Goethe's scientific studies as well as his literary writings, and to deal with his many relationships with women. It had been long known in literary circles in Germany—through Varnhagen von Ense—that Lewes was proposing to write Goethe's whole life. So intense was the patriotic feeling among German scholars that one, Heinrich Viehoff, hurried to publish the first of four proposed volumes of his own biography in 1847, declaring in his preface that the honour of German literature would be at risk if an Englishman were to be allowed to beat the Germans to it.[7]

Lewes interviewed everyone he could find who had known Goethe or who knew something about him. He was allowed to see Goethe's study and bedroom, and took notes which he reproduced in the *Life*. A letter to his two older sons, Charles, now nearly 12, and Thornie, aged ten, gives pleasant details of his life and work. It also shows—and it is the first surviving letter to his sons—that he was anything but a distant figure to them, despite his not having lived regularly at home for some time. He does not mention Marian, about whom they knew nothing. The letter, dated 27 September, begins:

My dear Boys

I suppose you will be glad to hear from Papsy as he would be glad to hug you! Here I am in the capital of the Grand duchy of Weimar, about which you, Thornie, know something already, I have no doubt—or soon will. It is a very queer little place although called the 'Athens of Germany' on account of the great poets who have lived here; one of them, the greatest of all, you know already by the portraits and little bust in our house—I mean *Goethe*. I am writing his Life, which work brought me to Weimar, to seek for materials. Fancy a little quiet town without cabs, omnibuses, very few carts and scarcely a carriage—with no gas lights for the streets, which are lighted (in winter only) by oil lamps, slung across the streets on a cord. These, which are rare, give so little light that when ladies go to the theatre they take a servant with them to carry a lantern. . . .

At Jena I visited the field of battle where Napoleon thrashed the Prussians so terribly. At the Wartburg I saw the room where Luther lived so long, as Squire George; they showed his inkstand, chair, footstool and the spot on the wall made by the Inkstand which Luther threw at the devil's head, when the devil came to tempt him. You know the story, don't you? I saw there portraits of Luther, of his mother and father; and a magnificent collection of ancient armour which would have pleased you more than anything else.

The other day the Grand Duke sent word that he should be glad to see me at his summer palace. As I had never paid a visit to a crowned head before I felt very uncomfortable lest I should not behave myself according to strict *etiquette*. How should you have felt, Charley? However the Grand Duke at once made me feel at home, and except that I called him 'Royal Highness', I did not behave otherwise than I should to any gentleman whom I might visit for the first time.[8]

Lewes goes on to ask the boys about their doings, referring to Thornie's having swallowed a tooth, encouraging them to work hard at school— Mr Pearce's Bayswater Grammar School—and sending them kisses. It is a loving letter, written to interest boys of their age, with nothing of the stern paterfamilias about it. One notes that though Lewes is keen to impress Charles and Thornie with his story of meeting royalty, he also makes a point of declaring his innocence of any conventional toadying.

While in Weimar, Lewes continued with his literature articles for the *Leader*, though these are noticeably fewer from July 1854. The absence of Vivian is striking on the theatre page. In any case, the *Leader*, like all the other papers, was much preoccupied with the progress of the Crimean War, so that the literature pages were considerably reduced during 1854 and 1855. Even in the literature section that remained, most of the books reviewed had something to do with the war. By 26 August Lewes, or perhaps Pigott in London, was despairing of receiving any new books to review: 'If the present famine in the publishing world is to continue, we shall soon be reduced to a review of the Iliad or the Pentateuch.'⁹ Late in September there appears a much-needed injection of liveliness in the form of a letter from Vivian in Weimar, entitled 'Vivian en Voyage'. It begins with a riddle about species:

The Greeks and Romans knew but one Rat, and that was a Mouse; a fact, *ami lecteur*, which may interest you beyond the application here to be made of it. How the ancients managed without that amiable Rodent, I know not; but as their Cat was a Weazel, they may very well have contented themselves with a Mouse for their sole Rat. If you want to puzzle a pundit, ask him what the Greek for Rat or Cat is: he will look foolish, and you will chuckle.

Vivian continues with a natural history lesson on how medieval Europe was contented with both the mouse and the black rat until the beginning of the eighteenth century, when a new rat was brought from India, and 'commenced internecine war against the Black Rat'. 'This new warrior, being equally at home on land and water, gradually spread over Europe, the Black Rat disappearing before him, as the Red Man disappears before the White.' All this is by way of introduction to the topic of European travel, in which the 'sentimental traveller' of the Grand Tour type has given way to other kinds of traveller—the political, the historical, the statistical, the geological, the zoological, and 'the traveller with black whiskers and large shirt-collars', of which species Vivian himself is a prominent member. He confesses, however, to being but a 'dilapidated Vivian' after his recent ill health, with his whiskers 'sadly out of curl'.¹⁰

A second Vivian letter tells of meeting Liszt. Vivian claims to have known the composer in Vienna in 1839, when Liszt was 'in the height of his popularity, in the maddest of all mad enthusiasms, a Viennese *furore*, when the women showed you with pride the bracelets made from the pianoforte strings he had broken; when everybody had some new anecdote of his capriciousness, coxcombry, or generosity'. Now, by contrast, 'he is here, in this quiet Weimar, leading the quietest of lives; grave, serious, and happy, entering on a new phase of existence; strong in conviction, happy in affection, resolute in ambition.'¹¹ The description might stand as well for the new G. H. Lewes.

Oddly enough, Lewes did not review *Hard Times* when it came out in September. Perhaps he had no heart for criticizing Dickens after the unfortunate *Bleak House* episode; perhaps war conditions made it impossible for books to be got to him. Most of his reviews from Weimar were of continental books readily available to him there. The best of these are two articles on the German poet Heinrich Heine, living in part-voluntary exile in Paris. Lewes writes brilliantly about Heine's recently published autobiographical fragments, noting the black humour of Heine, who was suffering from a spinal tuberculosis which kept him bedridden for the last seven or eight years of his life. Lewes translates from Heine's French, catching the teasing tone to perfection. He describes Heine's half-rude, half-playful attitude towards other writers like Goethe and Hegel. Of the latter Heine writes that as a young man he saw the philosopher 'sitting in his woeful way, like a hen, on his terrible eggs, and heard his clucking'. He liked Hegel's philosophy, not for its profundity, but because it tickled his vanity. 'I had never cared to believe that God had become man [a witty allusion to both his Jewishness and his atheism]; I taxed this sublime doctrine with superstition; but I latterly took Hegel's word for it when I heard him affirm that Man is God.' This pleased him, for it meant that 'I was myself the living and moral law; I was infallible.' However, since becoming so ill, Heine has thought seriously about returning to religion. Lewes notes his irony—'almost ghastly on such a subject'—and quotes Heine on his misfortunes:

Besides my financial deficiencies, I have not been in enjoyment of brilliant health; I am even affected with an indisposition, slight, it is true, according to what my physicians say, but which has now kept me more than five years in bed. In such a position it is a great comfort to me to have some one in heaven to whom I can address my groans and lamentations during the night, after my wife has gone to sleep.

As Lewes comments, 'in this strange, mocking way, Heine announces his recantation of scepticism, Hegelianism, and atheism, and his conversion—to what?' For the elusive Heine teases his readers about whether he means to return to the Judaism of his fathers, or to the Protestantism to which his family had prudently converted, or to the Catholic Church in which he had married his French wife. Lewes writes sympathetically of this most witty and dreadful of German writers, who, he remarks, when asked why he joined in the general detraction of Goethe's character and genius after the poet's death, replied simply, 'envy—sheer envy'.[12]

A second essay on Heine in December 1854 deals with the poetry which, as Lewes points out, 'defies translation'.[13] This is as true of Heine as it is of Goethe himself; and it goes some way towards explaining the general English lack of familiarity with the poetry of these two writers, now as then. Lewes, Marian Evans, who wrote four articles on Heine in 1855 and 1856,[14] and Matthew Arnold, whose famous essay appeared in *Essays in Criticism* (1865), were the most important writers on Heine in England in the nineteenth century.

Lewes's £20 a month from the *Leader* went to Agnes. His literary receipts for 1854 show that while in Weimar he earned £80 for two adaptations from French plays, one for Benjamin Webster of the Haymarket Theatre, the other for Alfred Wigan at the Olympic. But that was all. Marian had been paid £30 by Chapman for the Feuerbach translation; Bray had advanced her £50 against her half-yearly income from her father's estate; and she undertook an article for the *Westminster* on 'Woman in France', for which she received £15. But Chapman's, and the *Westminster*'s, affairs were in a crisis. James Martineau and W. B. Hodgson, leading Manchester Unitarians, were trying to buy the journal, supported by George Combe, who was exasperated by Chapman's lack of 'Conscientiousness', among other moral and intellectual faculties.[15] Chapman faced bankruptcy, but was disinclined to sell to Martineau and Hodgson. Harriet Martineau, the mortal enemy of her brother, stepped in with an advance of £500 and Chapman was once more saved. But during the summer and autumn of 1854 it was touch and go whether he would lose the *Review*. Marian's letters from Weimar to her old friend and employer are duly sympathetic, though it is striking that she cannot help letting her personal happiness shine through her concern for his financial affairs, which also had a bearing on hers, and to a lesser extent on Lewes's.[16]

Chapman and Bray were the two male friends (both of them unfortunately disliked by, and disliking, Lewes) on whom Marian relied for sympathetic understanding of her position. She also depended on them for news from England. For his part, Lewes wrote explaining himself to two of his oldest friends, Carlyle and Chambers. His letters and their replies have been lost, but we know that through Bray and Chapman the Leweses soon heard something of the furore which their relationship occasioned in London, even in the relatively avant-garde circles of the *Westminster Review* writers.

Inevitably, Lewes's past and in particular his well-known relationship with Thornton Hunt became the focus of further scandalized gossip. Some even supposed—though there is no evidence to support the supposition—that Lewes and Hunt had swapped wives. The sculptor Thomas Woolner, who was much later a regular visitor to the salons of Lewes and George Eliot, wrote to W. B. Scott, Lewes's old friend and neighbour, in October 1854:

By the way—have you heard of a—of two blackguard literary fellows, Lewes and Hunt? They seem to have used wives on the ancient Briton practice of having them in common: now blackguard Lewes has bolted with a——and is living in Germany with her. I believe it dangerous to write facts of anyone nowadays so I will not any further lift the mantle and display the filthy contaminations of these hideous satyrs and smirking moralists—these workers in the Agapemone—these Mormonites in another name—stink pots of humanity.[17]

Carlyle and his wife joined in the gossip. Charles Gavan Duffy remembered discussing the relationship with them; according to him, Jane said that hearing that 'the strong woman of the *Westminster Review* had gone off with a man whom we all knew' was 'as startling as if one heard that a woman of your acquaintance had gone off with the strong man at Astley's [the famous equestrian theatre]'. After some snide remarks from Duffy about Lewes's ugliness, Carlyle is supposed to have defended Lewes—a typical Carlyle twist—saying he was 'lively and pleasant' and not entirely to blame:

He originally married a bright little woman, daughter of Swynfen Jervis, a disreputable Welsh member; but everybody knows how that has turned out. Miss Evans advised him to quit a household which had broken bounds in every direction. His proceeding is not to be applauded, but it can scarcely be said that he has gone from bad to worse.[18]

Though this is hearsay, and written by a nasty gossip, it is true that Carlyle disapproved of the relationship while at the same time sympathizing with Lewes. He wrote to his brother in November, 'Lewes has cast away his wife—who indeed deserved it of him, having openly produced those dirty sooty skinned children which have Thornton Hunt for father, and being ready for a third; Lewes to pay the whole account, even the money part of it!'[19] Agnes already had three children by Hunt, and may have been pregnant with a fourth, which must in that case have miscarried.

That Carlyle responded to Lewes's letter of explanation we know because we have Lewes's touching reply of 19 October:

Your letter has been with me half an hour and I have not yet recovered the shock—delightful shock—it gave me. One must have been, like me, long misjudged and harshly judged without power of explanation, to understand the feelings which such a letter creates. My heart yearned towards you as I read it. It has given me new courage. I sat at your feet when my mind was first awakening; I have honoured and loved you ever since both as teacher and friend, and *now* to find that you judge me rightly, and are not estranged by what has estranged so many from me, gives me strength to bear what must yet be borne!

Lewes continues in a tougher tone. Carlyle has obviously asked him to refute the report that he left Agnes for Marian. This Lewes can emphatically do, though he remains vague about details, presumably out of loyalty to Agnes and a dislike of blaming others:

So much in gratitude. Now for justice: on my *word of honor* there is no foundation for the scandal as it runs. My separation was in no-wise caused by the lady named, nor by any other lady. It has always been imminent, always *threatened*, but never before carried out, because of those assailing pangs of anticipation which would not let me carry resolution into fact. At various epochs I have explicitly declared that unless a change took place I would not hold out. At last—and this more because some circumstances into which I do [not] wish to enter, happened to occur at a time when I was hypochondriacal and hopeless about myself, fearing lest a chronic disease would disable me from undertaking such responsibilities as those previously borne—at last, I say, the crisis came. But believe me the lady named had not only *nothing* whatever to do with it but was, I solemnly declare, ignorant of my own state of mind on the subject. She knew the previous state of things, as indeed others knew it, but that is all.[20]

Lewes appears to be referring to the 'dreary wasted time' of 1851 when he talks of a 'crisis'.

Carlyle was not wholly appeased. He wrote at the bottom of this letter, 'No answer to this second letter'. But he did not stop communicating with Lewes altogether. After Lewes's return from Germany Carlyle was generous with advice and praise for the *Life of Goethe*. He and Jane continued to invite Lewes—though not Marian—to their house. And, conventional as the Carlyles in some ways were, Jane Carlyle, for one, was not blind to the social hypocrisy practised by some married men and women. She wrote a sharp little riddle in her notebook in 1858, when it became known that Dickens had separated from his wife while publicly denying what many knew to be the case—that he had taken the actress Ellen Ternan as his mistress. 'When does a man really ill-use his wife?' goes the question. Answer: 'When he plays the Dickens with her.'[21] Jane would have supported Marian's brave remark in a letter to Cara Bray in September 1855: 'Light and easily broken ties are what I neither desire theoretically nor could live for practically. Women who are satisfied with such ties do *not* act as I have done—they obtain what they desire and are still invited to dinner.'[22]

More conservative in social *mores* than the Carlyles was the redoubtable George Combe. Chapman and Bray both tried to explain matters to him. He was shocked to hear the news of the woman whose intellect he had diagnosed as the greatest of any woman he knew, whose company he had enjoyed at the Brays' house, and whom he had invited into his own home and introduced to his friends in Edinburgh. He wrote to Bray to ask if she had gone mad. 'We are deeply mortified and distressed; and I should like to know whether there is insanity in Miss Evans's family; for her conduct, with *her* brain, seems to me like morbid mental aberration.' He could not bear to be proved wrong in his opinion of her, the more so as in his case opinions of others' characters were not merely a matter of personal preference but also of professional phrenological pride. Combe was also upset, with some reason, on behalf of radical free-thinking. 'T. Hunt, Lewes and Miss Evans have, in my opinion, by their practical conduct, inflicted a great injury on the cause of religious freedom.' He announced that he would give up forthwith his subscription to the *Leader*.[23]

Bray was loyal, though he was at first unable to tell Combe the whole truth, making it seem that Marian had accompanied Lewes merely as a friend:

I know he had a great friendship and respect for her. His health required that he should travel, he had overworked his brain, he had constant ringing in his ears and fear of apoplexy. Dr. Balbirnie, with whom he had been staying at Malvern, told us, that he feared serious injury to the brain. Miss Evans has long been wanting to go abroad, and Mr. Lewes offered to introduce her to friends of his in Germany . . .

To this excuse Bray adds his own, interesting, version of the state of things between Lewes and Agnes:

I have heard that Mr. and Mrs. Lewes have not been man and wife to each other for some years, but I do not see what that has to do with the case before us except to give plausibility and colour to scandal. What I have heard is that Mrs. Lewes after the birth of her 3rd child took one of those strong and unaccountable dislikes to her husband that sometimes does occur under similar circumstances amounting to monomania and that Lewes was most sincerely attached to his wife and greatly distressed by it.

If there is any truth in this account, which Bray may have got in part from Marian, the change in Agnes's feelings must be dated from the birth of her fourth child, St Vincent Arthy, in May 1848 rather than that of Herbert in July 1846. Bray finishes his letter by supporting Marian while regretting that she has been so imprudent as to lay herself open to 'evil report'.[24]

Undoubtedly Bray did his best to smoothe Combe down and to remain loyal to the woman he had known since she was a girl struggling against her father's religious orthodoxy and enduring his sternness towards her loss of it. He told Combe that 'as a daughter she was the most devoted I ever knew, and she is just as likely to devote herself to some *one* other, in preference to all the world, and without reference either to the regularity or legality of the connection'.[25] Magnanimous though this may seem, and certainly true in its analysis of Marian, we may note that the man who defended her conduct in this way had confided three years before a secret of his own to Combe, who in turn confided, in shorthand, to his diary:

At twelve years of age [Bray] was seduced by his father's cook and indulged extensively in illicit intercourse with women. He abstained from 18 to 22 but suffered in health. He married and his wife has no children. He consoled himself with another woman by whom he had a daughter. He adopted his child [Nelly Bray, born in 1846] with his wife's consent and she now lives with him. He still keeps the mother of the child and has another by her. I strongly objected to his being cooped up and recommended him to lower his diet increase his exercise and by every means lessen the vigour of his amativeness and be faithful to his wife.[26]

Combe continued to correspond amicably with Bray, but he never again invited Marian Evans to dinner.

Chapman also did his best to appease friends. He assured Robert Chambers of Marian's 'noble nature', while writing some weasel words about how much 'blame' should attach relatively to her and Lewes.[27] Even more than Bray, Chapman was anxious not to lose the support of radicals and free-thinkers on account of the scandal. They both tried hard according to their lights, though both were apt to fan the flames of gossip with ill-considered remarks, and neither could keep a confidence, as Marian was to find to her annoyance when the authorship of *Adam Bede* became the talk of England.

If Lewes's letters to Carlyle and Chambers brought only muted comfort to Weimar, and Marian's to Bray and Chapman also produced a mixed response—her journal for 11 October notes that 'a painful letter from London caused us both a bad night'[28]—her letters to the one female friend she was sure to find unshockable yielded generous moral support. Sara Hennell and Cara Bray were of course her oldest friends, but she dared not write to them without a hint from Charles Bray that they would find a letter acceptable. Sara soon began corresponding, but felt diffident, not liking Lewes, resenting Marian's flight without confiding in her, and feeling that she was now 'writing to some one in a book'.[29] It took Cara nearly a year to get over the shock; Marian's touching letter of September 1855, declaring her happiness with Lewes, the seriousness of their relationship, and her awareness that others were more secretive and continued to be asked to dinner, finally brought her round. But the friend to whom she wrote soon after her arrival in Weimar was the young feminist Bessie Rayner Parkes. Evidently Bessie wrote first, and Marian was grateful. Adopting the tone of an older sister, she told Bessie of her happiness and hopeful plans for the future.[30]

Bessie had to struggle mightily with her parents' disapproval of her friendship with Marian; she wrote without their permission, and when the Leweses returned to England she visited them without permission too. Letters flew during September and October 1854 between her and both her parents at their Midlands home. Mrs Parkes wrote at great length, regretting her daughter's friendship with one on whom such a 'stain' had appeared. She brought up the state of the Leweses' marriage, feared for Marian's soul, and, like Combe, foresaw a setback for the radical cause as a result of the liaison. She was also, naturally, anxious for her own daughter's reputation. Joseph Parkes also wrote to Bessie of his 'great sorrow & deep regret' at Miss Evans's 'folly, and I cannot but say *vice*'. He analysed the situation as he saw it:

Coming to London she set down exclusively among one set, equally a 'clique' of its kind; & among some men not of the best if not the worst morals. I have for years known something personally of Mr. Lewes, & always much about him. He is a man of great powers of mind & capacity for analysis & certain generalisations. But he is & always was *morally* a *bad man*. Of his domestic relations I know more than you as a woman can know. Of course you know the parentage of his children between himself & Mr. Thornton Hunt; an odious history, so far as concerns all partners . . . and which imitated by all the world would dissolve society & change human beings into brutes.

According to Parkes, Birmingham radical circles were buzzing with the scandal, which was, regrettably, injurious to 'general Liberalism'. Though he personally felt 'contempt & disgust' for Lewes, he did not wish to join in any 'hue & cry' against 'an unfortunate woman'. For all his vituperation of Lewes, Parkes was himself, according to his grand-daughter, not happy in his marriage and not a faithful husband.[31]

Bessie heroically withstood the onslaught. She did not know Lewes personally at this time—though she had seen him—and she largely accepted her parents' opinion of him. Indeed, she never came to like him, though this was probably more because of his lack of religion and lack of middle-class pedigree than because of his freedom in sexual relations. Her main aim was to defend Marian, which she did in a letter to her unofficial fiancé Sam Blackwell in September:

To represent that Marian ran off with a respectable married man after the manner in which 'the Dish ran away with the spoon' is most ludicrous to any one possessing the facts. Mr. Lewes had long been shaken from whatever hold he ever possessed on respectable domestic life; he was a clever man with a kind heart but never very well thought of.

Bessie was also clearly a little frightened of Lewes's sensuality. She describes him to the man to whom she was engaged but towards whom she felt no physical attraction, and with whom she finally, after many years, broke off the unhappy engagement:

Imagine a very short slender man, with blue eyes, large & full of meaning & feeling; very large mouth, expressive but quite too coarse; plain features deeply pitted with the small-pox, long dark hair waving into his neck; his face always reminded me of a Lions, & the hair was like a mane . . . excepting the mouth it was assuredly a winning face. Then imagine a wonderfully witty pen & tongue; conversation & light writing carried up to the pitch of perfection.

Bessie finishes off this most detailed and accurate pen-portrait of the man who held a kind of forbidden fascination for her: 'Religion, that of a Comtean Atheist, Morality, Honi soit qui mal y pense, but nobody thought well of it. Disposition very kind—one virtue, that of truth.'[32]

The subject of all this talk and correspondence in England, some of it hypocritical, some inaccurate, was meanwhile quietly getting on with writing on Goethe and making Marian Evans happy. While her friends babbled, she flourished. She wrote to Chapman in October that she was 'not mistaken in the person to whom I have attached myself. He is worthy of the sacrifice I have incurred, and my only anxiety is that he should be rightly judged.'[33]

Early in November the Leweses left Weimar, where they had been made so welcome, for Berlin. There Lewes renewed his acquaintance with Varnhagen, the man who more than any other could help him with his Goethe research. The broad-minded Varnhagen recorded in his diary for 5 November:

Met a gentleman accompanied by a lady on the street [Unter den Linden]. We recognized one another immediately; it was Mr Lewes, who arrived here yesterday from Weimar, where he has been for three months on account of his plan to write Goethe's life, a plan which he had long cherished, then postponed, and now is to carry out after all. His companion is an Englishwoman, a Miss Evans, editor of the *Westminster Review* and translator of Strauss's *Life of Jesus* and Feuerbach's *Essence of Christianity*.

The following day Lewes called on Varnhagen and 'made a great speech' in praise of Goethe.[34] Varnhagen's diary for the next few months contains several references to Lewes. He lent Lewes books; read the article on Goethe as a man of science, which he thought largely fair, but blinded by the Englishman's prejudice in favour of Newtonian physics, which Goethe had dared to question; and met Lewes and Miss Evans in Berlin society.

As in Weimar, the Leweses raised no eyebrows in Berlin. This was more significant among the bourgeois intellectuals of the capital than in the aristocratic circles in which they had moved in Weimar. It certainly brought out a difference in social tolerance between Berlin and London. While Liszt's unorthodox relationship with his princess may have been accepted partly on the grounds of his eccentric genius and the general laxity of the Weimar court, it says more for German tolerance in general that the ordinary citizen made no fuss about irregular partnerships such as that between Professor Adolf Stahr and the novelist Fanny Lewald in Berlin. The latter had known Lewes when she visited Britain in 1849–50, befriending Geraldine Jewsbury, among others, and researching for her book *England und Schottland* (1851–2). She and Stahr had lived together for nine years; when the Leweses heard in February 1855 that Stahr had been granted a divorce and that he and Fanny had at last got married, they had reason to be envious of the progressive divorce laws of Prussia. As Marian noted in her journal in March, shortly before they returned to England, Germany, for all its crude manners, 'questionable meat', poor beds, and 'indiscriminate smoking', was 'no bad place to live in'. And the Germans, 'to counterbalance their want of taste and politeness', were 'free from the bigotry and exclusiveness of their more refined cousins' in England.[35]

Lewes divided his time between visiting all his old Berlin friends and working hard, with Marian's help, on Goethe. She translated many of the prose passages for him, while he rendered extracts from Goethe's poetry into excellent English verse. The *Leader* carried a few more reviews by him, some of them dictated to Marian by Lewes, who still suffered from headaches. Their visits to the theatre were written up, and an occasional review of cultural events in Berlin was sent by 'V'. But Vivian had disappeared from the pages of the paper for good, and Lewes did very little work for it now.

The Goethe research completed, and with money running out, they left Berlin on 11 March 1855, travelling in intensely cold weather—the winter was one of the severest on record throughout Europe—arriving in Dover on 14 March. Marian found lodgings there while Lewes went to London to 'conclude some arrangements', that is, to visit Agnes and raise some much-needed cash. Agnes seems to have got into debt, and Thornton, now out of the *Leader* and writing leading articles for the *Daily*

Telegraph, was probably not paying his share.[36] Mathews gave Lewes
£39. 17s. od. for translating *The Cozy Couple*, a one-act farce about
domestic bliss (!), which had its opening night at the Lyceum on 15
March. Lewes also needed to find a publisher for the *Life of Goethe*. In
fact he did not reach an agreement with David Nutt until June, when it
was decided that 1,500 copies should be printed, with Lewes receiving
£250 on publication (in October) and a further £100 on the sale of the
first 1,000 copies.[37]

After visiting his friend Arthur Helps (perhaps to borrow money from
him), Lewes found lodgings in Bayswater. Marian joined him on 18
April; together they looked for more permanent accommodation, which
they found in East Sheen. Bessie Parkes visited them; Rufa Hennell,
sister-in-law of Sara and Cara, came, as did Chapman. Bray was invited
to stay for a few days during the summer, when Marian begged him not
to be indiscreet about something she had said 'two or three years ago,
which something you seem to have converted into a supercilious,
impertinent expression of disapprobation on my part'.[38] No doubt it was
an unflattering remark about Lewes uttered before she had come to like
him.

Bray did visit in July, without his wife. He and Lewes argued about
phrenology, and Marian, caught in the middle, had to defend herself
against Bray's charge that she had 'fallen off' from the 'physiological
basis'. On the contrary, she assured him after he had returned to
Coventry, she believed profoundly that 'character is based on organization', but she would not go the whole way, any more than Lewes would,
with phrenological explanations of character.[39] The difference between
her and Lewes on this matter, as on so many during their life together,
was not one of opinion but rather of the expression of opinion. Lewes
often offended by calling a spade a spade; Marian was more tactful in
her denunciation of quackery, especially when it was to be found in old
friends.

Both Lewes and Marian were kept busy during the summer, earning
money to support themselves and Agnes's family. In July Lewes was
paid £25 by Webster for adapting *Buckstone's Adventures with a Polish
Princess*, a broad farce for the comic actor John Baldwin Buckstone to
perform at the Haymarket.[40] Marian wrote several short reviews for the
Leader, including one of special interest for its bearing on her relationship
with Lewes: 'Life and Opinions of Milton' (4 August 1855). Here Marian
takes Milton's part on the question of divorce, arguing cleverly against
those who dismiss Milton's plea for a liberal divorce law on the grounds
that it came from a man with an unhappy marriage. 'There is much

unreasonable prejudice against this blending of personal interest with a general protest', she wrote. 'If we waited for the impulse of abstract benevolence or justice, we fear that most reforms would be postponed to the Greek Kalends.' Her remarks were timely, for Mrs Caroline Norton was even then petitioning the Queen in the course of her long battle against both the existing divorce law and the bill being put before Parliament to amend it. Marian expresses her support for Mrs Norton, adding with feeling, 'it is worth while to take up Milton's [plea], and consider what such a mind as his had to urge on the husband's side of this painful subject.'[41] Neither wives like Caroline Norton nor husbands like Lewes were to benefit from the limited Divorce Act which came into force two years later.

Marian stayed at home working on an article for the *Westminster Review* while Lewes spent a week in August with Charles, Thornie, and Bertie (Herbert) in Ramsgate. During his absence Carlyle kindly saw the manuscript of the *Life of Goethe* through the press. Whatever he thought of Lewes's private life, he was willing to help this book, which was dedicated to him as the man 'who first taught England to appreciate Goethe' and in which he could not but take an active interest.[42] In his gruff, half-negative way, he praised the work as 'a very good bit of Biography; far, far beyond the kind of stuff that usually bears that name in this country and in others'. He ended this encouraging letter of 7 August, 'Best speed to you, dear Lewes. Yours always truly, T. Carlyle.'[43]

The first complete biography of Goethe in any language duly appeared on 1 November 1855. It proved an immediate and lasting success, selling over 1,000 copies in the first three months, bringing Lewes mainly praise, spreading his reputation widely throughout Europe—for the book was translated into several languages—and eventually going into many editions, culminating in an Everyman reprint in 1906, which has itself been reprinted since.[44]

The book marks an important moment in Lewes's life and work. Unlike all his previous writings, this was a long time in gestation and was the product of real scholarship. Lewes finished it at a time of happiness and new life, having put the dreary wasted period of domestic unhappiness and frenetic activity behind him. Yet this past life, with all its variety of experience, fed into the work, for Lewes was undoubtedly equipped to understand the life of such a man as Goethe by a congeniality of shared experience as well as imaginative sympathy. Far from being unfitted for the task, as Margaret Fuller had declared, Lewes was, as Havelock Ellis much more shrewdly perceived when he came to write the introduction to the Everyman reprint of 1908, singularly well suited to it.[45]

Like Goethe, Lewes was widely read, if mainly self-educated; like Goethe, he was a student of science as well as literature; like Goethe, he was, or had been, a free lover. Both were dilettantes, in the sense that they loved knowledge in all its branches and each tried his hand at every kind of writing. Unlike the German professors who squabbled over details and demanded blind slavishness to Goethe's perfection as man and writer, and equally unlike some of the tight-lipped English reviewers of the *Life*, who disapproved of both Goethe's love affairs and Lewes's frank discussions of them, Lewes showed himself free from prejudices. He admired and understood Goethe, and wrote about him in a way which was remarkable then and remains remarkable today.

Lewes might have been thinking about his own work when he praised the first volume of Carlyle's *Frederick the Great* in 1858, asking 'Why, then, suppose that Biography must be false, and the hero idealized, in order to secure the reader's sympathy?'[46] Without worshipping Goethe or excusing his at times inexcusable behaviour, he seeks to bring us to an understanding of the man of genius. Of Goethe's unlovely treatment of a succession of girls and women whom he loved and left, Lewes writes unhysterically, refusing to join in the 'outcry of the sentimentalists' against the young Goethe's cruelty to Friederike Brion, while at the same time resisting the temptation to the cant of the sophists who maintain that 'to have been faithful to her he must have been faithless to his genius'.[47]

When dealing with the older Goethe's relationship with the mature, aristocratic, married Frau von Stein, Lewes punctures the usual view of her as a platonic friend encouraging Goethe's self-culture out of a purely high-minded desire to foster genius. His researches in Weimar had proved beyond doubt, as he told John Stuart Blackie, translator of *Faust*, that the liaison '*did* become more than platonic, as you will see I quietly indicate in one passage; but I was forced to keep that part in a subdued light because the British public would have gone into fits at the open avowal.' In the *Life* Lewes does indeed deal frankly but tactfully with the subject: 'Whoever reads with proper attention the letters published in the Stein correspondence will become aware of a notable change in their relation about this time (1781–2). The tone, which had grown calmer, now rises again into passionate fervour, and every note reveals the happy lover.'[48]

Having adroitly handled that problem, Lewes is also equal to the task of discussing Goethe's relationship with the socially inferior Christiane

Vulpius, the mother of his son in 1789, whom he married in haste in 1806 during the war between Prussia and France. Lewes rescues her reputation from those who snobbishly dismiss her as unworthy of Goethe; equally he explains, without excusing, Goethe's initial 'dread of marriage' and his disdain of public opinion. But 'the judgments of men are singular' in such matters, he writes, and who knew this better than Lewes himself? Society, which disliked Goethe's unofficial liaison with Christiane, was illogical enough to be even more outraged when he finally regularized the relationship during the uncertainties and upheavals of the war. Christiane might be tolerated, though ignored, while she was Goethe's mistress; how was she to be treated when she became his wife?[49]

It was for Christiane that the *Römische Elegien* (*Roman Elegies*) were written. These, says Lewes, are 'doubly interesting: first, as expressions of his feelings; secondly, as perhaps the most perfect poems of the kind in all literature'. Lewes does not shrink from giving an example from these frank love poems or praising their 'vivid sensuousness'. In the 1855 edition he himself renders the translation excellently, though in subsequent editions he substituted Theodore Martin's more stilted version. Here is a passage, with Lewes's own translation:

> Lass dich, Geliebte, nicht reu'n, dass du mir so schnell dich ergeben!
> Glaub' es, ich denke nicht frech, denke nicht niedrig von dir.
> Vielfach wirken die Pfeile des Amor: einige ritzen
> Und vom schleichenden Gift kranket auf Jahre das Herz.
> Aber mächtig befiedert, mit frisch geschliffener Schärfe,
> Dringen die andern ins Mark, zünden behende das Blut.
> *In der heroischen Zeit, da Götter und Göttinnen liebten,*
> *Folgte Begierde dem Blick, folgte Genuss dem Begier.*
> Glaubst du, es habe sich lange die Göttin der Liebe besonnen,
> Als in Idäischen Hain einst ihr Anchises gefiel?
> *Hätte Luna gesäumt, den schönen Schäfer zu küssen,*
> *O, so hätt' ihn geschwind, neidend, Aurora geweckt.*

> Let not my Loved One repent that she so quickly surrendered!
> Trust me, I think thee not *bold*,—think naught unworthy of thee.
> Amor has manifold shafts with manifold workings: some scratch,
> And with insidious steel poison the bosom for years.
> Others are mightily wing'd, and, keen in new-polished sharpness,
> Pierce to the innermost depths, kindling the blood into flame.
> In the Heroical Age, when the gods with goddesses wantoned,
> Passion was born in a glance, fruition followed desire.
> Think'st thou the goddess of love 'demanded time to consider',
> When in Idalian groves she gazed on Anchises with joy?

Luna delaying one moment to kiss the beautiful Sleeper,
Soon had seen him awake 'neath the kiss of eager Aurora.[50]

Throughout the *Life of Goethe* Lewes apologizes for his 'rough plaster-cast of translation' from the poetry, notoriously difficult to render into idiomatic or lyrical English. In fact his translations are very good indeed.

As a critic of Goethe's prose writings Lewes is equally impressive. Though acknowledging Goethe's own remark that all his works are 'fragments of a great confession', he nevertheless sees that life does not merely spill over into art. *Werther*, the sentimental cult novel throughout Europe in the 1780s and 1790s, was, however closely based on events in Goethe's own experience, a distillation, an '*ideal* expression of the age, as free from the disease which corrupted it, as Goethe was free from the weakness of his contemporaries. Wilkes used to say that he had never been a Wilkite. Goethe was never a Werther.' Again, 'Goethe, the strongest of men, makes heroes the footballs of circumstance. But he also draws from his other half the calm, self-sustaining characters.'[51]

Towards *Wilhelm Meister*, which Carlyle had translated in 1824, Lewes candidly admits that his feelings were 'at first tepid', but he has come to the view that it is a wonderful example of Goethe's unobtrusiveness, even elusiveness, as an author. 'I have only to refer to the marvellous art with which the characters unfold themselves. We see them, and see through them. They are never described, they exhibit themselves.' Lewes concedes that the complete absence of moral comment by the author is 'like the absence of salt at dinner' to many readers, but he does not count himself among them.[52]

Lewes and Marian agreed in this tolerant view of Goethe's 'morality' as a writer. Their discussions in Weimar bore fruit not only in this criticism in the *Life*, but also in a short but distinguished essay by Marian, 'The Morality of *Wilhelm Meister*', published in the *Leader* in July 1855 as a kind of trailer for 'Mr. Lewes's *Life of Goethe*, which we now see advertised'. In the article, Marian tackles the question of morality by reference to realism. Goethe shows 'large tolerance' of 'living, generous humanity—mixed and erring'; in so doing, he is following 'the stream of fact and of life', waiting patiently 'for the moral processes of nature as we all do for her material processes'. However, Goethe is not a realist at the expense of inculcating proper morality. On the contrary, those writers who reward and punish their characters are both ignoring probability and possibly encouraging the morally dubious satisfaction of vengeful feelings in their readers.[53] When she herself began writing fiction just over a year later, she put into artistic practice something of the complex view of realism and morality elicited here from her thinking, with Lewes, about Goethe.

The mutual fruitfulness of the Leweses' work on Goethe is evident again in Lewes's discussion of *Die Wahlverwandtschaften* (*Elective Affinities*), with its clash of duties and passions, its odd use of adulterous desire, and its tragic outcome which it is impossible to label either 'moral' or 'immoral'. Husband and wife in the novel are mutually attracted to two house guests; tragedy ensues, but it is not clear whether this is the result of the indulgence of the passion on the part of one attracted couple, the refusal to submit to it of the other, or the combination of both. Lewes judges the novel as neither moral nor immoral. 'Goethe was an Artist, not an Advocate.' As to the slow pace of the narrative, Lewes confesses to frequent boredom, but adds:

A dear friend of mine, whose criticism is always worthy of attention [thus in 1855; altered in subsequent editions to 'a great writer, and one very dear to me'], thinks that the long episodes which interrupt the progress of the story . . . are artistic devices for impressing the reader with a sense of the slow movement of life; and, in truth, it is only in fiction that the dénouement usually lies close to the exposition.[54]

This remark has a bearing on the early novels of George Eliot, with their leisurely evocation of the ordinary lives of carpenters, farmers, millers, and country families in general.

Lewes incorporated into the *Life* his 1852 essay on Goethe and science, being careful to update his references and information on the subject. The *rapport* between Lewes and his subject is most evident here. Goethe, like Lewes, gave up medical studies because he could not bear to inflict or observe pain.[55] It was not long before Lewes was nevertheless daily dissecting sea-creatures, frogs, and even—though with qualms—still-born puppies in the interests of scientific discovery.

Like Carlyle, Lewes knew German culture, appreciated its excellences, but was not entirely won over to its philosophy or its 'philosophical' criticism. When describing the idealist schools of thought and, more particularly, the critical school of the Schlegels and others, he introduces a parable of which he may well have been the originator—Francis Espinasse heard him tell a version of it at a party in Manchester in 1849[56] —and which certainly passed, in varying forms, into proverbial use:

A Frenchman, an Englishman, and a German were commissioned, it is said, to give the world the benefit of their views on that interesting animal the Camel. Away went the Frenchman to the *Jardin des Plantes*, spent an hour there in rapid investigation, returned and wrote a *feuilleton*, in which there was no phrase the

Academy could blame, but also no phrase which added to the general knowledge. He was perfectly satisfied, however, and said, *Le voilà, le chameau!* The Englishman packed up his tea-caddy and a magazine of comforts; pitched his tent in the East; remained there two years studying the Camel in its habits; and returned with a thick volume of facts, arranged without order, expounded without philosophy, but serving as valuable materials for all who came after him. The German, despising the frivolity of the Frenchman, and the unphilosophic matter-of-factness of the Englishman, retired to his study, there *to construct the Idea of a Camel from out of the depths of his Moral Consciousness.* And he is still at it.[57]

This pleasantly written work, undogmatic yet scholarly, admiring of Goethe but stopping short of idolatry, honest but not unnecessarily shocking, deserved the fame it achieved. Lewes's reviewer in the *British Quarterly Review*—Robert Vaughan, son of the editor—gave a striking statement of the magnitude of Lewes's achievement. What are the requirements of a biographer of Goethe? he asks:

The successful biographer of Goethe must possess no ordinary combination of qualities and accomplishments. He has to portray a literary career of twice the common duration, and of seven times the usual versatility.

How well is Lewes fitted to this daunting task?

In the case of Mr. Lewes, the tastes and the acquirements thus requisite, are assembled together with a felicity somewhat rare in the annals of biography. He is himself a man of letters. An acute critic, he possesses, at the same time, no mean power of original production. His literary knowledge is extensive; his taste catholic. The masterpieces of the modern literature of Europe are familiar to him in their original languages. His mind is clear-sighted and singularly agile. Such characteristics fit him readily to enter into the cosmopolitan manysidedness of Goethe. Stoicism is odious to him: enthusiasm is apt to awaken his quick sense of the ludicrous: speculation he will analyse for you to a nicety, and fling away the shreds as worthless. Here again is an advantage for the biographer of Goethe. The artist and the sage of Weimar—so little speculative, so active, and yet so calm—is a man after his own heart.

Finally, lest all this be taken too readily for granted, Vaughan reminds us that with all the secondary works already available on Goethe, all the controversies and the commentaries on his works, Lewes's two volumes might easily have been six; 'we shudder as we think of what we have escaped, and we style thrice-blessed Mr. Lewes's power of shelving the uninteresting.'[58]

Even this most sympathetic of Lewes's critics, however, protested mildly that Lewes was too tolerant of Goethe's defects of character. This was the main charge against Lewes among English critics. Sarah Austin, herself a translator from German, objected in the *Edinburgh Review* to Lewes's refusal to criticize Goethe's womanizing; John Oxenford in the *Athenaeum* also found him too 'placid' on the subject. Both, however, thought Lewes's criticism excellent.[59]

In Germany, a different set of prejudices was at work. Even among his acquaintances in Weimar and Berlin there was some annoyance. Varnhagen, though duly appreciative of the importance of the work in enhancing Goethe's reputation in England, thought Lewes occasionally superficial. He could not allow any criticism, however mild, of his hero. Others became apoplectic, writing pamphlets and critiques on the minutest details and Lewes's interpretation of them. Schöll, who had helped Lewes, claimed in his review in the *Weimarer Sonntagsblatt* in December 1857 that Lewes had picked up information from 'us in Weimar' but often misused it.[60]

Schöll and most other German reviewers had read the book in the German translation of Julius Frese (who later translated *Adam Bede*, *The Mill on the Floss*, and *Silas Marner*), in which the footnotes with their acknowledgement of help received from German scholars were unaccountably omitted. Lewes told his German publisher Franz Duncker in 1858 that the omission of such references was 'very painful to my feelings' and that 'much ill-feeling would have been spared in Germany, if the authors had seen their works acknowledged'.[61] Despite this unfortunate circumstance, the German translation went into several editions. When Lewes visited Germany during the 1860s and 1870s in order to discuss physiology with eminent scientists, he was lionized wherever he went as the biographer of 'unser Goethe'.

At home, Lewes was gratified to receive letters of congratulation from friends. Carlyle was generous with praise—'an excellent Biography', 'candid, well-informed, clear, free-flowing', he wrote on 3 November.[62] Marian sent a copy to Bray, hoping he would accept it 'as a keepsake from me'. 'I can't tell you how I value it, as the best product of a mind which I have every day more reason to admire and love.'[63] The *Life of Goethe* was thus a landmark in Lewes's life. Completed at a time of personal happiness, it brought him success and enough money to enable him to cut down somewhat on his miscellaneous journalism. He could begin to concentrate on the intellectual passion which increasingly claimed his attention—his Goethean love of science.

9

Natural History and the
Birth of George Eliot
(1856–1859)

ONE of the first things Lewes did on finishing the *Life of Goethe* was to borrow a microscope from Arthur Helps and set about a systematic study of biology. The immediate fruit of his researches, mainly carried out during a trip to Ilfracombe and Tenby from May to August 1856, was the series of popularizing articles in *Blackwood's Magazine* beginning in August called 'Sea-side Studies'. Together with a second series, 'New Sea-side Studies' (1857), the articles were published in book form by Blackwood in February 1858. This was the first result of Lewes's scientific research.

But he found he could not indulge in scientific study exclusively. Though he was soon paid £100 for the remainder of the first edition of the *Goethe* (in April 1856), increasing demands were made on him, so that he had to resort, as before, to magazine journey-work. During 1856 the *Leader* carried occasional reviews of his, as did the *Westminster*; he began writing for the new (politically conservative) *Saturday Review*; and he renewed his contacts with *Fraser's Magazine*, the *British Quarterly Review*, and—momentously—*Blackwood's Magazine*.

The financial burden was unexpectedly made heavier from late 1855 by the death of his brother Edward. Marian wrote to Bray in September:

Mr. Lewes has had a sad trouble within the last week—the death of his brother who died at sea, leaving at home a wife and two little children. The grief of his sister-in-law and mother has been very painful to him to witness, for he is a little like you in that matter—the suffering of others either bodily or mental is almost unendurable to him to witness unless he can be of practical use.[1]

Edward's young widow Susanna lived in Highgate with Vivian, aged three, and a baby daugther who did not survive infancy.[2]

Only two memorials of Edward survive, apart from the references to him as a child in his older brother Edgar's letters from Portugal. One is the pleasant note to him from Agnes, adorned by Thornton's sketch of Lewes, in reply to his request for a theatre ticket.[3] The second is a long letter from Edward himself to Edwin Chadwick in 1854. F. O. Ward enclosed Edward's letter in one of his own to his colleague on the Board of Health. Ward tells Chadwick that 'Mr E. C. Lewes' is the brother of 'Lewes the writer in the Leader, the Westminster Review &c., whom I have long known'. Edward had approached Ward 'desiring to be recommended by me' for employment as a sanitary inspector:

On enquiry I found that he had *voyaged* much—whence I inferred that he might probably prove most available as an inspector of *Shipping*—and to test in some degree his capacity I invited him to set down on paper his views on the subject— which he has accordingly done—& I now forward his letter for your inspection.

Edward's letter, written from Southwood Lane, Highgate, on 18 April, gives details of his experience of sanitary problems during 'two voyages [presumably as part of the ships' medical teams] to Australia one to India one to United States', in the course of which he 'visited New Zealand Chilian and Brazilian ports of S. America, Ceylon, Mauritius Ascension St. Helena Cape de Verde Isls. and Portugal', having sailed variously in 'schooner, brig, bark ship and steamer'. He proposes a method of improving sanitation in ships both at sea and, more particularly, in London's docks, and suggests siting a hospital ship off Gravesend to cope with sailors returning home with cholera or other epidemic diseases.[4]

Unfortunately for Edward, Chadwick was even then about to be ousted from the Board of Health, so that he was unable to further Edward's career. Whether the latter's death in 1855 occurred on a warship engaged in the Crimean War, or on a merchant vessel, is unknown. His loss upset Lewes; it also placed on him the added burden of supporting Susanna financially. He generously undertook to pay for his nephew Vivian's education as well as that of his own boys.

Lewes's sons were now reaching the ages at which decisions about their future must be made. He was anxious to remove Charles and Thornie from Mr Pearce's school, and thought of taking them to a school in Germany that summer. The Brays' friend John Sibree was considered as a temporary tutor; Marian asked Bray in April 1856 if Sibree still took pupils.[5] Lewes himself wrote to Sibree on 2 April, explaining his plans for the boys and describing the present state of their education:

The two eldest are at present at the Bayswater Grammar School. The youngest [Bertie] is at home and is *very* backward, because for some years his health was delicate, and I did not like his being at school. The elder boys are clever, and eager to get on. They are already tolerably grounded in Latin, and French, and have commenced German.[6]

There is proof of Thornie's prowess in French at the age of 11 in the form of a cheerful letter in that language written at school on 6 December 1855 and addressed to 'mes chers parents'. In it, Thornie has great pleasure in announcing that the school holidays are to begin on Friday 21 December. He thinks his best end-of-term marks will be in Latin, French, drawing, and arithmetic. After announcing his pious hope that 'ma conduite à la maison pendant les vacances' will show them that he is not ungrateful for all their goodness to him, he signs himself 'votre fils affectionné, Thornton Arnott Lewes'.[7]

This letter, among others, shows that despite his not living at home and his having spent nearly a year abroad, Lewes took a close interest in his children and seemed to them a normal loving father, in their ignorance of both Agnes's relationship with Hunt and Lewes's with Marian. From 1856 we have much more evidence than hitherto of Lewes's relations with his sons, in the form of letters and journals (for Lewes's journals from July 1856 have escaped destruction), though nothing now exists of the correspondence between Lewes and Agnes herself.

Sibree was unable to help, but Sara Hennell sent a prospectus for a school in Switzerland which friends had recommended to her. This was Dr Eduard Müller's establishment at Hofwyl, beautifully situated about six miles north of Berne, a school which attracted an international clientèle. Lewes finally fixed for Charles and Thornie to attend from late August 1856.[8] It must have seemed a good way of ensuring that the boys would receive a modern, secular education, while at the same time removing them from Kensington, where they would surely discover their parents' estrangement.

With all these commitments, both Lewes and Marian needed the regular income they received from reviewing. Both contributed occasionally to the *Leader*, though as Marian told her Coventry friends Lewes no longer had anything to do with the editorship, a fact which she wished to be 'generally known'.[9] It is not difficult to see why. The *Leader* was still associated in people's minds not only with intellectual radicalism but also with those brother-editors who had shared a wife or wives, though in fact neither Hunt nor Lewes now edited the paper. Both Leweses wrote some reviews for the *Saturday Review*, one of Lewes's first being a favourable article on Herbert Spencer's *Principles of Psychology* in March 1856.

Spencer was one of the old friends with whom they renewed contact after their time abroad. He had gone to Gloucestershire in search of quiet and improved health. Lewes, grateful to him for friendship at a difficult time and for having taken him along to visit Marian in 1852, wrote to Spencer in his country retreat a letter bubbling with the high spirits consequent on domestic happiness and the success of the *Goethe*:

And so you have become a hewer of wood and drawer of water? Is that the exodus of philosophy? It explains what in English life has hitherto been an obscurity to me, viz. the venerable old men who occupy themselves breaking stones on the Queen's highway—they are all ex-thinkers, broken down by large discourse of reason, decrepit with scepticism, used up from cerebral excitement. I shall take off my hat to the next I see; and ask him whether he has made any annotations on the Biog. Hist. of Phil. which invaluable work he will of course know by heart.

He answers Spencer's question about the authorship of an article on 'Lions and Lion Hunting' in the January number of the *Westminster*, adroitly turning from the metaphorical to the real:

We were amused by your asking if I had anything to do with the Lion article (which indeed I had—it was written in a hurry to stop a gap for J. C.) because you knew my 'weakness' for dancing before lions. Marry come up, weakness! You might have called it strength which your unfeline weakness couldn't sympathize with. There's a young lioness in the Z. Gardens just now more *kissable* than the loveliest Circassian in the Sultan's harem. Perhaps you think *that* a weakness? Do *you* never dance before noodles, and shall not I dance before majestic lions?[10]

He had been visiting the Zoo frequently, as befitted his natural historical interests. This happy letter ends with a light-hearted reminder to Spencer to call Marian 'Mrs. Lewes'—'in case the sagacious Philosopher should not think of it'—when writing or visiting them at their new lodgings in Richmond. One or two of their open-minded friends repeatedly embarrassed Marian with neighbours and landladies by addressing her as Miss Evans.[11]

Lewes's jovial mention of the *Biographical History of Philosophy* in his letter to Spencer was not entirely fortuitous. That work was on his mind. In January 1856 he had written to his friends the publishers J. W. Parker, father and son, suggesting they might like to bring out a library edition. He intended to add to the work, particularly to the very brief section on medieval and modern philosophy, so as to 'render it more worthy of acceptance in colleges and schools'. The book still had a healthy sale, being read even in Oxford and Cambridge colleges, which he had hardly expected when he wrote it. In all, the little volumes had sold an amazing 40,000 copies since publication ten years before.[12] Parker duly brought out the library edition, priced 16*s*., for which he paid Lewes a welcome £150 in March.

Already, however, Lewes's appetite for philosophy had waned. He wrote to George Tugwell, a 'charming little zoological curate' they met at Ilfracombe that summer, that the revision of the book weighed on him 'like a nightmare. Metaphysics is dry biscuit—especially to a man hungry for zoology!'[13] The visit to Ilfracombe and Tenby lasted three months. Lewes and Marian went for a combination of reasons. Lewes's health was still poor; he needed to study marine life *in situ* for his *Blackwood's* articles; lodgings were cheaper than in London; and they could get away from London gossip. Lewes's reopening of relations with the Blackwoods was to prove immeasurably significant, not so much for him as for Marian, whose emergence as George Eliot took place, via Lewes, with the publication of her first work of fiction, 'Scenes of Clerical Life', in serial form in *Blackwood's* from January 1857 (where it more than once appeared on adjacent pages with Lewes's own 'Sea-side Studies'). Blackwood published several of Lewes's subsequent books and all of George Eliot's except *Romola*. With his tact and kindness he proved, as they soon realized, the perfect publisher for the diffident, proud, socially outcast, sensitive, but strong-minded new novelist.

Lewes himself once more tried his hand at story-writing at this time. He sent Blackwood 'Metamorphoses', a story he had just adapted from his and Mathews's 1853 play *A Strange History*, in March 1856. Though Blackwood disliked the radical political views given an airing in this story of intrigue during the French Revolution, he accepted it for the magazine, where it appeared in three parts from May to July 1856.[14] He little knew that in acting so promptly in responding to Lewes's approach he was qualifying himself to become the publisher of George Eliot.

But this was still in the future. The couple set off for Ilfracombe early in May 1856. Marian noted in her journal the geological features of the area, describing the hunt for molluscs, sea-anemones, and other creatures along the seashore. For her, naturalizing with Lewes mingled fruitfully with her reading of two books on the history of German culture and society by Wilhelm von Riehl. Both she and Lewes noticed the 'strong family likeness between ourselves and all other building, burrowing house-appropriating and shell-secreting animals'. In the article she wrote on Riehl for the *Westminster*, 'The Natural History of German Life' (July 1856), she discussed the evolution of society in the naturalist's terms—the 'organism' and its 'medium'—and extended her discussion to the need for realism in the representation of country life in art and literature. Her own early fictions, especially *The Mill on the Floss* (1860), not only embody the theory sketched in this essay but are also written in language striking for its metaphorical use of natural historical example.[15]

In Ilfracombe they met Mr Tugwell, with whom they joined forces on their hunting expeditions. Lewes describes the three of them in his first 'Sea-side Studies' article:

We are a lady and two men. The lady, except that she carries a landing-net, and has taken the precaution of putting on the things which 'won't spoil', has nothing out of the ordinary in her costume. We are thus arrayed: a wide-awake hat; an old coat, with manifold pockets in unexpected places, over which T. has slung a leathern case, containing his hammer, chisel, oyster-knife, and paper-knife; trousers warranted not to spoil; *over* the trousers are drawn huge worsted stockings, over which again are drawn huge leathern boots. . . . Now these boots, with the worsted stocking peeping above, are not, it is true, eminently aesthetic. . . . Never mind the inelegance: handsome is as handsome does.

In this costume we wooed the mermaids.[16]

On 26 June they moved to Tenby, on the Welsh coast, to continue their marine studies there. Lewes's old friend Pigott joined them for a few days, as did Barbara Leigh Smith, whose affair with Chapman had recently ended. Marian sympathized with her 'sorrows and renunciations' and expressed a hope that they would become better acquainted, and 'that you will know Mr. Lewes too, for he is far better worth knowing than I', as she proudly and dotingly added.[17]

One unfortunate circumstance occurred during this otherwise idyllic summer of retirement and enthusiastic outdoor pursuit. Lewes engaged in a brief but acrimonious exchange of letters with Henry George Bohn, publisher of his *Comte*, with whom Lewes thought he had made a verbal arrangement to publish a translation of Spinoza's *Ethics*. Marian had spent much of her time in Germany on this work. No agreement in writing existed; Lewes's and Bohn's memories differed about what was required and what was to be paid; they corresponded between 3 and 18 June in an increasingly bad-tempered manner. Bohn reminded Lewes that nothing had been signed, Lewes shot off a reply about honourable men keeping their word, Bohn challenged Lewes to produce a bit of paper he claimed he had, Lewes took umbrage at Bohn's insulting tone and terminated his transaction with 'a man who shows such wonderful facility in forgetting' as Bohn showed in his letters. Lewes's hastiness meant that Marian's translation was never published during her lifetime, though Lewes did approach another publisher with it in 1859, without success.[18]

This was a rare example of the negative side of Lewes's otherwise admirable decisiveness. Charlotte Brontë had noticed that he always 'bolted his replies by return of post'. Marian herself assured Bray in August 1856 that Lewes *had* replied to some letters from Eliza Lynn: 'He answered them immediately on receiving them, as he does all letters, for he is promptitude, punctuality and diligence incarnate.'[19] She was to be the direct beneficiary of his promptitude when he undertook, as he soon did, to be her literary agent and financial manager, as well as the encourager of her genius for fiction. Indeed it was at Tenby that he first urged her to try writing a story, an ambition she had long cherished but never dared put to the test. She actually began the first of the *Scenes of Clerical Life*, 'The Sad Fortunes of the Reverend Amos Barton', soon after their return to Richmond in September.[20]

They left Tenby on 8 August. On the 25th Lewes set off for Switzerland with Charles and Thornie. 'Agnes & Baker [the children's nurse, Martha Baker, known to them as 'Nursie'] met me at London Bridge with the boys at 1. By 1 o'clock in the morning we were in Paris after a *very* rough passage.' They spent a day sightseeing in Paris, where the boys 'were in ecstasies with the shops, wanting to buy everything to send home to Mamma & the children [Bertie, now ten, Edmund, aged six, Rose, nearly five, and Ethel, nearly three]'.[21] At Hofwyl they settled in, exploring Berne, rowing on the lake in the school grounds, and rambling in the surrounding woods. Lewes, having taken to Dr Müller and his wife, was able to leave the boys cheerfully on 31 August. He met another old friend, Douglas Jerrold, on the boat from Boulogne, and arrived home on 4 September, pleased with this start in life for the boys in a healthy, beautiful environment.[22]

During September and October Lewes continued at the microscope— having returned Helps's and bought one of his own—paid frequent visits to Richard Owen to discuss his findings, and generously sent Mrs Gaskell all his letters from Charlotte Brontë for her biography. George Combe had unwittingly written Lewes a congratulatory letter on reading two articles in *Fraser's Magazine* in August and September, entitled 'Dwarfs and Giants' and signed, openly enough, 'GHL'. As Marian told Sara Hennell, Combe solemnly addressed a letter to 'GHL Esq. care of the Editor of Frazer, expressing very high admiration of the physiological essay' and asking if the author had written any more works on the subject. Lewes had replied with thanks, but, as Marian said, 'I fear Mr. Combe would be rather disappointed to find out whom he had been praising, Mr. Lewes being his favourite aversion, as a "shallow, flippant man". However, we should all of us pass very different judgments now and then, if the thing to be judged were anonymous.'[23]

Marian had good cause at this time—more than ever—to value Lewes as anything but shallow and flippant. He had early on recognized her extraordinary ability to write trenchant, witty, and thoughtful criticism. From a scrap of descriptive writing she read out to him one evening at Berlin in 1855, he thought she might be able to write novels. When he saw her wonderfully comic essay 'Evangelical Teaching: Dr. Cumming' (*Westminster Review*, October 1855), he knew she had genius, rather than just talent.[24] Lewes urged his diffident partner, over and over, to try her hand at fiction. In September 1856 she finally did. Sending off another fine essay to Chapman, the ebullient 'Silly Novels by Lady Novelists' with its division of silly novels into such sub-species as 'the *mind-and-millinery* species', 'the *oracular* species', and 'the *white neck-cloth* species', she sat down on 23 September to begin 'The Sad Fortunes of the Reverend Amos Barton', intended as the first story in a series to be called 'Scenes of Clerical Life'.[25]

On 6 November Lewes wrote to Blackwood about an article he proposed to write on sea-anemones to follow 'Sea-side Studies'. He also sent 'A m.s. of "Sketches of Clerical Life" which was submitted to me by a friend who desired my good offices with you'. Lewes is careful not to lead Blackwood to expect too much, but he skilfully drops references to *The Vicar of Wakefield* and 'Miss Austen' when describing this first of a series of tales 'illustrative of the actual life of our country clergy about a quarter of a century ago; but solely in its *human* and *not at all* in its *theological* aspect'. In his excellent way, Blackwood replied less than a week later: 'I am happy to say that I think your friend's reminiscences of Clerical Life will do.'[26]

From this exchange dates the celebrated partnership of George Eliot—though she did not take this name, chosen for love of Lewes and a good, plain, English-sounding surname, until February 1857—and Blackwood, with Lewes as indefatigable go-between. Marian kept her incognito as long as possible, but the 'veil of anonymity' proved transparent to the publisher during the course of their correspondence in 1857. For obvious social reasons, Blackwood was content not to lift it publicly sooner than could be helped. When Lewes wrote in November 1856 of the 'shy, shrinking, ambitious nature' of his friend, Blackwood took the hint and was careful not to be too critical of the stories.[27] Not that he was usually inclined to be slavish with authors, established or new. As Lewes told Tugwell, whose papers he was also trying to get Blackwood to take for the magazine, 'Blackwood is very critical; but when once you get your foot in his pages you are at ease for ever.'[28] But Blackwood at once recognized genius in this new 'unknown'. On 30 January 1857 he wrote to Marian, addressing her as 'My dear Amos', as he had no other name to use, announcing that he had shown part of 'Amos Barton' to Thackeray and had told him, 'I think I have lighted upon a new Author who is uncommonly like a first class passenger.' To this encouraging letter Marian replied on 4 February, using the chosen pseudonym for the first time: 'I subscribe myself, best and most sympathizing of editors, Yours very truly, George Eliot.'[29]

Lewes had read out his 'friend's' story when he spent his usual few days at Christmas with Arthur Helps in Hampshire (while Marian stayed quietly in Richmond and began her second story, 'Mr Gilfil's Love Story'). He reported that Helps's house guests were all sure that the author was a clergyman. Agnes, whom Lewes also visited over the Christmas period, thought it must be the work of a 'father of a family', a man who 'had seen a great deal of society'.[30]

Prompted by Lewes, Blackwood kept 'George Eliot' up to date with readers' responses to 'Amos Barton' as it appeared in the magazine in January and February; what must Lewes have felt on reading that of Albert Smith, poet, actor, wit, and fellow-member with Lewes, Thackeray, Ward, and others of the Fielding Club, who expressed his enthusiasm in a letter to Blackwood:

Nothing has delighted me so much for a long time as that story of 'Amos Barton' in the Magazine. The death of that sweet Milly made me blubber like a boy. I did not think, at forty, I had so many tears left in me; and was really glad to find, after my somewhat worn-out London life, I could still be so moved. You will be pleased to hear there is but one opinion about its excellence. Thack.'s eyes sparkled through his spectacles as he spoke of it yesterday.

Blackwood hastened to give the gist of this to George Eliot on 10 February, adding, 'It would be great fun if you are a member of that society [London's literary clubland] and hear yourself discussed.'[31]

Lewes—who had until recently been right at the centre of 'that society', having been characterized by Smith himself in a poem about the Fielding Club in 1852 as 'Vivian of the flowing locks'—wrote back jubilantly the next day, thanking Blackwood for his encouragement of 'that sensitive doubting fellow' Eliot:

You would never believe the work I have had to make him credit his own genius. He (very judiciously!) looks up to my critical opinion as oracular; but in spite of confidence in me he is so diffident of himself, that I had to *bully* him into acquiescence with the fact that I had discovered a genius. I cackle over my hatched chick; and so may you.[32]

So full are Lewes's letters of his genial friend that Blackwood shrewdly asked, 'Are you going to confine yourself to the character of intermediaire at present. Pray let me know if any subject occurs to you.' To which Lewes responded, 'It is very pleasant to have you asking if I am going to confine myself to the character of intermediaire. Think yourself lucky that I do! If I were to open the floodgates of my ink bottle, Maga [pet name for *Blackwood's Magazine*] would have enough to do to keep her course.'[33] Lewes's joy at his discovery of genius in the woman he loved sings out in every word, despite the subterfuge.

Buoyant as he felt, excited by Marian's success, and no doubt relieved that their tight financial situation was somewhat eased—Marian earned £52. 10s. od. in 1856 from the serialization of 'Amos Barton' and was to realize £443 for the completion of the series and its publication in book form during 1857—neither he nor she could have guessed at the end of 1856 or beginning of 1857 that she would soon be earning thousands of pounds for her writing. (Her literary receipts show that her earnings leapt from just over £300 in 1856 to £1,705 in 1858, peaking at an astonishing £7,000 in 1863.[34])

Lewes's financial affairs were precarious enough in December 1856 for him to have a contretemps with Thornton Hunt over money. In his journal of 5 December he writes that he has been 'agitated & distressed lately by finding Agnes £150 in debt mainly owing to T's defalcations. Angry correspondence & much discussion. Jervis has, however, given temporary aid, & more is hoped.'[35] Thornton was himself under pressure. Only a year before he had appealed to the Royal Literary Fund for a grant, declaring himself, in the fluent, mendicant Hunt way, 'at a most painful and parlous juncture in my personal affairs', and protesting that he worked a 16-hour day writing for the *Globe*, the *Spectator*, and the *Leader*. He described his life—'begun in poverty'—with seven children and some other relations to support; through his hard work he could earn a good salary, but the drain on it was too great. His immediate difficulties had been caused by his having stood guarantee for a friend for £80, and now that friend had let him down. Leigh Hunt himself wrote to the Committee of the Fund, supporting Thornton's application, and on 10 January 1856 Thornton received £50 from the Secretary, Octavian Blewitt.[36]

However, Thornton was not only unable to pay his share towards his family with Agnes, but he took a high tone with Lewes's complaints. On

16 December he sent Lewes a challenge, on the grounds that Lewes had refused to withdraw an 'offensive expression'. 'There is something ludicrous in the extravagance of this', wrote Lewes, comparatively mildly, in his journal. 'A challenge from him to me, & on such grounds!' Lewes wisely declined to fight, but offered to argue the case before a 'gentleman' to be named by Thornton as a court of honour. In the end, Lewes and Pigott met Thornton's friend George Redford to discuss the matter. It was agreed that Lewes could *not* be expected to withdraw the offensive expression, and the affair was dropped.[37]

Agnes was at this time pregnant with her fourth (and last) child by Hunt: Mildred, born 21 May 1857. She continued to get into financial difficulties; Lewes's journal records a rare expression of bitterness towards her in March 1858:

Another painful proof that my kindness to Agnes has not been appreciated. In spite of last year's affair, she is £184 beyond her increased income this year. Resolved to change my line of conduct altogether, until I see a different character in her. I fear she is quite *hardened*.[38]

Poor Agnes. Scarcely any documents remain to show her in an active light, rather than as a mere object of others' attention in their letters and journals. There is her short note to Edward about theatre tickets; the only other piece of writing by her is a pleasant letter of 1862 to a friend of Mrs Willim's, commiserating with her on the death of a brother. Surprisingly, she recommends her correspondent, Lizzie Gendle, to take comfort in the knowledge 'that God knows best'.[39] The letter shows Agnes to have remained in close contact with Lewes's mother, with whom Lizzie's cousin lived as a companion. Indeed, Lewes notes in his journal up to 1862 his frequent visits to his mother in St John's Wood and to Agnes in Kensington; often all three dined together at Mrs Willim's house. Lizzie's cousin, Mary Lee, had a daughter who recalled playing in the garden at St John's Wood with Agnes's younger children. According to this girl's account, written in old age for Lewes's granddaughter,

One sad day I learned that I was to lose my playfellows the children of Mrs. Lewes, since neither they nor their mother were to be allowed to come to the house to visit Mrs. Willim, that being the condition—as I was told afterwards— under which George Eliot would be introduced to her. The old lady extended a welcome to her son's clever companion, but to the end of her life—which came suddenly as her hand lay in blessing on my head—she regretted the loss of her daughter-in-law's loving attentions.[40]

It is probable that Mrs Willim did see less of Agnes after the meeting
with Marian, which seems not to have taken place until December 1860,
when Mrs Willim wrote to Lewes saying she was 'quite pleased to think
I shall be able to call and know your *aimable* Wife'.[41] We don't know why
they were not introduced sooner. Perhaps Marian was shy, and deliberately put off the occasion. From her own bitter experience—her brother
Isaac stopped communicating with her in June 1857 on hearing of her
'marriage' and prevailed on her sister Chrissey and half-sister Fanny to
do so too[42]—she would have expected a rebuff. Or Mrs Willim may have
felt diffident, since she was so fond of Agnes and her children, about
making Marian's acquaintance, an event which would inevitably change
the nature of her relations with Agnes, even if it is not true that Marian
refused to meet her unless she gave up seeing Agnes.

The complicated chemistry of Lewes's family life was changing in any
case in 1860, for another reason. Charles was coming home from Hofwyl
to begin living with Lewes and Marian, not with Agnes as before. When
Thornie and Bertie were in their turn to leave school, they too became
Lewes's responsibility, and did not return to Kensington, except to visit,
as Lewes himself still did. Amazingly, the younger children seem not to
have known that their father was not Lewes but Thornton Hunt. Ethel,
born in 1853, protested in old age to Blanche Colton Williams, a
biographer of George Eliot:

My Mother bore nine Children to my Father, George Henry Lewes—A little
Daughter, who died when two days old, Charles Lee Lewes, named after our
Great Grandfather, the original 'Young Marlow' in 'She Stoops to Conquer',
Thornton Arnott Lewes, Herbert Arthur, St. Vincent, who died when two
years old; Edmund Alfred, who was brought up with us three Girls; Rose
Agnes, called Rose after one of the Characters in my Father's novel 'Rose,
Blanche, and Violet'; Ethel after Thackeray's 'Ethel Newcome'; and Mildred
Jane. All are dead but myself [in 1938] . . .

My Mother was a most perfect Mother and the longer I live I realize what
fortunate Children we were. I remember my Father coming to see us until I was
going on for five [1858] and reading to him out of a book called 'Cobwebs to
Catch Flies'. I loved him very much; all children liked him.

But it was a most wicked thing to ever connect my Mother's and Mr.
Thornton Hunt's names together. . . .

My brother Charles visited us for years every Saturday afternoon at 3
Campden Hill Terrace, Kensington, my home until I came to America [c. 1890],
and I cannot believe he would visit a Mother who had committed adultery. My
two other Brothers on their return from Switzerland visited us frequently till
they went to Africa.[43]

It is a strange account, offering no reason for Lewes's not living with the children, but Ethel appears nevertheless to be sincere in her belief that he was her father.

Our picture of Agnes is unavoidably partial and unfocused. She appears chiefly as the recipient of letters from Charles and Thornie, away at school from 1856. Indeed, the choice of Hofwyl may have been made partly in order to remove them from Agnes's care without hurting her feelings. Of course it was natural for a man of Lewes's beliefs—and lack of wealth—to avoid the English public school system. A European education became increasingly the choice of radical and progressive Victorians. Meredith sent his son to Hofwyl in 1867, probably on Lewes's recommendation, and Trollope almost sent his boys there in 1860. Hofwyl was an understandable choice educationally for Lewes. But there is also a strong possibility that he wanted to remove them from Agnes's, and Thornton Hunt's, orbit. He reported to Blackwood in September 1857, after visiting the boys for the first time since they had started there, that he had felt 'the greatest pleasure a father's heart can feel, in seeing my boys robust in health, greatly improved, and perfectly happy'. Marian revealed slightly more to Sara Hennell: 'They can speak German quite well, and, what is better, their dispositions seem to be under a favourable influence.'[44]

The boys, ignorant of Marian's relationship with their father, who gradually introduced them in letters to the existence of his friend 'Miss Evans', wrote letters home to Agnes, showing great homesickness at first, but becoming more involved with school society as time went on. One feels sorry for them, for they saw their father only once or twice a year while they were away at school, and their mother not at all. Though the regime at Hofwyl was less brutal than that at many an English public school—where boys suffered torment as well as long absences from home—it seems hard on Lewes's sons to have seen so little of their parents and their home, however odd that 'home' may have been. In March 1857 Charles tells 'Mamma' of the boring Christmas he has had; asks how 'Mr. Bertie Lewes' is getting on at Bayswater Grammar School; inquires after Aunt Susanna, Grandmamma, Nursie, and the others, and writes: 'How is Papa's head? How are you yourself? And the children? Give my love and kisses to them all and tell Papa to kiss you for me.' He asks Agnes if any of his old school friends are to come to Hofwyl; there are only six English boys, including himself and Thornie.[45] Thornie wrote to Lewes on the same day that Charles wrote to Agnes. He had written a play which he had copied out for his father. This was not the only particular in which he was keen to follow in

Lewes's footsteps: 'Dear Daddy, will you please put in the box above all things for me, books of Natural History, in particular, if they do not *cost* too much a history of birds, butterflies and plants. I love natural History above all things, and when I grow up, it is my desire to become a naturalist.'[46]

Lewes himself was even then on the point of departing with Marian for the Scilly Isles and Jersey, where she wrote the second and third of her 'Scenes of Clerical Life' and he sent 'New Sea-side Studies' to *Blackwood's*. He was bullish about his work. Reviewing the achievements of 1856 in his journal, he expressed pleasure at having consolidated his 'greatest literary success—the *Life of Goethe*', and also at having 'learned to employ the *Microscope*, and inaugurated by "Seaside Studies" the entrance into the vast field of marine zoology'. Hopeful of success for himself and Marian, he confided his intention to have, for the first time in his life, a bank account.[47] He duly opened one with a deposit of £145 in the Charing Cross branch of the Union Bank of London in March 1857.

On Sunday 15 March the Leweses set off for the Scilly Isles. A typical day's work for Lewes there consisted of scrambling on the rocks looking for molluscs and sea-anemones all day, bringing home samples to his lodgings and arranging them in jars, then spending the evening viewing them under the microscope, reading works on physiology, and having Marian read aloud to him from some literary work.[48] On 9 April they began reading Mrs Gaskell's *Life of Charlotte Brontë*. When they had finished, Lewes wrote pleasantly to the author: 'The early part is a triumph for you; the rest a monument for your friend.' He requested that she consider inserting a phrase in the next editon to explain that his *Shirley* article was not intended to be disrespectful to women. 'I am ashamed to trouble you with so small a matter; but as I did not object to Currer Bell's uncomplimentary passages appearing, you will not, I hope, think me oversensitive in wishing not to be misrepresented on a subject which I feel to be momentous.'[49] Mrs Gaskell could not know how momentous the subject was to Lewes at that moment, with Marian already on her way to fame as a writer, thanks partly to Lewes's generous encouragement.

Mrs Gaskell duly toned down her criticism of him in subsequent editions, but she was shy of dealing personally with Lewes. She had asked George Smith to get Charlotte's letters to Lewes for her, and was grateful for Lewes's prompt co-operation in September 1856. 'Pray thank Mr. Lewes kindly for sending those letters,' she wrote to Smith, 'I think it was very frank & pleasant of him. (Only I don't wish to have anything direct or personal to do with him.)' When pressed by Smith to give a reason for her dislike, she said she had known him a little, but had not seen him for a long time. 'I did not like a certain familiarity of manner he assumed towards me then.' After finding out that *Scenes of Clerical Life* and *Adam Bede* were by Marian, she wrote to Smith agog for information about the relationship: *'How came she to like Mr. Lewes so much?* I know he has his good points but somehow he is so soiled for a woman like her to fancy.'[50]

Despite these feelings of fascinated repulsion, Mrs Gaskell recognized Lewes's generosity and lack of selfish pride in letting her publish freely Charlotte's acid comments about him. He was, indeed, remarkably free from *amour propre* in the matter. His journal records no feeling of annoyance at seeing Charlotte's unflattering remarks either to him or about him to other correspondents.

Having spent seven weeks in the Scilly Isles, the Leweses moved on to Jersey on 11 May for more marine biologizing. Here Lewes had the disconcerting experience of revisiting old haunts, finding them both familiar and yet much changed. The sight of Royal Square brought back 'the old boyish feelings' and a walk by the side of a particular pool bordered by a meadow of buttercups occasioned a 'sweet reminiscence'.[51] Marian, for her part, decided at this moment to renew her own links with the past. Perhaps emboldened by her new-found confidence as an author, as well as by her certainty about Lewes's love for her, she finally broke the silence that had existed between her and her brother Isaac for several years. Writing now to tell him of her relationship, she proudly described Lewes as her husband, but gave no details of a marriage, so as not to mislead Isaac about the unorthodox nature of the arrangement. He was clearly suspicious, waiting two weeks before getting his solicitor to reply coldly on his behalf, Isaac himself being unable to write 'in a Brotherly Spirit'. The solicitor begged to know 'when and where you were married'. To this Marian replied with a dignified admission that the marriage was not legal, though it was 'regarded by us both as a sacred bond'.

She received no answer. Isaac now rejected her completely, where before he had been merely angered into silence by her lack of religion and her decision to leave the Midlands and earn a living alone in London. Her sister Chrissey and half-sister Fanny also wrote, formally breaking off relations. This was particularly hurtful because Marian had sent a letter to Fanny, written on the same day as the more circumspect one to Isaac, appealing to her 'sisterly affection' and feeling sure that Fanny would be glad to hear of her having 'a kind husband to love me and take care of me'. Lewes, she said, was 'older than I am, not at all full of wealth or beauty, but very full indeed of literature and physiology and zoology and other invisible endowments, which happily have their market value'. Morover, he was 'a man of high honour and integrity and the kindest heart, of which of course, I think all the better because it is devoted to me'.[52]

Both Marian's and Lewes's journals are silent on the subject of this painful correspondence. Lewes's are full of his daily biologizing. He experimented endlessly, verifying his findings, taking detailed notes, and 'burying himself in big physiological books', German, French, and English, in the evenings.[53] He felt he had made a discovery concerning the nervous system of molluscs, and was not shy of claiming as much in his 'New Sea-side Studies' (June to October 1857). However, having been stung by Huxley's remarks about mere book-knowledge, he was careful to seek corroboration of his findings on his return to Richmond. At the end of July he visited Professor Owen with his evidence, 'with which he seemed greatly interested'. Lewes summed up his view of the year 1857 optimistically: 'Have dissected an immense quantity of animals, & used the microscope with daily diligence. Several not unimportant discoveries have rewarded this labor.'[54] He was hopeful of success with *Sea-Side Studies*, which Blackwood published in book form early in 1858.

The essays, and the book, are a curious amalgam of magazine chatter, which gently and humorously introduces the general reader to marine matters, and exceedingly detailed descriptions of species and their habits, buttressed by careful references to European physiologists of celebrity. In the preface Lewes claims to be appealing to natural history in its two aspects—as amusement and as science. He knows there is an increasingly large number of ordinary readers interested in popular books about beach-combing and its results; the 1850s saw such books published by Charles Kingsley, Philip Gosse, Tugwell, and others. Lewes aims at this audience too. Early in the book he reminisces about his boyhood by the sea; later, in the section on Jersey, he becomes quite confessional—for him—about his schoolday experiences of the theatre, the market-place, the public pillory which 'disgraced' Royal Square in those days. As for naturalizing, he confesses that his boyhood efforts in that direction consisted largely of hunting and torturing crabs, an occupation pursued 'by all amiable boys'. But now he has returned to the coast, 'desirous of ransacking the sea'.[55]

He does not scorn to tell readers what equipment and clothing they need; he seeks to interest them by the teasing use of anthropomorphic language about such species as the sea-anemones:

What a coquette is the Daisy (*Actinia bellis*), who displays her cinq-spotted bosom, beautiful as Imogen's, in the crystal pool. You are on your knees at once; but no sooner is your hand stretched towards her, than at the first touch she disappears in a hole. Nothing but chiselling out the piece of rock will secure her; your labour is the price paid for the capture, and the captive is prized accordingly . . .[56]

Such conversational writing draws the reader into the enthusiasms, joys, surprises, and disappointments of the search.

Like Darwin in the *Origin of Species*, published the following year, Lewes exudes enthusiasm for the wonders of the natural world: its variety, ingenuity of structure and function, the extraordinary interdependence of animals and plants which, sometimes 'remote in the scale of nature, are bound together by a web of complex relations', as Darwin says.[57] Both men wax lyrical about the beauties of organization: the 'plumed seed of the dandelion' and the 'flattened and fringed legs of the water-beetle', so well adapted to survival of the species (Darwin); the 'great drama which is incessantly enacted in every drop of water, on every inch of earth', made visible by the microscope (Lewes).[58]

Lewes combines this sense of wonder with a robust sense of humour. Sometimes this works well, as when he discusses the habits of the hermit crab, which lives in the empty shell of some mollusc, having no shell of its own. 'He looks fiercely upon the world from out of this apparently inconvenient tub, the Diogenes of Crustacea, and wears an expression of conscious yet defiant theft, as if he knew the rightful owner of the shell, or his relatives, were coming every moment to recover it, and he, for his part, very much wished they might get it.' Lewes observes two hermit crabs fighting for the same shell—'like Charles Kean and [Alfred] Wigan in the famous duel of the *Corsican Brothers*'. But he has a tendency to overdo the fun, to carry the whimsy too far from the accurate observation of natural processes, as when he ruminates on the mollusc as a 'moral individual' and the oyster or limpet as having a theory of life.[59]

Darwin, by contrast, more intent on instructing than amusing, and aiming to distil 20 years of research and experiment into support of a theory, naturally avoids such pleasantries. Besides, he is more squeamish than Lewes about drawing comparisons between animal species and mankind, being aware that he is likely enough to upset creationists by his view that species are 'produced and exterminated by slowly acting and still existing causes, and not by miraculous acts of creation and by catastrophes'.[60] Darwin carefully keeps man out of the *Origin of Species*, though even he cannot resist a certain anthropomorphism in his language, sometimes talking about the 'intentions' of plant or animal species.

Lewes chooses quite deliberately to encourage speculation about the habits of mankind and their relation to those of animals. As Marian did in her essay 'The Natural History of German Life', and as she was to do in *The Mill on the Floss*, he drew explicit parallels between species, describing the environs of Ilfracombe, for example, in terms of natural evolution: 'The houses all about naturally recall the curious shells and habitats with which our hunting has made us familiar.' He comes to the conclusion, also arrived at by Darwin, and more vociferously by Huxley, that 'man [is] a parasitic animal living on a grander creature—an epizoon nestling in the skin of this planetary organism, which rolls through space like a ciliated ovum rolling through a drop of water'.[61]

Lewes was a popularizer, but he demanded a great deal of his readers; there are many passages in *Sea-Side Studies* in which he discusses in painstaking detail his experiments on molluscs, and compares his findings with those of authorities like Owen, von Siebold, and Viktor Carus. He becomes quite technical on theories of parthenogenesis—the reproduction of offspring without resource to sexual union. Lewes's discussion of the theory is none the less serious for being introduced by a reference to Chamisso, author of *Peter Schlemihl* (the story of a man who sold his shadow for the inexhaustible purse of Fortunatus), who 'made a discovery in Natural History which was almost as incredible as his Shadowless Man', namely that a species of mollusc named *salpa* reproduces by 'budding' every second generation, and by the more conventional method of producing ova in the intervening generation.[62] Characteristically, Lewes puts in a word here for the literary man who makes a discovery in science; similarly, he frequently refers to Goethe, ending *Sea-Side Studies* with a quotation from Goethe's poem on contemplating Schiller's skull, in which he celebrates the revelation of the 'divine' (loosely understood) in Nature.

When Lewes uses language anthropomorphically, he does so in no unconscious or sentimental way. At least twice in *Sea-Side Studies* he draws attention to the way human beings attribute human tendencies to animals, as when he talks of sea-anemones being irritated or alarmed by enemies:

But as we are just now looking with scientific seriousness at our animals, we will discard all anthropomorphic interpretations, such as point to 'alarm', because they not only confuse the question, but lead to awkward issues; among others, that the Anemones have highly susceptible souls, as liable to emotions of alarm as a fine lady.

Again, molluscs, 'like [Jeremiah's] heathen idols', have eyes but do not see, organs of hearing but do not hear; these organs must have a function, but 'we speak with large latitude of anthropomorphism when we speak of the "vision" of these animals'. A mollusc's 'vision' is not seeing, but feeling.[63] The conscious attention to the terms 'anthropomorphic' and 'anthropomorphism' here not only shows a proper scientific rigour underlying Lewes's metaphorical fun, but also begins a trend towards the modern understanding of these terms as a transference of human attributes to animals or things, as opposed to the meaning they had hitherto had, that is, an attribution of human qualities to God. The Oxford English Dictionary cites Sea-Side Studies as the first work to use the words in the new sense.[64]

Altogether, Sea-Side Studies deserved its success. A print run of 1,250 copies was decided on, with Blackwood selling it at 10s. 6d.; a second edition was called for in 1860. Marian noted in her journal on 16 February 1858 that the book, which had only been out a fortnight, was already selling well, as was her own Scenes of Clerical Life.[65] Having appeared on adjacent pages in Blackwood's Magazine during 1857, the two works were now published almost simultaneously. Every letter from Blackwood to Lewes at this time contains references to the sales and criticisms of one or other of the books, or both. It was the beginning of literary success for Marian and a consolidation for Lewes of his reputation as the writer of bright, readable books. Both Leweses retained a soft spot for Sea-Side Studies. Marian told Bessie Rayner Parkes in 1859 that it was 'a pet book of mine: there is so much happiness condensed in it!' Years later, in 1876, Lewes confessed to a new friend, Alexander Main, that it was 'the book of all my books which was to me the most unalloyed delight'.[66] The happiness was the result partly of Lewes having found his feet in his beloved science and of Marian having found hers in fiction, and partly of their mutual love.

. The good opinion of others, especially scientists, mattered keenly to Lewes, strong-minded though he was. He recorded his delight in his journal on 19 February at receiving a complimentary letter from Huxley, accompanied by a present of some of Huxley's scientific papers. Putting the past firmly behind him, Lewes wrote to Huxley immediately, declaring 'I can honestly say there is no man in England whose favorable opinion on any question of biological science could be so gratifying to me as yours.'[67] Huxley's arch-enemy Owen, to whom the book was dedicated, also wrote in praise, as did other scientists like W. B. Carpenter, W. H. Harvey, and William Sharpey. Lewes reported to the boys at Hofwyl in March that the book was 'making money and glory'; even Lord John Russell had found time 'amid ministerial changes & excitements to read it with great enthusiasm'.[68]

Both Leweses were equally excited by the success of *Scenes of Clerical Life*. Dickens and Jane Carlyle, recipients of complimentary copies, wrote appreciative letters, the former astutely remarking that he was 'strongly disposed' to address the unknown author as a woman, the latter imagining 'a man of middle age, with a wife from whom he has got those beautiful *feminine* touches'.[69] Since Lewes and Marian planned to go to Germany in April, and had found it awkward work pretending to Blackwood that 'George Eliot' was merely a friend of Lewes's who had gone to the Scilly Isles and Jersey with him in 1857, they revealed the secret to him before going. He immediately wrote to his wife, telling her the news:

I drove to Richmond to see Lewes, and was introduced to George Eliot—a woman (the Mrs. Lewes whom we suspected). This is to be kept a profound secret, and on all accounts it is desirable, as you will readily imagine. . . . Lewes says he would do ten times the work for me that he would do for any other man, and he does not think any other editor in the world would have been able to induce George Eliot to go on. It was very flattering, as his experience of editors is very great, and he is a monstrous clever fellow.[70]

For most of the next 20 years the three-sided partnership—one of the most remarkable in the history of publishing—worked tremendously well, with Lewes and Blackwood combining to chivvy the often morbidly unconfident Marian through her regular periods of self-doubt. Blackwood was intelligent, generous though a shrewd businessman, fair, and genuinely admiring of her genius; Lewes was devoted to encouraging her, and also drove hard financial bargains on her behalf, partly to give tangible proof to her of what her genius was reckoned to be worth.[71]

Lewes had already agreed with Blackwood to write the introduction for a reissue of James Johnston's *Chemistry of Common Life*, which came out in monthly parts during 1859–60, and he also undertook to do a series of his own, called *The Physiology of Common Life*, which was to appear first in parts, then as a book. For this he wanted to consult physiologists in Munich and Dresden. Marian could write *Adam Bede*, begun before the end of 1857, as well in Germany as in England; the cost of living was less; and Marian could go into society with Lewes in a way she could not in England. In any case, she was anxious about the reception of *Scenes*, and this journey set a precedent, which she and Lewes were to follow after the conclusion of every novel, of escaping to the continent.

They seemed once more fated to leave behind speculation and rumour, as they had done in 1854. This time the question was: Who is George Eliot? Claims for a half-crazed Midlands man, Joseph Liggins, were already being made, reaching *The Times* in April 1859, by which time the phenomenally successful *Adam Bede* had been added to Liggins's achievement.[72] Starting as a joke, this affair gradually became an embarrassment and annoyance, only to be finally got rid of when 'George Eliot' reluctantly went public in June 1859. To the rumours circulating in Warwickshire about Liggins were soon added inspired guesses among their old *Westminster Review* colleagues, Chapman, Spencer, and Bray, until the secret was no longer worthy of the name.

In Munich they met several distinguished scientists, including Karl von Siebold, Professor of Comparative Anatomy and Zoology, and the famous chemist Justus von Liebig. After a day spent in the fossil department of the Academy looking at specimens of Ichthyosaurus and Pterodactylus on 27 April, they went to an evening party where they met Liebig, who spoke highly of the *Life of Goethe*, as did all their German acquaintances. Lewes recounted his social success to the boys:

Every body is so extremely kind; and the author of the 'Life of Goethe' is naturally an object of interest & attention to all cultivated Germans. Indeed everyone seems anxious to show the said author every possible attention, and as my work could only be furthered by much personal assistance, this is extremely satisfactory. You ask me what book I am writing—do you not guess that it can be no other than

The Tadpoles of Peloponnessus
Und ihre Beziehung zur Weltgeschichte!!!
[And their relation to world history]

I am sure Thornie as Rex Ranarum [king of the frogs] will feel the deepest interest in this work.[73]

Marian, now beginning to be called Polly by Lewes, a name she had used for herself for several years with Sara Hennell, wrote to Sara on 13 May that Lewes was 'in a state of perfect bliss', having gone to the Academy 'to see wonders through von Siebold's microscope and watch him dissecting'. He also collaborated with Liebig, as he told J. W. Parker:

I am getting very thick with Liebig, who is going to perform some experiments I have devised, with me, on Animal Heat. If they turn out striking, wont *that* be a feather in my cap? I have already been operating on Lizards and Salamanders with Von Siebold, but without arriving at any new results. Àpropos, what should *we* think if some lunar professor were to clutch one of us, and quietly insert a thermometer up the anus, allowing it to remain there till he had satisfied himself of *our* Animal Heat? 'Tis a question![74]

If Lewes was in a state of bliss in the laboratory, Marian was in an equivalent state in the drawing rooms of Munich, for the wives of Lewes's professorial friends had no qualms about inviting her to dinner. In Marian's detailed account of their doings to Sara Hennell there is a carefully placed reference to their dining with Liebig and his family on 9 May.[75] She wanted to inform her old friend—and through her Cara Bray, who had not visited or invited the Leweses together since their liaison became known in 1854—that German society easily tolerated such relationships. In fact, Marian was enjoying a twofold recognition in Munich: she was accepted socially, as a wife, but she was also treated seriously, unlike the other wives, in intellectual discussions. Lewes expressed his pride in her in this respect in a journal entry for 5 May:

After dinner we called on the *Liebigs*—the wife, a typical Frau. Having done the requisite small talk with her we descended into the laboratory and stayed there with Liebig, one hour & a half. He explained to Marian the whole process of silver mirror manufacture, & gave her one as a remembrance.[76]

Whereas in England he could not take Marian to visit Mrs Helps or Mrs Owen or even Mrs Carlyle, in Germany she was welcome everywhere, both socially and professionally.

Not only was social life easier than at home; so also was the working life of the scientist. Lewes described to Blackwood how well equipped the Munich laboratories were, with 'extensive apparatus and no end of frogs' put at his disposal. 'When government establishes a physiological Institute professors (and amateurs) can work in clover.'[77] Not so at home. Lewes made do with accepting—with mixed feelings—a still-born puppy from a neighbour's litter; in 1859, when they moved to Holly Lodge, Wimbledon, he employed boys to bring him frogs.[78] Even professional scientists in England might envy their German colleagues' facilities, not to mention their salaries. Celebrated as Richard Owen was as Hunterian Professor at the Royal College of Surgeons from 1836 to 1856, he was paid too little to live on; he only became comfortably off when the Queen granted him a grace-and-favour residence at Sheen

Lodge, Richmond Park, in 1852. Others, including Huxley and Tyndall, were also poorly paid.[79]

Lewes's health while at Munich was not good. He suffered from his old singing in the ears and deafness; but he kept on working. On 13 June he discussed 'Physiology, Poisoning, Coagulation of Blood &c.' with Liebig. The following day the two men met again, and 'spoke sorrowfully of Dickens's public separation from his wife, which is making a scandal here as well as in England'.[80] Such news, as Lewes well knew, travelled fast. It was only on 12 June that Dickens made his disingenuous statement in *Household Words*, after rumours had spread through the Garrick Club and beyond, that his 'domestic trouble' had been 'made the occasion of misrepresentations, most grossly false, most monstrous, and most cruel'. The statement went on to deny categorically the fact that he was having an affair.[81]

On 18 June Lewes, on a sudden impulse, set off alone from Munich to see his sons at Hofwyl. The three boys—Bertie had joined his brothers in August 1857—were delighted to see him. He stayed a few days, rambling and naturalizing with them in the woods surrounding the school. On the way back to Munich, Lewes dropped in on Jacob Moleschott, Professor of Physiology at Zurich, who welcomed the biographer of Goethe with open arms, and introduced him to the architect Gottfried Semper and the poet Georg Herwegh.[82] Early in July the Leweses left Munich for Salzburg, then Vienna, where they—or 'I', as Lewes reported the journey to his sons—stayed three days: 'I lived there six months more than eighteen years ago, when I was a "gay young bachelor"—and you can imagine the interest with which I sought out my old lodgings & the old familiar places.'[83] From Vienna they went to Prague and Dresden, where they worked away, he at the *Physiology* and an article on modern German novels, she at *Adam Bede*.

Lewes's article, 'Realism in Art: Recent German Fiction', was published in the *Westminster* in October 1858. It was to be his last review for Chapman, and almost his last literary review, so engrossed was he now in his scientific work. Lewes speaks up for realism as Marian had done in her article on Riehl and as she was doing even now in *Adam Bede*. His argument not only agrees with hers; he probably has her current novel, with its defence of 'Dutch realism' in art, its descriptions of the working-day life of carpenters, and its bold use of dialect, in the forefront of his mind as an example of what a novel should be:

Realism is thus the basis of all Art, and its antithesis is not Idealism, but *Falsism*. When our painters represent peasants with regular features and irreproachable linen; when their milkmaids have the air of Keepsake beauties, whose costume is picturesque, and never old or dirty; when Hodge is made to speak fine sentiments in unexceptionable English, and children utter long speeches of religious and poetic enthusiasm; when the conversation of the parlour and drawing-room is a succession of philosophical remarks, expressed with great clearness and logic, an attempt is made to idealize, but the result is simply falsification and bad art. . . . Either give us true peasants, or leave them untouched; either paint no drapery at all, or paint it with the utmost fidelity; either keep your people silent, or make them speak the idiom of their class.

Of Otto Ludwig's tiresome novel *Zwischen Himmel und Erde* (*Between Heaven and Earth*) he complains: 'He cannot tell the story simply, but must be incessantly interrupting it with wearisome pages of "psychological" narrative, setting forth what the characters *would* have felt, did *not* feel, and did *not* see'—much as Lewes himself had done in his own youthful novels. Lewes was clear-sighted about his criteria; he was living with a woman who was at that very moment fulfilling his prescription for 'true psychology in a novel', namely that it should consist in 'the presentation of the actual emotions, motives, and thoughts at work in the action of the drama'.[84] This was the gift he recognized in Marian, as he had recognized it in Jane Austen, and, partially, in Charlotte Brontë and Mrs Gaskell.

The Leweses returned home at the beginning of September. Lewes told Blackwood that he was preparing a paper for the British Association for the Advancement of Science, which was to meet in Leeds under Professor Owen's presidency at the end of the month. 'I wish to give that *official* publication to some very astounding results I got in Munich and in the book [*The Physiology of Common Life*] I can then refer to that official publication.'[85] According to Lewes's journal of 5 September Owen, with whom he dined—without Marian, for they were now in England—advised him to submit his paper 'On the Spinal Chord as a Sensational and Volitional Centre'. Lewes did not attend the meeting, probably because of ill health. Owen read out his paper for him, replying to some objections from the floor. Lewes reported to Blackwood on 8 October:

It was pronounced 'most valuable' by the chairman, and will doubtless do good although the *Times* did spoil my advertisement by calling me G. A. Lewes. That puts me in mind of poor R. H. Horne who went nearly distracted because when he played Shylock one night at Sadler's Wells (because I had done it) [he] found to his horror that the walls were placarded with the announcement of Shylock by Mr. R. J. Horne. This comes of having initials![86]

Lewes also expressed his pleasure that Blackwood expected the forthcoming *Physiology* to be a success. 'I put my whole soul into it and expect it will be a property to us, for it has no real rival.' Through this book, and through offering papers to the British Association, which he did again in 1859, Lewes hoped to be taken seriously by professional scientists. Blackwood was encouraging, though he had already made it plain that he thought Lewes's forte was rather the light exposition of science for amateurs of the *Sea-Side Studies* kind. He had written frankly in 1857 after meeting Professor Owen:

He spoke very highly of your papers and said that you had so great a turn for scientific research and Analysis that he hopes you might some day contribute papers for some of their philosophical transactions where discoveries might be discussed and tested. The reflection that passed through my mind was a hope that you would not be such a donkey as to waste your time on such dryasdust publications. The Professor was busy over some old bones from Egypt.[87]

Well, Lewes, who had often enough defended Goethe's love of old bones, *was* such a donkey. He wanted the *Physiology* to be a useful book for students, which it was—Blackwood told him in May 1859 that the medical students of Edinburgh were buying it in large numbers.[88] He also wished it to impress experts, in which he also had some success. Charles Kingsley wrote pleasantly on seeing the announcement of the book. 'I know no one more fitted to do the thing as it should be done than you are. Pray put me down as a subscriber' (for the publication in monthly numbers which preceded the two-volume edition of 1859–60).[89]

The book, like all Lewes's previous works, is a clear, fluently written account of his subject, intended to interest the general reader while offering something for experts too. His discussions of the nervous system of various species, the chapters on hunger and thirst, digestion, circulation of the blood, respiration, and so on, embrace, as he proudly asserts, 'molluscs, bees, beetles, spiders, locusts, crabs, fishes, frogs, tritons, lizards, chickens, moles, mice, rats, cats, dogs, sheep, pigs, calves, oxen, and men'.[90] In the second volume Lewes writes about contentious and undecided issues such as inheritance of characteristics from parents, the relations between the mind and the brain, between feeling and thinking, and the mechanism of sleep and dreams. His discussions are sensible, though much of the argument is now outdated, of course, for Lewes lacked, as did all his contemporaries, a knowledge of genetics to explain the transmission of inheritance. His work on sleep and dreams is firmly in the tradition of English empirical physiology which Freud studied as a young man, and which formed part of the background to his interpretation of dreams and the unconscious. In Russia, Ivan Petrovitch Pavlov, a student in a theological seminary in 1864–5, came across the work and was induced by reading it to swap theology for physiology. Lewes's discussions of the phenomena of hunger and thirst influenced his famous theory of the conditioned reflex.[91]

Lewes was gratified by the attention his work received on publication. He told Blackwood in January 1859 that 'several things that have dropped lately from various eminent scientific men . . . have assured me that I am no longer considered by them as a literary alien, as formerly, but have won my "freedom of the city" in their community & am treated by them as a colleague.'[92] When Owen again read out Lewes's papers on nerve physiology and the muscular sense at the 1859 meeting of the British Association at Aberdeen, there was criticism but also appreciation. Lewes was told that Huxley, among others, had warmly supported his theory that sensory information arose in muscles—a discovery of Lewes's which held sway for some years, though the mechanism which he proposed for the process has since been proved wrong[93]—and he was able to report proudly to his sons how his papers were read 'before the Prince' (Prince Albert being president that year) and caused a stir.[94]

1859 thus marked a change in Lewes's perception of his place in the world of authorship. He was now a scientist, spending most of his time at the microscope, reading the works of the scientific authorities—he was much more *au fait* with the progress of science in Germany than were many of his contemporaries—writing books and articles, but content now with a literary output much less in volume, and much more slowly produced, than in earlier years. Such changes were not unrelated to his herculean task as the defender and encourager of Marian, whose *Adam Bede* appeared in February 1859 to a chorus of praise, curiosity, and false claims of authorship. It was an odd role for someone of Lewes's forcefulness, vitality, and original talent. To his credit, he entered into the unsought profession of 'minder' with gusto and generosity; not a word can be found in his papers of resentment at the considerable time given over to it or of envy of the greater gifts, fame, and fortune of his beloved Marian. 'To know her was to love her', he wrote in January 1859. 'To her I owe all my prosperity & all my happiness. God bless her!'[95] She, in return, paid frequent tribute to her generous, cheerful, unjealous husband.

PART III

FULFILMENT

Family Matters

(1859–1864)

ADAM BEDE, published on 1 February 1859, produced a sensation. It established the reputation of 'George Eliot' as a great new rival to Dickens and Thackeray, both of whom were generous in their admiration. So also was Mrs Gaskell, who wrote to the mysterious author on 3 June saying she had 'had the greatest compliment paid me I ever had in my life. I have been suspected of having written "Adam Bede".'[1] Blackwood was kept busy throughout the year issuing new editions and satisfying the voracious demands of Mudie's circulating library. By the end of October he was proposing to give Marian an extra £400 in addition to the £800 agreed before publication, in recognition of the book's runaway success.[2] Lewes's confidence in her genius was being triumphantly justified.

Much has been written about Lewes's role in the astonishing emergence of a great Victorian novelist. His careful nurturing and even more careful defending of her sensibilities against all adverse criticism—the 'mental greenhouse' (in Mrs Oliphant's words) in which he kept his tender plant—have been blamed for the strains evident in some of the novels.[3] Speculation about whether she would ever have written fiction at all if she had not had Lewes to 'lean upon' has also been rife since her own day, with most commentators believing she would not have gained courage to write without his company, protection, and encouragement, while a minority, many of them feminists, have disagreed. The question must, of course, remain open. Marian Evans, with her wonderful gifts, lived under certain circumstances; these embraced Lewes's invaluable support and her happiness with him, but also the pains of social isolation. For good or ill, it was under this particular set of circumstances that she was enabled to become George Eliot.

Marian herself was sure she would never have written a word without Lewes's encouragement. She inscribed the manuscript of *Adam Bede*, which Blackwood returned to her for the purpose: 'To my dear husband, George Henry Lewes, I give this M.S. of a work which would never have been written but for the happiness which his love has conferred on my life. March 23, 1859.' Later in the year she renewed her correspondence with her Genevan friend François D'Albert-Durade, telling him that 'under the influence of the intense happiness I have enjoyed in my married life from thorough moral and intellectual sympathy, I have at last found out my true vocation.'[4]

Marian also enjoyed, for the first time since she began living openly with Lewes, the friendship of a woman. Cara and Sara continued to correspond, but she seldom saw them, and their dislike of Lewes kept them from renewing the old warm relationship. Bessie Rayner Parkes was an enthusiastic visitor; Rufa Hennell, now married to Lewes's acquaintance W. M. W. Call, bravely invited both Leweses to dinner in September 1857—she was the first woman to do so—and Barbara Leigh Smith was a staunch supporter. But Barbara now lived most of the time in Algiers, where she had met and married Dr Eugène Bodichon in 1857. Marian missed close female companionship. In the months following the spectacular success of *Adam Bede*, she could not fully enjoy her success because of her sensitivity about remaining anonymous and her realization that she could not remain anonymous for long. The Leweses' oldest friend, Herbert Spencer, disappointed her. He was told the secret early in 1859—the only friend to whom they divulged it—and reacted with coldness and jealousy. Marian needed a new friend; she found one in her new neighbour in Wimbledon, Maria Congreve, wife of the positivist (and fellow-shareholder in the original *Leader* company in 1850) Richard Congreve. She invited both Leweses to her home in March 1859, and she immediately became a warm friend and admirer of Marian, though her husband and Lewes got on less well, the one being an ardent disciple of Comte and the other an emphatic ex-Comtist.[5]

The success of *Adam Bede* brought problems aplenty. All England began to gossip about who George Eliot might be; the rumour that Joseph Liggins was the author took a firm hold in the Midlands, with people who knew him insisting publicly that he *was* George Eliot, and adding that Blackwood had obviously treated him shabbily, since he was living in abject poverty! Blackwood and Lewes did their best to scotch this with denials in the press and in letters to well-meaning interferers, such as Bray's friend Charles Bracebridge. Letters flew this way and that, but the rumour would not die. Sara Hennell even passed it on to Marian, who was at first inclined to shelter behind the smokescreen offered by the Liggins myth. At the same time, a counter-rumour was circulating in London, namely that the author of *Adam Bede* was the strong-minded woman who was living with Lewes. The Blackwoods feared the effect of the inevitable lifting of the incognito on the sales of future novels, particularly to the fastidious Mudie; Marian herself shrank from the exposure.[6]

While she avoided all publicity, Lewes, as usual, went out into society, where he heard golden opinions of the novel. He also faced awkward questions from Chapman and others. Spencer had allowed Chapman, who was wondering why Marian no longer sent him articles for the *Review*, to wheedle the secret out of him, and Chapman gave a broad hint about the authorship in the *Review* itself. Angry though they were with both old friends—and Lewes wrote a 'stinger' to Chapman in February, saying point-blank that she was *not* the author[7]—they could not stop others from finding out. They could hardly be annoyed by Barbara Bodichon writing from Algiers in April to say that on reading an extract from the book, she was immediately convinced that it was written by her friend, 'whom they spit at'.[8] Lewes recorded in his journal their pleasure at Barbara's 'wild triumph and delight', but he wrote privately to her asking her to moderate her feminism so far as to stop addressing Marian as 'Marian Evans'—'that individual is extinct, rolled up, mashed, absorbed in the Lewesian magnificence!'—and, what was even more desirable, to resist telling Marian any nasty gossip.[9]

Lewes himself seems to have given away the secret unintentionally. When visiting at the house of his old friend Owen Jones (chief designer of the Crystal Palace), he was observed by Mrs Jones, who noted that 'his eyes kindled at any praises of A. B. or C. Scenes'. Sharp-eyed friends also noticed that the Leweses' style of living had changed; and indeed the move to Holly Lodge on 11 February was significant. It was the first time they had taken a whole house, rather than renting merely a few rooms.[10] From 1859, George Eliot was to make them very comfortably off, in contrast to the early years of their relationship.

Other changes were taking place. If life with Lewes provided the happy environment in which Marian was enabled to fulfil her ambition of writing fiction, life with Marian wrought its changes in his life too. He no longer needed to write so feverishly for periodicals to earn money, though he did, as a matter of choice, continue as a journalist. Indeed, he was increasingly in demand during the 1860s, not only to contribute to journals, but to edit them. But he could also indulge his passion for science, making up for his lack of formal training by constant work at the microscope and keeping his reading up to date. By October 1859 he had perfected his microscopic technique. 'He is wonderfully clever now at the dissection of these delicate things [dragonflies]', wrote Marian. Lewes had 'attained this cleverness entirely by devoted practice during the last three years'.[11]

Perhaps also under her influence, Lewes was now less inclined than formerly to rush into print, and when he did write he found it necessary to 'rewrite almost everything, except quite unimportant articles. This I formerly never did.' He also allowed Marian to persuade him to tone down attacks on others. When writing about W. B. Carpenter's work, 'I had laughed at him for a bit of his usual pretension & nonsense; but she, always alarmed lest people should misconstrue what I do, urged me to cut that out.'[12] Old enthusiasms had waned too. In March 1859 the Leweses read Leigh Hunt's *Autobiography*, but 'fairly broke down' with it.[13] Leigh Hunt died later that year.

Changes were looming within the family. In 1859 Charles was 16, and plans had to be made for a career for him when he left Hofwyl, which would be in spring 1860. A pleasant, willing, hard-working boy, he was not academic, as his reports from Hofwyl showed. Lewes thought of setting up a publishing house, in which Charles would be trained, but Blackwood, whom he consulted in May 1859, advised against the idea.[14] He probably did so because of the expense involved. Trollope confided to Lewes in 1869 that he was starting *his* eldest son, Harry, in the business, as a partner with Frederick Chapman. 'I pay £10,000—(of course this is private)—and he has a third of the business.'[15]

Lewes next seems to have considered, with Charles, the possibility of his son's fulfilling his old abandoned ambition of becoming a doctor. Charles rather charmingly discounted this notion in a letter from Hofwyl in July 1859:

I think its better not to think of: Istly. I should be rather old to begin especially as I don't know Greek and ought to know better Latin; IIndly. I should not have a firm enough and at the same time not a gentle enough touch and I don't think I should get many patients; IIIrdly. There are so many of the profession struggling for their daily bread, that I think I should be but hardly off.

He added that Agnes had suggested a cadetship to go to India. He was attracted to the idea, and had written to her to ask her to find out whether he should go into the army or the navy, and whether he would have to pass an examination. 'But I think she never has any letters before her when she writes for I seldom get my questions answered unless I ask 4 or 5 times.'[16] Charles's future was left undecided for the moment.

Lewes now came to the momentous decision that it was time to tell the boys about his relationship with Marian. He had carefully included in his letters mentions of Miss Evans and her interest in their progress, and had even sent them small presents from her. Now the success of *Adam Bede*, of which the boys had heard, would make it easier to tell them, for it would give them something to be proud of as a counterweight to any feelings of shame or embarrassment they might experience. Lewes prepared to make his usual summer visit to Switzerland; this time he took Marian with him. She was so upset by the annoyances about her authorship, which they had just been forced to make public, that she could not bear to stay behind. She remained in Lucerne while Lewes visited Hofwyl. He met the boys on 13 July, took them walking in the woods, and 'there lying on the moss I unburthened myself about Agnes to them. They were less distressed than I had anticipated and were delighted to hear about Marian.' The news about George Eliot did indeed help. On his return to London Lewes reported to Blackwood that the fame of *Adam Bede* had reached even Hofwyl, 'for on telling my second son I had brought him a novel all three shouted "Is it Adam Bede?"'[17]

The boys were soon writing to 'Mother' (Agnes remained 'Mamma'). Charles thanks her on 24 July for the watch she sent via Lewes and hopes to see her on Lewes's next visit. He says he has read *Adam Bede* and likes it, promises to play piano duets with her when they meet, and asks if she plays chess. It is an honest, awkward little letter, ending 'Yours affectionately, Charles Lewes'. Thornie's style is different. He begins with a flourish: 'For the first time do I seize the pen to begin a correspondence which is to be lasting, and which affords me much pleasure.' He asks her for stamps for his collection, and tells her of a felonious usher at the school: 'Tell Father ["Papa" is scored out] that the old brute of a Dr. Stamm has been convicted of stealing silver spoons, and will therefore of course never return.'[18]

It was not long before Thornie was wheedling and coaxing Marian into interceding with Lewes—'the schnurrbarttragende Alte' (the mustachioed old man)—to get him a rise in pocket-money so that he could add to his collection of butterflies and birds to stuff.[19] Thornie was to cause his parents much worry with his whims and his irresponsibility; his letters are delightful, cheerful, ebullient, and manipulative, showing him to be of all the sons the one most like his father. Bertie, younger and still very backward at spelling and expression, wrote more babyish letters. His thoughts were, naturally, mostly of Agnes and his little brother and sisters at home. A rare letter from him written on 21 November 1859 shows him homesick—'I long to come to England again, it is 3 jearys that I have not seen England' (actually two years and three months).[20]

When Lewes and Marian returned from Switzerland at the end of July, a present from Blackwood greeted them—a 'real pug dog'. Marian expressed her gratitude in rather bitter terms. 'Pug is come!' she told Blackwood, 'come to fill up the void left by false and narrow-hearted friends. I see already that he is without envy, hatred, or malice—that he will betray no secrets, and feel neither pain at my success nor pleasure in my chagrin!'[21] Herbert Spencer was in her mind here; also the Brays and Sara, who were not entirely delighted at the news of her celebrity. She was thinking, too, of her estranged brother Isaac, whom Sara reported as having said, on reading *Adam Bede*, that 'no one but his sister could write the book'. (Sara also told her in September that when she tried to borrow *Sea-Side Studies* from Coventry Library, she was told it was out to Mrs Evans of Griff, Isaac's wife.)[22]

The estrangement had weighed heavily on Marian's mind since February, when their sister Chrissey had broken her long silence to tell Marian that she was ill and regretted the breach. Chrissey died on 15 March without seeing her sister. Small wonder that there is bitterness in the humour of *The Mill on the Floss*, which was being written throughout 1859, or that the painful brother–sister relationship should be the chief theme of that wonderful book.

Editors and publishers now began to beat a path to George Eliot's door. Dickens wanted a story for his journal *All the Year Round*; the publisher Samuel Lucas wanted one (and one from Lewes too!) for his rival paper, *Once a Week*. Both approached Marian via Lewes, who did agree to write some light scientific articles for their journals. As relations with the Blackwoods were somewhat strained in October 1859 from Lewes's dissatisfaction with their efforts at stopping the Liggins story and from their obvious fear of dropping the incognito—a fear which accorded with, but also chafed, Marian's own sensitivity about her social position—Lewes and Marian were open to suggestions from elsewhere.

But John Blackwood's patient handling of the situation won through; by the end of November they had agreed on a contract for *The Mill on the Floss*, which was now almost finished. Between themselves, Blackwood and his brother William—'the Major'—together with their London manager Joseph Langford and the manager of their printing office, George Simpson, grumbled about 'GE' preparing to sell herself to the highest bidder and being tempted by 'that fallen angel C.D.' (Dickens).[23] But Blackwood finally told Marian in December that in his opinion 'George Eliot has only to write her book quietly without disturbing herself about what people are saying and she can command success.'[24]

Though Dickens did not in the end prevail on her to write for his paper, he was happy to renew his old acquaintance with Lewes and to meet Marian. He dined with them in November, when he reminded Lewes of their first meeting at his Twickenham home 23 years before. Lewes told his sons of the impending visit of the great writer: 'He is an intense admirer of your mother, whom he has never seen; and we expect a very pleasant dinner, at which two such novelists will gobble and gabble!'[25]

In the same letter Lewes brings the boys up to date with family news:

Yesterday I dined with Mother. Agnes was there. From her I learned that Vivian had had the Meazles; Edmund was still away with the coast guardsman at Goring; and the baby was very poorly. Captain Willim has been suffering severely from the gout, several *chalk stones* having come from his foot! Imagine that! Mother was in good spirits, but very feeble.

He tells them of Mrs Willim's pride at hearing that the ex-royal family of France has admired the *Life of Goethe*. 'Dear mother! she thinks the admiration of royalty so much more complimentary than the admiration of other mortals: a feeling I do not share.' In November 1859 the Leweses made their wills. He bequeathed his copyright interests to his three sons and 'all other estate to Mary Ann Evans, spinster'. The wills were witnessed by Henry Sheard, their solicitor, and Maria Congreve.[26]

One publisher who had not as yet tried to poach George Eliot from Blackwood was Lewes's old friend from the Museum Club days, George Smith. It was Lewes's talent he was seeking when he came to Holly Lodge on 27 October. He had agreed with Thackeray to start a new literary magazine, the *Cornhill Magazine*, named after the City street where Smith, Elder had their publishing business. Thackeray was to edit it, at the astonishing salary of £1,000 a year.[27] Smith wanted Lewes to contribute a series of papers on natural history, to be published separately as a book after appearing in the magazine. Lewes accepted the proposal, stating that the series should be called 'Studies in Animal Life' and should be prefaced by a motto from Wordsworth's *Excursion*:

> Authentic tidings of invisible things;
> Of ebb and flow, and ever-during power,
> And central peace subsisting at the heart
> Of endless agitation.

The terms Lewes stipulated were 25s. a page for the magazine articles and half profits on the book.[28]

The new magazine appeared in January 1860 with a serial story, 'Lovel the Widower', by Thackeray, and a novel, *Framley Parsonage*, by Trollope, who was paid £1,000 for it, twice as much as he had ever had for a novel. There was also an article by Thornton Hunt about his father ('A Man of Letters'); and Part 1 of Lewes's 'Studies in Animal Life' appeared, with its appealing opening:

Come with me, and lovingly study Nature, as she breathes, palpitates, and works under myriad forms of Life—forms unseen, unsuspected, or unheeded by the mass of ordinary men. Our course may be through park and meadow, garden and lane, over the swelling hills and spacious heaths, beside the running and sequestered streams, along the tawny coast, out on the dark and dangerous reefs, or under dripping caves and slippery ledges. It matters little where we go: everywhere—in the air above, the earth beneath, and waters under the earth— we are surrounded with Life.

Lewes continues to engage the reader's sense of wonder, of paradox, of the amazing truths to be found out through the study of biology. He explains the laws of development and differentiation, with references to Goethe, von Baer, and—later in the series—Darwin. He combines clarity with humour, but is also uncompromising about the conclusions we are to draw from our study of animals, from the lowest to the highest: man 'forms but the apex of the animal world'.[29] Lewes was to run into trouble with the orthodox Smith on this subject; the series ended, rather abruptly, after six numbers, in June 1860.

But it is nevertheless an important work. It lays before the general reader the great arguments of the day in the natural sciences, taking particular account of Darwin's *Origin of Species*, so recently published and so controversial among scientists and laymen alike. The necessity, and difficulty, of classifying species is discussed with reference to Linnaeus, Cuvier, Owen, and Darwin. Though Lewes is cautious, even perhaps a little grudging, about Darwin's achievement, he firmly takes Darwin's side on the question of the variability or fixity of species. Of course species are variable, he says, and Darwin is at least *probably* correct in his hypothesis that specific forms have developed out of one common stock. Lewes draws an interesting parallel here with philology, quoting Friedrich Max Müller on the familial relations of languages. These pro-Darwinian remarks were made in April 1860, two months before Huxley's famous trouncing of Samuel Wilberforce, Bishop of Oxford, at the meeting of the British Association in Oxford, at which Wilberforce turned to Huxley to ask in crude terms whether he was related to an ape on his grandfather's or his grandmother's side. Huxley's victorious reply was reported to have been as follows:

I asserted . . . that a man has no reason to be ashamed of having an ape for his grandfather. If there were an ancestor whom I should feel shame in recalling, it would be a *man*, a man of restless and versatile intellect, who, not content with an equivocal success in his own sphere of activity, plunges into scientific questions with which he has no real acquaintance, only to obscure them by an aimless rhetoric, and distract the attention of his hearers from the real point at issue by eloquent digressions, and skilled appeals to religious prejudice.[30]

The *Cornhill Magazine* was a great success. Lewes wrote to Smith in congratulation:

Bravo, bravissimo!
Bravo Figaro!
A te fortuna non manchera!
70000 is a pretty number to break into. Helps writes me word that he had read parts of Animal Studies three times; & I hear nothing but golden opinions of the Magazine. Our newsman says he sells it like bread. But considering that it comes from the Hill of Corn . . .![31]

On 14 January Smith held a dinner in celebration. Lewes was there, as were Thackeray, Trollope, Millais, Oxenford, Henry Cole, and others. 'Came away at ½ past 11 with a commencing headache, which grew crescendo all night & became splitting towards morning', wrote Lewes in his journal. 'Vowed never to "dine out" again!'[32]

While Marian finished the last chapters of *The Mill on the Floss*—Lewes told Blackwood that her eyes were getting 'redder and *swollener* every morning as she lives through her tragic story', adding, 'the more she cries, and the readers cry, the better say I'—Lewes was busy on both their behalfs. His journal for 1 March reads:

Yesterday I had a busy day in town. First I went by appointment to Trübner who wanted me to write a preface to the translation he proposes to issue of Humboldt's letters [to Varnhagen von Ense]. But as I object altogether to the system of preface writing, I acknowledged the compliment and declined. Promised him, however, to read the book and give him my opinion on it, and on the necessary omissions. He then went with me to Appleton's agent [i.e. Appleton & Co., the New York publishers], who is very anxious to secure the early sheets of 'The Mill on the Floss'. He said he could give as much as £300 if he were protected against Harper's reprinting the book; but I could not take *that* risk, so I went to Sampson Low, Harper's agent, who agreed to give £300 without any conditions. This is 100 more than he offered some days ago.— Called on Langford and on Lucas, smoked a cigar with the latter, who again returned to the charge about my writing a novel for 'Once a Week' and made me promise that if I should change my mind, and think of writing one, he should have the refusal of it. Went to Williams and Norgate, who have been trying to bargain for Tauchnitz, offering only £80 for the right of reprinting 'The Mill' in Germany; but I stood out for £100 and to that they now agree.[33]

They had already planned to go abroad as soon as *The Mill* was finished. This time they chose Italy, aiming to visit several cities, then come home by way of Switzerland, visiting the D'Albert-Durades in Geneva (François was translating *Adam Bede* into French) and the boys at Hofwyl. It would be Marian's first meeting with her stepsons, and Charles was to leave school and come home with them for good. Thornie made his own plans for their journey, writing to Marian on 23 January, 'When you go to Italy, it is understood that we three imps should go with you, is it not? I suppose it is! For if Father won't have it, you must make him agree.'[34] Father would not have it.

In his next letter, Thornie had a new idea. He and Charles wanted to be confirmed with some other boys from the school. 'If you consent, which I hope you will, please send us our Taufschein [certificate of baptism], I don't know how they are called in English.' To this Lewes quickly replied in a letter addressed to the more obedient Charles: 'Thornie asked whether I had any objection to your being confirmed at Bern. *Yes, I have*; and intend it to take place in England—where you will become a "confirmed" musician and he a "confirmed" poet.'[35]

Lewes instructs Charles to let his hair grow 'nice and long, so that when your mother embraces you, she may embrace a good-looking chap!' He reports that he has dined with Mrs Willim and the Captain, who is 'very shaky indeed and in low spirits—I'm afraid he will not last many years'. As for his and Marian's affairs, Lewes fills in the details: he has been approached for permission to translate the *Goethe* into French and the *History of Philosophy* into German; Viktor Carus is already translating the *Physiology* into German, and the English reprint is to be published in Germany; *Adam Bede* is now available in Hungarian and Dutch as well as French and German:

So you see we are becoming quite European celebrities; and Thornie will have a hard task of it to keep up and *extend* the family fame—he must work hard now, while he has the chance! As for you, you do not need to be told to work, you have done it manfully.

Lewes sends an admonishment to Bertie, 'the young rascal', who hardly ever writes letters. He announces that the *Cornhill* sells 100,000 copies, the most ever sold by a magazine. Finally, 'all England is on tiptoe with expectation for the "Mill on the Floss".'

Lewes's firmness could not put an end to Thornie's bright ideas. Reluctantly dropping the confirmation plan, he then proposed that it would be necessary to tell a departing schoolfellow the secret of his stepmother's identity.[36] Lewes had to squash this ingenious plan. Thornie replied humorously on 16 May, glad to hear that they were enjoying Rome, but warning, 'Ah! well, the time may come, when Mr. and Mrs. Thornton Lewes have fat pups at Hofwyl and go over to Italy "to ride in the path you rode in", and leave poor old Pater at home thinking how unkind his son is not to take him with him.' He also announced that he had been phrenologized by the new fencing master at Hofwyl, with the following revealing results:

Muth (ziemlich)	Eitelkeit (stark)
Religiosität (schwach)	Gutmütligkeit (entschieden)
Scharfsinn (sehr stark)	Mordsinn (schwach)
Dichtersinn (entschieden)	Zahlensinn (stark)
Nachahmungsinn (gut)	Beständigkeit (stark)
[Courage (fair)	Vanity (strong)
Religious feeling (weak)	Good humour (decided)
Astuteness (very strong)	Murderous feelings (weak)
Poetic feeling (decided)	Head for figures (strong)
Ability to mimic (good)	Constancy (strong)][37]

Meanwhile, Lewes and Marian were enjoying their first experience of Rome, though Lewes was again suffering from headaches and partial deafness. Among other sights, they visited the graves of Keats and Shelley. Lewes found Shelley's grave 'simple and affecting'. Other aspects of Rome shocked Marian (as they were to shock Dorothea in *Middlemarch*) and disgusted Lewes:

Good Friday. From ½8 to 1 at St Peter's, wearied with the hollow sham of shams in the shape of Papal Ceremonies, washing the feet of the Apostles &c. Thoroughly disgusted with the whole business.[38]

Lewes summed up his sense of the city on 18 April, his forty-third birthday:

The disappointment, & almost dislike, created by the city has not worn off: it is ugly, colourless, dirty, incommodious, with none of the advantages of a capital. . . . The antiquities are deeply interesting, & make Roman History & Literature living things for one. The art is of a 'mingled woof'—immense quantities of bad & detestable, & some few supreme works. . . . Papal Rome is very odious; built on shams. But the Roman people, like the Italians generally, seem remarkably good natured, easy, happy, & unintellectual.[39]

At the end of April they left Rome for Naples. Here they visited the ruins of Pompeii, where Lewes noted 'the schoolboy like tendency in these Pompeians, to ornament their bedrooms with pictures of hideous obscenity'. The unprudish Lewes felt that 'the phallus outside the lupanar [brothel] is very well, and innocent enough' but he objected to 'amorous donkeys and satyrs with naked women' in the ordinary bedrooms of Pompeii.[40] After Naples came Florence, where Lewes suggested that the story of Savonarola would make a good germ for a novel. The notion bore fruit in due course in *Romola*. Good news came from the Blackwoods about the sale and reception of *The Mill on the Floss*. Though less rapturous than was the case with *Adam Bede*, the response was satisfactory. Lewes noted in his journal, in an uncharacteristic mood of anxiety perhaps caught from Marian, perhaps caused by his poor health, that 6,000 copies had been sold and a further 500 reprinted. 'Last night I dreamt that John Blackwood told me "we can do nothing with the Mill". Polly has been anxious of late, believing, as usual, in failure.'[41]

By the end of June they were in Berne. Lewes 'rushed to Hofwyl. Boys much grown. Spoke to Dr. M. about removing Thornie. Heard Charley play.' On 24 June the boys came to Berne to meet Marian. Lewes's journal is reticent, merely revealing that the boys spent the day with them, after which Lewes went to an evening party given by Professor Moritz Lazarus, at which he was complimented on the *Physiology*.[42] On the way home with Charles they stopped in Geneva so that Lewes could be introduced to Marian's old friends, the D'Albert-Durades. She had described him to them in a letter as a 'very airy, bright, versatile creature—not at all a formidable personage'[43] (and not, in fact, unlike Will Ladislaw in *Middlemarch*). The possibility of Thornie coming to them as a paying pupil was discussed, but Lewes could not afford M. D'Albert-Durade's terms. Thornie was due to leave Hofwyl in September 1860; Lewes was probably worried about having him to live with them when he finished there. They were willing to give the quiet Charles a home while he studied for the Civil Service examinations on which they had now decided, but the prospect of having the more unmanageable Thornie with them as well was too daunting. He was to spend a year preparing for the East Indian service. When the Geneva plan fell through, Lewes decided instead to send him to Edinburgh High School, the headmaster, Dr Leonhard Schmitz, being an old acquaintance from Lewes's acting, lecturing, and fund-raising days in that city.

The next few months after their return to England were largely taken up with arranging the futures of the two boys, though Lewes did manage to write some light articles for *Blackwood's*, and he edited *Selections from the Modern British Dramatists*, which was published in Brockhaus's Library of

British Poets in 1861. (Lewes included plays by Bulwer, Jerrold, Charles Reade, Boucicault, and—for old times' sake—Leigh Hunt.)

Trollope, his fellow-contributor to the *Cornhill Magazine* and fast becoming a good friend, helped Lewes with information about the Post Office, where he worked. 'He most kindly interested himself and wrote to the Duke of Argyll [Postmaster General] for a nomination to compete for a vacancy', wrote Lewes in his journal. 'We have been much occupied training Charley for the examination, and I have dictated to him every day.'[44] Trollope warned them of the need for good handwriting, spelling, and arithmetic. 'The danger to young men educated on the continent is in spelling & in ordinary English idioms', he told Lewes, who knew this to be his sons' weaknesses, for all the advantages he felt they had gained from their Swiss education. When Charles came top in the exam, Trollope was quick to congratulate him and to remind him, through Lewes, that a job at the Post Office was nothing to be ashamed of. Men 'may live as vegetables, or worse again as dead sticks, in the Civil Service'. But opportunities existed for excellence both in the Service and in the generous spare time allowed. 'One such man in our days edits the Edinbro [Henry Reeve], a great gun in his own way; another has written the best poem of these days [perhaps Matthew Arnold]; a third supplies all our theatres with their new plays [Tom Taylor]; and a fourth plies a small literary trade as a novelist.'[45]

Charles started work as a clerk in the Secretary's Office on 15 August. His salary was £80. His working in the City meant that the Leweses had to consider moving into town, the journey from Wimbledon being too long. They took a furnished house in Harewood Square, Marylebone, at the end of September, moving once more to nearby Blandford Square in December. It was a sacrifice for them, particularly Marian, who hated living in London; they took the Blandford Square house for three years, hoping that by the end of that time they would have done their duty by the boys and could then choose 'to live where we list', as Marian wrote in her journal.[46]

Thornie was harder to settle than Charles. He wrote cheerfully from Hofwyl on 11 September, seeing himself already in imagination as an Edinburgh student, 'kicking up rows, and attacking the peelers, the most poetic part of student life. I am very glad there is a Garibaldi there, I hope he is a good fellow, if so, I shall fraternize with him with a vengeance, and who knows if I don't run away some day with him to Sicily, and make the world ring with the glory of my name.'[47]

Meanwhile, Lewes, finding that Dr Schmitz could not put Thornie up in his house—'He has daughters growing up and does not therefore take puberty into his family circle'—asked Blackwood if he knew of a suitable family. 'I want him to have the advantages of family life; and at the same time to have someone over him to replace me.' The father should be 'NOT *Calvinistic*', but if possible 'Episcopalian and gentlemanly', wrote the anxious father who had once been something of a rebel himself.[48] A classics master, George Robertson, was found, and on 30 September Lewes took Thornie, newly arrived from Hofwyl, to Edinburgh to settle him in. He took the opportunity of visiting old friends like John Stuart Blackie, and various scientists at the University. Blackwood gave a dinner for him and Thornie, and they managed some business talk too.

An index of the changed financial status of the Leweses—Marian earned nearly £4,000 in 1860 and Lewes nearly £600—and their desire to provide in the long term for their many dependants is the fact that Lewes, on his return to London, visited a City solicitor to consult about investments. 'He took me to a stockbroker, who undertook to purchase 95 shares in the Great Indian Peninsular Railway for Polly. For £1825 she gets £1900 worth of stock guaranteed 5%.'[49] They would never be hard up again, but on the other hand the drain on their resources would increase for some years to come as the children grew up.

Once installed in Edinburgh, Thornie wrote high-spirited letters home. To Marian, the 'dear Mother' whom he hardly knew, having seen her for only one day in Berne and three days in London on his return, he announced that he was 'very celebrated through Edinburgh and Leith as being a tough customer for the Gold medal, only think. But please don't be jealous of my reputation, it does not equal yours yet.' He also teased her with the news that one of Dr Schmitz's daughters was said to have fallen in love with him already.[50]

Trollope and Lewes became firm friends. They met often at the offices of the *Cornhill*, and in November Trollope asked Lewes's advice about schools for his sons Harry and Frederic. Lewes recommended Hofwyl highly, despite its weakness in English idiom and spelling. In the end, however, Trollope left his sons where they were, at a boarding school near Reading.[51] Trollope invited Lewes to give a lecture at the Post Office in aid of funds for the clerks' library. Thackeray, Tom Hughes, and Trollope himself were also giving lectures. Lewes duly gave his, 'Life from the Simple Cell to Man', on 15 February 1861 to a full audience. He was uncharacteristically nervous (and Marian was too worried even to attend), but reported in his journal that it had been 'immensely successful', despite his having handled chalk and blackboard for the first time.[52]

Two articles for Blackwood, on Jane Austen (July 1859) and *Tom Jones*

12. G. H. Lewes with Pug, 1859. Photograph by J. C. Watkins.

13. George Eliot 1860. Drawing by Samuel Laurence, misdated 1857.

14. Herbert Arthur Lewes as a boy.

15. Thornton Arnott Lewes, *c*.1861.

16. Charles Lee Lewes, *c*.1864.

17. George Eliot, 1865. Drawing in chalks by Sir Frederic Burton.

18. G. H. Lewes, 1867. Drawing by Rudolph Lehmann.

19. 'Prof.' G. H. Lewes (1870s?).

20. George Eliot, 16 March 1877.
Sketch by Princess Louise.

21. Agnes Lewes, *c.*1888.

(March 1860), were an exception to his general practice now of avoiding literary subjects. Neither essay is very well constructed, and in both Lewes is at first sight surprisingly unenthusiastic about authors he had previously admired. The reason, however, is not far to seek. Lewes knew a novelist whom he felt to be superior to both Fielding and Jane Austen. Even before Marian had become famous with *Adam Bede*, Lewes cited *Scenes of Clerical Life* as an example of 'truthfulness, ventriloquism, and humour' equal to Jane Austen's, though he conceded that the latter was better at telling a story.[53]

From now on, Lewes took every opportunity of praising George Eliot in print—though always indirectly—while he encouraged her often flagging spirits in private. In January 1860 he had bought her a set of the Waverley Novels by her favourite author, Scott, inscribing the first volume 'To Marian Evans Lewes, The best of Novelists and Wives, These works of Her longest-venerated and best-loved Romanticist are given by her grateful Husband 1 January 1860.'[54] Lewes knew that she was often depressed, not just about her writing, but also about her social status. Visited by only a few female friends, seldom invited to others' houses, the subject of gossip which was a torment to her, she was—as many contemporaries noticed —deeply sad in spite of the love and care of Lewes. Samuel Laurence, the portrait painter Lewes had known in the days of Hunt–Gliddon communal living, asked to do a portrait of her in 1860. She sat to him in August, but Lewes disliked the result. However, Blackwood stepped in and bought the painting; he felt that the 'pensive and sad look' to which Lewes objected was true to his impression of her from their very first meeting (see Plate 13).[55]

It seems that an attempt was made at this time to regularize the Leweses' relationship. A lawyer, 'very accomplished in foreign and English law', looked into the possibilities—presumably of a divorce for Lewes and a subsequent marriage in England, or, failing that, abroad— but 'pronounced it *impossible*'. Marian wrote proudly, and rather piously, to Barbara Bodichon:

I am not sorry. I think the boys will not suffer, and for myself I prefer excommunication. I have no earthly thing that I care for, to gain by being brought within the pale of people's personal attention, and I have many things to care for that I should lose—my freedom from petty worldly torments, commonly called pleasures, and that isolation which really keeps my charity warm instead of chilling it, as much contact with frivolous women would do.[56]

There is an air of whistling in the dark about this. George Smith recalled in his memoirs that 'a rumour got about that Mr. and Mrs. Lewes were at last married, and many ladies gladly hastened to call upon her.' Smith thought the Leweses actually did get married 'on the Continent'. But even if they had done, such a marriage would have counted for nothing in England. Although, as Smith notes, the 'social disabilities' under which Marian lived were gradually lightened as she became more celebrated, he himself did not for many years introduce his wife and daughters to her: 'social considerations somehow rendered that impossible.' There was no escape from her anomalous situation, the 'awkward blot in her life', as the charitable but conventional Mrs Gaskell described it to Smith.[57]

During the last months of 1860 Marian interrupted her mammoth task of researching into fifteenth-century Florence for *Romola* in order to write *Silas Marner*, which 'came across [her] other plans by a sudden inspiration', as she told Blackwood in January 1861.[58] Her spirits were kept up as usual by Lewes's prompting and praise, and she finished her short 'Wordsworthian' fable in time for it to be published, to universal critical acclaim, in April 1861. Meanwhile, Lewes produced some lively articles for Blackwood, including 'Seeing is Believing' (October 1860), written, as he told Blackwood, with a view to making people understand

the difference between a *fact* and an *inference*. It is with especial reference to the monstrous folly of Table-turning and Spirit-rapping which has revived—and which the 'Cornhill Mag.' has the immorality (I can call it nothing else) to assist by a paper in its favor, although Thackeray does not *pretend* to believe it.

Lewes cites cases of supposed defiance of physiological laws, taking a sceptical view and offering explanations of a 'conspiracy' between trickery on the part of those orchestrating the phenomena and gullibility on the part of those watching.[59]

Lewes and Blackwood were planning a book on physiology for schools, on which Lewes set 'fiercely' to work in October 1860, finishing it and delivering it to Blackwood's London office on 13 November.[60] On 5 December Blackwood wrote with kind words about Thornie, to whom he was acting as a kind of Edinburgh uncle, but bad news about the textbook. Blackwood's two readers did not like it, thinking it unsuitable for schoolboys, whereupon Blackwood had read it himself. He was sorry to say that he agreed with them; there was too much statement of opinion (possibly of a kind bearing at least indirectly on religion, in which Blackwood was orthodox), and not enough facts. Lewes was dashed. 'This evening an unpleasant letter came from Blackwood announcing that he thought my "Physiology for Schools" a mistake,' he wrote in his journal.[61] To Blackwood he replied in his usual straightforward, unruffled manner:

What you say of the Physiology is to me surpising, & of course unpleasant; but as there are three of you strong in opinion against it, I must suppose I have made a mistake. The truth is I purposely did *not* write such a book as is ordinarily written for scientific school books. According to my experience they never do teach any boy anything. And it lies in the very way such books are written that they should not be intelligible & interesting to boys. I do not mean to say that I have succeeded; but my object was to write such a book as a boy would read with some pleasure, & understand. If I have failed in this—or if I have written what teachers would not accept—the best thing would be to burke it altogether. Better for me to put up with the present failure than have the greater failure after publication.[62]

Nevertheless, it was a disappointment after his hard work, and a jar to his usually confident and unerring judgment. Lewes noted in the end-of-year summary in his journal that the book would 'probably not appear'. It did not, and the manuscript has been lost.

Some depression is apparent in Lewes's journal during the early 1860s. Worry about the boys; the need to be constantly bolstering Marian in her despondency about her work (always a problem, but most acute while she was writing *Romola*); a duty, too, to be always making up to her for her irregular social position—to these concerns were added the disappointment about his work and the onset of serious ill health. During 1861 he tried many cures: Italy in spring, Malvern and the water cure in summer, a walking tour with Spencer as of old in September. In August 1862 he even went alone to Spa in Belgium to try to recover from his chronic headaches and indigestion. Marian wrote to their Munich friend Frau von Siebold in August 1861: 'for years he has been delicate, but I think I have never seen him so weak and so frequently reduced to inactivity by headache and other ailments as he is now.' Through it all, however, as she told Sara Hennell a few months later, 'he is better-tempered and more cheerful *with* headache than most people are without it.'[63]

To add to his problems, Lewes's mother, whom he visited regularly and who now dined at their house quite frequently, came to consult him about the not very amiable 83-year-old Captain Willim. On 16 April 1861 she 'gave a very painful picture of her life with the Capt. who wont let anyone come to the house, & is so irritable that she cant sit in the room with him'. Lewes told her to tell the Captain that if he did not behave better, she would leave him to live with the Leweses.[64] It did not come to that, though there was another flurry in September when Mrs

Willim's companion, Mary Lee, nearly took a job as housekeeper to Barbara Bodichon. Marian told Barbara that 'old Captain Willim is in a state of great bitterness about Mrs. Lee's taking a situation, as she has been a sort of factotum for him, going into the city about money business, etc.' In the end, the Captain offered to raise her salary if she stayed, and Barbara gracefully gave her up.[65]

The news in July 1861 that Elizabeth Barrett Browning had died in Italy caused Lewes to write to Tom Trollope, whom they had visited in Florence that spring, in sombre and confessional mood:

Poor Browning! that was my first, and remains my constant reflection. When people love each other, and have lived together any time, they ought to die together. For myself I should not care in the least about dying;—the dreadful thing to me would be to live after losing, if I ever should lose the one who has made life for me.[66]

Though Lewes was writing light scientific articles for Blackwood, he had no 'big book' in preparation. But he followed keenly the scientific debates in the early 1860s, watching Huxley defend Darwin, and, more awkwardly, seeing him trounce Lewes's old friend and mentor, Professor Owen. In June 1858 Huxley had given the annual Croonian Lecture, with Owen taking the chair. The young giant-slayer lectured on 'The Theory of the Vertebrate Skull', rejecting Owen's theory that the skull was simply an extended anterior portion of the vertebral column, and putting forward his own counter-theory that the skull and spinal column, though starting from the same primitive condition, immediately begin to diverge.[67] Lewes had not attended the lecture, being in Munich at the time. In his subsequent articles, however, he quietly sided with Huxley, while giving careful praise, wherever he could, to Owen's work in paleontology.

Owen, ultra-sensitive about his reputation, was already the sworn enemy of Huxley. Their feud became public knowledge, and a source of public sport, in 1861. The affair of 'hippocampus minor' brought forth a rash of broadsheets and satirical poems. According to Owen, this small bone occurs only in the human brain, and marks off the human species from the apes. Huxley, rightly, declared that it exists in the higher monkeys and apes too. In lectures and articles he hammered home his message about the relations between man and the rest of the animal kingdom. Lewes visited him on 18 April 1861 (his forty-fourth birthday) and was shown 'the half dissected brains of a spider monkey & a man in order to point out the respective sizes of the hippocampus, descending cornea, & cerebellum'.[68]

Lewes and Huxley became increasingly friendly, though Lewes maintained cordial relations with Owen too. He kept out of the hippo-campus controversy, which afforded much matter for general fun. Kingsley talks tongue-in-cheek in *The Water Babies* (1863) about the 'hippopotamus major' of the water baby and speculates on the possibility of sending a specimen to Professor Owen and another to Professor Huxley, to see what each would make of it. An elaborate pamphlet, entitled *A Report of a Sad Case, Recently tried before the Lord Mayor, Owen versus Huxley, in which will be found fully given the Merits of the great Recent Bone Case*, appeared in 1863. In it, Tom Huxley, 'well known about the town in connection with monkeys', and Dick Owen, 'in the old bone and bird-stuffing line', are arrested for causing a disturbance. Each puts his case in street Cockney.[69] The scientific argument thus spilled out of the academy and into the streets, both because of the potential for satire in the stance of the two antagonists and because of the implications of the argument for man's place in nature. Christians like Owen wanted to see an anatomical difference between man and the other animals. Agnostics like Huxley—who coined the word—and Lewes accepted with equan-imity evidence to the contrary.

Reviewing the year 1861, Lewes noted his health problems and the relative dearth of writing on his part. But he described his 'deep wedded happiness' and was hopeful about a new task he had taken on. This was to be a large history of science. 'For this latter I have made minute & extensive studies on *Aristotle* whose scientific works I am analysing.'[70] The only part of this work to be published was *Aristotle: A Chapter from the History of Science*, which Smith, Elder brought out in 1864.

George Smith called on Lewes in January 1862, wanting him to continue with 'Studies in Animal Life' in the *Cornhill*, the sixth and last of the series having appeared in June 1860. Lewes declined, 'as I have been disgusted with his behaviour'.[71] Smith had in all probability complained about Lewes's heterodoxy and Darwinism. However, as an agreement existed between them to republish the articles in a volume, Lewes allowed Smith to go ahead and bring out *Studies in Animal Life* with the briefest of prefaces, a few endnotes adding new materials to the individual chapters, and the original abrupt ending of the series.

No doubt Smith had reopened the relationship with the ulterior motive of catching George Eliot. He needed a new novel for the magazine, to follow *Framley Parsonage*, and he offered Marian, through Lewes, an amazing £10,000 for the whole copyright of her next work. After much thought, they accepted.[72] Blackwood was told in a business-like, if slightly awkward, letter from Marian in May. Though he grumbled to his colleagues about 'our friends in Blandford Square' and complained of Lewes's 'voracity' on Marian's behalf, his reply to the guilt-ridden author herself was restrained, even heroic. He was sorry that her new novel was not to come out 'under the old colours' but was glad for her that she had been made such a magnificent offer.[73] After a short break, he continued to correspond courteously about Lewes's essays for the magazine, and also continued to be hospitable to Thornie in Edinburgh. If ever virtue were rewarded, Blackwood's patience and good humour were when, after losing Smith money on the not very popular *Romola* (for which she took in the end only £7,000 in consideration of Smith's loss), Marian returned to her first, best publisher in 1866 with *Felix Holt*.

Not content with securing George Eliot and pouring money into her lap for *Romola*, the magnanimous Smith also offered Lewes tempting terms to edit the *Cornhill*. Thackeray had finally resigned in March 1862, having been a very unsuitable editor. His work habits were chaotic, he was highly strung, and he could not bring himself to refuse a contribution without first agonizing and equivocating, then wrapping up the rejection in gracious terms. Smith remembered how he had screwed himself up at last to reject something of Elizabeth Barrett Browning's. Thackeray had begun the painful letter with an analogy:

My dear, kind Mrs. Browning,
   Has Browning ever had an aching tooth which must come out (I don't say 'Mrs. Browning' for women are more courageous)—a tooth which must come out, and which he has kept for months and months away from the dentist? I have had such a tooth a long time, and have sat down in this chair, and never had courage to undergo the pull.[74]

Right at the beginning Thackeray had squirmed wittily about his editorial duties. Respecting the first number he had written to Smith, 'In the name of Allah let go!—I can't pretend to correct the other Contributors proofs—and wouldnt no not for 10000 a year.'[75]

Lewes, much better fitted for the office of editor—one cannot imagine him letting his editorial toothache drag on—had to refuse because of his poor health and his desire to get on with his history of science. But he let Smith persuade him in May 1862 to act as his chief literary adviser for £600 per annum. 'This is very handsome', wrote Lewes, 'as the work promises to be light, and not disagreeable.'[76]

The arrangement, by which Lewes's annual income soared in almost inverse proportion to the work required of him, was satisfactory to both. Lewes's natural industry and astute judgment meant that he gave Smith value for money over the next few years. His letters advising Smith were shrewd and decisive; he did not hesitate to make criticisms and suggestions, even about works by Thackeray and Trollope. He also wrote miscellaneous articles for the magazine until 1865, and took charge of the 'Literature and Science' section generally. By the summer of 1863, however, the circulation had dropped from its early record numbers, and Smith was losing money and beginning to think of making the magazine 'trashy', in Lewes's view. Lewes analysed the decline in a thoughtful letter of August 1864. Other magazines had sprung up in imitation of the *Cornhill* and now shared its market. Moreover, the illustrations were too lavish and expensive and should be cut to save money. Lewes himself offered to retire, leaving Smith and his other adviser, Frederick Greenwood, to share the editing. He generously offered to help unofficially, 'purely as a matter of friendship'.[77]

During 1862 the Leweses began to go into society more than previously. They were living in town now, and had Charlie to take out to opera, concerts, museums, and so on. Smith had regular seats at Covent Garden, which he sometimes let them have. When they wanted to visit an art exhibition they could now afford to do so in comfort, hiring a brougham for the day. Since February 1861 Lewes had been a Fellow of the Zoological Gardens, which they often visited, sometimes taking Mrs Willim.[78] Around this time, too, they began to have semi-regular evening parties at home, a practice which became institutionalized when they bought The Priory in Regent's Park in 1863. More women began to visit and invite Marian, though progress in that respect was slow. Those who could not approve of her life found themselves in the odd position of admiring her works—for moral as well as aesthetic reasons. As Lewes told Smith, after Marian had received a letter of praise for *Romola* from the theologian F. D. Maurice:

As you may imagine Maurice's letter has made my dear wife supremely happy. What a noble letter it was for a clergyman, an old man, and a celebrated man to write to a woman frowned on by the world, precisely on the grounds of morality! It brought the tears into my eyes, as much out of delight in his nobleness, as of pleasure in the recognition of her.[79]

Domestic life necessarily changed now that they had Charles living with them and Thornie to be steered into a career, while Bertie, still at Hofwyl, would be coming home in July 1863. Charles proved quiet and undemanding; he 'worshipped' Marian, as Lewes told Blackwood, and she described him as 'one of those creatures to whom goodness comes naturally. Not any exalted goodness, but everyday serviceable goodness such as wears through life.'[80] He was soon to be invaluable to them as a housesitter during their frequent trips abroad. In May 1862, however, they faced a temporary worry over his career. Trollope wrote to tell Lewes that Charles was not doing well at the Post Office; he was thought to be careless and slow. Trollope believed the defect to be that he was 'more au fait in French and German than he is in English, and that he is awkward and slow in the use of his own language'. Lewes was grateful for the kind warning, but was so upset that he suffered a bilious attack.[81] Charles's good nature and willingness to improve got him through this setback; he was promoted in 1863, again in 1868, and became a Principal Clerk in 1880.

Thornie, otherwise known as 'Caliban' or 'Sturm und Drang' to his family and friends, caused Lewes, as ever, greater problems than Charles. While studying in Edinburgh he did well academically but had a brush with authority in the person of his landlord Mr Robertson. In December 1861 there was a locking-out episode when Thornie came home late from the theatre. The next morning tempers ran high. Thornie was rude, and Mr Robertson, 'calling me an insolent dog', as Thornie wrote to his father unabashed, 'made his shoeleather acquainted with my posterity. You need not ask me what I did; I did what you would have done in my place—knocked him down.' Here Thornie drew a sketch of Mr Robertson's face with black eye and bruises. A reconciliation had been effected, as he hastened to assure Lewes; a postscript adds: 'Charles will no doubt be desirous of knowing whether I got any blow, so you can inform him that I got one on the cheek, which cut it slightly internally. That is all, as Sayers said to Heenan, when he split the latter's eye open' (a reference to a famous prize fight in 1860 between the small Englishman Tom Sayers and the huge American John Heenan).[82] What Lewes thought of Thornie's adventure is not recorded, but it is unlikely that he was entirely comfortable about this example of teenage rebellion against a father substitute.

At first it looked as though Thornie would do well in his examinations. In June 1862 he easily passed the first, coming thirty-eighth out of 270 candidates. He had to spend a further year studying Sanskrit and Indian law, and was to take his final examination in the summer of 1863. This he failed, and he refused to retake the exam, having set his mind, as Lewes noted in his journal in August 1863, 'on going out to Poland to fight the Russians. The idea of his enlisting in a guerrilla band, & in such a cause was too preposterous, & afflicted us greatly. But for some time we feared that he would set us at defiance & start.'[83] At the same time Lewes was trying to find something for Bertie, whom he had brought home from Hofwyl, aged just 17, in July. The idea at first was that he should learn farming in Algeria or Australia. Lewes consulted Bulwer-Lytton and others. In the end, Bertie was sent to learn farming near Glasgow, with Robert Chambers's son as a companion. Meanwhile, Thornie agreed to go out to Natal to farm, some contacts having been made through Barbara Bodichon. Bertie would join him on finishing his Scottish apprenticeship.

Despite the risks of the long journey and the climate and conditions in Africa, the Leweses, like many of their contemporaries in those days of expansive British activity abroad, sent him off with more hope than fear in their hearts. Marian wrote to Sara Hennell on 16 October 1863:

Well, our poor boy Thornie parted from us today and set out on his voyage to Natal. I say 'poor' as one does about all beings that are gone away from us for a long while. But he went in excellent spirits with a large packet of recommendatory letters to all sorts of people, and with what he cares much more for—a first-rate rifle and revolver—and already with a smattering of Dutch and Zulu picked up from his grammars and dictionaries.

Lewes wrote in his journal, showing some of the exasperation he felt with his son: 'Thornie *at last* shipped off to Natal, well equipped with funds, outfit, and letters, to seek a career for himself there.'[84]

In November 1863 the Leweses moved into The Priory, for which they paid £2,000 for a 49-year lease. Their friend Owen Jones was commmissioned to decorate the living rooms, and they thus entered on a splendid style of living, as well they might, since Marian had accepted the £7,000 for *Romola*, and Lewes's earnings from the *Cornhill*, with an additional £250 from Smith for a revised edition of the *Life of Goethe*, reached over £1,000 in 1863. November 1863 also saw Charles's coming-of-age, and a joint twenty-first birthday party and housewarming was held. Trollope, Owen Jones, Spencer, and Pigott were among the guests. Bessie Rayner Parkes was invited, but could not go. She told Barbara Bodichon how she felt, making no attempt to hide her irritation with Lewes:

She has written to ask me to go to Charleys birthday evening next week; but I cant go to an evening party there without worrying my Father & Mother; & I was thankful to be going out of town for a few days, to Kate Webber, as a real excuse. . . .

Indeed only people like yourself & me who know Marian well, can see her excuses for what she has done. I speak more especially of Lewes' previous character. Rightly or wrongly the wretched little man has continued to damn himself so completely in public opinion, that it makes it more difficult to frequent *his* house than dear Marian's. You remember what Mrs. Noel said to you; & Mrs. Gaskell said just the same thing to me, only much more strongly. I dont think Lewes deserves the whole of it; at all events not now since Marian took him in hand; but there is the fact of the public opinion, and it creates a double difficulty, especially for an unmarried woman . . .

I can conceive no more painful life for a woman of Marians wide affectionate sympathies and high culture, than exclusion from the best society and the best movements of the day.

If Lewes died she would recover part of her ground. But now she must have many and sad moments which she would hardly detail to you; little rebuffs, or perhaps little exclusions. For instance, Anthony Trollope goes there next week; but will he take his wife?[85]

These comments have their truth—Trollope, and Owen Jones, too, visited The Priory without their wives, and Bessie was right about Marian's sensitivity and the torture it must have been to her to put up with small rebuffs. But it was petty of her to drag up Lewes's former life; if any rumours still existed about him, they were of this old kind which people like Bessie would not allow to be forgotten. And as for hoping Lewes might die so that Marian could 'recover part of her ground'—here Bessie showed that she had little understanding either of her friend or of the nature of her relationship with Lewes.

We have only the merest glimpse into Lewes's relations with his mother, with Agnes, and with his sister-in-law Susanna at this time. Mrs Willim received regular visits and was often taken out by Lewes and Marian. Lewes continued to support Agnes and also to visit her, though less frequently than in the early years of their separation. In November 1862 he took her some clothes for Edmund, and found her in bed after a fall in the street the previous day. 'Chatted with her for a couple of hours', wrote Lewes in his unrancorous, laconic way. Relations with Susanna were strained. Marian noted on 16 March 1863 that Lewes visited her and found her 'very ill from anxiety and attendance on her boy'—Vivian, now aged 10 or 11. Lewes himself mentioned in his journal in April that he had made up some quarrel with Susanna, though he did not specify the cause of the estrangement. That Christmas Bertie, being the nearest in age to Vivian, visited his cousin while he was home for the holidays.[86]

On Christmas Eve 1863, Thackeray died suddenly. Lewes attended the funeral at Kensal Green on 31 December. 'There was a very large gathering—between 1000 and 1500 people; among them most of the literary and artistic celebrities', he noted.[87] Death came in the family too. 'While I was at work this morning', he wrote on 11 February 1864, 'mother sent word that Capt. Willim was dead. I went up to her at once, to keep her up. She was not a little gratified when we found the will & learned that everything was left to her.' The estate amounted to nearly £5,000.[88] Perhaps Mrs Willim was afraid that her husband, with whom she had clearly had a troubled and not very close relationship, might leave his money elsewhere out of pique. His death at 86 was neither a shock nor a sorrow. As Lewes told Blackwood, his stepfather's death was a loss to no one, but it kept him busy about his mother's affairs.[89] There were problems about the will. A Mr Evans of Hereford intended to dispute it, believing Captain Willim 'meant to leave him the reversion of the Estate'. Lewes wrote to him 'in scarifying terms'. In April Lewes had to visit Hereford to sort things out.[90] Meanwhile, on 16 February, the funeral took place, and Captain Willim became the first member of the family to be buried, as they all were in time, in Highgate Cemetery.

Editing the *Fortnightly Review*
(1865–1866)

IN June 1864 Marian wrote to D'Albert-Durade, telling him of their recent trip to Italy, which had been delayed till May by the 'large demands' made on Lewes's time by the death of his stepfather and the needs of his 'aged mother'. She also told her friend of their surprise, on returning home from their trip, to be told by Charles that he was engaged to a 'young lady, for whom we had observed that he had a growing penchant, but who we suspected would hardly fall in love with our amiable bit of crudity'. Lewes's revealing comment in his journal was that the news 'made Polly happy, and me rather melancholy—the thought of marriage is always a solemn and melancholy thought to me'.[1]

Charles's fiancée was Gertrude Hill, granddaughter of the reforming Southwood Smith, whom Lewes had known in his youth. The Leweses liked her; they were also, as Marian confessed, not sorry to enjoy once more their 'dear old tête-à-tête', now that Charles was always visiting Gertrude at Hampstead, where she lived with two 'aunts', Margaret and Mary Gillies, friends of her late grandfather.[2]

Thornie sent good news too. He had written an ebullient letter from on board ship, announcing that he had started up a newspaper, in which he preached 'a lot of the "Vestige of Creation" opinions', in consequence of which 'I have been set down as an Atheist & a fool, but that does not matter as it furnishes subjects for chaffing me, & as I stand it of course, you know how, I am very popular'. Another shipboard activity in which he took a leading part was acting: 'Last night we performed Buckstone's farce of "Shocking Events" to an enthusiastic audience, I taking the part of Mr. Puggs (Keeley's original part) & sending the spectators into roars.' Once arrived in Pietermaritzburg in January 1864, Thornie wrote again, describing his reception there and in Durban by the friends to whom letters from Barbara Bodichon, Pigott, and Bulwer-Lytton had introduced him.[3] Lewes, receiving the January letter on 4 April, recorded his delight at Thornie's high spirits and 'manly determination to work out some career for himself, after a thorough survey of the conditions'.[4]

For some months Thornie travelled around looking at farms, reporting in October that a fellow passenger on his ship was to become his partner and that they were off to the Transvaal for a few weeks, after which 'you may expect a long and interesting letter'.[5] Thornie was indeed to send his father interesting letters, with much adventure, mishap, comedy, and tragedy told in their pages.

Lewes began at this time to frequent the famous unconventional breakfasts of Richard Monckton Milnes, now Lord Houghton. There he met artists and writers, politicians, journalists, and literary members of the aristocracy. Matthew Arnold described one such party in June 1863, at which were gathered 'all the advanced liberals in religion and politics, and a Cingalese in full costume'. The philosophers, said Arnold, were 'fearful! G. Lewes, Herbert Spencer, a sort of pseudo-Shelley called Swinburne, and so on. Froude, however, was there, and Browning, and Ruskin.'[6] Lewes breakfasted with Lord Houghton twice in June 1864, joining Browning, with whom he had become friendly since the latter's return, a widower, from Italy, Spencer, the painter Holman Hunt, the liberal MP Grant Duff, Bulwer-Lytton's son Robert, and Huxley.[7]

Lewes's relations with Huxley were growing closer; they were on the same side in the controversy surrounding Darwinism, and they moved more and more in the same circles, both scientific and social. Lewes and Marian gradually entertained more at home, and Huxley was often one of their guests. Lewes sent him a copy of *Aristotle* in March 1864. He had been careful to have the work read over in proof by no less an authority than the astronomer Sir John Herschel, who reported to George Smith that he found 'a great deal to approve and admire' in Lewes's account of Aristotle's place in the history of science. Huxley, too, had been consulted, and he wrote pleasantly on receiving his copy:

My dear Lewes

Accept my best congratulations on your safe delivery of the infant, some stages of whose development I have had the privilege of inspecting. I hope soon to return the compliment —after the manner of Du Chaillu's pond newts who don't eat their own progeny but swop babies with their neighbours.[8]

Lewes thus pleased scientific authorities with his book; and, though it could not hope for a popular sale, it was praised by non-scientists too. Trollope wrote in genuine admiration in March, 'On Sunday I got your Aristotle and went at it at once. It is wonderfully and deliciously lucid. Indeed I know no one so lucid—and at the same time so graphic—as you are. Your Goethe was charming to me as combining those two qualifications.'⁹

These qualities of Lewes's writing were much in demand at a time when several new publishing ventures were afoot. Lewes no sooner gave up his advisory post on the *Cornhill* in October 1864, because the magazine was losing money, than he was being requested on all sides to edit new journals. Smith himself was eager to sink yet more of his seemingly limitless wealth into a new evening paper, the *Pall Mall Gazette*. Frederick Greenwood was to be editor, with Lewes again acting as adviser, for which he would receive £300 a year. He would also write miscellaneous articles for the paper, as well as doing most of the regular drama criticism. Smith even suggested that 'Vivian' be revived, but Lewes's reply shows how much he felt the changes in his life since 1850:

My objection to Vivian is first that V. was a personality which I can no longer maintain being too airy & foppish for a grave signior about to be a grandfather [a proleptic remark, as Charles and Gertrude were not to be married until March 1865]. Moreover it looks like connecting the PMG with the *Leader* which wd. be a mistake.¹⁰

Lewes's articles, for which he resumed with gusto his old habit of theatre-going, became almost as celebrated as Vivian's had been. Smith brought them out in a volume, *On Actors and the Art of Acting*, in 1875, following a suggestion from Trollope.

At the same time, at the end of 1864, Trollope was leaning on Lewes to agree to edit a new liberal periodical, the *Fortnightly Review*. The plan was to emulate the *Revue des Deux Mondes* in giving contributors complete freedom from editorial interference or party adherence. To this end all articles would be signed—an innovation in English periodical history. Lewes was tempted, and 'accepted rather imprudently, seduced by the prospect of a good income and pleasant work'. But, he continued in his journal entry for Christmas Day 1864, 'my fears lest it should be too much for my health, and disturb our domestic habits, have made me resign.'¹¹

Trollope was disappointed, having set his heart on having his friend as editor. He wrote a skilful letter on 24 December:

I cannot deny that I am disappointed and grieved by your letter; but you are not to suppose that I shall either find fault with you or argue with you. I know well how these things go, and do not think that a man is open to censure because he changes his views. . . . So much, I say, to quell any fear that you may have that I should condemn you—believing that you would not willingly be condemned by one who regards you as well as I do.

But having said that I must go on to declare that I greatly regret your defection. I have felt the necessity of the aid of some one who would know what he was about in arranging the work of such a venture as we propose . . .

He ended by begging Lewes to attend a meeting of the founders, Danby Seymour MP, Laurence Oliphant the traveller and writer, Frederic Chapman the publisher, and Trollope himself, so that Lewes could 'state his withdrawal' for himself.[12]

Lewes attended the meeting on 30 December and swallowed the bait: 'I have given a *provisional* adhesion to the proposal of my editing this, they offering me a subeditor and every facility.'[13] By 13 January 1865 Lewes had drafted the Prospectus for the *Fortnightly*, in which he adverted to the 'important changes, both at home and abroad'—a reference in particular to the inevitability that one of Gladstone's bills for electoral reform would soon be passed. The *Review* would keep itself 'untrammelled by the limitations of a party or a sect'; the old Comtean motto—now completely detached from Comtism—of Progress and Order was invoked. Lewes quotes Tennyson's optimistic if conservative lines about England

> Where Freedom slowly broadens down
> From precedent to precedent

and reiterates the importance of individual responsibility for articles and the refusal to advocate any 'ism', whether political or theological. Characteristically, Lewes includes science among the subjects with which the journal will deal, perhaps controversially.[14]

With Lewes as editor at £600 a year and John Dennis as sub-editor, the *Fortnightly* made its appearance on 15 May 1865. Marian was worried about the effect of the work on Lewes's health: 'Dear George is all activity, yet is in very frail health. How I worship his good humour, his good sense, his affectionate care for every one who has claims on him! That worship is my best life,' she wrote in her journal.[15] Though Lewes was finally forced by ill health to give up the editorship at the end of 1866, he began the venture in better spirits than he had enjoyed for some time. His journals testify to that, as does the strong, buoyant tone of his letters as editor, whether praising articles, chivvying late or lazy authors, or refusing offers from unwanted quarters. Lewes was in his element as editor. Having founded and co-edited the best political paper of the 1850s and been a constant contributor to the best quarterly journal of the mid-century, he was now in charge of the journal which quickly became the most distinguished general periodical of the later years of the century.

Under Lewes, the *Fortnightly* was open-minded and wide-ranging, with tendencies towards free-thinking and liberalism. Contributors included Trollope, Huxley, Spencer, George Eliot—who wrote 'The Influence of Rationalism' for the first number to help it make its mark—Meredith, Frederic Harrison the Comtist, Arnold, Swinburne, and John Morley, who took over the editorship from Lewes at the end of 1866.[16] Morley described Lewes as 'that wonder of versatile talents', and his evaluation of Lewes as a colleague was echoed by Greenwood, who later marvelled at his ability to 'get up anything', 'so versatile was he, so lucid, so sparkling and adept'.[17]

There were those who thought that the *Fortnightly* was indeed a party organ—radical and atheistic. Among these were the peculiar Sir Edward Bulwer-Lytton, who wrote to his son Robert in September 1865:

I am very much touched by your wish not to go against my inclinations as to the *Fortnightly* review. I can assure you however that two of your warmest admirers and both liberals expressed to me regret at your name appearing in that review and in the same number which contained what is generally considered an attack on the Bible, as well as one politically hazardous by that ass Amberley [Viscount Amberley, father of Bertrand Russell]. You must remember that Lewes himself tho' a clever and a nice fellow is deconseded by the higher class of Liberals—while by Conservatives he is regarded as a determined free thinker and a defier of the general laws of Society.[18]

Thus Bulwer, who had publicly and nastily separated from his wife 30 years before, later committed her to a lunatic asylum, taken mistresses before, during, and after his disastrous marriage, regularly rouged himself and generally acted the fop. Moreover, he had abandoned the upbringing of his son to others. John Forster had been Robert's chief father-substitute, and Lewes himself—though we know little about the details—was another. When Lewes died, Robert wrote not only to Marian about his sorrow at the loss of one 'to whom from boyhood I have looked up', but also, in great distress, to Sir James Fitzjames Stephen, saying he felt 'as if a spring had snapped somewhere in my own life'.[19]

Perhaps in deference to his father, Robert did not contribute to the *Fortnightly* during Lewes's editorship. But he did correspond regularly with Lewes in the 1860s and 1870s, sending screeds from his various diplomatic postings around the world. In February 1866 he wrote from Cintra that he had 'strong yearnings for reference to your opinion'; in June he confessed from Lisbon that he had 'a thousand motives for strongly wishing to see you', his desire being that of 'the moth for the star' (from Shelley's 'One word is too often profaned'), or 'to put it less poetically, of a young frog to get to the water in spring'. Lytton described his 'instinctive wishing that I could sometimes sun myself in your fullness of knowledge and freedom from prejudice, and test the temper of certain instincts in myself by the edge of your keen conclusive intellect'.[20]

Lewes was touched by the younger man's outpourings. Comforting Lytton over the temporary loss of sight in one eye, he himself waxes confessional:

When I tell you that some years ago Greek type and midnight metaphysics brought on a somewhat similar terror to me—and that for weeks I was forced to abstain altogether from reading or writing, you will understand that over and above my old personal regard for you there was a cause for sympathy in your affliction. As Mr. Winkle passionately urged the drowning Pickwick to save himself for his (Winkle's) sake so I urge you to be careful for my sake—and your wife's—whom I hope some day to know.

He also encourages Lytton to confide in him: 'It has been my lot in life to be a large receptacle of confidence—and I like it. Probably it's because I like it that it comes to me.'[21]

Lewes's dining out—bad for his dyspepsia but good for his morale— increased once more, having very often an additional editorial purpose. His journal for the weekend 12–14 May 1865 shows how busy he was:

May 12th. Sat to Watkins for my photograph. Dined with Spencer at the St. George's Hotel, Albemarle Street—present Huxley, Tyndall, Hooker, Masson, Bain, an American (Prof. Youmans), and ourselves. Got Huxley, Tyndall and Spencer to promise contributions to the *Fortnightly*.
Saturday 13 May. The *First Number of the Fortnightly* appeared. We went to the Royal Academy. Charles and Gertrude dined with us and the Aunts came in the evening.
Sunday 14 May. Wrote letters. Spencer came to lunch. In the afternoon Lord Houghton, Crompton, Beesly, FitzJames Stephen, Warren, Bagehot, and Mr. and Mrs. Martin called. Kept up talk and tea from three to 7![22]

The first number of the *Fortnightly* opened with Part I of Walter Bagehot's work on the English Constitution, later published as a book. Next came the beginning of Trollope's novel *The Belton Estate*; then George Eliot on rationalism; Lewes, 'The Heart and the Brain'; Sir John Herschel on atoms; Lewes again with Part I of 'Principles of Success in Literature'; Frederic Harrison on the ironmasters' trade union; and brief notices of recent books done by Lewes, George Eliot, Dennis, and Francis Palgrave. Bagehot's articles on British political history, Lewes's on literature, and Trollope's novel were three very strong series for the first few numbers of a new journal. Lewes recorded the 'great success' of the *Fortnightly* in his journal on 13 June. 'I rather like the work,' he added.

Thanks to his *Fortnightly* work and his *Pall Mall Gazette* work, he netted the largest annual income of his life in 1865: £1,300.[23] This would have seemed an enormous sum to the young Lewes who had found it hard to make £300 a year 20 years before. Beside Marian's income, however, it looked modest, though 1865 was, as it happens, a lean year for her. Since *Romola* had been published in 1863, she had been working on her poem 'The Spanish Gypsy', but got stuck. As *Silas Marner* had intervened during the struggles with *Romola*, so *Felix Holt* now came across her unrewarding work on the poem during 1865, but the new novel was not published until June 1866, and in 1865 nothing new appeared by George Eliot.

Lewes's six articles, 'The Principles of Success in Literature', published between May and November, were expressions of his literary creed, incorporating notes and plans he had been writing since 1856.[24] The essays were admired by Trollope, who urged Lewes to collect them in a volume. Oddly, Lewes did not, but after his death the articles were collected together and reprinted 'for the use of the students of the University of California' by Albert S. Cook in 1885, and subsequently reprinted, again in California, by W. D. Armes in 1901. A Boston publisher also printed editions in 1891, 1892, and 1917.[25] In England, T. Sharper Knowlson added in 1898 an introduction and notes, as well as an essay, 'The Inner Life of Art', which was the first part of Lewes's Hegel article of 1842. This book, which Lewes never published as a book, is still in print, having been issued with an introduction by Geoffrey Tillotson in 1969.[26]

In his essays Lewes attempts to describe, rather than prescribe, what makes literature great. As if realizing that his title is somewhat unfortunate, he early on insists that he is not writing a primer, a how-to-do-it book: 'No man is made a discoverer by learning the principles of scientific Method; but only by those principles can discoveries be made.' The scientific analogy is not accidental, for the novelty of Lewes's approach is that he proposes to look at literature in terms of its foundation on 'psychological laws' and 'principles which are true for all peoples and for all times'.[27] Lewes is here adding to the long history of attempts to define literature and assign value to examples of it, a history which runs from Plato and Aristotle to Coleridge and Hegel. But, unlike these predecessors, Lewes seeks to demystify literature by studying it in terms of scientific laws. Not surprisingly, complete success eludes him. But, though the grand attempt to categorize falls to pieces in the course of the articles, many excellent remarks and analyses occur, as we might expect from a man of Lewes's wide reading and long literary and critical career.

Lewes commits himself to the realist school: 'Personal experience is the basis of all real Literature.' The greatest writers—not named here, but we can guess at least one whom he has in mind—are able to 'see deep significance in what is common'. Those who are unable to do so often turn to the uncommon and try for novelty. But Lewes does not advocate what he calls 'coat-and-waistcoat realism', the result of 'a creeping timidity of invention', by which 'artists have become photographers'.[28] He handles the notoriously difficult topic of Imagination, what it is and how it works. George Eliot, coyly referred to not by name but as 'a very imaginative writer', is quoted from her article on Young's poety in the *Westminster Review* (1857); Ruskin on Turner is also brought to bear. In the end, however, Lewes can only describe the *effect* which great literature and painting may have on our emotions as a result of the operation of the artist's imagination.[29]

Perhaps Lewes felt he had not quite succeeded in his aim, and so did not reprint the essays himself. The fact that others revived them later in the century is interesting. Since Coleridge, no English critic—not even Arnold—had produced a sustained attempt at defining the essence and function of art. Lewes's contribution was thought to fill a gap. Also, like all Lewes's writing, it is clear, concise, and easy to follow, and therefore suitable for students. As Trollope said, congratulating him on chapter 2 in May 1865, 'Your style leaves nothing to be desired.'[30]

The *Fortnightly Review* gave Lewes an opportunity to become once more the miscellaneous critic, a role which suited him wonderfully. In September 1865 he found space, for old times' sake, to review John Chapman's book on curing diarrhoea and cholera by means of ice. Chapman, now a medical doctor, was treated kindly, if sceptically, by his old acquaintance. Lewes praises Chapman's 'wise candour' in confessing that though his method of treating the aforesaid diseases 'has been effective within his experience, the range of his experience is but small'.[31] To another 'old friend', Charles Bray, Lewes wrote an excoriating criticism, fortunately in a private letter rather than in the pages of the *Fortnightly*, though Bray may have been hoping for a review when he sent Lewes his pamphlet *On Force, Its Mental and Moral Correlatives; and on That Which Is Supposed to Underlie All Phenomena; with Speculations on Spiritualism, and Other Abnormal Conditions of Mind*, in which he argued that thought and electricity are different manifestations of the same force. Lewes's usual heroic self-restraint with Bray, exercised for Marian's sake, was thrown to the winds on this occasion. Perhaps Lewes felt

no need to keep the velvet gloves on since Bray had attacked his revised
History of Philosophy in the 1863 edition of his *Philosophy of Necessity*:

My dear Mr. Bray

Your discovery is a very old friend with a new face—and the new face one
not presentable in scientific circles. I have no time if I had the desire for
discussion of the various hazy conceptions and misconceptions of your pamphlet,
but with regard to the new face on 'the discovery' which is to bridge over physics
and metaphysics, let me point out this glaring logical error.

Mental force you first declare to be force 'conditioned' by the brain. You then
suppose this force can exist apart from its conditions—floating free of brains like
a bird in the air. Now the a.b.c. of logic affirms that this force when no longer
conditioned will no longer present the qualities it presented when conditioned. . . . Ergo the idea of emanation of mental states to form a thought
atmosphere, is tantamount to the emanation of *spectral brains spectrally active*—
which for those who believe in spirits and rappers may be acceptable enough,
but for those who are to follow the methods of science is an 'unpresentable'
idea. . . .

In a word while I sympathize with the pleasure you must have felt in weaving
these speculations, I cannot but regret that you should have wasted money in
printing anything so crude, and am quite sure you will get no man of science to
pay the slightest attention to it.

Yours faithfully
G. H. Lewes.[32]

Lewes exercised his considerable sharpness once again when he attacked
Victor Hugo's latest poems in the *Fortnightly* in December 1865. In the
course of his witty negative piece, he puts into good practice the
principles enunciated in his 'Success in Literature' articles. That is to
say, he finds Hugo everywhere lacking in the necessary principles.
Conceding that Hugo is 'gifted with extraordinary powers of language',
he shows how he misuses these powers. 'His imagery is all the more
inexhaustible because for the most part it is not drawn from actual
experience of nature or human nature, but compounded out of verbal
suggestions.' Mischievously quoting verses in which metaphors are piled
on one another, he proceeds to annotate them in common-sense fashion:

You cannot think yourself in the 'grand smile of the Ideal', for you cannot
understand it; you have no idea of 'quitting the scale of animated beings which
is plunged in the gulf named God', for you never heard God called a gulf, do
not understand in what sense God is a gulf, and cannot picture the scale plunged
into it.

Again, if April can be called 'the porter of summer' in one place, and 'un
vieil intrigant' in another, why not, asks Lewes, 'a poor-law commis-

sioner'? In short, '"imaginative poetry" (of this kind) may be produced by the yard.'[33]

In January 1866 Lewes introduced a regular column under the title 'Varia', soon changed to 'Causeries', in which he, as editor, sought to 'chat' with his readers about 'passing events in Literature, Science, and Art'. He surveyed these miscellaneous events in authoritative, wide-ranging, witty fashion. The Bishop of Oxford (Huxley's old adversary) is castigated for his 'tawdry rhetoric'. 'The orator who said, "I smell a rat—it's brewing a storm—but I'll crush it in the bud", had no great regard for sequence in his metaphors, but a strong feeling that metaphors were ornamental. Are they?' A notable event in January 1866 which Lewes does not let pass is the first of a series of Lay Sermons, given over to science and general knowledge, planned for Sunday evenings at St Martin's Hall. Huxley gave the introductory lecture, 'The Advisableness of Improving Natural Knowledge', on 7 January, and other scientists were to follow.[34]

Lewes's confidence and happiness, noted in his journal on 1 January 1866, particularly with reference to his and Marian's delight about 'Charles's happy marriage', and evident in letters such as those to Robert Lytton, can also be felt in two long articles he wrote for the *Fortnightly* early in 1866. 'Auguste Comte' (1 January) and 'Spinoza' (1 April) are two of the best essays he ever wrote. Both view their subjects from a certain distance; in both the memory of previous intellectual and emotional engagement with the subject is balanced by objective criticism and historical placing. Both follow the life-and-works method in which Lewes was so skilful. He shows no rancour towards Comte, who had treated him shabbily; rather he sympathizes with Comte's unhappy marriage, his attacks of insanity, and his suicide attempts. He vigorously defends Comte's work from the cheap charge of incoherence because written 'by a madman'. 'If they are products of madness, we could wish that madness were occasionally epidemic.' He remembers his visit to Comte when Clotilde de Vaux was dying; while Comte's subsequent immortalizing of her was, in Lewes's view, a wrong turn, it is understandable and pitiable. As for the infamous Religion of Humanity, Lewes describes it lucidly, announcing his own acceptance of the 'cardinal views' of the historical part, but dissociating himself from the mumbo-jumbo of secular saints and rites of worship which Comte introduced in his *Politique positive*. He takes his stand as an ex-disciple who retains his respect while maintaining a critical distance from his erstwhile mentor.[35]

On Spinoza, too, Lewes writes knowledgeably and maturely. He tells of his early introduction to the philosopher in the Red Lion Square debating club; gives a sympathetic account of Spinoza's life; and expounds the philosophy with rare clarity. In the course of describing orthodox antagonism to Spinoza's pantheism, he argues strongly against 'the rooted prejudice that morality is inseparable from certain special dogmas which, if rejected, leave the man a prey to all animal and ignoble passions'.[36]

Lewes was reminded of his youth at this time not only by undertaking these surveys of his earlier intellectual enthusiasms, but also by the appearance of a ghost from the past in the person of Richard Henry (now Hengist) Horne, who wrote to him from Australia. Horne had heard that Lewes was refusing to carry a review of his poem *Prometheus* in the *Fortnightly*. His letter to Lewes must have been accusatory, for Lewes's reply is an attempt to mollify him. Lewes explains that he tried to get someone to review Horne's poems, but failed. Expressing his regret, he adds, 'As for me I am a shadow of what I was—dyspeptic and feeble; but I rub on from day to day, resolved to wear out rather than rust out.' Remembering that when Horne left England he had still been married to Agnes, he proudly describes his new wife as 'a Mediaeval Saint with a grand genius'.[37] The description seems fanciful, yet if one looks at the famous portrait of George Eliot done by Frederic Burton in 1865, and now in the National Portrait Gallery in London, one sees its aptness (see Plate 17). Lewes was 'in raptures with it', as Marian told Barbara Bodichon while the portrait was in progress, though she herself did not know 'whether it is good or not'.[38]

With Charles happily married and living in Hampstead, and Thornie apparently cheerful in Natal, it was Bertie about whom Lewes and Marian now had to take decisions, though these depended on the news that came every few months from Thornie. In December 1865 the plan to send Bertie out to join him was postponed because of a war against the Basuto people in which Thornie took part with relish, sending news of his first battle 'From Your Own Correspondent'. Bertie was not clever. Marian told D'Albert-Durade that he was 'a fine fellow physically', with 'pleasant social qualities', but was 'not suited to any other life than that of a farmer'.[39] His emigration was delayed until more settled news came from Thornie. Meanwhile he went off to Warwickshire to work on a farm near Stratford-upon-Avon.

Thornie sent detailed descriptions of his 'wonderful doings' in the war between the Orange Free State and the Basutos. Soon he was in debt but his problems appeared to be solved in June 1866, when, at the end of the war, the Government of the Orange Free State promised him land to farm in recognition of his services and in fulfilment of a plan to protect itself against future wars by parcelling out land to white men on a semi-military footing. Thornie urged Bertie to come out now to join him.[40] On receipt of this letter, Lewes decided that Bertie should go; after a family party, Bertie sailed for Natal on 9 September. By December, however, it was apparent that his departure had been premature. 'The prospect of the farm seems to have been imaginary—at any rate Thornton now gives up all hope of getting one except by purchase. This, and his neglect of letters worried me somewhat,' wrote Lewes in his journal on Christmas Day.[41] However, the brothers were soon sending back cheerful letters, as they set about finding a farm together.

1866 was a happy year for the Leweses' relationship with their old friend John Blackwood. After the break over *Romola* in 1862, Lewes had ceased to write for *Blackwood's Magazine* and correspondence was reduced to occasional letters about the sales progress of the other novels and about Lewes's *Physiology*, with both parties maintaining a polite interest in one another's health and family affairs. But the constant eager toing and froing of letters encouraging, praising, shrewdly criticizing, and in every way facilitating the painful procedure of bringing forth another novel by George Eliot had ceased.

Early in 1866, with *Felix Holt* nearly finished, Lewes offered it to George Smith. According to the latter, he 'gave me to understand she expected £5000 for it. I read the MS to my wife, and we came to the conclusion it would not be a profitable venture and I declined it.'[42] Though relations with Smith remained friendly, they never had the special character of those with Blackwood, which Lewes now undertook to renew. He wrote to Blackwood in April that Marian was finishing 'a novel of English Provincial Life just after the passing of the Reform Bill in '32'. In case Blackwood should think the politics would be too left-wing for his liking, Lewes added that 'the political tone is as *dramatic* and impartial as her tone has been in all her writings'.[43] Certainly Felix Holt is as conservative a radical as one could hope to meet, in life or literature.

Blackwood replied immediately, feeling sure that the novel would be 'first rate' and offering, without seeing it, 'from four to five thousand Pounds for the copyright for five years'. He made it clear that he could not offer more, but finished with his usual deftness of touch.

Will you give her my regards and tell her that I have been thinking so much of her Novel since receiving your note that I have found it very difficult to attend to my ordinary work, of which I have more than enough at this period of the month.[44]

The first two volumes were immediately sent off to Edinburgh, where they were consumed in a matter of hours, so that Blackwood was writing again on 22 April, only four days after Lewes had broached the subject, talking of how beautiful the novel was. Lewes accepted the offer on Marian's behalf, avowing that Blackwood's two letters had given her 'a glass of moral champagne'.[45] The novel was published on 15 June 1866, just at the time when the second great Reform Bill of the century was being drafted and redrafted for discussion in Parliament. Blackwood was delighted, praising Marian's politics: 'I suppose I am a radical of the Felix Holt breed, and so was my father before me.'[46]

As always, Lewes and Marian escaped abroad at the moment of publication. Lewes's health was anyway breaking down again, and he left the *Fortnightly* in Trollope's hands while he was away. They set off on 7 June for a leisurely trip to Germany. The day before their departure Lewes met Dickens on his way home. Dickens told him 'curious stories of dreams, etc.'—a case of an inconsequential dream seeming to come true in the most minute details, and examples of the strange effect which shock could have on people's behaviour and perception of themselves.[47] The examples fed Lewes's interest in psychology; after Dickens's death, Lewes related in his *Fortnightly Review* article on his friend, in 1872, other instances of dreams Dickens had described to him.

They were away for two months, stopping off in Amsterdam, where they visited Spinoza's birthplace and the site of the Portuguese synagogue from which he was expelled. In Germany their route was determined by the need to avoid the venues of battles in the newly begun Austro-Prussian War. From Schlangenbad they wrote to Charles and Gertrude of their lazy existence as 'two old lovers' in 'this sequestered paradise'.[48]

Trollope greeted them on their return early in August with a letter to Marian praising *Felix Holt*, asking after 'the Master's' health, and offering him some cigars from a batch of 8,000 (!) which he had just received from Cuba. Marian thanked him 'for the regard I think you bear towards that (to me) best of men, my dear husband'.[49] The event which Trollope most feared—Lewes's resignation as editor of the *Fortnightly*—could not be delayed much longer. From now on Lewes was in more or less constant ill health, with symptoms of chronic headaches and dyspepsia, and by November 1866 Trollope was bowing to the inevitable. He expressed his sorrow at the *Fortnightly*'s loss, and questioned Lewes nervously about a possible successor. John Morley, a disciple of Mill, was chosen, but Trollope was afraid he might not like 'the nose on his face', editorially speaking.[50] He didn't. Soon he was writing to the

Fortnightly under its new management to protest against an article attacking fox-hunting, an amusement 'which I love'. He remembered in his *Autobiography* his sense that 'our loss in him [Lewes] was very great', adding that Lewes was one of his dearest friends and 'the acutest critic I know'.[51]

Lewes's health was so poor that Marian wrote to Sara Hennell on 22 November, her forty-seventh birthday:

I have been telling Mr. Lewes that it is my birthday, and at the news he smiled through the sad look of head-ache as he lay on his pillow. It is the second morning that he has been unable to get up to breakfast, from the presence of that horrible demon, who has taken possession of his poor body as a penalty for our entertainment of a gentlemen's party on Tuesday. A little extra excitement— or a morsel of mutton fat—will lay him prostrate for days. . . .

However, I am comparatively at ease now that he has given up his editorship and has nearly finished his History. He will be able then to think of nothing but what he likes best, and we shall probably go southward.[52]

The 'History' was the third revised edition of Lewes's first book, the *Biographical History of Philosophy*, now published, in 1867, minus the adjective 'Biographical', much revised, and with the recent Comte article added.

Lewes bowed out of the *Fortnightly* in December with a 'Farewell Causerie' which looks back on the first two years of the periodical with justifiable pride in its achievements: bringing in contributors 'so varied in opinion and so distinguished in power', allowing writers 'perfect freedom', having them sign their articles, and generally contributing to the 'civilising influence' which periodical literature should have. Lewes was not being pompous; his own practice had always been to be honest and take the consequences. As a contributor to the periodicals of others he had always advocated, and practised (when allowed) full freedom of expression on every subject. He could afford to be pleased that he had extended that right to the writers in *his* journal.

It is worth noting that though Lewes was no longer quite the radical he had been in his *Leader* days, he was still alert to political trends, and was not at all conservative in his views. The last Causerie is remarkable for the surefootedness of his analysis of the past year and his prescience about the future of England politically:

Students of History well know the difficulty of fixing on a date which shall mark a new epoch. . . . The noisiest currents are not the deepest and broadest, but they attract most attention by reason of their noise. A study of history will, however, disclose to the philosophic eye certain characteristics which give significance to phenomena seemingly unimportant; and this study will enable us to see something eminently significant in one of the events of 1866—not noisy at all, not discussed in newspapers and public meetings, but certain to be one day referred to as the starting-point of a new epoch. What is this? Ask the press what have been the great topics of this year of noises. They have been the cattle-plague, the [financial] panic, the disclosures of railway mismanagement, the agitation for Reform, the Fenians, the conflict of the President with Congress, the Seven Days' War, ending in the expulsion of Austria from Germany, and the freedom of Italy from a foreign yoke. These are, some of them at least, events of importance, but the philosophic student will probably see far more significance in an event which was neither imposing in outward aspect, nor suggestive in its prophecies to the ordinary mind: that event is the Congress of Workmen at Geneva.

Continuing with his assessment of the importance of the International Working Men's Association, Karl Marx's brainchild, Lewes prophesied the importance of trade unions in the future. The formation of trade unions had been momentous:

The English plan is nothing less than that of making Strikes universal; the French plan is nothing less than that of removing Industry from its present conditions of Capital and Labour, and substituting universal co-operation. That neither plan could be at present carried out is obvious enough; but nothing is more clear to the prophetic eye than that if once the workmen of Europe combine, they will ultimately adopt one or both of these plans; and that what they resolve on must be realised.

As for the progress made during 1866 in his beloved science, Lewes points to Huxley's work in the only genre in which he himself had failed to write successfully—the school textbook. He generously praises Huxley's *Lessons in Elementary Physiology*, saying: 'teachers may read it with profit, to learn from it the art of popular exposition.'[53] With this Lewes ceased his distinguished editorship of the *Fortnightly Review*. Carlyle, whom Lewes saw only occasionally these days, told his brother in January 1867 that 'Lewes is quite out of it;—poor Lewes, I hear, is dangerously ill of liver, face of him quite shrunk away &c., a dreary bit of news in its sort.'[54]

Immediately after Christmas the Leweses went to France, planning to go on to Spain if he was well enough, so that Marian could get a feeling for the country and might then be able to resume her half-written poem, 'The Spanish Gypsy'. Blackwood wrote to Lewes, 'People are very fond of writing books to teach others to think, but if some one could teach you not to think for a spell it would be doing you a good turn.'[55] There was little hope of that. But though Lewes's activity was maintained at his usual rate in the intervals between illnesses, his output from now on was much reduced. This was not entirely due to ill health. He had embarked on his most ambitious project yet: a comprehensive study of the human organism, physiological and psychological, which he would finally publish during the 1870s in the five volumes of *Problems of Life and Mind* (1874–9).

More Family Matters

(1867–1875)

THE Leweses reached Biarritz on 6 January 1867. Not only was Lewes's physical health poor; so also were his spirits, according to Nina Lehmann—daughter of Robert Chambers and one of an increasing number of young women who sought out Marian's company—whom they visited for a few days at Pau.[1] Nevertheless, they pressed on into Spain, a country neither had visited before, where they wished to fulfil 'a dream of many years'—to visit the Alhambra in Granada.[2] Bravely ignoring the horror stories they had heard about 'Spanish hotels and cookery' and the hardships of Spanish travel, they endured a 16-hour journey from Malaga to Granada, their diligence being drawn up the mountains by a team of ten mules. Their 'rickety bodies' survived the ordeal, and the beauty of the Alhambra made the effort worthwhile.[3]

Marian wrote to Blackwood that she felt invigorated enough to finish the work which had been laid aside for nearly three years. Only when she returned from Spain in March did she divulge for the first time that it was—'prepare your fortitude'—a poem.[4] Everywhere they went in Spain they were struck by the beauty and unusualness of the scenery and the people. At Lerida Lewes saw in the groups of beggars, gamblers, children playing, shepherds, and gypsies examples from Spanish art—'Murillo everywhere'. Spanish literature, too, came to life: 'met an old usurer in large horn spectacles seated on a donkey with a boy walking behind—we settled he *was* an usurer from Gil Blas. Indeed we are constantly meeting the people of Gil Blas & Don Quixote.'[5]

At Barcelona they heard from Charles that the old eccentric, Swynfen Jervis, had died. He had long ago retired from public life, married his third wife in 1857, lived on his Staffordshire estate, busying himself with publishing pseudo-scholarly works on his beloved Shakespeare. Jervis's will, proved at Lichfield on 5 February, was exceedingly complicated. Four of the seven children by his first wife, including

Agnes, were still alive. Of these the eldest son, John, inherited Darlaston Hall. A sister Emily, being a nun, was not a beneficiary. Jervis left his personal estate to be divided among Agnes's youngest sister Florence, his third wife, Catherine, and the two children born to his second wife. Agnes alone received nothing.[6] Perhaps Jervis took this way of showing his disapproval of her way of life. What is certain is that Agnes did not become independent on her father's death. Lewes continued to support her until his death, as did Marian until hers, and after that Charles, who himself predeceased her by 11 years, he dying in 1891 and his mother not until 1902.

Family matters were much on Lewes's mind in another, more pleasant, connection. In a letter to Mrs Willim from Barcelona—one of only two surviving letters from son to mother—he writes:

You were often told that you had a Spanish look when young; & it is true; & it is not (what I used to think it) a poor compliment, for the Spanish women are very lovely, some of them we have seen are quite ideal; & in general good looks are more abundant than in any other country I know—far more so.

He adds, for his mother's interest, that unfortunately all the ladies '*trail their dress yards behind them in the dirt after the Parisian fashion, which is painful to see*'. Lewes also reports that his health is much improved, '& I expect to get back to you as brown—as *your* son ought to be. I am getting flesh on my bones too!' He ends his pleasant letter, 'God bless you, Your loving Son, GHL'.[7]

They returned, fitter and happier for their trip despite the extraordinarily long journeys and a hectic round of sightseeing. Lewes immediately got on with the revision of the *History of Philosophy* and the English text to Kaulbach's illustrations from Goethe, *Female Characters of Goethe*, for which he was paid £100 by Trübner.[8] Marian resumed *The Spanish Gypsy*, which was eventually published to a polite but hardly rapturous response in May 1868.

They also re-entered their ever-widening social circle. After hearing Richard Congreve lecture on Positivism on 5 May, along with Lord Houghton, Frederic Harrison, Edward Beesly, Professor of History at University College London and a leading Comtist, Lord and Lady Amberley, and 'sixty or seventy others', Lewes introduced Marian to Lady Amberley, who invited them back to lunch with her. This was significant socially. It meant that Marian might be received in aristocratic circles—at least liberal ones. Even so, there were shades of difference. Though she might invite both Leweses to a quiet Sunday lunch, Lady

Amberley seems to have invited only Lewes to her large evening party the following Tuesday. At any rate, only Lewes went:

Dined at the Amberleys—Lord and Lady Russell, Lady Airlie, Sir J. Bowring, W. E. Forster, Prof. Frazer, Dr. Hanna, Crompton, and several others at dinner and in the evening. Lady Amberley more charming than ever, but her sister Lady Airlie even pleased me more—perhaps because her talk was mainly about Polly, whom she seems thoroughly to appreciate.[9]

Lewes wrote thanking Lady Amberley for the party, mentioning his pleasure at being able to talk about 'my Madonna' to her sister, and signing himself 'Your very obedient and faithful philosopher'. At some later date she annotated the letter with the remark: 'The correct etiquette about Lewes and George Eliot appears to have been somewhat undecided.'[10] Even progressive aristocrats, it seems, were stumped about how to fit this unusual yet desirable couple into their social milieu.

As well as moving, however problematically, in these exalted circles, Lewes was also catching up with the news about the *Fortnightly Review*. Despite his poor digestion, he dined at the Garrick Club with Browning, Forster, Fitzjames Stephen, Beesly, Meredith, and Trollope on the evening before Lady Amberley's party.[11] Though now out of the editorial office, Lewes was still a contributor to the *Review*. In July 1867 his article on the Duke of Argyll's pamphlet, *The Reign of Law*, appeared. In this admirably clear essay, Lewes praises the Duke's scholarly interest in science, while respectfully claiming that, though laws are operating everywhere in the physical world, it is unscientific, and unwise, to speak of a lawmaker. Stressing a point Darwin had made in the *Origin of Species*, Lewes eloquently presses for theology and metaphysics to be left out of the question:

The prodigality of waste is far more conspicuous than the wise economy of which so much is said; no one would applaud the wisdom and skill of a man who wasted a pipe of wine every time he desired to fill a glass. It must strike every reflective mind as humanly speaking strangely at variance with a wise vision of ends, that structures so marvellously complex and capable of so complete an existence as those of man and animals, should be formed by millions under conditions which prevent their development; not only are ova sacrificed by millions, but even when the ova have been fertilised this 'end' is frustrated—the embryo perishes, the infant perishes, the child perishes, the youth perishes, and the organisation we are called upon to marvel at as a work of 'exquisite contrivance', attains its 'end' as an exception to the general failure. . . . Design, contrivance, skill, are phrases to denote human, not Divine, agencies.[12]

Lewes's old friend Richard Owen replied in *Fraser's Magazine* to what he took to be an indirect assault on his own creationist views. Lewes hastened to put things right:

My dear Owen

I hope I am wrong in my uncomfortable notion that you have interpreted a phrase or two of mine into a covert allusion of contempt or sarcasm against your sincerely respected self. That we differ profoundly respecting Design and the Creator is an old story—*that* difference never yet has disturbed our harmony— but what is new is the suspicion (it is not more) that you interpret my language as covertly attacking you, and above all as imputing 'infirmity' to you. . . . I don't want our old friendship to be crossed by a misunderstanding. By a difference of opinion it won't be.[13]

Owen seems to have been mollified, for the two men continued to meet, and to correspond, amicably.

With the Reform Bill extending the franchise finally on its way into law, Marian was approached by those supporting Mill's intended amendment to include women. Disappointingly for Mill, his friend Morley, and her many feminist women friends, Marian felt unable to join them. Not only did she consider her anomalous social position—'the peculiarities of my own lot', as she termed it in reply to Morley's request for support in May 1867—to be a bar to her speaking out publicly, but she also believed that woman's function, biologically and morally determined, was 'to mitigate the harshness of all fatalities'.[14]

It is hard to see exactly what she meant by this. Certainly, it is clear from her novels, particularly *The Mill on the Floss* and the as yet unwritten *Middlemarch*, that she resented the lack of educational and professional opportunities for women. 'You are a man, and can do something,' says Maggie Tulliver in frustration to her brother Tom; Dorothea Casaubon can only busy herself doing random good works in the parish, though she is shown to be capable of, and anxious for, more regular and professional work. Yet in the end, even the narrator of *Middlemarch*, though ambivalent, appears to believe that Dorothea's life as the wife of Will Ladislaw—'an ardent public man'—a life hampered by the conditions of 'an imperfect social state', is worthwhile. George Eliot, fully aware of the disadvantages for women in such an imperfect social state, cannot bring herself, in life or in her fiction, to advocate strenuous efforts to change that state, to set about perfecting the imperfect.

Unfortunately, we don't know what Lewes's view of the enfranchisement of women was at this time; earlier, when married to Agnes and encouraging her to view him as something less than her lord and master, he had paradoxically adhered to the Comtean view—not very different in this respect from the traditional Christian one—that women are made to be wives and mothers. Now Marian, technically speaking not a wife, and for that very reason not a mother, took the same view. Being a reluctant social rebel, she refused to profess rebellion as a creed. She did, however, give more hearty support, though still privately, to Barbara Bodichon and Emily Davies in those efforts on behalf of higher education for women which resulted in the founding of Girton College, Cambridge, in 1869.[15]

Both Leweses had become more conservative politically as, on the one hand, they got older, and, on the other, political progress was, however slowly, being made. Lewes even seems to have lost on occasion his customary sense of the ridiculous when he went into the highest of high society. His journal for 18 May describes a garden party at Lady Airlie's with no trace of self-irony:

Nothing could exceed the attention with which I was treated. As the servant announced my name I heard a woman's voice in the conservatory say 'Here he is', so that they had been talking about me. Lady Amberley & Lady Airlie seemed anxious to introduce me to every one, first to their whole family & then to all the more distinguished guests, so that I had to bow to more Lords & Ladies than I ever met before.[16]

During the summer of 1867, Lewes became a member of the Committee of the London Library, having been proposed by Lord Stanley. He and Marian took a couple of short trips abroad for his health and Marian's flagging inspiration, and in October Lewes went on a walking expedition with Spencer. They went to Surrey, where they met friends of Spencer's, the Cross family, who received Lewes 'like an old friend—they knowing my books and worshipping Polly'.[17] John Cross was to become intimate with both Leweses, who later relied on his financial skills to manage their investments and wrote familiarly to him, signing themselves 'Aunt' and 'Uncle' to this adopted nephew.

Lewes began zoologizing again in preparation for the part of his great work called 'The Physical Basis of Mind'. Marian reported to Cara Bray in December that one of Lewes's victims, known as 'Froggie', had just died of starvation after living for months without his brain.[18] In December Lewes planned a quick trip to Germany to discuss his physiological work with his German colleagues in Bonn and Heidelberg. His journal for Christmas Day 1867 shows him to have regained some of his old buoyancy after a chequered year:

Health on the whole improved, though a great many days of forced idleness from headache & indigestion. Work includes the completion of the 'History of Philosophy', two or three papers in the 'Pall Mall Gazette', & long laborious researches into the *Nervous System* for my work on Physiology. Latterly I have had such illuminations on this subject, completely reshaping the whole scheme of nervous anatomy, that I have resolved to run over to Germany to inspect the preparations &c of the best men there, in the hope of finding bricks ready made for my purpose.[19]

Lewes's optimism about his findings, his sense of having made genuine discoveries in scientific research, generally met with a muted response among the British scientific community. Its members allowed Lewes to be a clever popularizer, but no more. As Alexander Bain, the disciple of Mill and writer on associational psychology, put it in a letter to his colleague George Croom Robertson, Professor of Mental Philosophy and Logic at University College London, in 1877:

Not surprised that you find Lewes uncomfortable. His affectation being always beyond his powers, and always after the appearance of novelty, it is hard to give him the credit that he expects.[20]

There is some truth in this, especially with reference to *Problems of Life and Mind*, on which Lewes worked so hard for ten or more years, and which made less of a mark than he felt it deserved. On the other hand, there was an element of professional snobbery at work against him. Refreshingly for Lewes, when he went to Germany he was well received by the many eminent scientists there. On the occasion of this brief visit in December 1867, Lewes was gratified to be told that his *Sea-Side Studies* and *Physiology of Common Life* were 'universally known to the men of Science', as well as the *Life of Goethe*, which 'still continues to be read by everyone'.[21]

Blackwood, who had just printed in the magazine 'Felix Holt's Address to the Working Men'—which Marian wrote at his request to remind the newly-enfranchised and those not yet admitted to the vote what their responsibilities were—welcomed Lewes back in a letter of 22 January 1868: 'In probing the nervous system of the human race take care that you do not overwork your own. You do work very hard but it is both nature and habit with you.'[22] The warning was timely. By March the Leweses were off on another enforced holiday, to Torquay, though Lewes was to combine rest with some gentle zoologizing. As in the days of Tenby and Ilfracombe, he hunted among the rocks by day and studied the results under a microscope in the evenings. He was also writing. 'Having something that he wanted to say on Darwin and Darwinism',

Marian told Sara Hennell in March, 'he is finishing two long articles on the subject—the first will appear in the next Fortnightly.'[23]

Lewes had already written three short review articles of Darwin's new work, *The Variation of Animals and Plants under Domestication*, in the *Pall Mall Gazette* on 10, 15, and 17 February. In these he welcomed the new book with its addition to the evidence given in *Origin of Species* to support natural selection. Lewes praises Darwin's thoroughness and clarity; provisionally accepts the hypothesis of natural selection as 'the most plausible one that has yet been propounded'; agrees with Darwin's view of the variability of species; and admires 'the noble calmness with which he expounds his own views, undisturbed by the heats of polemical agitation which those views have excited, and persistently refusing to retort on his antagonists by ridicule, by indignation, or by contempt'. He discusses the vexed question of what constitutes a species, finding Darwin to have added greatly to the methods of definition. While accepting Darwin's stress on the interaction of external conditions and internal organization in the production of variety, he rightly doubts the 'ingenious hypothesis of Pangenesis, in which every cell of the organism is made to throw off a gemmule capable of reproducing it'.[24] Neither Darwin nor Lewes, of course, knew of the genetic transmission of internal characteristics, which the Austrian monk Gregor Mendel was even then studying. Darwin saw the first of Lewes's articles and wrote immediately to his friend Joseph Hooker: 'If by any chance you should hear who wrote the article in the *Pall Mall*, do please tell me; it is some one who writes capitally, and who knows the subject.' Darwin signed his letter 'Your cock-a-hoop friend C. D.'.[25]

For the *Fortnightly* Lewes set about 'a more elaborate consideration' of Darwinism, as he told Darwin in a letter of 2 March. He had heard—through Smith, probably—that Darwin was pleased with his *Pall Mall Gazette* papers, and wrote to express his intention of doing more. Lewes finished this, his first, letter to Darwin with an apology for 'trespassing on your valuable time'.[26] The two men had not met in London scientific circles because Darwin's ill health (and shyness) kept him in the country, where he could continue with his studies and writing more or less undisturbed by the excitement his work caused. From this time Lewes and Darwin became friendly, meeting occasionally when Darwin came to London, and occasionally in the country too. In November 1868, after one of his visits to town, Darwin called on the Leweses, writing to Lewes afterwards to say he would be delighted to propose him for membership of the Linnaean Society.[27]

Lewes's articles, entitled 'Mr. Darwin's Hypotheses', appeared in

April, June, July, and November 1868. He takes the large view of the
Origin of Species, stating unequivocally that 'no work of our time has
been so general in its influence', and noting that that influence 'rapidly
became European'. (To Darwin himself he wrote in July that he had
'found all young scientific Germany Darwinian'.)[28] In the four long
essays Lewes explains the Development Hypothesis and Darwin's
version of it, placing it in the context of philosophical questions about
the origin and function of life. He tackles at some length the difficulty
of deciding how to define species, particularly where animals have
become extinct and so cannot be studied in their breeding groups, and
more generally where there are gaps in the genealogical record of plants
and animals. The question of waste, nature's 'trial and error', and
atrophied or useless appendages such as the toes and nails of the seal—
'obvious superfluities'—is put to warn those, like Philip Gosse, who
liked to think that God created species ready-made and adapted to their
conditions.[29]

Lewes considers the complex relationship between an organism and its
medium, referring not only to Darwin but also to Huxley and the leading
European scientific thinkers, as well as to Herbert Spencer's social theory
and his phrase (often wrongly attributed to Darwin) 'the survival of the
fittest'. As to Darwin's cautious embracing of the likelihood that all
species are descended from one or a few originals, Lewes is sceptical.
But he pays tribute throughout to Darwin's 'large and conscientious'
mind, 'wide-sweeping in its circuit and patient in research'.[30] Apart from
Huxley, no other scientific writer dealt with Darwin's theory with such
fairness and knowledge as Lewes in these articles. Darwin had every
reason to be cock-a-hoop. He thanked Lewes in some letters of July
1868, encouraging him to publish the articles as a separate book. If only
Lewes had done so! Parts of the articles were eventually incorporated in
volume iii of *Problems* (*The Physical Basis of Mind*, 1877), but they scarcely
reached a wider audience in that form than they had in the original
Fortnightly Review.

While these articles were appearing, Lewes was gratified to be asked
by Henry Acland to attend the August 1868 meeting of the British
Medical Association at Oxford. Lewes felt that his physiological
researches were now receiving due recognition from the scientific and
medical establishment. In his Christmas journal entry he recorded his
pleasure at the meeting with Darwin as a result of his articles and at his
own progress with the work on *Problems*—'some of the conclusions are
quite novel—may they prove true!' He had the satisfaction, too, of
knowing that all his works 'were translated into Russian, the Physiology

having had two translations', as he was told by a Russian friend of Spencer's.[31]

The Spanish Gypsy was published in May, the sign for the Leweses to disappear to the continent for two months—this time to Germany and Switzerland. Though Lewes and Blackwood had kept up Marian's spirits with praise of the poem (did they *really* think it a successful effort?), she was right to fear that others would not like it as much as the novels. Reviews were on the whole polite, but a nasty one in the *Pall Mall Gazette* had Lewes writing sharply to George Smith in October:

Your sending Mrs. Lewes a remembrance urges me to speak frankly on a subject on which otherwise I should have preferred keeping silence to you as to others; and to explain why such a token of friendliness cannot be received with the same pleasure which many former tokens have given while we are inwardly supposing the giver to have acted in a way which our best judgment pronounces *un*friendly.

The injured tone on Marian's behalf is one Lewes would not have adopted had the attack been on one of his own books. But his protective feelings towards her, and his knowledge that adverse criticism made her threaten to give up writing altogether, caused him to tell Smith that he could no longer write for the *Pall Mall Gazette*. Smith must have replied immediately, for two days later Lewes wrote again, still smarting about the review but saying 'my relations to you are another matter. I am not disposed to give up a friend because of *one* unfriendly manifestation.'[32] Relations with Smith were therefore resumed.

There was, too, a resumption of relations with W. B. Scott, the painter, now returned to London after 20 years of teaching design at Newcastle. He wrote to Lewes in May 1868, and Lewes promised to visit him and his wife in Chelsea. They saw one another occasionally thereafter. Scott remembered that in these meetings 'there was a sort of self-complacent feeling between us of two old fellows who had not stuck in the world, but had made some considerable way since we used to meet in my first studio' off Hampstead Road. Writing up his memories soon after Lewes's death, Scott summed up his view of his friend's career:

At first he was only the clever fellow, but at a very early time he became the literary adept, then the able investigator, and lastly, the scientific thinker and philosopher, one of the most trenchant and advanced minds in the science of this country.[33]

The family news during 1868 had been on the whole good. Lewes visited his mother often, though he seems to have given up visiting Agnes at the end of 1862. In her old age Mrs Willim was becoming increasingly dependent on him. Marian told Cara Bray in October 1868 that their trips abroad, now two or three a year, had to be kept short because Mrs Willim was now 'so aged [81] and fidgetty that she is never long satisfied in her son's absence'.[34] Charles had been promoted at the Post Office in January, and was happy in his marriage, though as yet without a child to replace the first one, which had strangled at birth in September 1866. Thornie and Bertie seemed to be prospering in Natal.[35]

But in March Thornie wrote from their farm, which they had called 'The Falls of the Assagai', a letter light-hearted in tone but containing ominous news. He had consulted a doctor in Pietermaritzburg

as the idea had been gaining on me, that my complaint was not sciatica at all, but something else. Sure enough, tho' the old woman of a doctor could not make out my complaint at all, on my getting hold of a medical book, I soon found out what was the matter, something more serious than sciatica—stone in the kidney.

He was hopeful of curing it homeopathically, and sent a riddle, 'composed by the undersigned, when suffering from an unusually sharp attack: What is the difference between my complaint & the highest form of mathematics? Answer—my complaint is *calculus* of one kidney, & the other is calculus of quite another kidney.' The rest of the letter is cheerful, though a sense of loneliness comes through, despite his having Bertie as a companion. He thanks Lewes for the books on distilling and other farming subjects. Most of the crops have failed this year, he says, but potatoes, peas, and turnips have done well. Bertie has discovered a talent for building, and they are both looking forward to a hunting trip.[36]

Lewes and Marian appear not to have been unduly worried about Thornie. The next letter they received, written on 12 October 1868 but not received until 6 January 1869, therefore gave Lewes a mighty shock. It begins with adventure, speculation, and hopes, but moves to doubt, despair, and a shamefaced request for money. As one reads the letter, one readily imagines the feelings it aroused in Lewes:

Dear Pater

You will doubtless be surprised at not having heard from either of us before, as I promised to write when we came back from our buffalo hunt in the Amaswazi country, but when we came back we heard on the road of a speculation, which had all the elements of success and which if carried out, would have made writing unnecessary. You would have seen me walk into the Priory to communicate viva voce, what this letter must now do. This speculation was as follows . . .

Thornie gives a long, lively account of how the brothers were persuaded to travel to the Amaswazi capital to offer the chief blankets, which they had been told he needed, in return for ivory—an exchange which would have made their fortune. After a long journey and much expense, they found that some other adventurers had got there before them. 'The consequence is', wrote Thornie, 'that instead of having money in our pockets, to enable me to go to England as we had intended, *why*, I will tell you farther on, we are on our last legs':

Our hunting trip was a failure, we had heavy expenses, and the buffalo skins we got fetched literally nothing, and the consequences of the trip: 9 days trekking with the oxen through a country without a mouthful of grass, were that a lot of our oxen died from exhaustion.

He and Bertie urgently needed £200 to buy 'blankets, powder, lead, guns, and provisions for 4 months. If therefore you can oblige us with the loan we shall be very obliged indeed, as it will be a great help, and we will repay it when we come back from our great trip next year.' Then comes the shock:

So much for that: the next I am sorry to say is again a demand for money but of such vital importance that I do not hesitate in applying to you. I had hoped to have been able to come home to England with the proceeds of the trip but 'l'homme propose et Dieu dispose'. The fact is this, that what with this stone in the kidney and other internal complications, for there is something serious besides the stone, I am gradually wasting away. I eat almost nothing, nothing but delicacies tempt me, and those we can't afford. I can't do a stroke of work of any sort, I can hardly stoop to touch the ground, I can't sit up for half an hour, all I can do is lie down, then get up and walk about for half an hour, then lie down again. Every evening about sundown when the paroxysms come on, I can hardly turn myself over, and if I want to sit up, I must push myself up with my hands, from my shoulder blades downwards I am powerless; and I have a sort of shooting compression of the chest, which makes breathing difficult, and makes me shout with pain. And as this lasts usually for 2 to 3 hours, and sometimes there is more or less pain all night long, so that I can get no sleep, and sometimes I have slight attacks in the day time—you can fancy that my life is not a pleasant one. In fact if I were 50 instead of 24, I should have quietly walked some fine day over our waterfall; but while there is youth there is hope; and I hope and trust that a trip to England, to consult one or two of the best doctors may do me good . . . I know this trip, seeing physicians etc., perhaps undergoing some operation will cost a great deal of money, but—que voulez vous. It is my last chance in life, and you are the only person I can apply to, so I don't hesitate to make the application. . . .

Hoping to hear from you at once, with love to Mutter [i.e. Marian], Grandmamma and everybody else, I remain, Dear Pater

Your affectionate Son
Thornton A. Lewes.

Lewes noted in his diary, 'Letter from Thornie made me very miserable. Went into the city to send him £250.' To Blackwood Lewes wrote simply, 'The vision of him haunts me incessantly.'[37]

Thornie was expected to arrive home in June or July 1869. Meanwhile, Lewes tried to get on with his work on *Problems* and Marian with her new novel of English life—how Blackwood's heart must have leapt when he heard in February that she had started one![38] Mrs Willim became ill at the end of January, and Lewes visited her almost every day. By the end of February she was sufficiently recovered for them to feel that they could go to Italy. They stayed with Tom Trollope in Florence, then went on to Naples and Rome. The weather was poor; Lewes was often ill; their spirits were low. By 5 May they were home again, not much the better for this trip.

Three days later they came home from visiting Mrs Willim to find that Thornie had arrived home unexpectedly early. 'Dreadfully shocked to see him so worn', wrote Lewes in his diary. When Charles first saw his brother on 1 June—he and Gertrude were abroad when Thornie arrived and Lewes did not tell them how bad he was—he was so shocked that he fainted.[39] Thornie was at first cheerful, but the very day after his return, Sunday 9 May, he had a 'dreadful day' of rolling on the floor in agony.

Some American friends, not knowing of the domestic crisis, called that afternoon to enjoy one of the regular Priory gatherings. Among them was Henry James, only one year older than Thornie himself (and, like Thornie and Charles, educated in Switzerland), calling to meet for the first time the famous writer whose works he admired and on whom he had already written some critical articles. For James the occasion was momentous; he later devoted several pages of his *Autobiography* to an account of the odd turn of events from an expected audience with a great writer to a domestic crisis in which he played his small part, cherishing, as he says, 'for the rest of the day the particular quality of my vibration'. Lewes had to rush out to find a chemist who was open on a Sunday to dispense a drug for Thornie's pain. Meanwhile, as James describes it, he continued his small talk with Marian for a while, then offered to take a cab to fetch James Paget, the Leweses' doctor; he did so, only to find that after 'crawling' to Hanover Square—'or was it Cavendish?'—the doctor was not at home.[40] Lewes's diary makes no mention of James's visit, merely recounting Thornie's terrible pain and the arrival of Paget that evening.

For the next five months Thornie veered between cheerfulness and hysteria, temporary absence of suffering and the return of excruciating pain only controllable by frequent doses of morphia. Lewes and Marian nursed him day and night, with Lewes often getting up four times in the night to administer morphia. They hired a nurse to help, but still gave as much time as they could to Thornie. The family rallied round, with Charles and Gertrude relieving their parents occasionally to let them go to the country for a day or two. Susanna and Thornie's cousin Vivian came to sit with him. So did Barbara Bodichon, who was in London, and Owen Jones, who had known Thornie since he was a child. On 18 May Thornie's condition was so bad that Agnes was called for. She stayed for two-and-a-half hours. On the whole, Thornie kept cheerful, but he became hysterical when in severe pain; Lewes noted on 29 May that Thornie's shrieks in the night made him feel sick. On 4 June he wrote, 'I had a severe shock last night, suddenly awakened by the nurse calling me to give Thornie morphia. It seemed to ice my heart; & I was a long while getting over it.'[41]

Lewes kept Agnes informed by letter. On 8 August Thornie became hysterical, 'unable to pass his urine, very flatulent'. As Paget was away, Sir Henry Holland was consulted. Both doctors were rather baffled. Paget, who visited again on 27 September, 'could form no idea of Thornie's disease. "Watch & wait".' By 11 October Paget was confirming Lewes's suspicion that Thornie was 'drifting away'. Lewes wrote to Agnes on 17 and again on 18 October. Next day Thornie 'did not seem to know me this morning. Died at 7 this evening.'[42] Thornie had had Heine's terrible disease, tuberculosis of the spine.

Marian confessed to friends that she had not been so close to death since her father died 20 years before. She had felt almost a mother's love for Thornie, who, she noted in her journal on the day of his death, was 'still a boy though he had lived for 25 years and a half'.[43] Thornie was buried in Highgate Cemetery, after which the exhausted parents went to the country to try to recover. Lewes's journal for 1 January 1870 records the past year as 'a wasted and painful one', but writes of the 'deepening love' sustaining him and Marian. 'No money earned this year at all, except £20 from the Dramatic Authors Society. Such work as I have done has been solely relating to the "Problems of Life & Mind".'[44]

Lewes himself was now ill again. He fainted in bed on 17 February 1870, and became nervously exhausted after 'even an hour & a half's writing'.[45] As usual when illness overcame him at home, he took the drastic measure of travelling abroad. They went to Germany in March. Shortly before leaving they had Dickens to lunch. He told them a 'fine story of Lincoln's *dream*', and said he had given up the public readings of his novels 'on a warning as to his nervous condition'.[46] It was the last time they would see Dickens; he died, worn out, on 10 June 1870.

In Berlin they met old and new friends, including the American Ambassador to Germany, George Bancroft, the historian Theodor Mommsen, Emil Du Bois Reymond the physiologist, as well as assorted members of the Prussian royal family. Knowing his mother's pride in him and her enjoyment of royal stories, Lewes wrote to her cheerfully on 28 March, giving news of the lionizing he and Marian were enjoying:

Dearest Mother

If your son comes back 'with his head where his tail ought to be' you must not be surprised; in any case you must expect him to have his head *turned* from all the flattery and attention which is momently paid him here. After writing to you on Tuesday, I went to the University Festival of which I spoke, and there found myself seated apart from the public among the Princes, Professors, Ambassadors, and persons covered with stars and decorations. The American Ambassador and myself were the only *un*decorated persons there—as Talleyrand said of Castlereagh at the Congress of Vienna 'the absence of decoration was a distinction'. Several of the potentates in science came up and were introduced to me and began compliments.[47]

Lewes spent his days visiting hospitals, lunatic asylums, and laboratories. In the evenings they attended parties and went to the opera. As in 1854, they tried Wagner, hearing *Tannhäuser*; as in 1854, they decided that 'Wagner's music is not for us.'[48] Marian had written in *Fraser's* in July 1855 in an article on Liszt, Wagner, and Weimar, how she missed in *Lohengrin* the melody her ear required: 'We are but in "the morning of the times", and must learn to think of ourselves as tadpoles unprescient of the future frog. Still the tadpole is limited to tadpole pleasures; and so, in our state of development, we are swayed by melody.'[49] Sixteen years on they were still arrested in the tadpole stage of development with regard to Wagner's music.

In April they moved on to Vienna, where they were met by Lewes's old friend Robert Lytton, then home to find, as Lewes told Lytton in a letter of 9 May, 'a heap of some 60 letters' waiting:

Somebody I have heard of used only to answer his letters once a fortnight on the ground that in the interim the majority answered themselves. *Mine* don't—d – – n their souls!—My plan is to make literary sandwiches, namely between two tiresome or uninteresting letters to insert one which has either friendship or interest to give it flavour—(*this* letter is a slice of ham, with mustard).[50]

After ceasing to entertain or go out while they had been nursing Thornie, they now resumed their Sunday afternoons at The Priory. A few favoured friends, among them Spencer, Pigott, and Barbara Bodichon when she was in England, would be invited to lunch; in the afternoon there was open house for their larger circle of friends, many of whom would bring a guest to meet George Eliot. This was how Henry James had come on the fateful Sunday a year previously, being a guest of his fellow Americans, Charles Eliot Norton and his wife. By 1870 notable changes had taken place in 'society's' attitude towards George Eliot. Whereas in the early 1860s Bessie Rayner Parkes had had to deceive her parents in order to visit Marian, and when men visited they came without their wives, the people who turned up now were as likely to be women as men. They were also as likely to be members of the liberal and intellectual aristocracy—the Amberleys and the Russells, Lord and Lady Houghton—as the intellectual middle class. Though Marian still shrank from her novel-reading public, and still had her mail and the critical reviews of her works censored for her by Lewes, she now sometimes dined out and went to public places more than she had done in the early years of her life with Lewes.

The Leweses' gatherings became famous. Dozens of Victorians who were lucky enough to be invited or to go along with friends remembered their visits in memoirs written, for the most part, long after both Lewes and Marian were dead. Some of them were unable to resist the temptation to metaphor offered by the fact that the Leweses lived in a house called The Priory, had their gatherings on Sunday, and attracted a varied group of lay 'worshippers' of George Eliot's genius. Needless to say, many of those who later ridiculed the process of being ushered into the temple of the goddess by her devoted high priest had themselves been devout worshippers once. Among these were the minor poet Robert Buchanan, whom Lewes praised in the *Fortnightly*, the artists P. G. Hamerton and Rudolf Lehmann, the journalist T. H. S. Escott, the distinguished critic Sidney Colvin, and various American visitors, including the Nortons.[51]

Indeed, Charles Eliot Norton was one of the Priory visitors who sometimes changed the metaphor from church to stage. He described to a friend in 1869 his first visit to the house, 'a little, square, two storey dwelling standing in a half garden, surrounded with one of those high brick walls of which one grows so impatient in England':

Lewes received us at the door with characteristic animation; he looks and moves like an old-fashioned French barber or dancing-master, very ugly, very vivacious, very entertaining. You expect to see him take up his fiddle and begin to play.

Most famously of all, and much later, Meredith told Leslie Stephen àpropos of the latter's book on George Eliot in the English Men (!) of Letters series:

I could not have refrained from touches on the comic scene of the Priory—with the dais, and the mercurial little showman, and the Bishops about the feet of an erratic woman worshipped as a literary idol and light of philosophy. No stage has had anything so poignant for satire.[52]

Funny as this is, it is a little treacherous to old friends to whom he owed a debt of gratitude: to Lewes for encouraging his contributions to the *Fortnightly* and for suggesting Hofwyl for his son, and to Marian for setting a novelistic example he was eager to follow.

Though it is undoubtedly true that Marian became increasingly dependent on the reverence of her visitors, particularly that of a group of younger women who threw themselves at her feet—Edith Simcox, Elma Stuart, Georgiana Burne-Jones—Lewes kept some part of his old sense of the ridiculous at the same time as he unashamedly encouraged this serious adoration of his wife. To Lord Houghton he wrote in February 1872, 'That "Sunday Services for the People" (pleasant people!) are held at the Priory has not, we hope, been wholly forgotten by one whose "voice may have grown hoarse with singing of Anthems", but whose wit made very good incense!'[53]

Witty, sceptical, tough, and unfussy as Lewes was, he knew that the woman he loved was morbidly sensitive about her work and her social position; when the need seemed to him to arise, he gladly sacrificed his scepticism for the sake of bolstering her confidence. Not that Marian herself lacked humour, even humour directed against herself. Her novels are proof enough, but so also are her letters, in which her humour tends to take a self-scourging, inward, negative turn. When writing to old friends like Sara Hennell and Cara Bray, or to her closest friend Barbara Bodichon, she habitually referred to her anxieties with a wry laugh at the egotism which underlay them. But all the more because she recognized this trait in herself did she need Lewes to foster the sentiment and adoration of others towards her.

It was under these conditions that Marian accepted and Lewes promoted the attentions of the young Scot, Alexander Main, who asked in 1871 to be allowed to publish a selection of sayings from George Eliot's works. Blackwood diplomatically acquiesced in the publication of Main's *Wise, Witty, and Tender Sayings of George Eliot* (1872), though privately he described Main as 'the Worshipper of Genius' and 'the Gusher'.[54] As always, Blackwood knew how to soothe and flatter his diffident author, believing that was the way to get the best out of her. His judgement was rewarded with the appearance in eight parts of *Middlemarch* during 1871 and 1872, of which he wrote when he had seen only two portions, 'It is a most wonderful study of human life and nature. You are like a great giant walking among us.'[55] The publication in half-volume parts at 5*s*. each was Lewes's idea, formed in May 1871 when it became clear that two stories on which Marian was working, 'Miss Brooke' and 'Middlemarch', had come together and would make a long novel. Lewes and Blackwood agreed that it would be a good idea to 'circumvent the Libraries and make the public *buy* instead of borrowing'. Lewes got the idea, he said, from Victor Hugo's method of publishing *Les Misérables*.[56]

Middlemarch took a long time to write and caused Marian more than her usual share of despair. Lewes told Blackwood in February 1872, when she was half-way through the writing:

Your letters always welcome and generally cheering could not have come at a time when they were more needed; for partly from health and this damp damnable weather, she is in one of her most depressed moods. Reading 'Felix Holt' the other morning made her *thin* with misery, so deeply impressed was she with the fact that she could never write like that again and that what is now in hand is rinsings of the cask! How battle against such an art of ingeniously self tormenting?[57]

Mrs Willim, whom Lewes had continued to visit frequently in St John's Wood, died unexpectedly and calmly in her chair on 10 December 1870. As Marian told Sara Hennell, she was 83 and ready to 'go to rest, so that this death has none of the bitterness that belonged to the parting with Thornie'.[58] Lewes had been a dutiful and loving son, aware of his importance to her as her only surviving child after 1855. In a rare confessional moment he told Main in 1873 about his relationship with his mother:

For some years my mother used to watch for my visits like a girl watching for her lover: she would sit at the window for hours before my regular time, and with the first glimpse of my 'wide-awake' in the distance she would exclaim to her maid 'There he is'—and be happy for the rest of the day. You can imagine how I look back on those days and what a comfort it is to me to think that I never allowed other attractions to rob her of her one remaining joy. My father died when I was two years old, and with my mother were bound up all my early recollections. We lived together till I married. Her belief in me, and pride in me, you may estimate when I tell you that secretly she thought not of what a prize I had secured, but of the prize Dorothea [i.e. Marian] had secured![59]

It seems from this, Lewes's only surviving reference to his father, that his mother kept the secret of her relationship with John Lee Lewes, carrying it to the grave with her. Lewes clearly took great pleasure in remembering his mother's love for him.

During 1871 they came to have reason to worry about Bertie. His infrequent letters, arriving three months after they were written, tell of his engagement in August 1870 to Eliza Harrison, the daughter of an English settler in Natal, and his marriage to her in May 1871. But they also tell of Mr Harrison's opposition to the match, 'because I am poor'; of her leaving home and marrying him in spite of her father; of his moving from the Falls of the Assagai to a farm less deep in the bush and therefore safer for his wife; of being cheated by the vendor of the new farm; of losing many of his 130 sheep; and of generally finding life hard. Lewes had sent him £200 on hearing he was to be married; thanking him, Bertie wrote, 'I hope I shall make better use of it than the money I have had before.'[60] Bertie's letters are dutiful but distant. He seems awed by his parents, and not at all close to them. Marian he hardly knew, of course, and even Lewes had been a rather distant and intermittent figure since he was a child of eight. Of the three sons he had stayed longest at Bedford Place with Agnes. Then came Hofwyl, followed by farming in Scotland and the Midlands, and finally Natal. He cannot have spent many days of his young life with his father and 'mother'. Perhaps his letters to Agnes—lost, of course—would have shown him in a more intimate light.

In 1870 Lewes published nothing except a few scientific letters to a new periodical, *Nature*, and he earned nothing. Early in 1871 a fourth edition of the *History of Philosophy* appeared, for which he was paid £150 by Longman. Lewes revised it again, adding material on Hegel, whose philosophy was enjoying a vogue in Oxford and on whom J. H. Stirling had recently published *The Secret of Hegel* (1865), a book Lewes described as 'even less intelligible than Hegel'.[61] Otherwise, Lewes was carrying on with his study of psychology, learning maths to help with his work, and feeling cheerful. To Mrs Cross, whose son John was now a close friend, he wrote in the teasing, familiar manner for which he was so well known:

Mrs. Lewes is decidedly stronger and has got rid of her *tic*; but she is still not flourishing as she could, should, might, ought to be. But then you women are so unreasoning and unreasonable! The Saturday Review says so—and it must know. You, for instance, whom we had almost learned to regard as a judicious woman—could any thing be more irrational, misplaced, intempestive, *a crosstic*—than your taking to yourself a Bronchitis. . . . Now look at me—a male and rational animal—see how I brown here like a well fried sole—how I 'put on flesh' like a prize pig (of the Breton sort, I regret to say, that is rather lanky, all ribs and ears)—how I digest (when I can get the food) and work at mathematics as if I were going in for honors. You don't see any injudiciousness in me. *I* don't coquette with Bronchitis or any other itis. I say unto them 'get thee behind me; or visit some less rational party'. Make me your model and it will be well with you![62]

This was written from Haslemere, where the Leweses spent the summer of 1871 while alterations were being carried out at home. They were also escaping once more from their hectic social life in London. In April they had entertained Turgenev, whom Lewes had known in Berlin in 1839, and Pauline Viardot, the famous soprano (whose much older husband tolerated her relationship with Turgenev), as well as their usual guests. They had met Jenny Lind at a matinee and heard Adelina Patti sing *La Sonnambula* at Covent Garden. They even contemplated accepting an invitation to attend the centenary celebrations for Sir Walter Scott in Edinburgh in August, though in the end Marian's suffering from a sudden intestinal illness forced them to cancel.[63]

Lewes made an exception to his habit of not writing articles, particularly literary ones, when Forster's *Life of Dickens* began to appear, the first of three volumes being published in December 1871 (though dated 1872). Forster, who had acted as Dickens's agent and legal adviser—and whom Dickens had caricatured as Podsnap, the self-important 'gent' in *Our Mutual Friend*, also characterizing him to friends as 'the Mogul'—produced his biography without referring for help, as was the custom, to others who had known Dickens well. At a *Punch* dinner on 7 December 1871 all the talk was of volume i and the obtrusive way in which Forster indicated his own importance in Dickens's life. Lewes was there, and so was Wilkie Collins. *Punch*'s editor, Shirley Brooks, noted in his diary that after most people had gone home, 'Collins & Lewes stayed till 12. Forster & Dickens talked of—they call it "Life of J. F. with notices of C. D.".' Lewes was seized by a desire to write about Dickens, but not, he assured John Morley, in the form of a review of Forster's *Life*.[64]

The article came out in the *Fortnightly* in February 1872. Entitled 'Dickens in Relation to Criticism', it is an interesting piece of work. It incensed Forster, who subsequently attacked Lewes savagely in the third volume of the biography. Some Dickens scholars and critics still describe Lewes's article, as Forster did, as a slur on Dickens as man and writer. On the other hand, Trollope took Lewes's part in the row with Forster, defending Lewes's essay as 'the best analysis we have yet had of the genius of that wonderful man'.[65]

Lewes opens with general reflections on the relationship between authors and their critics, complaining of the penchant shown by many critics to 'pronounce absolute verdicts' where really they are expressing personal taste. Though this leads on to a discussion of Dickens and his critics (unnamed) it is hard not to see in Lewes's uncharacteristic sensitivity on behalf of authors some expression of feelings which he found close to home. Both here and later in the article, when he dwells, while protesting his admiration for Dickens's genius, on Dickens's faults and omissions, there is reason to think that foremost in his mind is the genius of George Eliot. Even as he wrote the article, Marian was deep in the writing of *Middlemarch*, describing in wonderful detail—emotional, psychological, social, even physiological—the progress of the unhappy marriages of Dorothea and Casaubon and Lydgate and Rosamond. How could Lewes avoid judging other novelists by the standard he saw his remarkable wife setting for the English novel as an imaginative expression of psychological realism? He nowhere mentions George Eliot, but it is noticeable that he finds Dickens lacking in the very qualities she has in abundance:

The writer presents an almost unique example of a mind of singular force in which, so to speak, sensations never passed into ideas. Dickens sees and feels, but the logic of feeling seems the only logic he can manage. Thought is strangely absent from his works. I do not suppose a single thoughtful remark on life or character could be found throughout the twenty volumes. Not only is there a marked absence of the reflective tendency, but one sees no indication of the past life of humanity having ever occupied him; keenly as he observes the objects before him, he never connects his observations into a general expression, never seems interested in general relations of things.[66]

This reads, inside out, as it were, like the analysis of George Eliot's genius Lewes would have written if he had ever put pen to paper directly on that subject.

Yet Lewes began the article with the avowed intention of *defending* Dickens against criticisms of his exaggeration, vulgarity, and so on; or at least of explaining how those who criticize Dickens are nevertheless likely to be bowled over by his marvellous power. And here another of Lewes's own enthusiasms—obsessions even—finds expression, somewhat to Dickens's disadvantage. Lewes's studies for the past several years had been into curious psychological phenomena and their basis in physiological conditions. With German professors, English scientists, with Dickens himself shortly before his death, Lewes had discussed dreams and psychological curiosities. He recounts in the article two of

Dickens's dreams as told to him, and their relation to the waking life. And he suggests that the solution to the puzzle of Dickens's genius is that he possessed a 'vividness of imagination approaching closely to hallucination'. Though Lewes is at pains to assure readers that he 'never observed any trace of the insane temperament in Dickens's works, or life', he finds in Dickens's unusual faculty for *seeing* and *hearing* his characters in vivid detail the key to appreciating the power of his novels.[67]

It is an intelligent analysis of Dickens's genius, readily acceptable to modern readers made aware by Freud of the potency of dreams in the mental economy of all of us. But Lewes, while laying bare an undeniable element in Dickens's greatness, takes an example from his recent physiological researches which he should have known would have an unfortunate effect. Talking of Micawber's 'always presenting himself in the same situation, moved with the same springs, and uttering the same sounds, always confident on something turning up, always crushed and rebounding, always making punch', Lewes says he is reminded 'of the frogs whose brains have been taken out for physiological purposes, and whose actions henceforth want the distinctive peculiarity of organic action, that of fluctuating spontaneity':

It is the complexity of the organism which Dickens wholly fails to conceive; his characters have nothing fluctuating and incalculable in them, even when they embody true observations; and very often they are creations so fantastic that one is at a loss to understand how he could, without hallucination, believe them to be like reality.[68]

It is hardly surprising that this article, which was undoubtedly one of the most insightful studies of Dickens, should have raised Forster's hackles. He made rather too much of it in volume iii of his biography, which came out in February 1874. Despite Lewes's careful protestations, Forster paraphrases his argument as being that Dickens's imagination was 'merely hallucinative'. He quotes the trenchant passage about the brainless frogs, and, wittily enough, asserts that 'since Trinculo and Caliban were under one cloak, there has been no such delicate monster with two voices', the forward voice speaking well of his friend, the backward uttering foul speeches and detracting.[69] Though excessive, this verdict is not without truth. Lewes seems indeed to have been in two minds when writing his piece.

He was stung by Forster's reply. Trollope, who helped him to write a letter to Forster (now lost), remembered in his obituary article that Lewes was 'greatly hurt' by Forster's attack. 'On behalf of Lewes I find myself bound to say that his was the simple expression of his critical intellect dealing with the work of a man he loved and admired,—work which he thought worthy of the thoughtful analysis which he applied to it.'[70] On the whole I agree with Trollope, though I think Lewes's article was in fact one of the *least* simple expressions of his critical intellect, being, whether he knew it or not, both a literary application of his recent psychological researches and an indirect celebration of George Eliot's genius, so different in kind from Dickens's.

After this foray into the old field of literary criticism, Lewes quickly returned to his scientific labours. He signed himself in a letter to Spencer about this time 'The Problematical Thinker'. And he was so bound up in the progress of *Middlemarch* that he took to identifying himself with the dryasdust scholar Casaubon, and referring to *Problems* (alas, not entirely inappropriately) as his 'Key to all Psychologies'—a pun on Casaubon's unfinished life's work, 'The Key to all Mythologies'. He even made a prophetic joke to Blackwood in July 1872: 'The shadow of old Casaubon hangs over me and I fear my "Key to all Psychologies" will have to be left to Dorothea!'[71] His Dorothea, however, was quick to point out, in reply to a naïve question from Harriet Beecher Stowe, that Casaubon was *not* drawn from Lewes, adding one of those ironic, self-knowing remarks of hers:

Impossible to conceive any creature less like Mr. Casaubon than my warm, enthusiastic husband, who cares much more for my doing than for his own, and is a miracle of freedom from all author's jealousy and all suspicion. I fear that the Casaubon tints are not quite foreign to my own mental complexion.[72]

By November 1872, with *Middlemarch* finished and winning golden opinions—Blackwood told her on 31 December that the publication of the novel would be one of the events by which 1872 would be remembered—Marian and Lewes reversed their usual roles. She became his reader and encourager, suffering, as Lewes cheerfully told Blackwood, '(silently, as Mrs. Casaubon would) under an oppression of marital m.s. with no permission to "omit the second excursus on Crete"'—an allusion to Casaubon's instruction to Dorothea when she is reading aloud his manuscript to him in the middle of the night.[73]

The plan was for Blackwood to publish *Problems* one volume at a time. Lewes offered him the first volume in January 1873. Blackwood replied warmly, agreeing to the half-profits system, and joking that 'if the lamented Casaubon had written it I should have insisted on his publishing at his own risk'. But he was confident of Lewes's proven ability to write clearly and interestingly on any scientific or philosophical subject, and agreed to publish it without having seen any of it, though Lewes had warned him that he might object on religious grounds to some of the material. Blackwood brushed aside the warning, assuring Lewes that he could 'not imagine the cause of real religion being injured by any amount of free and fair discussion such as yours is sure to be'.[74] Lewes asked Blackwood to get Professor Tait, mathematician and physicist at Edinburgh University, to look over the proofs, casting an eye over the 'mathematical & physical illustrations to see if they are correct' and making sure nothing Lewes says would 'make the mathematicians wince'. Tait should be severe—'it is correction I hunger for' and 'the harder he hits the more I shall rub my hands & say "frappy Monsieur, frappy toujours".' Tait took Lewes at his word, marking points of disagreement and telling Blackwood, 'I found it pretty stiff reading, far worse than double its amount of analytical formulae: but it is very interesting indeed, and will thoroughly rile the so-called Metaphysicians.'[75]

It riled Blackwood too. It took him until 24 May 1873, when the volume was already being printed, to work up courage to tell Lewes how much the book 'grated' on him. He objected to Lewes's 'assumption on page 2 that those are the most weighty thinkers who believe that the world would be better without religion', and disliked the tone of an anecdote about 'the Author of Creation'. Lewes, as always, rose to the unpleasant occasion. Though annoyed that Blackwood had not spoken up earlier, he accepted without rancour the termination of the agreement—'treat it as if it had never been'. He invited Blackwood, who was in London, to come and visit at The Priory without embarrassment. But he denied the specific charges made by Blackwood, who, he thought, must have misunderstood his tone because he had 'started with a preconception'.[76] Lewes wasted no time. On 25 May he saw Nikolaus Trübner and arranged to transfer publication of *Problems* to him. It was early in 1874 before volume i, *The Foundations of a Creed*, was finally published.

In the meantime Marian enjoyed, in her doubting way, the greatest success she had ever had with a novel. *Middlemarch* ousted even *Adam Bede* as the favourite George Eliot book of readers and critics. Letters of praise flowed in from old and new friends; Lewes was kept busy answering them, sometimes merely politely, occasionally more welcomingly. John Cross—'nephew Johnny'—invested the proceeds from *Middlemarch* in American railway stock in January 1873. By the end of the year the Leweses were hiring a carriage, with 'man, horse, harness, and stabling', for £140 per annum.[77]

Family news was mixed. Charles and Gertrude had had a child, Blanche, born safely in July 1872, nearly six years after their first baby had died at birth. Bertie's wife Eliza also bore a daughter, named Marian, in December 1872. But Bertie's letters were few and brief. He was not doing well financially; when he wrote in October 1873 to thank Lewes for £50 sent to buy a piano, he told his father in his offhand way that he was suffering from neuralgia in his back and hips, could not sleep at night for the pain, and had 'got quite a skeleton'.[78] Except for the difference in tone, the letter reminds one of Thornie's fateful one five years earlier. In less than two years Bertie too was dead, just a few days short of his twenty-ninth birthday. Lewes's diaries contain no hint that he was afraid his youngest son would not live much longer in the hard conditions of Africa.

July and August 1873 saw the Leweses abroad again, travelling without a specific plan in France and Germany. Marian was in the early stages of her research for *Daniel Deronda*. At Frankfurt they bought books on Jewish subjects and saw round the synagogue (which Daniel was to visit in his search for Jewish relations). Lewes was ill again, suffering from deafness and earache. On their return home, they heard of the death on 25 June of Thornton Hunt. The leader-writing machine had worked himself to death; as Carlyle, who had hardly seen him since the end of the *Leader* days, eloquently expressed it, Thornton had been 'given up to *Journalism* this long while past'.[79] Always improvident, somewhat complaining, yet working manically to earn by his 'treadmill life' enough to keep his large family, Thornton died at the age of 62, leaving no will. Administration of his estate, valued at less than £1,000, was granted to his widow in September 1873.[80]

As Agnes held an insurance policy on Thornton's life, Lewes met her in August, and again in October, to visit the insurance office and claim her money, which she received on 3 November. Lewes, however, did not give up his contributions towards her and the children. His cash accounts in the diaries show that he continued his regular payments to Agnes and gave occasional gifts of money to the children. Edmund, now 25, received over £100 in 1875, perhaps to help him set up his dental practice. Rose, Ethel, and Mildred were given the odd £10 or £20, and their cousin Vivian also received financial assistance with his chemistry studies at London University. In April Lewes transferred £1,800 in stocks and shares to Vivian's name, probably as a twenty-first birthday present.[81] Of course, Lewes's generosity no longer represented a financial sacrifice; his later diaries contain pages listing the returns on the investment of Marian's considerable income. Nevertheless, his unrepining temperament is admirably demonstrated in these gifts, by which children not his own benefited more than his sons had done.

Bertie, however, received generous help with his farming and family needs. Eliza expected a second child in May 1875. On 8 August Lewes's diary records, in the laconic manner of his descriptions of disaster, 'News came of *Bertie's Death*. 29th June. Aged 29.'[82] Bertie's last two brief letters were written on 17 May and 24 June from Durban, where he had gone to seek medical help. His childhood glandular disease had returned, his weight was down, he had mumps and 'Natal sores' (a kind of boil), but was cheered at hearing from Eliza of the birth of their second child, George Herbert, on 16 May.[83] Bertie never saw this child. He died in Durban of an attack of bronchitis, leaving his young wife nearly penniless with her two infants, touchingly called after Lewes and Marian. The Durban newspaper editor John Sanderson wrote on 2 July with news of Bertie's death. Mrs Sanderson added her memories of seeing Thornie and Bertie for the first time in 1866, and went on to describe the sad decline of both young men. Her letter contains one of the few verbal protraits we have of Bertie, and it is of interest both for that reason and for the comparison and contrast she draws between the two brothers:

The last time we had seen him, previous to his last sad visit, was in '66 when Thornton and he dined and slept at Bishopstown where Mr. Sanderson and I were staying at the time—they were both full of life and energy then and we were particularly struck by Herbert's good sense and quiet cheerfulness, which contrasted well with but did not spoil Thornton's gay, good natured, winning manner; you can understand how shocked we were when the latter came down here evidently in the last stages of his fatal disease; he came in to our house, looking like the ghost of his former self, quite suddenly one day and I shall never forget the shock it gave me, but when a few short weeks ago the same thing happened with Herbert I was almost too much overpowered to greet him; he was very cheerful and hopeful about himself and as he said that he had gained flesh since he came down I tried to hope that he was not so bad as he appeared to be. . . . his last visit will ever be one of my saddest recollections; he was so much exhausted when he came in that he fell into a deep sleep while sitting in an easy chair . . .[84]

Charles wanted to go to Natal to bring Eliza and the children to England, but Lewes thought it better to wait. He sent Eliza money, and she began writing shy, confiding letters about the children's progress. She eventually came to England in 1879, after Lewes's death, and became rather a burden on Marian and Charles, who did not take to her, though they did everything they could to help her financially. Marian told Blackwood of this new financial responsibility more than a year after

Bertie's death, in explanation of what seemed like greed on her part in querying his offer of £4,000 for a further ten years' lease on her works. She spoke of the entire dependence of Eliza and the children on her and Lewes. 'We told hardly anyone at the time (because Mr. Lewes dreaded letters of condolence).'[85] Only Barbara Bodichon and Johnny Cross were told immediately. Marian gave expression in a letter to Cross on 14 August 1875 to their sorrow (and guilt):

He was a sweet-natured creature—not clever, but diligent and well-judging about the things of daily life, and we felt ten years ago that a colony with a fine climate, like Natal, offered him the only fair prospect within his reach. What can we do more than try to arrive at the best conclusion from the conditions as they are known to us?[86]

Now only Charles was left. He was thriving, as Marian had told Blackwood in November 1874:

He is the father of two children, wears spectacles, and has just been appointed head of a department in the P.O. with twenty men under his direction. And it seems to us but the other day when we brought him from Hofwyl looking like a crude German lad of seventeen. He is not, thank Heaven, a literary dabbler, but he sometimes writes on practical questions that interest him.[87]

Charles had recently published an article in the *Edinburgh Review* supporting reform in the education of girls. He was also the translator of various German works, including Lessing's play, *Emilia Galotti*, in 1867, and a life of Bismarck in 1869. In the 1880s he campaigned with his sister-in-law Octavia Hill (one of the founders of the National Trust) to save Parliament Hill Fields from development; he was also one of the first members of the London County Council in 1889. Not only did he thus become a minor public figure of liberal social and political views; he was to prove as generous and unselfish as his father when Marian needed sympathy and practical help after Lewes's death. Marian's remark to Sara Hennell in November 1875 that though Charles was well, 'the boys seem all to have inherited an untrustworthy physique',[88] was borne out when Charles became ill in his mid-forties, retired early from the Post Office, and died in 1891 in Egypt, where he had gone on doctor's orders.

Another sad event occurred in May 1875—sad and bizarre. The *Daily News* announced on 12 May that there had been an incident at the London Library the previous day:

On some person entering the magazine room, a gentleman was discovered lying on the floor with a pistol by his side. The apparently lifeless body was recognized as that of Mr. Leigh Hunt [Bryan Courthope Leigh Hunt, born in 1852], a son of Mr. Thornton Hunt . . .

Bryan Hunt had failed to find regular employment, and felt he was a burden to his family. One wonders if there is any significance in the fact, noted by the assistant librarian and also by Lewes in his diary when he heard the news a week later, that the book Hunt had borrowed and was returning to the library was volume i of *Problems of Life and Mind*.[89]

Lewes himself was becoming thinner and feebler. To his old symptoms of headache and dyspepsia were added attacks of lumbago, and in December 1875 he had intimations of mortality: 'After dinner while dozing in my chair', he wrote in his diary on 14 December, 'felt a strange pressure inside the ears accompanied by inability to move or speak. Thought paralysis had come on or Death.'[90] But there was still work to do. In January 1875 he had been visited by George Croom Robertson of University College London, who wanted to discuss the setting up of a new review of psychology. Lewes 'battered his brain till it [was] sore' to think of a title.[91] The periodical was called *Mind*, and its first number appeared in January 1876. Lewes contributed to it, offering his articles and reviews for nothing. He was pleased to be involved in the project, since his own interests lay so close to the aims of its founders— Robertson, Bain, and Sully—now that he was at last bringing out his five volumes of physiological psychology, *Problems of Life and Mind*.

13

The Problematical Thinker
(1874–1878)

BRINGING out *Problems* was itself not achieved without problems. Volume i appeared at the beginning of 1874, and Marian marvelled at her husband's calmness as publication day approached, so different from her own panic and depression on these occasions. She told their medical friend Thomas Clifford Allbutt that Lewes 'is calmly certain that very few will care about its discussions. No human being can be more happily constituted than he in relation to his work. He has quite an exceptional enjoyment in the doing, and has no irritable anxieties about it when done.'[1] This was true in the relative perspective of her own feelings on completing a book, but not true absolutely. Actually Lewes cared very much about the reception of *Problems*. Changing the successful habits of a lifetime, during which he had seized on a subject, studied it rapidly, and written brightly and boldly in less time than it takes most people to acquaint themselves with a new topic, he had now spent years amassing information, stuffing notebooks full of psychological case histories, holding off the writing to the last possible moment. In May 1873 Marian had told Benjamin Jowett that Lewes was busy 'pruning his too abundant manuscript'.[2] These were new signs, and they were in a sense ominous.

Of course, Lewes had got tired of hopping from one subject to another, and tired of being decried in some quarters as a jack-of-all-trades, a mere popularizer. Successive editions of the *History of Philosophy* chart his movement away from the popular towards the serious and scholarly mode of writing. While acknowledging that the book had been able to reach its second, third, and fourth editions (in 1857, 1867, and 1871 respectively) precisely because of its huge success in the original form of 1845–6, Lewes nevertheless claimed in his prefaces that he was aiming not only to add new material to take account of newly available information, but also to reach a more discriminating audience. Hence the dropping in 1867 of the word 'Biographical' from the title; hence the addition of a more serious discussion of Kant and Hegel in 1871—though Lewes had not changed his views on these philosophers. He simply felt that their systems were complex enough, and by the 1870s influential enough—particularly through the interest taken in them by the Oxford philosophers T. H. Green, Edward Caird, and William Wallace—to merit more than cursory discussion.[3]

Perhaps Lewes's becoming more circumspect about his writing and his reputation was a natural result of his reaching middle age and beyond and wishing to make his mark before he died. (Both he and Marian talked frequently in their letters and diaries now of their enduring happiness in one another's company, clouded only by the fear of their own, or—worse—the other's death.) But it may be that even so strong and positive a personality as Lewes's was showing signs of erosion by the pride and self-doubt—and the success—of the great writer at his side. However it came about, this change in Lewes meant, as his friends and his not-so-friendly scientific acquaintances noticed, that he hoped for a more admiring response to his late work than it was likely to receive.

The first two volumes of *Problems*, published in 1874 and 1875, were entitled *The Foundations of a Creed*. Blackwood may have been intitially misled by the title into thinking that the book would not be inimical to Christianity. Francis Espinasse later speculated that volume i succeeded at first in selling well because of the groping need felt by post-Darwinian Victorians for a consolatory creed to replace traditional belief:

No young author, flushed with the success of a first effort, could have shown more elation than Lewes when, verging on sixty, he saw vol.i of his *Problems of Life and Mind* reach a second edition soon after it was issued. At the time I suspected that this success was due less to an appreciation of the philosophical acumen displayed in the volume than to the attractiveness of its sub-title, 'The Foundations of a Creed', and that many of its readers may have been disappointed on finding in it, not a new religion, but abstruse discussions on the first principles which the author intended to apply in the subsequent treatment of biological and physiological questions.[4]

Though Blackwood was, as Lewes had retorted to him, wrong in seeing an anti-religious animus in the first volume, he was nevertheless not being entirely naïve in rejecting it. He may have felt, but dared not express the feeling, that for once Lewes was *not* writing clearly and readably. Whereas the heavy matter of the subsequent volumes, *The Physical Basis of Mind* and *The Study of Psychology*, is periodically lightened by interesting examples in the field of human and animal cognition, emotion, motive, and so on, the first two volumes comprise an ambitious and surprisingly abstract attempt to lay a theoretical basis for the following discussions. Though keen as ever to dismiss idealism and all fruitless speculation about the unknowable, Lewes now endeavours to extend his lifelong adherence to empirical method beyond the study of 'experience' in the narrow sense of impressions on the five senses. While still an empiricist, he now accepts what he had previously rejected under the name of metaphysics. It might, he felt, be admissible to study phenomena outside the range of immediate sense experience; we might properly study the relations between subject and object, mind and matter, without betraying the methods of science. Instead of banishing metaphysics from the discussion, then, Lewes proposes a new enemy to be excluded. He coins the word 'metempirics' for this.[5] Though a few reviewers took up the distinction offered by Lewes, most felt he was over-reaching himself in trying to supersede the old empirical–metaphysical distinction. The ordinary reader finds it difficult to grasp the superfine distinction, while philosophers after Lewes declined, on the whole, to take up the new term.

Friendly reviewers gave Lewes some praise for his labours. William Kingdon Clifford, writing in the *Academy*, thought the volume represented 'an advance of the empirical front' but could not endorse the novelty of the terminology. Douglas Spalding gave two feeble cheers in *Nature*, though he felt that much was obscure. James Sully welcomed the term 'metempirical' but did not agree with Lewes on causation. The loyal Frederic Harrison praised *Problems* in the *Fortnightly*, but avoided the metaphysical/metempirical controversy altogether, preferring to read the work as a positivist document.[6] Lewes had hoped for more; he even expected to stir up a controversy. But beyond lukewarm notices in the specialist press, Lewes's first two volumes received little attention.

Lewes, though disappointed, was not entirely surprised. Despite his ingenious attempt to rescue a part of metaphysics, he knew he was not really in his element. He confessed to Alexander Main in November 1874, when he was correcting the proofs of the second volume of *Foundations of a Creed*, that 'all seems so dull and incomplete'. Once the volume was out, Lewes breathed a sigh of relief, for he could now get away from 'hated metaphysics' to 'dear Biology and Psychology'.[7] If Lewes himself felt so, it is not surprising that readers experience some relief on closing the first two volumes.

In March 1875 one of Lewes's oldest friends, Arthur Helps, died. Two years before he had published *Some Talk about Animals and Their Masters*, for which Lewes had thanked him as an 'animal lover'. Helps had written about the horrors of vivisection—a topic which occupied scientists, Parliament, and the ordinary British animal owner throughout the 1870s. Cara Bray was involved in 1874 in founding the Society for the Prevention of Cruelty to Animals, to which Marian loyally made a financial contribution.[8] In 1875, when a Royal Commission was set up to look into the use of animals in laboratories, Lewes was among the experimental scientists who gave evidence before it. With Darwin and most of the scientific experts, he favoured vivisection as a necessary mode of furthering knowledge, though he disliked causing pain.

Lewes's testimony to the Commission on 15 December 1875 defended vivisection under strict conditions, but opposed any law-making on the subject. As he had said to Helps in March 1873:

All physiological discovery was made through experiment, and of experiment the greater part is Vivisection. Since the discovery of anaesthetics almost all experimenters render the animals unconscious, not only for the sake of sparing pain, but for the precision of the operation. I have performed hundreds, and never once, except in very trifling cases, operated without anaesthesia. Nor indeed could I *see* another operate without it. There are some experiments which do not admit of the application of anaesthesia but these are few and one of the very greatest living experimenters, Schiff, *always* narcotizes. In France they are culpably reckless on this point—a tradition with them.[9]

The anti-vivisection lobby gained ground, with the result that a Cruelty to Animals Act came into force in 1876.[10] It was in the end a compromise between the two sides, with the scientists forming a Physiological Society in March 1876 to defend the rights of scientists while not opposing a Bill placing restrictions on the number of experiments to be carried out and the places where they might occur. Lewes was on the council of the Society, taking the chair for the first time on 5 May 1876.[11]

Apart from reviving his own interest in physiology and defending the rights of others to practise it, Lewes responded in 1875–6 to two requests to reissue old works in a new form. Smith, Elder wanted a third edition of the *Life of Goethe*, and Lewes felt obliged to update it with references to the 'latest documents', which involved 'the wearisome toil of going through more than 20 volumes of German dreariness—indispensable!' This was 'a hateful task, though I cannot but be grateful for the necessity of a new edition', as he told W. B. Scott. In 1873 he had been persuaded by Smith to issue an abridged version, *The Story of Goethe's Life*, omitting the critical sections, and this had stimulated interest in the unabridged *Life*, which sold 600 copies in 1874, thus necessitating the new edition.[12]

The second reissue was suggested by Trollope. He thought Lewes's theatre reviews in the *Pall Mall Gazette* would make an interesting volume. Lewes addressed his friend in his preface to the work, *On Actors and the Art of Acting*, published by Smith, Elder in July 1875, saying he had decided to take Trollope's advice because of recent signs of a revival in the British theatre. The essays became, according to William Archer, writing in 1896, 'one of the not too numerous classics of English dramatic criticism'.[13] They are still in print. In them, Lewes combines memories of seeing the Keans, Macready, Charles Mathews, and the other great actors of his time with remarks on Shakespeare, on drama in France, Germany, and Spain, and on styles of acting. On the last point he advocates a compromise between 'coat-and-waistcoat' naturalism and too lofty an idealism on the part of the actor, leaving it to the actor's tact to decide how much he should 'select and heighten in his characterisation'.[14]

Marian was despairing more than ever about the progress of *Daniel Deronda*, aware that readers would find uninteresting the 'Jewish part', with its pages of Mordecai's reflections on Hebrew philosophy and the future of a possible Jewish state, but needing to be told by Lewes and Blackwood that it would be a roaring success. Blackwood listed the delights of the first volume, which he read in May 1875, having been prompted by Lewes to do so, lest she give up while the book was still unfinished. Blackwood responded easily, believing that Lewes was right about the greatness to be found in the novel. 'I have never found [Lewes] wrong on the subject', he told Marian.[15] Lewes himself was enthusiastic, even ebullient. He told Blackwood in July, while they were staying at a house in Rickmansworth, that Marian was constantly snubbing him for being 'cockaloop' about the novel, and for 'not adopting the despondent view of *other people*—but on that subject my estimate of the estimate of *other people* is that it isn't worth two peas!'[16]

Like *Middlemarch*, *Daniel Deronda* was to appear in eight parts. Blackwood's experts in the office thought the parts should appear every two months, but Lewes preferred monthly publication. Blackwood agreed—'there can be no better judge of such a point than Lewes'—and the novel duly appeared monthly between February and September 1876.[17] When Blackwood wondered how Marian had come to know so much about the Jews, Lewes crowed, 'You are surprised at her knowledge of the Jews? But only learned Rabbis are so profoundly versed in Jewish history and literature as she is.' He also prophesied that the novel would

rouse all the Jews of Europe to a fervor of admiration for the great artist who can—without disguising the ludicrous and ugly aspects—so marvellously present the ideal side of that strange life. Lydgate in Middlemarch conquered all the medical profession—and Mordecai will in like manner conquer all the Jews. What a stupendous genius it is!'[18]

Lewes was right. Jews, Rabbis among them, wrote gratefully to George Eliot, and though many other readers and critics were less enthusiastic about the Mordecai episodes, the general reception of the novel justified Lewes's faith and echoed Blackwood's remark to Lewes—'She is *A Magician*'. To the doubts expressed by Langford about parts of the novel, Blackwood replied—and in this he agreed with Lewes—'she is so great a giant that there is nothing for it but to accept her inspirations and leave criticism alone.'[19] If we feel inclined to blame Lewes for not alerting her to the *longueurs* and over-reachings evident in *Daniel Deronda*, we should remember that Lewes and Blackwood both knew that she *had* to write as she did and that any but the gentlest criticism would have had her putting away her pen for ever.

Lewes left their Rickmansworth refuge for a day in July 1875 to move in high society once more. Lady Airlie was giving her annual garden party, and Lewes, but not Marian, accepted the invitation. His funny report to Mary Cross, one of Johnny's sisters, shows that he had not lost all his old irreverence now that he, a member of Ranthorpe's 'aristocracy of intellect', was mixing easily with the 'aristocracy of birth':

Know then that being invited to meet the Queen of Holland, and finding I could run up to town comfortably after lunch, and be back home again by 8, I arrayed myself in my 'war paint', and presented myself at Airlie Lodge. To my surprise I found that the Queen had expressed a special wish that I should be presented to her, so immediately on her arrival that ceremony took place. You must imagine a pale plain elderly woman of somewhat feeble and certainly unenchant-ing aspect—and opposite her stands—The Matchless! Then this dialogue ensues.

Queen. Very glad to see you, Mr. Lewes. I saw you in 1871 at Florence. You were there were you not?

The M. I was, your Majesty.

Q. You were pointed out to me at the theatre, you and your wife. Lady Airlie (not having caught the word 'Florence' or because 'Weimar' was running in her head, we having been talking of it when the Q. arrived) 'Mr. Lewes says they were so very kind to him at Weimar.'

Q. (*with something like fretful impatience*) I don't want to hear about Weimar! (*loftily*) I have done with them. (*Family quarrel*)—So you like Weimar, Mr. Lewes? (*a touch of sarcasm in the tone*)

The M. Well, your Majesty, I was very happy there and much interested in everything.

Q. It's a very ugly place. You can't say it's beautiful!

The M. No, not beautiful, certainly not like Florence.

Q. Oh! Florence is charming. (*a pause*) I admire your writings—as to your wife's, all the world admires them. Here the Matchless bows, and begins to think 'when will this come to an end'. . . .

It was a brilliant sight that garden dotted with lovely women and lovely dresses (with some *not* so lovely!) and celebrated men and 'nobs'. I enjoyed an hour and a half of it; and came away wondering whether I had produced anything like the same impression on Royalty that Royalty had produced on me.[20]

In November 1876 Lewes visited Cambridge to work with the physiologist Michael Foster in his laboratory. 'Glorious physiological talk', he noted on 9 November; the next day he spent 'all day from 9 to ¼ past 4 in the Laboratory working with Foster on frogs and snails— capital talk the while'. But he was unwell, being exhausted before he went and suffering from 'the fiercest cramp I ever had' while there.[21]

His work on volume iii of *Problems—The Physical Basis of Mind*—went on slowly. During 1876 he published a few articles from his work in progress, including two essays on 'Spiritualism and Materialism' in the *Fortnightly Review* in April and May. In these papers he describes himself as no longer a complete materialist, but of course not a spiritualist either. Rather he calls himself—as did many of the German scientific philosophers whose works he knew—an organicist. That is, Lewes takes the view that to define man as a machine, an aggregate of cells, is inadequate, while to talk of the unknowable soul is equally unhelpful:

The organicist applauds every attempt to detect the agency of physical and chemical processes in the complex physiological process; he only protests against the notion that a physiological process can be interpreted without taking in all the organic conditions.[22]

The stress is on the importance of not ignoring the social factor in psychology. Lewes thought he was being original here, as an exchange of letters with G. C. Robertson shows. Robertson, editor of *Mind*, obligingly published brief extracts from Lewes's forthcoming volume in 1876 and 1877. While encouraging Lewes to write for *Mind*, he was critical of Lewes's organicist views, being with his professional colleagues Bain and Sully a more orthodox associational psychologist in the British empirical tradition of Locke, Hume, and Hartley. Robertson, like Bain, felt suspicious of Lewes's conclusions and objected to his claims of originality. Lewes took his criticisms seriously. 'Can you give me the titles of the books and essays you seem to refer to as having preceded me in the discovery of the social factor in Psychology?' he asked in March 1877. Robertson replied with an apologetic remark about the idea appearing in odd essays by Clifford and Pollock, in Leslie Stephen's recent book on English thought in the eighteenth century, and in Spencer's works. He soothed Lewes by saying he ought to have done more justice to Lewes's 'emphatic statement of the position' in volume i of *Problems*.[23]

Volume iii, *The Physical Basis of Mind*, came out in July 1877. It was a study of the 'group of material conditions which constitute the organism in relation to the physical world'.[24] Incorporating his earlier articles on Darwin and some passages and illustrations from the *Physiology of Common Life*, the work includes discussions of the nervous mechanism and reflex theory. Less wholly abstract than volumes i and ii, the new volume is altogether more readable, though not by any means so much so as Lewes's earlier works. It received few notices, Robertson delaying his obscure, detailed, polite, but unenthusiastic review in *Mind* until January 1878. Allowing Lewes to occupy an 'almost unique position' in England as a philosophical thinker, a psychological inquirer, and a practical worker, Robertson nevertheless finds Lewes's work incomplete in any of these fields separately and largely unsuccessful in combining them.[25] Lewes accepted the criticism with a good grace, telling Robertson that he had had a much more negative review by William Stanley Jevons, Professor of Logic at Manchester, which he called 'calmly crushing.'[26] Lewes was not one to show his disappointment, and Marian's remark in her journal for 10 November 1877 that volume iii had 'sold satisfactorily for a book so little in the popular taste' suggests they were putting a brave face on things.[27]

Socially, they were busier than ever. On 30 March 1877 they had a party to hear Tennyson read *Maud*; among the guests were Charles and Gertrude, the Crosses, Barbara Bodichon, Professor Beesly, the painter Frederic Burton, and F. W. Myers of Cambridge. On 20 April Lewes went to dine at Lord Charlemont's. 'There were present the Marquis of Sligo, Lord Houghton, Lady Barron, Mad. Du Quairo, Mr. and Mrs. Fellows and two other gentlemen. A quiet but very pleasant dinner. Good stories and I had a good innings.'[28] He had not lost his gift for jokes, imitations, and anecdotes. For the past few years he had been writing down in his diary stories he heard; he and Robert Lytton—Lord Lytton since the death of Bulwer-Lytton in 1873 and Viceroy of India since 1876—had for a long time swapped anecdotes in their letters. One such is the one about the Spanish princess 'whom they tried to enlighten on marital duties' and who exclaimed 'Sleep in the same room with him! I thought only poor people did that!'[29]

In May Richard Wagner came to give a concert season. Despite their deafness to his music, the Leweses entertained him for the sake of his second wife, Liszt's daughter Cosima. The Wagners were frequent Sunday guests at The Priory during their stay, and Lewes and Marian attended several rehearsals and concerts.[30] On 15 May, after attending one of these rehearsals, the Leweses were guests at a party given so that Princess Louise, Queen Victoria's fourth daughter, could meet George Eliot. The Princess set a precedent, being not only the first member of the royal family to meet the woman who was once known as the strong-minded blue-stocking of the *Westminster Review* and blackguard Lewes's infidel concubine, but also desiring, against etiquette, that *she* be pre-sented to George Eliot, rather than the other way round. Lewes recorded the momentous, even symbolic, event with due pride in his diary. Princess Louise had already seen Marian at a charity concert in St James's Hall in March, on which occasion she had drawn a sketch of the novelist on her programme (see Plate 20).[31]

By June 1877 the Leweses were installed in their new country house, The Heights, Witley, in Surrey. They had been looking for years for a house to buy, so that they could spend several months of the year out of London. In November 1876 John Cross found the house—near his own home in Weybridge—and negotiated its purchase for £4,950.[32] Settling in during the summer of 1877, they described the place as 'Paradise'. Cross persuaded them to learn tennis, fixing up a court for them on the lawn.[33] Tennyson was a near neighbour and freqent visitor, and selected friends were invited to stay. In a clever pastiche of Wordworth's 'She dwelt among the untrodden ways', Lewes petitioned Eleanor and Emily Cross (known in the family as 'the Doves'):

> There dwelt beside the Weybridge ways
>   (And often called 'the Doves')
> Maidens who seeking no man's praise
>   Gained everybody's loves.
> Their Uncle dwelt on Witley Heights,
>   Who loved these maidens well
> Though why they ne'er shared his delight,
>   Of home—no man can tell.
> Was it because he lived retired
>   With brain too much o'ertasked?
> Or that they ne'er to come desired?
>   Or—were they never asked?[34]

Their oldest friend, Herbert Spencer, still visited them, though only occasionally. As Marian told Sara Hennell, from whom she had also grown apart rather, corresponding only infrequently, Spencer was an idiosyncratic friend:

We have long given up vain expectations from him and can therefore enjoy our regard for him without disturbance by his negations. He comes and consults about his own affairs, and that is his way of showing friendship. We never dream of telling him *our* affairs, which would certainly not interest him.[35]

Marian's remarks about Spencer were marked by a sharp sense of irony; they always had been, even when she had been unhappily in love with him. In November 1876 she noted in another letter to Sara that he who 'used to despise biography as the least profitable occupation of the brain' was now busily collecting materials for his own autobiography (begun in May 1875, circulated from time to time among a few friends abjured to keep it under lock and key, continued until 1893, and finally published after his death, in 1904). In an aside to Sara, in 1868, she had written that Spencer always asked after Sara 'with sympathetic interest', adding, in brackets, '*proportion gardée*, for you know his feelings are never too much for him'.[36]

Once at The Priory again, in November 1877, Lewes busied himself with work and society. He heard he had been proposed, in company with Browning, Arnold, Tyndall, Lord Selborne, and two others, for the Rectorship of St Andrew's University. He was flattered, but neither surprised nor disappointed when Lord Selborne was elected.[37] While Marian worked at a new book, not a novel but a collection of thoughts of the fictitious 'Theophrastus Such', Lewes carried on with his studies. In January 1878, as he told Baraba Bodichon, he was invited with Huxley and Paget to 'see a patient from whom a Glasgow surgeon had removed the *whole of the larynx*, and this he had supplied by an artificial larynx with which the man could speak. It was most interesting. He spoke in a monotone but with perfect distinctness. What will science do next?'[38]

Lewes's only writing at this time was an essay in the *Fortnightly Review*. Called 'On the Dread and Dislike of Science', it was published in June 1878. It was to be Lewes's last essay, and, looked at now it represents, I think, a fitting end to his astonishing literary career. The old Lewes virtues of clarity and lightness of touch yet trenchancy in argument are present throughout. 'In the struggle of life with the facts of existence', it begins, 'Science is a bringer of aid'; in the struggle of the soul with the mystery of existence, 'Science is a bringer of light'. Yet science has been viewed with suspicion, particularly by those who see it as a threat to religion. Lewes launches into a statement of the case as he sees it.

Calling as of old on the historical insights of Comte, Lewes claims that science is 'Common-Sense methodised and extended'. It ought not to be seen as being in necessary conflict with religion, but only with the claims of theology to explain the natural world, which is the proper province of science. Not at all intent on denying the importance of religion as a force in men's moral and spiritual lives, Lewes on the contrary sees in science, with its extension of knowledge and its social and medical usefulness, an ally of religion, though he himself holds no religious belief other than a faith in the progress of humanity. The essay ends on a ringing note of optimism, which sounds odd to our ears, though it represents the hopes of many Victorians:

When Science has fairly mastered the principles of moral relations as it has mastered the principles of physical relations, all Knowledge will be incorporated in a homogeneous doctrine rivalling that of the old theologies in its comprehensiveness, and surpassing it in the authority of its credentials. 'Christian Ethics' will then no longer mean Ethics founded on the principles of Christian Theology, but on the principles expressing the social relations and duties of man in Christianised society. Then, and not till then, will the conflict between Theology and Science finally cease; then, and not till then, will the dread and dislike of Science disappear.[39]

In February Lewes attended dinners with Trollope—recently returned from six months in South Africa—Leslie Stephen, Browning, Lord Houghton, and other worthies; and both he and Marian were guests at the wedding in Westminster Abbey of Tennyson's son Lionel.[40] On 15 March Lewes was the guest of honour at a dinner given by the German Athenaeum club—'a noisy & very German supper of 60, all shouting at once, so that one could barely hear one's neighbour'. Lewes's health was drunk as the 'illustrious guest, the representative of English Literature', and, of course, the biographer of Goethe.[41]

In April Cross gave a dinner at the Devonshire Club. 'Capital talk and stories', wrote Lewes in his diary. A fellow guest was Henry James, who described the occasion to his mother:

very pleasant dinner of men given by the good John Cross at the Devonshire Club—G. H. Lewes, Henry Sidgwick & others more obscure. I sat next to Lewes, who is personally repulsive; (as Mrs. Kemble says 'He looks as if he had been gnawed by the rats'—& left;) but most clever & entertaining. He is rather too much the professional *raconteur*—he told lots of stories; but he recounts very well—chiefly in French. He remembered as soon as I was introduced to him, my queer visit to GE in 1869 with Grace Norton, & asked me to come back, which I shall do.

James duly visited The Priory on Sunday 28 April, reporting that he felt he had the right henceforth to consider himself 'a Sunday *habitué*'.[42]

Lewes spent his sixty-first birthday on 18 April quietly at home. In June he and Marian moved to Witley for the summer, planning to spend some time later in the year with Blackwood in Edinburgh. But Lewes's health began to decline. At first he showed signs of having gout and cramps and 'feeling his inward economy all wrong', as Marian noted on 27 June.[43] By mid-July Lewes was feeling ill enough to tell P. G. Hamerton that he was 'vegetating' and unable to do much work. But he was still cheerful, giving accounts of 'sauntering and pottering' in the mornings, though the fact that he quoted John 9 : 4—saying 'the night in which no man can work' was fast approaching—may suggest he suspected the seriousness of his condition.[44] To Blackwood, who was planning to reprint two of Lewes's 'Maga' stories in the *Tales from Blackwood* series and who expressed disappointment that the Leweses were not after all coming to stay with him, Lewes wrote frankly on 6 August, 'You do not realize my state':

If I could even read an amusing book for three hours I should consider myself strong enough to come. But I can't work at all, and can't read for more than an hour. Walking is what I do best—(*no*, sleeping is my forte!)—even listening to Mrs. Lewes reading soon wearies me.[45]

Marian seems not to have realized, or not to have admitted to herself, how ill he was. His high spirits when not in pain kept her hopeful. Lewes's diary records anecdotes, meetings with Tennyson and others, and bits and pieces of reading. In September he sent Agnes her regular cheque for £43. 2s. 6d.; Susanna received £18. 15s. od. On 30 October Susanna visited to talk about Vivian's engagement to Constance Abraham; ill as he was, Lewes found time to write to Mr Abraham asking him to drop his opposition to the marriage.[46] He attended a concert on 16 November, but 'came home feeling very unwell'. On 18 November he consulted Paget: 'Examined me and pronounced it not Piles but thickening of the mucus membrane.' He took castor oil, but 'without any effect'. Tuesday 19 November was 'a wretched day. No motion from a blue pill two doses of castor oil and two of water! Only blood and mucus. Paget came. Bed at 9 and till 3.30 in agony.' The following day he wrote his last entry in the diary: 'Awoke very quiet. Paget came before breakfast. The storm has passed I think! Got up to lunch.'[47]

Lewes's last act as Marian's literary agent was to write, on 21 November, a note to Blackwood accompanying the manuscript of her compilation of aphorisms, *The Impressions of Theophrastus Such*. By 25 November Marian acknowledged that she had 'a deep sense of change within, and of a permanently closer relationship with death'.[48] Johnnie

Cross and Charles were the only friends she saw. She was the one who would be left behind, the fate Lewes had dreaded for himself.

On 30 November Lewes died, aged 61, of enteritis. He was buried in the dissenters' part of Highgate Cemetery on 4 December after a simple Unitarian service given by Dr Sadler of Rosslyn Chapel.[49] Marian did not go. Neither did Agnes. Charles was the chief mourner; Herbert Spencer attended, as did, among others, Cross, Browning, Trollope, Pigott, George Smith, Joseph Langford, the Burne-Joneses, and Frederic Harrison and his wife. Many other friends, including Rudolf Lehmann, Edward Beesly, and the loyal Holyoake—who ensured that he himself would be buried next to Lewes and Marian—missed the announcement in *The Times*. Holyoake wrote in distress to Spencer on 15 December, having learned of the funeral too late to attend:

I never felt a pang before at being absent from a grave. Lewes's friendship for me made my life brighter in the evil days. I had an affection for him. I did not imagine he had died in London or I should have been an outside mourner. Lewes was my first friend in opinion. I wish you would tell Mrs. Lewes how sorry I am for her and how much I regarded him.[50]

Epilogue

Lewes's friends were eloquent in their grief and consolation. Even Spencer, so lacking in imaginative sympathy, wrote with touching frankness to Marian:

I can but dimly conceive what such a parting must be, even in an ordinary case. Still more dimly can I conceive what it must be in a case where two lives have been so long bound together so closely, in such multitudinous ways. But I can conceive it with clearness enough to enable me to say, with more than conventional truth, that I grieve with you.[1]

One of Lewes's other oldest friends, Edward Pigott, told Charles that he was overwhelmed by the news: 'The earth seems crumbling around me.' He recalled the old *Leader* days:

Is it possible that your dear father—my dear friend of five and twenty years—the friend and comrade of the happiest, though the most anxious, years of my life, has departed; and that I shall never set eyes on him again?[2]

Everyone found it hard to believe that Lewes was dead. Though they knew how fragile his health was, his friends had detected no change in his cheerful, optimistic, busy demeanour. Browning wrote to Lady Lindsay on 2 December, 'I was laughing, a week ago, over a bright clever epistle congratulatory which he sent to Leighton—one would not have expected that the light was to go out so soon.'[3] And Blackwood, who was too ill to leave Edinburgh for the funeral, and who was himself dead within the year, wrote simply to Marian, 'I sit very sad thinking of you. With all his illness & sufferings there was so much vitality about him that I never feared the event was so near.'[4]

Robert Lytton wrote briefly to Marian from Calcutta about his feelings for one whom he had admired since he was a boy; to a third party, Fitzjames Stephen, he wrote more fully:

I am terribly cut up by the death of my dear old friend, George Lewes. I have known and loved him since childhood. He had the most omnivorous intellectual appetite of any man I ever knew; a rare freedom from prejudice; soundness of judgment in criticism, and a singularly wide and quick sympathy in all departments of science and literature.[5]

This was to be the note sounded in all the obituaries. They marvelled at Lewes's brightness, quickness, versatility, and omnicompetence. For some, like the writer in *Nature*, the *Life of Goethe* was his best work; others, including Frederic Harrison in the *Academy*, thought the *Biographical History of Philosophy* his most characteristic achievement. In Trollope's view, many of Lewes's books were of equal importance: 'There was no form of literary expression in which he did not delight and instruct.' The *Biographical History of Philosophy* 'made philosophy readable, reasonable, lively, almost as exciting as a good novel'; *Sea-Side Studies* and the *Physiology of Common Life* did for science what the *Biographical History* had done for philosophy; the *Life of Goethe* was 'almost perfect' as a critical biography, being 'short, easily understood by common readers, singularly graphic, exhaustive, and altogether devoted to the subject'.[6]

Trollope's tribute is not only the most touching, describing, as it does, 'the leading incidents' of the 'peculiarly valuable literary life' of his 'most dear friend and cherished companion';[7] it is also the most fair and shrewd. Lewes ought indeed to be remembered chiefly for the works Trollope selects for special mention, as he ought also for his miscellaneous criticism and his editorial and journalistic work on the *Leader* and later the *Fortnightly Review*. His life was both idiosyncratic, given his familial and social background, his early bohemianism, his political radicalism, his atheism, his embracing of Darwinism, his entering into two irregular marriages—in short, given his enduring capacity to be unorthodox in his views and behaviour—and yet it was also strangely typical of the age in which he lived. This is partly because, being so often ahead of his age in his views, he found that his age sometimes —as in the case of political reform, religious tolerance, acceptance of scientific discoveries, and the gradual acceptance also of the 'aristocracy of intellect'—came to the same opinions on these subjects as he had already embraced. Moreover, a man of such varied interests and such a bright intelligence could hardly avoid making his mark in contemporary discussions, whether the subject be literary, scientific, philosophical, or psychological.

To *Problems* obituarists were polite, knowing how hard Lewes had worked, and knowing, too, that Marian was planning to arrange Lewes's remaining notes for publication. The last two volumes appeared during 1879—*The Study of Psychology* and *Mind as a Function of the Organism*. Working on these, as well as discussing with some of Lewes's scientific colleagues the setting up of a physiology studentship in Lewes's name, kept her going in her desolation after his death. Michael Foster of Cambridge offered to help her with *Problems*, adding that he owed more to Lewes's *History of Philosophy* 'than to any other one book'.[8] And Clifford Allbutt wrote from Leeds about Lewes's 'indomitable and noble spirit', telling her that some of his best young biologists had named the *Physiology of Common Life* as the book from which they had learned most.[9]

Encouraged by such testimonies to his influence, Marian asked both Foster and Allbutt to help her set up the George Henry Lewes Studentship 'in memory of my husband'. The recipient should be a young scientist 'working in the way he would have liked to work', enabled by the studentship to have full access to a laboratory.[10] After much discussion between Marian and Foster, with Henry Sidgwick and Huxley also being consulted, the terms of the Studentship were decided. It was to be held at Cambridge for a term of three years, was to be open to women as well as men, and was to be financed by a fund of £5,000 held under the trusteeship of five scientists, including Huxley and Sidgwick.[11] Dr Charles Roy was chosen in October as the first holder of the Studentship; he later became Professor of Pathology at Cambridge.[12]

Allbutt wrote to Marian again in April 1879, at her request, giving his opinion of Lewes's contribution to science. He spoke of Lewes as having the clarity of a good teacher and the enthusiasm of an expert, while avoiding the heaviness of some scholars. He also sketched for her Lewes's demeanour at the meeting of the British Medical Association in Oxford in 1868, where he had first met Lewes. The French physiologist Guillaume Duchenne was also there:

Nervous diseases were the chief theme & surely even poor Duchenne never knew before the full heat of his own enthusiasm. And the bright fun so irresistible in [Lewes]—how charmed he was with the loss of Duchenne's undirected portmanteau somewhere on the railway—where—on what line even, the poor man gifted with one tongue only couldn't tell. And how we were horrified because he had no toilette, & because his portmanteau contained pieces of limbs and all sorts of anatomical horrors (& some said nothing else) which would certainly electrify the officials & how Duchenne was naively unconscious of the possible effects of his 'preparations' & equally indifferent to the toilet requisites & only yearned after his bones! What playful kindly fun [Lewes] made of all this & how in discussion he brought out the best meanings of each of us and welded us together & how he took this ascendancy by sympathetic insight & by very little formal speech-making.[13]

On 6 May 1880 Marian, who had changed her name by deed poll in January 1879 to 'Mary Ann Evans Lewes' in order to set up the

Studentship trust fund, changed it once more when she married John Cross at St George's, Hanover Square. He was 21 years younger than she. By taking this step she shocked the Comtists, who believed in the principle of 'perpetual widowhood'; amazed her friends; and pleased her brother Isaac, who broke his long silence, unbroken by the news of Lewes's death (though his wife had written kindly), to write her a letter of congratulation.[14]

John Cross had been the only person apart from Charles to see her for some months after Lewes's death. He took on most of her business correspondence and was a consoling presence. She herself could not explain why she eventually came to think of marrying him. (Cross saw marriage to her as a 'high calling'.)[15] As she told Georgiana Burne-Jones, 'Explanations of these crises, which seem sudden though they are slowly dimly prepared, are impossible.'[16] The remark, so close to the spirit of her novels in their delineation of the chemistry of human relations, is reinforced by another she reportedly made to Charles—that 'if she hadn't been human with feelings and failings like other people, how could she have written her books?'[17]

While the Congreves, Beeslys, Harrisons, and other positivists were variously horrified and disappointed at what they saw as weakness or disrespect for Lewes's memory, and the gossips took pleasure in discussing Johnnie Cross's gallantry in throwing a rope to the 'heavily laden but interesting derelict, tossing among the breakers, without oars or rudder' and 'towing her into harbour',[18] Charles Lee Lewes acted supportively and generously. The true son of his father, he welcomed the new hope of happiness for Marian. Thackeray's daughter Annie, herself married to a man 18 years her junior, described hearing the news from Charles two weeks after the wedding:

I am still thrrrrrrilling over a conversation I had yesterday with Charles Lewes. Lionel Tennyson was here; he declared that his hair stood on end as he listened. Charles Lewes said he wished to tell me all about the wedding. He gave her away, and looks upon Mr. Cross as an elder brother. . . .
Young Lewes is generous about the marriage. He says he owes everything to her, his Gertrude included, and that his father had no grain of jealousy in him, and only would have wished her happy. . . . He talked about his own mother in confidence, but his eyes all filled up with tears over George Eliot, and altogether it was the strangest page of life I ever skimmed over.[19]

The marriage fuelled rumours already doing the rounds that Marian had become disillusioned with Lewes before his death or with his memory soon after it. George Smith thought so; Frederic Harrison's wife also. The gossipy Oscar Browning picked up the story, and Henry James heard it from him. James wrote to his sister Alice in January 1881, 'Browning has a theory that she "went back on" Lewes after his death: i.e. made discoveries among his papers which caused her to wish to sink him in oblivion.'[20] Though this remark is followed by a disclaimer—'but this, I think, is Browningish and fabulous'—it has been taken up and repeated endlessly.

Marian's surviving letters and diaries give no hint of any disillusionment on her part. More tellingly, since papers can be destroyed, her idolatrous young admirer, Edith Simcox, who haunted The Priory during Lewes's illness and for months after his death, and who would have been the first to notice (and revel in) any suggestion of disaffection, gives evidence in her autobiography quite to the contrary. In May 1878, shortly before the onset of Lewes's last illness, she noted on a visit 'the perfectness of the love binding those two together'. After Lewes's death, in April 1879, she reported Marian as saying with reference to 'the step she had taken' in choosing to live with Lewes that the unorthodoxy of the union had caused them to 'live for each other and in such complete independence of the outer world that the world could be nothing for them'. While this might, Marian conceded shrewdly, be considered 'a sort of dual egotism', it was surely better 'to make the nearest relation perfect' than for husbands and wives to run away from one another 'after philanthropic works while the true life was left unblessed'.[21] No doubt the very fact of their union being unorthodox made it imperative for the Leweses to remain constant to one another. On the other hand, there is no evidence that either of them felt inclined otherwise. Edith Simcox, Blackwood, Spencer, and all their closest friends observed the genuine devotion of this most 'married' of couples.

Charles Lewes got it right. Lewes himself would not have been offended or jealous that Marian had found another man to love and live with. As it turned out, her second marriage lasted only seven months. After spending their honeymoon in Italy, followed by some weeks at Witley, she and Cross moved into their new home in Cheyne Walk, Chelsea, on 3 December 1880. Marian died suddenly, of kidney failure, on 22 December. She was buried next to Lewes in Highgate Cemetry, along with his letters to her, which she had packed up for that purpose on the first anniversary of his death.[22]

Naturally enough, George Eliot has had her biographers, while Lewes has not hitherto been memorialized at length. Trollope was the contemporary who gave, in the space of a short essay, the best sense of what it was like to know Lewes. We who can only know him in his writings and in those of his contemporaries may turn to the brief verbal portrait with which Trollope ended his obituary notice of his friend: 'There was never a man so pleasant as he with whom to sit and talk vague literary gossip over a cup of coffee and a cigar . . . he has left behind him here in London no pleasanter companion with whom to while away an hour.'[23] It is a fitting epitaph to add to Trollope's remarks about his friend's great achievements in philosophy, biography, and criticism, and his particular contribution to the culture of his age. Lewes would have been pleased with such a summary of his intellectual and social life; which of us would not?

LIST OF ABBREVIATIONS USED
IN THE NOTES

———⟢⟢⟢———

A short form of reference to manuscript sources has been used in the notes (e.g. MS Hertford); the full forms are given in the list which may be found in the first section of the Bibliography.

BL	British Library
GE	George Eliot
GE	Gordon S. Haight, *George Eliot: A Biography* (Oxford, 1969)
GEL	*The George Eliot Letters*, ed. Gordon S. Haight, 9 vols. (New Haven, Conn., 1954–6, 1978)
GHL	George Henry Lewes
Letters, Pilgrim Edn.	*Letters of Charles Dickens*, Pilgrim Edition, ed. Madeleine House, Graham Storey, *et al.*, 6 vols. so far (Oxford, 1965–)
MLR	*Modern Language Review*
NLS	National Library of Scotland
NYPL	New York Public Library
PMLA	*Publications of the Modern Language Association of America*
PRO	Public Records Office, Chancery Lane, London
SDUK	Society for the Diffusion of Useful Knowledge
UCL	University College London
UCLA	University of California at Los Angeles
V. & A.	Victoria and Albert Museum, London

NOTES

CHAPTER I

1. Dickens, *A Tale of Two Cities* (London, 1859, repr. Harmondsworth, 1970), 35.

2. The phrase 'strong-minded woman' was Carlyle's, see *GEL*, ii. 177 n.

3. See Francis Espinasse, *Literary Recollections and Sketches* (London, 1893), 276, 282.

4. George Sand and Jules Sandeau, *Rose et Blanche* (Paris, 1831). See Patricia Thomson, *George Sand and the Victorians: Her Influence and Reputation in Nineteenth-century England* (London, 1977).

5. Charlotte Brontë to William Smith Williams, 5 Apr. 1849, *The Brontës: Their Lives, Friendships and Correspondence*, ed. T. J. Wise and J. A. Symington, 4 vols. (Oxford, 1932), ii. 322; Jane Welsh Carlyle to Jeannie Welsh, 5 Feb. 1849, *Jane Welsh Carlyle: Letters to her Family 1839–1863*, ed. Leonard Huxley (London, 1924), 319–20.

6. Carlyle to Mrs Aitken, 25 Apr. 1850, *New Letters of Thomas Carlyle*, ed. Alexander Carlyle, 2 vols. (London, 1904), ii. 93.

7. See Ivan Petrovitch Pavlov, *Lectures on Conditioned Reflexes*, trans. and ed. W. Horsley Gantt, 2 vols. (London, 1928, 1941, repr. 1963), i. 13.

8. Anthony Trollope, 'George Henry Lewes', *Fortnightly Review*, 25 NS (Jan. 1879), 15.

9. [Joseph] Jacobs, *Athenaeum*, 27 Sept. 1879, 398. Author identified from the marked copy of the *Athenaeum* in the City University, London.

10. For an account of Charles Lee Lewes's career see *A Biographical Dictionary of Actors, Actresses, Musicians, Dancers, Managers and Other Stage Personnel in London 1660–1800*, ed. P. H. Highfill Jun., Kalman A. Burnim, and Edward A. Langhans, 12 vols. so far (Carbondale, Ill. 1973–), ix. 271, 273–4.

11. See Alexander Kilham, *The Hypocrite detected and exposed; and the True Christian vindicated and supported* (Aberdeen, 1794), and Charles Lee Lewes's reply, published in *Memoirs of Charles Lee Lewes*, ed. John Lee Lewes, 4 vols. (London, 1805), ii. 236 ff.

12. Thornton Arnott Lewes to GHL, 13 Oct. 1860, MS Yale.

13. The genealogical material in this Chapter has been collected from the

following sources: *The International Genealogical Index*, a most useful but unfortunately not comprehensive guide to baptisms and marriages compiled by the Mormons; the PRO, where records of wills and administrations up to 1857 are held; the Greater London Record Office, which holds copies of most London parish registers; the Guildhall Library, which has registers for the City of London parishes; Westminster City Libraries, where parish registers for Westminster are held; and the Liverpool Record Office. For other information, chiefly relating to the addresses of members of the Lewes family, I have consulted Post Office Directories for London and Liverpool, as well as the 1851 Census, copies of which are held in the Census Room, Portugal St., London.

14. Gore's Liverpool Directory has John Lee Lewes living at Brownlow Hill, Liverpool, from 1803 to 1811.

15. John Lee Lewes, *Poems* (Liverpool, 1811), ix.

16. John Lee Lewes, *National Melodies and Other Poems* (London, 1817), 1–3.

17. The four children were baptised at St Nicholas Church, Liverpool, according to the register now in the Liverpool Record Office. All the information about John Lee Lewes in this chapter is new, nothing having hitherto been known about him.

18. Despite searching through the available parish registers of baptisms in Liverpool and London, I have been unable to find a record of the baptisms of Edgar, Edward, and GHL.

19. Information from Sister Jean de Chantal Kennedy, *Frith of Bermuda: Gentleman Privateer; a Biography of Hezekiah Frith 1763–1848* (Hamilton, Bermuda, 1964), 149–50; Henry C. Wilkinson, *Bermuda from Sail to Steam: The History of the Island from 1784 to 1901*, 2 vols. (London, 1973), ii. 464; the Bermuda Archives, Hamilton; *Bermuda Index 1784–1914*, compiled by C. F. E. Hollis Hallett, ii. 795, a copy of which was kindly sent me by Mrs Sandra Roiya of the Bermuda Archives; Administration of John Lee Lewes, 3 Jan. 1832, PRO.

20. GE to François D'Albert-Durade, 1 Aug. 1878, *GEL*, vii. 46.

21. See GHL to Alexander Main, 2 Jan. 1873, ibid. v. 361.

22. A copy of the St Pancras marriage register is in the Greater London Record Office. This is the source of my information that Elizabeth Ashweek was not married previously. Information about Captain Willim is from *Gentleman's Magazine*, 16 NS (Mar. 1864), 405, and V. C. P. Hodson, *List of Officers of the Bengal Army 1758–1834*, 4 vols. (London, 1928–47), iv. 484–5.

23. GHL Jour., 16 Apr. 1861, *GE*, 337.

24. GHL to John Blackwood, 8 Mar. 1864, MS Blackwood Papers, NLS.

25. Thornton Arnott Lewes to GHL, 29 Aug. 1864, *GEL*, vii. 322.

26. Edgar James Lewes to Mrs Willim, 2 Aug. 1825, MS Yale.

27. All the information about Mrs Willim's whereabouts comes from Edgar's letters at Yale. Captain Willim's will is at Somerset House, London.

28. Edgar James Lewes to Mrs Willim, 4 Aug. 1828, MS Yale.

29. *Memoirs of Margaret Fuller Ossoli*, ed. R. W. Emerson and W. E. Channing, 3 vols. (London, 1852), iii. 98; Henry James to his mother, 12 Apr. 1878, MS Houghton.

30. Thackeray, *Vanity Fair* (London, 1848, repr. Harmondsworth, 1968), 740; Dante Gabriel Rossetti to Philip Webb, 23 Sept. 1867, *Letters of Dante Gabriel Rossetti*, ed. Oswald Doughty and John Robert Wahl, 4 vols. (Oxford, 1965–7), ii. 634. For Boulogne and bankruptcy in the nineteenth century see Barbara Weiss, *The Hell of the English: Bankruptcy and the Victorian Novel* (London and Toronto, 1986).

31. GHL, *The Life and Works of Goethe*, 2 vols. (London, 1855), i. 37 n.

32. GHL Jour., 15 May 1857, *GEL*, ii. 327.

33. GHL, *Sea-Side Studies at Ilfracombe, Tenby, the Scilly Isles, and Jersey* (London, 1858), 270, 271.

34. Edgar James Lewes to Mrs Willim, 20 Jan. 1829 and 10 Feb. 1830, MSS Yale.

35. GE to Charles Lee Lewes, 23/4 Sept. 1880, *GEL*, vii. 327. Mrs Ouvry, Charles Lee Lewes's youngest daughter, gave the information about Edgar to Anna Kitchel, see Kitchel, *George Lewes and George Eliot: A Review of Records* (New York, 1933), xii. 7.

36. Frederick Locker-Lampson, *My Confidences* (London, 1896), 114 ff.

37. James Sully, 'George Henry Lewes', *New Quarterly Magazine*, 2 NS (Oct. 1879), 357. The proof copy, annotated by GE, is in the Sully Collection, UCL. There is also a draft of a biographical essay on GHL, *c.* 1859, with corrections probably in GHL's hand, for a proposed volume of 'Contemporary Biography' by the publisher R. Griffin & Co., MS BL. The 'Biography' was not published.

38. Richard Quain to Sir James Paget, 22 Apr. 1879, MS Yale. Many London hospitals had medical schools in the 1830s, among them Guy's, St Thomas's, St George's, the Middlesex, and St Bartholomew's. The records of all these schools are incomplete; no Lewes appears on the registers which do survive.

39. See William Bell Scott, *Autobiographical Notes*, ed. W. Minto, 2 vols. (London, 1892), i. 130; GHL, review of Scott's work, *Leader*, 5 July 1851, 638.

40. GHL, *Ranthorpe* (London, 1847, repr. with introd. by Barbara Smalley, Athens, Ohio, 1974), 6, 218, 65; Henry Vizetelly, *Glances Back through Seventy Years*, 2 vols. (London, 1893), i. 135.

41. GE to Sara Hennell, 22 Nov. 1869, *GEL*, v. 69.

42. GHL to Leigh Hunt, 2 Oct. 1834, MS Leigh Hunt Collection, BL.

43. GHL, 'Spinoza', *Fortnightly Review*, 4 (Apr. 1866), 385. The quotation is from Pope's *Epistle to Dr Arbuthnot* (l. 18).

44. Ibid. 386–8.

45. See introd. to J. A. Froude, *The Nemesis of Faith*, ed. Rosemary Ashton (London, 1988); *GE*, 40–4.

46. Lord Acton, 'George Eliot's "Life"', *Nineteenth Century*, 17 (Mar. 1885), 478–9.

CHAPTER 2

1. Carlyle to John Carlyle, 22 June 1840, and to John Stuart Mill, 21 Mar. 1833, *The Collected Letters of Thomas and Jane Welsh Carlyle*, ed. C. R. Sanders and K. J. Fielding, 18 vols. (Durham, NC, 1970–), xii. 17, vi. 350.

2. Dickens, *Bleak House* (London, 1853, repr. Harmondsworth, 1987), 119.

3. George Smith, 'Recollections of a Long and Busy Life', unpublished TS, NLS, 9–10; part published in [Leonard Huxley] *The House of Smith Elder* (privately printed, London, 1923), 36–7.

4. GHL Jour., 19 Feb. and 2 Mar. 1859, MS Yale.

5. Leigh Hunt to GHL, 12 July [1837], MS Yale.

6. GHL to Leigh Hunt, 15 Nov. 1838, MS BL.

7. Leigh Hunt to GHL, 23 Mar. [1839], MS Yale. For Leigh Hunt's relationship with Mary Shelley 1838–9, see *The Letters of Mary Wollstonecraft Shelley*, ed. Betty T. Bennett, 2 vols. so far (Baltimore, Md., 1980–), ii. 304–5, 318, 319. For Leigh Hunt's continued begging in 1843–4, when Mary Shelley told him she could not help until after Sir Timothy Shelley's death, which finally occurred in Apr. 1844, see *The Letters of Mary W. Shelley*, ed. Frederick L. Jones, 2 vols. (Norman, Okla., 1944), ii. 210, 217–18, 223.

8. GHL to Leigh Hunt, 21 Dec. 1839, MS BL; Mary Shelley to Leigh Hunt, c. 23 Dec. 1839, *Letters of Mary Wollstonecraft Shelley*, ii. 334–5.

9. GHL to Varnhagen von Ense, 27 Mar. 1844, T. H. Pickett, 'George Henry Lewes's Letters to K. A. Varnhagen von Ense', *MLR*, 80 (July 1985), 522. The letters are in the Jagiellonian.

10. GHL's own file of his contributions to the *Penny Cyclopaedia* 1842–3 is in the Dr Williams's Library in London; it is part of Lewes's library, which his son Charles deposited there in 1882. See William Baker, *The George Eliot–George Henry Lewes Library: An Annotated Catalogue of their Books at Dr Williams's Library, London* (London, 1977), and 'G. H. Lewes and the *Penny*

Cyclopaedia: 27 Unattributed Articles', *Victorian Periodicals Newsletter*, 7 (Sept. 1974), 15–18.

11. GHL, 'Percy Bysshe Shelley', *Westminster Review*, 35 (Apr. 1841), 303–44.

12. Mill to GHL, [late 1840], *The Collected Works of John Stuart Mill*, ed. F. E. L. Priestley, 25 vols. (Toronto, 1963–86), xiii (*Earlier Letters*, ed. F. E. Mineka), 448–9.

13. Letters from all these young men to Leigh Hunt in the 1830s are in the Leigh Hunt MS Collection, BL.

14. GHL to W. B. Scott, [Nov. 1837?], MS Princeton.

15. W. B. Scott, *Autobiographical Notes*, ii. 246.

16. Ibid. i. 130.

17. Ibid. i. 131.

18. GHL, *Leader*, 5 July 1851, 638.

19. The book is in Dr Williams's Library.

20. Egerton Webbe to GHL, 25 Mar. 1839 (on the verso of a letter from Leigh Hunt), MS Carl H. Pforzheimer Collection, NYPL.

21. GHL, *National Magazine and Monthly Critic*, 1 (Oct. 1837), 257. GHL's cuttings of his contributions to this and other periodicals are in the Folger.

22. Thornton Hunt to GHL, 6 July 1838, MS Yale.

23. GHL, 'Review of Books', *National Magazine and Monthly Critic*, 1 (Dec. 1837), 446.

24. See GHL, 'Dickens in Relation to Criticism', *Fortnightly Review*, 11 NS (Feb. 1872), 151–2. Dickens's earliest surviving letter to GHL is dated 9 June 1838, *Letters*, Pilgrim Edn. i. 403.

25. Leigh Hunt presented GHL with a copy of Thomas Keightley, *The Mythology of Ancient Greece and Italy* (1831), which he inscribed 'That all the Gods may conspire to bless the Greek and German of G. H. Lewes is the fervent wish of his friend, Leigh Hunt. August 9, 1838', see Baker, *George Eliot-G. H. Lewes Library*, 108.

26. For Carlyle's and GHL's importance as mediators of German literature see Rosemary Ashton, *The German Idea: Four English Writers and the Reception of German Thought 1800–1860* (Cambridge, 1980). The four writers are Coleridge, Carlyle, GE, and GHL.

27. GHL, *Ranthorpe*, 284.

28. GHL to Leigh Hunt, 3 Oct. 1838, MS Keats Memorial House.

29. GHL, 'A Night in a German Swamp', *Douglas Jerrold's Shilling Magazine*, 5 (Feb. 1847), 170.

30. Professor G. Ziegengeist of the Akademie der Wissenschaften der DDR, East Berlin, kindly gave me an extract from an unpublished letter of

Henriette Solmar, 21 Oct. 1838, in which she invites Turgenev and his friend Neverov to meet 'Herr Lewes'.

31. GHL to Leigh Hunt, 15 Nov. 1838, MS BL.

32. GHL to his sons, remembering his time in Vienna, 20 July 1858, MS Yale.

33. GHL to Leigh Hunt, 15 Nov. 1838, MS BL.

34. For full details of Richard Henry (later Hengist) Horne see Ann Blainey, *The Farthing Poet: A Biography of Richard Hengist Horne 1802–84* (London, 1968).

35. GHL to Horne, 10 Mar. 1840, MS Iowa.

36. GHL to Horne, 1 May 1840, MS Iowa.

37. GHL, *Monthly Chronicle*, 6 (July 1840), 17–32.

38. Carlyle to W. D. Christie, ?7 May 1840, *Collected Letters*, xii. 138.

39. GHL, 'Old English Ballads, by Professor Bibundtücker', *British Miscellany*, 1 (Apr. 1841), 185–8. GHL also published a 'Prospectus of an intended course of lectures on the philosophy of humbug' by Professor Bibundtücker in *Bentley's Miscellany*, 6 (1839), 599–602, and two articles entitled 'Professor Bibundtücker's Remains' in the *Monthly Magazine*, 7 NS (Feb. and Mar. 1842), 148–52, 238–42.

40. GHL's copy of the article, with a note that it was written in Berlin and Vienna, is in the Folger.

41. GHL, 'The French Drama', *Westminster Review*, 34 (Sept. 1840), 287–324.

42. GHL to Horne, 8 May 1840, MS Iowa.

43. GHL to Horne, [?12 Aug. 1850], ibid.

44. George Smith, 'Recollections', TS NLS, 44–5.

45. See GHL to Leigh Hunt, 10 Apr. 1840, MS BL.

46. GHL to Horne, 12 June [1840], MS Iowa, and to Varnhagen von Ense, 3 Jan. 1841, Pickett, 'Lewes's Letters to Varnhagen', 517.

CHAPTER 3

1. GHL to Horne, 17 Feb. 1841, MS Iowa.

2. Southwood Smith was Leigh Hunt's doctor; in 1840 he invited Leigh Hunt to meet Mr and Mrs Jervis, Smith to Leigh Hunt, 1 Apr. 1840, MS BL. Arnott wrote to Swynfen Jervis about the smokeless stove he had invented, 1 Feb. 1841, MS Wellcome Institute.

3. For details of Swynfen Jervis's career see obituary in *Gentleman's Magazine*, 3 NS (Feb. 1867), 265, and *Who's Who of British Members of Parliament*, ed. M. Stenton and S. Lees, 4 vols. (Hassocks, Sussex, 1976–81), i. 212.

4. Carlyle to John Carlyle, 3 June 1840, *Collected Letters*, xii. 158–9.

5. There are two letters from Jervis to the Secretary of the Society for the Diffusion of Useful Knowledge, 7 Oct. 1832 and 1 Jan. 1835, MS SDUK Papers, UCL.

6. Thornton Arnott Lewes to GHL, 20 Oct. 1861, MS Yale.

7. Swynfen Jervis, 'A Thought in Spring', *Leader*, 13 Apr. 1850, 67.

8. D. G. Rossetti to Christina Rossetti, 4 Aug. 1852, *The Family Letters of C. G. Rossetti*, ed. W. M. Rossetti (London, 1908), 20–2.

9. D. G. Rossetti to Jane Morris, 3 Sept. 1880, *Dante Gabriel Rossetti and Jane Morris: Their Correspondence*, ed. John Bryson and Janet Camp Troxell (Oxford, 1976), 158.

10. 'My dear Leontius, I am again going to Germany shortly for 8 or 9 months', wrote GHL to Leigh Hunt, 10 Apr. 1840, MS BL. But GHL wrote to Horne from Hampstead Rd. in May and June 1840, and there is no evidence to suggest he actually went to Germany.

11. George Smith, 'Recollections', TS NLS, 220.

12. Marie Belloc Lowndes, 'Notes for an Article on George Eliot', unpublished TS, Girton.

13. Details of the wedding at St Margaret's, Westminster (the parish church for MPs) are in the Library of Westminster Abbey.

14. GHL, *Rose, Blanche, and Violet*, 3 vols. in 1 (London, 1848), i. 6–7.

15. Ibid. 76–7.

16. George Smith, 'Recollections', TS NLS, 221–2.

17. GHL, *Ranthorpe*, 86–7.

18. Ibid. 107–11.

19. GHL's notebook, 'Personal Expenses', records 'Agnes from her father £200' in 1842, *GEL*, vii. 365.

20. See GHL's 'Literary Receipts', ibid. 365–8.

21. W. B. Scott, *Autobiographical Notes*, i. 134; George Jacob Holyoake, *Sixty Years of an Agitator's Life*, 2 vols. (London, 1892), i. 239; Jane Welsh Carlyle to Jeannie Welsh, 5 Feb. 1849, *Letters to her Family*, 320.

22. Leigh Hunt, 'Epithalamiums—Wedding-days—Vivia Perpetua', *British Miscellany*, 1 (Apr. 1841), 291–2.

23. The London Post Office Directory for 1842 has Mrs Willim (not Captain Willim) as the occupant of 3 Pembroke Square.

24. Leigh Hunt to GHL and Agnes Lewes, 19 Feb. 1841, MS Yale.

25. Mill to GHL, Feb. 1841, *Collected Works*, xiii. 463–4.

26. Mill to GHL, 1 Mar. 1841 and [April 1841], ibid. 466, 471. For Jeffrey,

Carlyle, and German literature in the *Edinburgh Review* see Ashton, *The German Idea*, 67–76.

27. Mill to GHL, 24 Apr. 1841, *Collected Works*, xiii. 470.

28. Mill to J. M. Kemble, 7 May 1841, ibid. 475–6.

29. GHL's copy of Coleridge's *Literary Remains* is richly annotated; many of the comments on Shakespeare are praised by GHL, but the remarks on other prose and poetry are often criticized in the margin, see GHL's collection of his articles, Folger.

30. GHL, 'Hegel's Aesthetics', *British and Foreign Review*, 13 (Oct. 1842), 14–15, 19–20.

31. Ibid. 44.

32. GHL, *A Biographical History of Philosophy*, 4 vols. in 2 (London, 1845–6), iv. 213. GHL's heavily annotated copy of Hegel's work is in Dr Williams's Library.

33. GHL, 'Hegel's Aesthetics', 49.

34. GHL to Macvey Napier, 11 Nov. 1841, MS Macvey Napier Papers, BL.

35. Mill to Macvey Napier, 18 Feb. 1842, *Collected Works*, xiii. 499.

36. Mill to Agnes Lewes, 16 July and 20 Dec. 1841, copies of MSS in the possession of the late Gordon S. Haight.

37. See Mill's disciple-like letters to Carlyle 1832–4, culminating in a letter of 12 Jan. 1834, in which Mill tries to extricate himself, *Collected Works*, xii. 204–9.

38. GHL to Horne, 22 July 1841, MS Iowa.

39. GHL to Varnhagen, 5 Dec. 1841, Pickett, 'Lewes's Letters to Varnhagen', 518.

40. Ibid.

41. GHL to Charles James Mathews, 19 Oct. 1841, MS Mathews Family Papers, William Seymour Theatre Collection, Princeton. The quotation 'breathless as a nun' is from Wordsworth's sonnet beginning 'It is a beauteous evening, calm and free, | The holy time is quiet as a Nun | Breathless with adoration' (1802).

42. GHL to Mathews, 16 Oct. [1842], MS Princeton. For Mathews's career, and that of his wife, Madame Vestris, see William W. Appleton, *Madame Vestris and the London Stage* (New York, 1974).

43. GHL to Varnhagen, 2 Mar. 1842, Pickett, 'Lewes's Letters to Varnhagen', 519.

44. Ibid.

45. GHL, 'The Character and Works of Göthe', *British and Foreign Review*, 14 (Mar. 1843), 78.

46. Ibid. 111–12.

47. Mill to GHL, 25? Nov. 1842, *Collected Works*, xiii. 557–8.

48. GHL to J. M. Kemble, 23 Mar. [1843], MS Yale.

49. GHL to William Hickson, [June 1842], MS Henry W. and Albert A. Berg Collection, NYPL. There are also several letters from GHL to Hickson 1843–9 at Yale.

50. GHL to Macvey Napier, 7 Nov. 1842, *Selection from the Correspondence of the late Macvey Napier*, ed. (his son) Macvey Napier (London, 1879), 413. For the Act of 1843 removing the monopoly from the two patent theatres see John Russell Stephens, *The Censorship of English Drama 1824–1901* (Cambridge, 1980), 5–16.

51. GHL to Macvey Napier, 24 Oct. 1843 and 7 June 1844, *Correspondence of Macvey Napier*, 445, 464.

52. GHL, 'The Life and Works of Leopardi', *Fraser's Magazine*, 38 (Dec. 1848), 659–69, and 'Spinoza's Life and Works', *Westminster Review*, 39 (May 1843), 372–407. For GHL as the best early critic of George Sand see Thomson, *George Sand and the Victorians*, 21 ff.

53. GHL, 'Spinoza's Life and Works', *Westminster Review*, 39 (May 1843), 382, 403, 406.

54. GHL to Horne, 4 Jan. 1843, MS Iowa, and to Varnhagen, 17 July 1843, Pickett, 'Lewes's Letters to Varnhagen', 521.

55. GHL to Varnhagen, 2 Mar. 1842, ibid. 519.

56. GHL to Hickson, [Apr. 1842], MS Yale.

57. See Mill to Victor Cousin, 27 Apr. 1842, and to Auguste Comte, 9 June 1842, *Collected Works*, xiii. 517, 527.

58. Comte to Mill, 29 May 1842, Auguste Comte, *Correspondance générale et confessions*, ed. Paulo E. de Berrêdo Carneiro and Pierre Arnaud, 7 vols. (Paris, 1973–), ii. 49.

59. GHL to Jules Michelet, 26 May 1842, MS Michelet Papers, Bibliothèque Historique de la Ville de Paris. See also Michelet, *Journal*, ed. Paul Viallaneix, 2 vols. (Paris, 1959, 1962), i. 398–404, 538, for references to GHL's visits to him in May 1842 and again in Sept. 1843.

60. GHL, 'The Modern Metaphysics and Moral Philosophy of France', *British and Foreign Review*, 15 (July 1843), 401.

61. Mill to Comte, 13 July 1843, *Collected Works*, xiii. 591; Comte to Mill, 16 July 1843, *Correspondance générale*, ii. 178–9.

62. Mill to Comte, 21 June 1845, *Collected Works*, xiii. 667. See also Mill to Alexander Bain, 22 Nov. 1863, ibid, xv, 903 (*Later Letters*).

63. GHL, *Biographical History of Philosophy*, i. 11, 6, 7.

64. Ibid. iii. 7.

65. Ibid. 109.

66. Ibid. iv. 95.

67. Ibid. 245, 250.

68. For accounts of the widespread influence of Comte's system see W. M. Simon, *European Positivism in the 19th Century: An Essay in Intellectual History* (Ithaca, NY, 1963), and T. R. Wright, *The Religion of Humanity: The Impact of Comtean Positivism on Victorian Britain* (Cambridge, 1986).

69. *Classical Museum*, 3 (1846), 220. (The review may have been by Thomas Dyer, see K. K. Collins and Frederick Williams, 'Lewes at Colonnus: An Early Victorian View of Translation from the Greek', *Modern Language Review*, 82 (Apr. 1987), 295.) See also *Oxford and Cambridge Review*, 2 (Feb. 1846), 168–91.

70. GHL to Varnhagen, 2 Aug. 1845, Pickett, 'Lewes's Letters to Varnhagen', 523; GHL to W. B. Scott, [June 1846], MS Princeton; GHL to Macvey Napier, 16 July 1846, MS BL.

71. Comte to GHL, 4 July 1846, and GHL to Comte, 10 July 1846, *Correspondance générale*, iv. 20, 225.

72. John Sharpe to J. W. Parker & Son, 12 Nov. 1857, MS Yale; Harriet Martineau, *Autobiography*, 2 vols. (London, 1877, repr. 1983), ii. 371; and R. K. Webb, *Harriet Martineau: A Radical Victorian* (London, 1960), 303.

73. Herbert Spencer, *An Autobiography*, 2 vols. (London, 1904), i. 378, 379.

74. See GHL Jour., 1 Jan. 1866, MS Yale.

75. Frederic Harrison, 'G. H. Lewes', *Academy*, 14 (Dec. 1878), 543.

76. Lord Acton, 'George Eliot's "Life"', *Nineteenth Century*, 17 (Mar. 1885), 478; E. Abbott and L. Campbell, *The Life and Letters of Benjamin Jowett*, 2 vols. (London, 1897), i. 261.

77. Holyoake, *Sixty Years of an Agitator's Life*, i. 244.

CHAPTER 4

1. GHL, *Biographical History of Philosophy*, iv. 257.

2. Charles Lee Lewes was born at 3 Pembroke Square, Kensington, in Nov. 1842; in June 1843 the Leweses moved to nearby Campden Hill Terrace, where Thornie was born in Apr. 1844. The family moved to 26 Bedford Place, Kensington, in June 1846, and Herbert was born there in July 1846. Information about their addresses is from Lewes's letter headings and from London Post Office Directories. Thornton and Kate Hunt lived in Church Lane, Kensington, moving to nearby Queen's Road, Bayswater, some time

in 1844, and to Hammersmith in 1849, see Molly Tatchell, *Leigh Hunt and his Family in Hammersmith* (London, 1969), 59.

3. Arthur Helps to John Anster, 27 Nov. 1843, *Correspondence of Sir Arthur Helps*, ed. E. A. Helps (London, 1917), 40–1. The editor gives the date as 1844 but it is clear from the reference to GHL's article on dramatic reform in the *Edinburgh Review* that the year is 1843.

4. GHL to Agnes Lewes, n.d. [Dec. 1843?], copy of MS in the possession of the late Gordon S. Haight.

5. See GHL, 'Literary Receipts', *GEL*, vii. 366–8.

6. See Comte to GHL, 1 Apr. 1846, and to Mill, 6 May 1846, *Correspondance générale*, iii. 365; iv. 6.

7. See GHL to Varnhagen, 29 Apr. 1846, Pickett, 'Lewes's Letters to Varnhagen', 526.

8. GHL, 'George Sand', *Monthly Magazine*, 7 (May 1842), 578–91.

9. GHL, 'Balzac and George Sand', *Foreign Quarterly Review*, 33 (July 1844), 265–98.

10. George Sand to GHL, 6 May 1843, MS Pierpont Morgan.

11. GHL to George Sand, 30 Mar. [1846], MS Bibliothèque Historique de la Ville de Paris, published with the wrong date—1847—in George Sand, *Correspondance*, ed. Georges Lubin, 19 vols. (Paris, 1964–), vii. 645.

12. George Sand to Charles Duvernet, *c.* 25 April 1846, ibid. 321; Harriet Grote to Varnhagen, 20 May 1846, MS Jagiellonian. I am indebted to Terry Pickett of the University of Alabama for the text of this letter.

13. George Sand to Charles Duvernet, *c.* 25 Apr. 1846, *Correspondance*, vii. 321.

14. Edward Lytton-Bulwer to GHL, n.d. (probably 1849, when GHL was planning the *Leader*), MS Bodleian. For details of Bulwer's life see Michael Sadleir, *Bulwer: A Panorama* (London, 1931).

15. Carlyle, 'Model Prisons', *Latter-Day Pamphlets* (London, 1850, repr. by the Canadian Federation for the Humanities, 1983), 101–2, 103. See also Fred Kaplan, '"Phallus-Worship" (1848): Unpublished Manuscripts III—A Response to the Revolution of 1848', *Carlyle Newsletter*, 2 (1980), 19–23, for Carlyle's fragmentary rant against Phallus-worship in novels.

16. See Jane Welsh Carlyle to Jeannie Welsh, 18 Jan. 1843, *Collected Letters of Thomas and Jane Welsh Carlyle*, xvi. 20.

17. GHL to Varnhagen, 26 Apr. 1847, Pickett, 'Lewes's Letters to Varnhagen', 530.

18. Jane Welsh Carlyle to Jeannie Welsh, 1–4 Apr. 1849, *Letters to her Family*, 329.

19. For the complicated arrangements of the Hunt and Gliddon families, see Tatchell, *Leigh Hunt and his Family*, 58 ff.

20. Frederick Locker-Lampson, *My Confidences*, 312.

21. George Smith, 'Recollections', TS NLS, 220–1.

22. Ibid. 221.

23. Bessie Rayner Parkes to Barbara Leigh Smith, 18 Nov. 1863, and an unpublished TS by Bessie's daughter Marie Belloc Lowndes, MSS Girton. See also *Diaries and Letters of Marie Belloc Lowndes*, ed. Susan Lowndes (London, 1971), 100.

24. Halcott Glover, *Both Sides of the Blanket* (London, 1945), 3, 7, 10, 15, 21–2, 46, 132, 144–5, 157.

25. *New Statesman and Nation*, 16 Aug. 1947; see also Gordon S. Haight's reply, ibid. 20 Sept. 1947, casting doubt on Glover's story. I am indebted to Mrs Kathleen Adams of the George Eliot Fellowship for cuttings of these letters.

26. Eliza Lynn, *Realities, a Tale*, 3 vols. in 1 (London, 1851); *The Autobiography of Christopher Kirkland*, 3 vols. (London, 1885), i. 280–1.

27. E. M. Whitty, *Friends of Bohemia: or, Phases of London Life*, 2 vols. (London, 1857), i. 180.

28. Quoted in [GE] 'Belles Lettres', *Westminster Review*, 67 NS (Jan. 1857), 313, 314. Mrs Phillipson's pamphlet is unobtainable, but GE in her review quotes amply from it.

29. GHL to W. B. Scott, [June 1846], MS Princeton.

30. GHL, *The Spanish Drama: Lope de Vega and Calderon* (London, 1846), and 'The Spanish Drama: Lope de Vega and Calderon', *Foreign Quarterly Review*, 31 (July 1843), 502–39.

31. GHL to Varnhagen, 19 Nov. 1846, Pickett, 'Lewes's Letters to Varnhagen', 527.

32. GHL, 'Friends in Council', *British Quarterly Review*, 6 (Aug. 1847), 134.

33. GHL, 'Charles Lamb—His Genius and Writings', ibid. 7 (May 1848), 306.

34. GHL, 'Charles Lamb and his Friends', ibid. 8 (Nov. 1848), 382.

35. GHL, 'Historical Romance—Alexandre Dumas', ibid. 7 (Feb. 1848), 184, 185.

36. Ibid. 193, 186–7.

37. GHL, 'T. B. Macaulay—History of England', ibid. 9 (Feb. 1849), 4–5, 27.

38. For the history of Chartism in London see David Goodway, *London Chartism 1838–1848* (Cambridge, 1982).

39. GHL to Hickson, 5 Mar. 1848, MS Yale; GHL, 'Historical Romance—Alexandre Dumas', *British Quarterly Review*, 7. 194.

40. GHL, 'Benjamin D'Israeli', ibid. 10 (Aug. 1849), 118, 120.

41. GHL to Napier, endorsed 15 Aug. 1846, MS BL.

42. William Blackwood to GHL, 12 July 1878, *GEL*, vii. 41; GHL to William Blackwood [summer 1878], MS Blackwood Papers, NLS. Two stories, 'Falsely Accused' (Feb. 1849) and 'Metamorphoses' (May–July 1856), were printed in *Tales from Blackwood* (1879).

43. See GHL, 'Literary Receipts', *GEL*, vii. 368.

44. Douglas Jerrold to GHL, n.d. (either 1847 or 1848), MS Brotherton.

45. George Smith, 'Recollections', TS NLS, 73–4, 77.

46. Jerrold to GHL, 11 Sept. [1848], MS Pierpont Morgan.

47. The MS diary of Henry Silver is in the London office of *Punch*.

48. GHL, *Morning Chronicle*, 6 Mar. 1848, 3; Thackeray to GHL, 6 Mar. 1848, *Letters and Private Papers of W. M. Thackeray*, ed. Gordon N. Ray, 4 vols. (London, 1945–6), ii. 354.

49. GHL, 'Pendennis', *Leader*, 21 Dec. 1850, 929–30, and 'Henry Esmond', ibid. 6 Nov. 1852, 1071–3.

50. GHL to Elizabeth Gaskell, [1857], quoted in her *Life of Charlotte Brontë* (London, 1857, repr. 1984), 233.

51. Charlotte Brontë to William Smith Williams, 6 Nov. 1847, *The Brontës*, ii. 151–2. Charlotte Brontë's letters to GHL are in the British Library; the editors of *The Brontës* give inaccurate transcriptions and omit portions of the letters. I quote in every case from the MS, giving volume and page reference to the published version except in cases where the text has been omitted from it, when I give the MS reference only.

52. Charlotte Brontë to GHL, 6 Nov. 1847, *The Brontës*, ii. 152–3.

53. GHL, 'Recent Novels: French and English', *Fraser's Magazine*, 36 (Dec. 1847), 690–1.

54. Charlotte Brontë to Williams, 11 Dec. 1847, *The Brontës*, ii. 159–60. For GHL as the best contemporary reviewer of Charlotte Brontë see Miriam Allott, introd. to *The Brontës: The Critical Heritage* (London, 1974), 15.

55. See Charlotte Brontë to GHL, 12 and 18 Jan. 1848, *The Brontës*, ii. 178–81. For an account of the Brontë–GHL correspondence see Franklin Gary, 'Charlotte Brontë and George Henry Lewes', PMLA, 51 (1936), 518–42.

56. Charlotte Brontë to Williams, 14 and 23 Dec. 1847 and 4 Jan. 1848, *The Brontës*, ii. 162, 166, 174.

57. Charlotte Brontë to Williams, 22 Feb. 1850, ibid. iii. 79–80.

58. Agnes Lewes to Edward Lewes, n.d. (but probably *c.* 1849), MS Co-operative Union.

CHAPTER 5

1. GHL, *Ranthorpe*, vi.

2. GHL to Leigh Hunt, 3 Oct. 1838, MS Keats Memorial House; GHL to Varnhagen, 2 Mar. 1842, Pickett, 'Lewes's Letters to Varnhagen', 519–20.

3. Bulwer's note, dated 1869, is filed with GHL's letters to him, MS Hertford; Bulwer to his son Robert, 20 Aug. 1866, Victor A. G. R. Lytton, *The Life of Edward Bulwer, First Lord Lytton*, 2 vols. (London, 1913), ii. 438.

4. GHL to Bulwer, 15 Feb 1843, MS Hertford.

5. Bulwer to GHL, postmarked 1 Dec. 1846, MS Bodleian.

6. GHL to Bulwer, 22 Dec. 1846, MS Hertford.

7. See Robert Vaughan, *British Quarterly Review*, 7 (May 1848), 332–46; GHL to John Blackwood, 22 May [1847], MS Boston.

8. Arthur Helps to John Anster, 31 May 1847, MS in the possession of Dr Peter Helps. I am indebted to Dr Helps and to his sister Mrs Ann Thornton, for allowing me to study the Helps papers. GHL to Varnhagen, 26 Apr. 1847, Pickett, 'Lewes's Letters to Varnhagen', 529. Jane Welsh Carlyle's copy of *Ranthorpe* is in the Carlyle House, Chelsea; see Fred Kaplan, 'Carlyle's Marginalia and George Henry Lewes's Fiction', *Carlyle Newsletter*, 5 (1984), 21.

9. Ibid. 23, 25.

10. Vaughan, *British Quarterly Review*, 7 (May 1848), 335.

11. Charlotte Brontë to GHL, 18 Jan. 1848, MS BL (this part of the letter is omitted by the editors of *The Brontës*); and to Williams, 29 Mar. 1848, *The Brontës*, ii. 200.

12. GHL, *Ranthorpe*, 113.

13. Mill to GHL, May 1847, *Collected Works*, xvii. 2003 (*Later Letters*); Dickens to GHL, 7 Nov. 1847, *Letters*, Pilgrim Edn. v. 190–1.

14. GHL to Horne, n.d. (summer 1852), MS Harry Ransom Humanities Research Center.

15. GHL, *Ranthorpe*, 142, 146–7.

16. John Forster to Samuel Phelps, 27 Nov. 1846, MS Yale. See also James A. Davies, *John Forster: A Literary Life* (Leicester, 1983), 86, 272.

17. Peter Conrad, reviewing the Ohio 1974 reprint of *Ranthorpe*, *Times Literary Supplement*, 9 May 1975.

18. Lady Blessington to GHL, 7 Apr. 1848, MS UCLA.

19. Geraldine Jewsbury to Jane Welsh Carlyle, 29 Mar. 1849, *Selections from the Letters of G. E. Jewsbury to Jane Welsh Carlyle*, ed. Mrs Alexander Ireland (London, 1892), 288.

20. Jane Welsh Carlyle to Carlyle, 13 Apr. 1848, *Letters and Memorials of Jane Welsh Carlyle*, prepared for publication by Carlyle, ed. J. A. Froude, 3 vols. (London, 1883), ii. 34.

21. See Kaplan, 'Carlyle's Marginalia', 26–7.

22. GHL, *Rose, Blanche, and Violet*, i. pp. v, vi.

23. Dickens to GHL, 20 May 1848, *Letters*, Pilgrim Edn. v. 312–13.

24. Charlotte Brontë to Williams, 26 Apr. and 1 May 1848, *The Brontës*, ii. 206–7, 208–9.

25. GHL to Bulwer, 14 Apr. 1848, MS Hertford; Bulwer to GHL, postmarked 24 Apr. 1848, MS Bodleian.

26. GHL Diary, 6 Dec. 1875, MS Yale.

27. Dickens to GHL, 15 June 1847, *Letters*, Pilgrim Edn. v. 91.

28. Dickens to Mark Lemon, 4 July 1847, ibid. 115, and to GHL, 9 July 1847, ibid. 122.

29. Dickens to Alexander Ireland, 11 July 1847, ibid. 125.

30. Dickens to Forster, 9–19 July 1847, ibid. 131.

31. Christiana Thompson's diary for 26 July 1847, ibid. 133 n.

32. See Dickens to Thomas Beard, 2 Aug. 1847, ibid. 136; Walter Dexter, 'For One Night Only: Dickens's Appearances as an Amateur Actor', *The Dickensian*, 36 (1940), 20.

33. Dickens to GHL, 3 Aug. 1847, *Letters*, Pilgrim Edn. v. 139.

34. Holyoake, *Sixty Years of an Agitator's Life*, i. 227.

35. Dickens to GHL, 11 Aug. 1847, *Letters*, Pilgrim Edn. v. 147.

36. GHL to Hickson, 12 Sept. [1847], MS Yale.

37. See Jerrold to GHL, 27 Sept. [1847], MS Yale Medical Library.

38. GHL to Hickson, 6 Dec. 1847, MS Yale.

39. Dickens to GHL, 31 Jan. 1848, *Letters*, Pilgrim Edn. v. 242 and n.; see also Dickens to John Hullah, 31 Jan. 1848, ibid. 241 and n.

40. Dickens to GHL, 28 Feb. and 2 Mar. 1848, ibid. 252–3, 258.

41. Dickens to GHL, 12 Apr. 1848, ibid. 277, and to Mrs Cowden Clarke, 14 Apr. 1848, ibid. 278.

42. Ibid. v. 307 n.

43. See Dexter, 'For One Night Only', 22–30, for details of playbills, performances, and receipts in 1848.

44. Unidentified newspaper cuttings in Forster's collection of Amateur Theatrical Performances, Forster Collection, V. & A.

45. Ibid. Geraldine Jewsbury praised GHL's acting in his own play, *The Noble Heart*, in the *Manchester Examiner and Times* in Apr. 1849, see Susanne Howe, *Geraldine Jewsbury: Her Life and Errors* (London, 1935), 70.

46. GHL wrote to Comte, 9 Oct. 1848, saying he was to introduce positivism to England's provincial cities; Comte replied graciously, 15 Oct. 1848, *Correspondance générale*, iv. 195, 256.

47. The first version is in 'Plays from the Lord Chamberlain's Office', vol. cxlvi, Mar. 1848, and the final version is in vol. clxi, Feb. 1850, MSS BL.

48. Text of 12 Feb. 1850, ibid. vol. clxi.

49. Espinasse, *Literary Recollections*, 286; Jane Welsh Carlyle to Jeannie Welsh, 1 and 4 Apr. 1849, *Letters to her Family*, 329.

50. See GE's annotations to the proof copy of Sully's article on GHL, *New Quarterly Magazine* (Oct. 1879), Sully Collection, UCL. She corrects Sully's remark that GHL gave up his theatrical ambitions in 1851: 'No—he did not *soon* abandon it. He continued it till 1853, in the last 4 or 5 years up to that period more diligently than other forms of literature. He gave it up simply because his *habits*, *tastes* and *opportunities* had altered.'

51. Elizabeth Gaskell to Edward Chapman, 9 Mar. 1849, *The Letters of Mrs Gaskell*, ed. J. A. V. Chapple and Arthur Pollard (Manchester, 1966), 72; Espinasse, *Literary Recollections*, 283.

52. *Manchester Courier*, 14 Mar. 1849, 164.

53. Espinasse, *Literary Recollections*, 284.

54. GHL, 'Macready's Shylock', *Leader*, 9 Nov. 1850, 787.

55. See W. J. Lawrence, *Barry Sullivan: A Biograpahical Sketch* (London, 1893), 34.

56. Forster to Macready, 4 May 1849, quoted from a sale catalogue in Dickens, *Letters*, Pilgrim Edn. v. 550 n.

57. *Manchester Guardian*, 18 Apr. 1849, 6.

58. See Susanne Howe, *Geraldine Jewsbury*, 70; Espinasse, *Literary Recollections*, 284–5.

59. Dickens to Sheridan Muspratt, 4 June 1849, *Letters*, Pilgrim Edn. v. 550.

60. *Edinburgh News and Literary Chronicle*, 24 Nov. 1849, 4; *Scotsman*, 24 Nov. 1849, 2.

61. GHL, *On Actors and the Art of Acting* (London, 1875), 55, 56.

62. Ibid. 61–2.

63. GHL, 'On the Fame of Actors', *Leader*, 8 Mar. 1851, 228.

64. GHL to Benjamin Webster, n.d. (late 1849): 'Have the Keans read "The Noble Heart" and decided?', MS UCLA.

65. GHL to Robert Chambers, 8 Feb. [1850], MS W. and R. Chambers Papers, NLS.

66. Holyoake's diary for 18 Feb. 1850 notes his attendance, MS Bishopsgate Institute; Dickens to Frank Stone, 18 Feb. 1850, *Letters*, Pilgrim Edn. vi. 38.

67. See *Athenaeum*, 22 Feb. 1850, 211–12, and *Examiner*, 23 Feb. 1850, 117.

68. See Stephens, *The Censorship of English Drama*, 28.

69. GHL, *The Noble Heart*, a tragedy in 3 acts, as performed at the Royal Olympic Theatre (London, 1850), iii.

70. See Edmund Yates, *Recollections and Experiences*, 2 vols. (London, 1884), i. 207–8; *Dramatic Essays by John Forster and George Henry Lewes*, ed. William Archer and Robert W. Lowe (London, 1896), xxiii.

71. See John Hopkin, 'George Henry Lewes as Playwright: A Register of Pieces', *Essays on Nineteenth-Century British Theatre*, ed. Kenneth Richards and Peter Thomson (London, 1971), 113.

CHAPTER 6

1. For accounts of European refugees in England after 1848 see Bernard Porter, *The Refugee Question in Mid-Victorian Politics* (Cambridge, 1979), and Rosemary Ashton, *Little Germany: Exile and Asylum in Victorian England* (Oxford, 1986).

2. GHL, 'Prospectus for "The Free Speaker"', MS Berg Collection, NYPL.

3. Charlotte Brontë to James Taylor, 22 May 1850, and to GHL, 23 Nov. 1850, *The Brontës*, iii. 111, 183.

4. See *The Unknown Mayhew: Selections from the Morning Chronicle 1849–1850*, ed. E. P. Thompson and Eileen Yeo (London, 1984); Carlyle, *Past and Present* (London, 1843), bk. iii, ch. 7, 'Over-Production'.

5. Carlyle, *Latter-Day Pamphlets*, 'Downing Street' (Apr. 1850), 197, 113; 'The Present Time' (Feb. 1850), 14; 'Model Prisons' (Mar. 1850), 87.

6. Dickens, 'The Last Words of the Old Year', *Household Words*, 4 Jan. 1851, in Dickens, *Collected Papers*, 2 vols. (London, 1937), i. 341–3.

7. 'Prospectus', *Leader*, 30 Mar. 1850, 22.

8. Holyoake, *Sixty Years of an Agitator's Life*, i. 237.

9. See Thomson, *George Sand and the Victorians*, 24.

10. Holyoake, *Sixty Years*, ii. 232.

11. GHL, 'Lyell and Owen on Development', *Leader*, 18 Oct. 1851, 996.

12. GHL to Chambers, 8 Feb. 1850, MS NLS.

13. Mill, *On Liberty* (1854), ch. 2 ('Of the Liberty of Thought and Discussion'), *Collected Works*, xviii. 241.

14. See *Leader*, 5 Apr. 1850, 318.

15. GHL, 'Literature', ibid. 1 June 1850, 231.

16. For a discussion of the work of Combe, Chambers, Spencer, and others see Diana Postlethwaite, *Making It Whole: A Victorian Circle and the Shape of Their World* (Columbus, Ohio, 1984).

17. GHL to Thornton Hunt, Sat. [24 Nov. 1849], MS Berg, NYPL.

18. Ibid.

19. See introduction to Froude's *Nemesis of Faith*, 7–8; Edmund Larken to Thornton Hunt, 24 Dec. 1849, MS Berg, NYPL.

20. GHL to Hunt, Wed. [28 Nov. or 5 Dec. 1849], MS Berg, NYPL.

21. GHL to Hunt, Sat. [1 or 8 Dec. 1849], MS Berg, NYPL.

22. GHL to Holyoake, 8 Aug. 1849, MS Co-operative Union.

23. Holyoake to Herbert Spencer, 15 Dec. 1878, MS Yale.

24. See Holyoake, *Bygones Worth Remembering*, 2 vols. (London, 1905), i. 64.

25. Holyoake, *Sixty Years of an Agitator's Life*, i. 243, 241.

26. W. J. Linton to Thornton Hunt, 11 Oct. 1849, Miscellaneous MSS Yale. This is one of 8 lengthy fanatical letters between 9 Oct. 1849 and 22 Feb. 1850.

27. Mazzini to James Stansfeld, 20 Jan. 1850, *Mazzini's Letters to an English Family*, ed. E. F. Richards, 3 vols. (London, 1920–2), i. 144.

28. W. J. Linton to Edmund Larken, two undated letters [Feb. 1850], Miscellaneous MSS Yale.

29. GHL to Hunt, [1 or 8 Dec. 1849], MS Berg, NYPL.

30. See F. B. Smith, *Radical Artisan: W. J. Linton 1812–1897* (Manchester, 1973), 96.

31. Larken to Hunt, 24 Dec. 1849, MS Berg, NYPL.

32. Ibid.

33. GHL to Hunt, Saturday [29 Dec. 1849], MS Berg, NYPL.

34. See GHL, 'Literary Receipts', *GEL*, vii. 369.

35. GHL to Hunt, [29 Dec. 1849], MS Berg, NYPL.

36. Larken to Hunt, 4 Jan. 1850, MS Berg, NYPL.

37. Leigh Hunt, *Autobiography*, 3 vols. (London, 1850), ii. 149–50.

38. See *The Autobiography and Letters of Mrs M. O. W. Oliphant*, ed. Mrs Harry

Coghill (Edinburgh and London, 1899), 419, for Mrs Oliphant's report of Jane Welsh Carlyle on the Hunts.

39. Leigh Hunt to Carlyle, 29 July 1833, in C. R. Sanders, *Carlyle's Friendships and Other Studies* (Durham, NC, 1977), 118. Thornton Hunt's epilepsy is mentioned in 1860 by his American friend Benjamin Moran, *The Journal of Benjamin Moran 1857–1865*, ed. S. A. Wallace and F. E. Gillespie, 2 vols. (Chicago, Ill., 1948), i. 638.

40. Carlyle to John Carlyle, 5 Mar. 1850, and to Mrs Aitken, 25 Apr. 1850, *New Letters*, ii. 90–1, 93–4.

41. Holyoake, *Sixty Years of an Agitator's Life*, i. 227.

42. Holyoake Diary 1850, MS Bishopsgate Institute.

43. A copy of the deed is in the Bishopsgate Institute.

44. GHL, 'Literature', *Leader*, 30 Mar. 1850, 14.

45. GHL, 'The Apprenticeship of Life', ch. 11, ibid. 8 June 1850, 261.

46. GHL, 'Confessions of a Timid Lover', part i, ibid. 7 Sept. 1850, 573.

47. Vivian, 'The Beauty of Married Men', ibid. 13 Apr. 1850, 68–9.

48. GHL, 'Two Magnetic Seances', ibid. 15 June 1850, 285.

49. GHL, 'Leigh Hunt's *Autobiography*', ibid. 6 July 1850, 353.

50. Charlotte Brontë to GHL, 1 Nov. 1849, *The Brontës*, iii. 31.

51. GHL, 'Currer Bell's *Shirley*', *Edinburgh Review*, 91 (Jan. 1850), 155, 157–8, 160.

52. Charlotte Brontë to GHL, Jan. 1850, *The Brontës*, iii. 67.

53. Charlotte Brontë to GHL, 19 Jan. 1850, ibid. 68.

54. GHL to Elizabeth Gaskell, 15 Apr. 1857, *GEL*, ii. 315–16.

55. GHL, 'The Drama before Easter', *Leader*, 30 Mar. 1850, 19.

56. GHL, 'Wordsworth's *Prelude*', ibid. 17 Aug. 1850, 496–7.

57. GHL, 'Literature', ibid. 8 June 1850, 254.

58. GHL, 'Leigh Hunt's *Autobiography*', ibid. 29 June 1850, 328–9.

59. GHL, 'Tennyson's New Poem', ibid. 22 June 1850, 303.

60. GHL, 'Browning's New Poem', ibid. 27 Apr. 1850, 111; 'Elizabeth Barrett Browning', ibid. 30 Nov. 1850, 856–7.

61. See GE's essays, 'Evangelical Teaching: Dr Cumming' (1855) and 'Silly Novels by Lady Novelists' (1856), repr. in *Essays of George Eliot*, ed. Thomas Pinney (London, 1963), especially 302 and n. The phrase 'this working-day world' comes originally from *As You Like It*, i. iii. 12.

62. GHL, '*Wuthering Heights*', *Leader*, 28 Dec. 1850, 953.

63. Charlotte Brontë to Ellen Nussey, 12 June 1850, *The Brontës*, iii. 118.

64. Vivian, 'Charles Kean's Hamlet', *Leader*, 12 Oct. 1850, 692, and 'Macready's Shylock', ibid. 9 Nov. 1850, 787.

65. See Archer's introd., *Dramatic Essays of John Forster and George Henry Lewes*, xxiv.

66. G. B. Shaw, reviews in *Saturday Review*, 20 June 1896 and 5 June 1897, repr. in *Our Theatres in the Nineties*, 3 vols. (London, 1932), ii. 161, iii. 155.

67. Froude to GHL, 7 Feb. [1851], MS Yale.

68. Froude to Kingsley, 10 Nov. 1849, Waldo Hilary Dunn, *James Anthony Froude: A Biography*, 2 vols. (Oxford, 1961, 1963), i. 164.

69. Ibid. ii. 274; Espinasse, *Literary Recollections*, 289.

70. Thornton Hunt, 'The New Catholic Episcopacy', *Leader*, 26 Oct. 1850, 731; 'News of the Week', ibid. 9 Nov. 1850, 769.

71. GHL, 'Literature', ibid. 9 Nov. 1850, 783.

72. Charlotte Brontë to GHL, 23 Nov. 1850, *The Brontës*, iii. 183–4.

73. Harriet Martineau to GHL, 10 Dec. [1850], MS Yale.

74. See the letter from 'Alfred' to 'Open Council', *Leader*, 6 Apr. 1850, 36–7.

75. GHL, 'Social Reform: Communism as an Ideal', ibid. 26 Oct. 1850, 734.

76. Thornton Hunt, 'The Law of Divorce', ibid. 14 Dec. 1850, 898.

77. See *Mazzini's Letters to an English Family*, i. 193–4. The Freemason's Hall meeting was reported in the *Leader*, 15 Mar. 1851, 243.

78. A printed account of the meeting is in the Holyoake Papers, Bishopsgate Institute.

79. George Combe to GHL, 10 Apr. 1850, (carbon copy) MS Combe Papers, NLS.

80. GHL to Combe, 5 May 1850, MS Combe Papers, NLS; GHL, '*Life of Andrew Combe*', *Leader*, 18 May 1850, 185.

81. Information about the sales of the *Leader* comes from Robert B. Doremus, 'George Henry Lewes: A Descriptive Biography, with Especial Attention to his Interest in the Theatre', unpublished Harvard PhD thesis (1940). For an account of the Stamp Act and its repeal see William Thomas, *The Philosophical Radicals* (Oxford, 1979), 317.

82. See *London Gazette*, 10 June 1851, 1529.

83. See GHL, 'Literary Receipts', *GEL*, vii. 371–2.

84. The fullest account of the *Leader*'s complicated financial and management history is Alan R. Brick's unpublished thesis, '*The Leader*: Organ of Radicalism', Yale PhD thesis (1958).

85. Vivian, 'The Beauty of Married Men' and 'Whitebait at Greenwich', *Leader*, 15 Apr. 1850, 69, and 19 Nov. 1853, 1124. See Eric Partridge, *A*

Dictionary of Slang and Unconventional English, 8th edn. (London, 1984), for the sexual slang used by Lewes and Whitty.

86. E. M. Whitty, *Friends of Bohemia*, i. 179–82.

CHAPTER 7

1. For Chapman's domestic arrangements, and GE's part in them, see Gordon S. Haight, *George Eliot and John Chapman* (New Haven, Conn., 1940, repr. 1969), 15 ff; *GE*, 94 ff.

2. GE left for Coventry on 24 Mar. 1851, returning at the end of Sept., see Haight, *George Eliot and John Chapman*, 22.

3. [William Hale White], *The Autobiography of Mark Rutherford* (London, 1881, repr. Leicester, 1969), 123.

4. Chapman to Chambers, 16 Oct. 1854, see *GE*, 167.

5. Haight, *George Eliot and John Chapman*, 89, 91.

6. Ibid. 130, 131.

7. Ibid. 133–4, 135.

8. *Autobiography of Mark Rutherford*, 122.

9. Combe to Chapman, 7 Dec. 1851, *GEL*, viii. 33.

10. GE to Chapman, 1 Aug. 1851, ibid. i. 357.

11. *GE*, 127.

12. Spencer, *Autobiography*, i. 348.

13. Ibid. 376.

14. Ibid. 376–7, 378, 379.

15. Ibid. 377.

16. GHL Jour., 28 Jan. 1859, MS Yale.

17. GHL, 'Literature', *Leader*, 4 Jan. 1851, 15; 20 Sept. 1851, 897.

18. Vivian, 'Merry Wives of Windsor', ibid. 29 Nov. 1851, 1142.

19. GE to Cara Bray, 27 Nov. 1851, *GEL*, i. 377.

20. *Leader*, 8 Feb. 1851, 132–3; 8 Mar. 1851, 228.

21. 'Vivian in his Easy Chair', ibid. 19 Apr. 1851, 373.

22. 'The Bachelor's Evening', ibid. 25 Oct. 1851, 1022.

23. Spencer, *Autobiography*, i. 377.

24. GHL, 'Lyell and Owen on Development', *Leader*, 18 Oct. 1851, 996.

25. GHL to Richard Owen, n.d. (probably Sept. or Oct. 1851), copy of MS in the possession of the late Gordon S. Haight.

26. GHL to Owen, n.d. (probably 1852), MS Yale.

27. See introduction to Dion Boucicault's *London Assurance*, ed. James L. Smith (London, 1984), xi.

28. See Hopkin, 'G. H. Lewes as Playwright', 113–14.

29. Thornton Hunt, 'The Game of Speculation', *Leader*, 4 Oct. 1851, 949.

30. See, for example, Edmund Yates, *Recollections and Experiences*, i. 192–3; John Westland Marston, *Our Recent Actors: Being Recollections Critical, and, in Many Cases, Personal, of Late Distinguished Performers of Both Sexes*, 2 vols. (London, 1888), i. 164–5, 166–7.

31. GHL, *On Actors and the Art of Acting*, 65.

32. GHL, 'The Game of Speculation', I. i. and III. i, 'Plays from the Lord Chamberlain's Office', vol. clxxiii, MS BL.

33. See Hopkin, 'GHL as Playwright', 113.

34. John Hollingshead, *My Lifetime*, 2 vols. (London, 1895), i. 65–6.

35. Vivian, 'The Lyceum Reopened', *Leader*, 20 Dec. 1851, 1214.

36. GHL to W. M. W. Call, Mar. or Apr. 1852, MS Houghton.

37. Hopkin, 'GHL as Playwright', 115.

38. GHL to J. Stirling Coyne, n.d. (1852), MS Iowa.

39. John Coleman, *Players and Playwrights I Have Known*, 2 vols. (London, 1888), i. 217.

40. Blanchard Jerrold, *The Life and Remains of Douglas Jerrold* (London, 1859), 324; GE to Charles Bray, 17 Apr. 1852, *GEL*, ii. 18.

41. GHL, *On Actors*, 16.

42. See introduction to *Dramatic Essays by John Forster and G. H. Lewes*, xl.

43. 'Vivian in Tears!', *Leader*, 7 Feb. 1852, 137.

44. GHL, 'King John', ibid. 14 Feb. 1852, 161–2.

45. GHL to Robert Chambers, [19 Feb. 1852], MS NLS (dated from Chambers's Journal, also in NLS).

46. Vivian, *Leader*, 28 Feb. 1852, 209; 25 Sept. 1852, 930; 9 Oct. 1852, 978.

47. GHL to Kean, 18 Oct. 1852, and copy of Kean to GHL, 18 Oct. 1852, MSS Yale.

48. GE to the Brays, 5 May 1852, *GEL*, ii. 23–4.

49. GHL, 'Shelley and the Letters of Poets', *Westminster Review*, 1 NS (Apr. 1852), 502–11; 'The Lady Novelists', ibid. 2 NS (July 1852), 129–41.

50. Comte to GHL, 28 Jan. 1847, and GHL to Comte, [Feb. 1847], *Correspondance générale*, iv. 98–100, 240–1.

51. Comte to GHL, 15 Oct. 1848, ibid. 198.

52. See Wright, *Religion of Humanity*, 52 ff.

53. GHL, 'Comte's Positive Philosophy, Part I—Biographical', *Leader*, 3 Apr. 1852, 327–8.

54. GHL, 'Comte's Positive Philosophy, Part XVIII—Vital Dynamics: Instinct and Intelligence. Conclusion', ibid. 14 Aug. 1852, 786.

55. Thomas Baynes, 'An Evening with Carlyle', *Athenaeum*, 2 Apr. 1887, 450.

56. GHL to Horne, n.d. (mid-1852), MS Harry Ransom Humanities Research Center.

57. See Kitchel, *George Lewes and George Eliot*, xii. She had the information from Lewes's granddaughter, Mrs Elinor Ouvry.

58. J. W. Cross, *George Eliot's Life as Related in her Letters and Journals*, 3 vols. (Edinburgh and London, 1885), i. 326.

59. Spencer, *Autobiography*, i. 394–5.

60. GE to the Brays, 14 June 1852, *GEL*, ii. 34; Herbert Spencer to Cross, 2 Feb. 1885, quoted in *GE*, 121–2. See also *GE*, 112–22, for a cogent discussion of GE's relationship with Spencer.

61. Spencer to E. L. Youmans, 3 Feb. 1881, quoted in *GEL*, viii. 42–3 n.

62. See *GE*, 71.

63. GE to the Brays, 27 Apr. 1852, and to Spencer, 21 Apr. 1852, *GEL*, ii. 22, viii. 42. GE's letters to Spencer in 1852 were held in reserve in the MS department of the BL, not to be opened until 1985, at the request of the trustees. They became available for Haight to publish in his supplementary vol. viii of *GEL* in 1978.

64. GE to Spencer, 16? July 1852, *GEL*, viii. 56–7.

65. GE to Spencer, 8? July 1852, ibid. 51.

66. See Virginia Woolf, 'Modern Fiction' (1919), *The Common Reader*, First Series (London, 1925, repr. 1957), 190.

67. GE to the Brays, 27 Apr. 1852, *GEL*, ii. 22.

68. GE to the Brays, 14 June 1852, ibid. 35.

69. GE to Charles Bray, 23 June 1852, ibid. 37.

70. GE to Spencer, 8? July 1852, ibid. viii. 50–1.

71. GHL, 'Literature', *Leader*, 10 July 1852, 663; GE to Chapman, 24–5 July 1852, *GEL*, ii. 49.

72. GE to Sara Hennell, 2 Sept. 1852, ibid. 54.

73. Thomas Adolphus Trollope, *What I Remember*, 2 vols. (London, 1887), ii. 299.

74. David Masson to Robert Vaughan, 8 May 1852, MS Yale.

75. Margaret Fuller to R. W. Emerson, 16 Nov. 1846, *Memoirs of Margaret Fuller Ossoli*, iii. 98; GHL, 'Literature', *Leader*, 14 Feb. 1852, 158–9.

76. GE to the Brays, 22 Nov. 1852, and to Sara Hennell, 28 Mar. 1853, *GEL*, ii. 68, 94. The references to GHL increase throughout 1853.

77. GE to Sara Hennell, 1 Oct. 1853, ibid. 118–19.

78. See Oscar Browning, *Life of George Eliot* (London, 1890), 37; *GE*, 134.

79. Bessie Rayner Parkes Belloc, *In a Walled Garden* (London, 1895, repr. 1900), 17.

80. William Hale White, letter to *Athenaeum*, 28 Nov. 1885, 702.

81. GE to Bray, 8 Oct. 1851, *GEL*, i. 366.

82. GHL to F. O. Ward ('FOW'), n.d., MS Harry Ransom Humanities Research Center. The letter is one of several association items— MS letters of nineteenth-century celebrities—stuck into a first edition of Forster's *Life of Dickens*.

83. See Partridge, *Dictionary of Slang and Unconventional English*.

84. GHL to Chapman, 16 and 18 July 1853, *GEL*, viii. 77–8; GHL to J. W. Parker, 23 Dec. 1853, MS Princeton.

85. See Vivian, *Leader*, 21 May 1853, 501.

86. GE to the Brays, 5 and 12 Mar. 1853, *GEL*, ii. 91, 92.

87. GE to Sara Hennell, 10 July 1854, ibid. 165.

88. GHL, 'Currer Bell's New Novel', *Leader*, 12 Feb. 1853, 163, and '*Ruth* and *Villette*', *Westminster Review*, 3 NS (Apr. 1853), 485, 491.

89. Carlyle, *The French Revolution*, 2 vols. (London, 1837, repr. 1888), i. 108; GE to Bray, 8 Oct. 1851, *GEL*, i. 367.

90. GHL, '*Ruth* and *Villette*', *Westminster Review*, 3 NS, 477, 485; see also '*Ruth*', *Leader*, 22 Jan. 1853, 90.

91. Vivian, *Leader*, 12 Nov. 1853, 1099; 'Two Old Owls', ibid. 19 Nov. 1853, 1123–5; 'The Hope of the Family', ibid. 10 Dec. 1853, 1195.

92. GHL Jour., 28 Jan. 1859, *GE*, 271.

93. See GHL to Varnhagen, 3 Aug. 1853, Pickett, 'Letters to Varnhagen', 530; *GE*, 70; GE to Combe, 23 Sept. 1853, to Sara Hennell, 25 Nov. 1853, and to Cara Bray, 14 Apr. 1854, *GEL*, viii. 78, ii. 127, 149; GHL, 'Literary Receipts', ibid. vii. 383.

94. GHL, 'Literature', *Leader*, 11 Dec. 1852, 1189.

95. Dickens, *Bleak House*, 523 (ch. 33).

96. GHL, 'Literature', *Leader*, 5 and 12 Feb. 1853, 137, 163.

97. Dickens to John Elliotson, 7 Feb. 1853, *The Letters of Charles Dickens*, ed. Walter Dexter, 3 vols. (London, 1938), ii. 446–7; Dickens to GHL, 25

Feb. 1853, published by Gordon S. Haight, 'Dickens and Lewes on Spontaneous Combustion', *Nineteenth Century Fiction*, 10 (1955–6), 58. Several scholars have investigated the GHL–Dickens argument, all of them finding in GHL's favour: Trevor Blount, 'Dickens and Mr Krook's Spontaneous Combustion', *Dickens Studies Annual*, 1 (1970), 183–213; E. Gaskell, 'More About Spontaneous Combustion', *The Dickensian*, 69 (1973), 25–35; Peter Denman, 'Krook's Death and Dickens's Authorities', *The Dickensian*, 83 (1987), 131–41.

98. GHL, 'Goethe as a Man of Science', *Westminster Review*, 2 NS (Oct. 1852), 479, 481, 483, 500. Owen and Huxley became enemies in the later 1850s. Studies of the arguments and personalities in Victorian science include William Irvine, *Apes, Angels, and Victorians: A Joint Biography of Darwin and Huxley* (London, 1955); Adrian Desmond, *Archetypes and Ancestors: Palaeontology in Victorian London 1850–1875* (London, 1982); Mario di Gregorio, *T. H. Huxley's Place in Natural Science* (New Haven, Conn., 1984).

99. GE to Combe, 25 Nov. 1853, *GEL*, viii. 89 and n.

100. GE to Chapman, 17? and 19 Dec. 1853, ibid. ii. 132, 133; GE to Chapman, Dec. 1853, MS Henry E. Huntington Library.

101. T. H. Huxley, *Westminster Review*, 5 NS (Jan. 1854), 254–6.

102. GHL, 'Literature', *Leader*, 14 Jan. 1854, 40.

103. GHL to Chapman, 1 Feb. 1854, *GEL*, ii. 139.

104. GE to Cara Bray, 18 Apr. and 19 May 1854, ibid. 150, 157, 155–6.

105. GE to Bray, 27 May 1854, and to the Brays and Sara Hennell, 19 July 1854, ibid. 158, 166.

CHAPTER 8

1. *GE*, 153.

2. GHL, *Life of Goethe*, i. 310.

3. Carlyle to James Marshall, 14 July 1854, in Fred Kaplan, *Thomas Carlyle: A Biography* (Ithaca, NY, 1983), 433.

4. GHL, *Life of Goethe*, i. 96 n.

5. See Ottilie von Goethe to GHL, 10 Aug. 1854, *GEL*, viii. 117.

6. GE to Bray, 16 Aug. 1854, ibid. ii. 171.

7. GHL quotes Viehoff in the preface to *Life of Goethe* (1855), i. pp. v–vi.

8. GHL to Charles and Thornie Lewes, 27 Sept. 1854, *GEL*, viii. 120–1.

9. *Leader*, 26 Aug. 1854, 809.

10. 'Vivian en Voyage', ibid. 23 Sept. 1854, 909.

11. Ibid.

12. GHL, 'Henri Heine', ibid. 4 Nov. 1854, 1047.

13. GHL, 'Heinrich Heine', ibid. 2 Dec. 1854, 1143–4.

14. GE wrote on Heine in *Leader*, 1 Sept. 1855 and 23 Aug. 1856, in *Westminster Review*, Jan. 1856, and in *Saturday Review*, 26 Apr. 1856, see *Essays of George Eliot*, 216 and n.

15. There is an extensive correspondence between Combe and Chapman on the subject of the latter's faults, Combe Papers, NLS; see also Combe Jour., 15 Sept. 1854, *GEL*, viii. 118.

16. See, for example, GE to Chapman, 6 Aug. 1854, ibid. 115–17.

17. Thomas Woolner to W. B. Scott, 4 Oct. 1854, ibid. ii. 175–6.

18. Sir Charles Gavan Duffy, *Conversations with Carlyle* (London, 1892), 222–3.

19. Carlyle to John Carlyle, 2 Nov. 1854, *GE*, 163.

20. GHL to Carlyle, 19 Oct. 1854, *GEL*, ii. 176–7.

21. Jane Welsh Carlyle in her notebook, *New Letters and Memorials of Jane Welsh Carlyle*, annotated by Carlyle, ed. Alexander Carlyle, 2 vols. (London, 1903), ii. 115.

22. GE to Cara Bray, 4 Sept. 1855, *GEL*, ii. 214.

23. Combe to Bray, 15 Nov. 1854, ibid. viii. 129.

24. Bray to Combe, 8 Oct. 1854, ibid. 122–3.

25. Bray to Combe, 28 Oct. 1854, ibid. 128.

26. Combe's diary, 18 Sept. 1851, MS NLS. I am indebted to the late Gordon S. Haight for the translation of Combe's shorthand.

27. Chapman to Chambers, 16 Oct. 1854, *GEL*, viii. 126.

28. GE Jour., 11 Oct. 1854, *GE*, 160.

29. Sara Hennell to GE, 15 Nov. 1854, *GEL*, ii. 186.

30. GE to Bessie Rayner Parkes, 10 Sept. 1854, ibid. 173–4.

31. Elizabeth Parkes to Bessie Rayner Parkes, 22 and 23 Sept. 1854; Joseph Parkes to Bessie, 1 and 14 Oct. 1854, MSS Girton; Marie Belloc Lowndes, *I, Too, Have Lived in Arcadia* (London, 1941), 39.

32. Bessie Rayner Parkes to Sam Blackwell, 28 Sept. 1854, MS Girton.

33. GE to Chapman, 15 Oct. 1854, *GEL*, viii. 124–5.

34. Varnhagen von Ense Diary (my translation), 5 and 6 Nov. 1854, *Aus dem Nachlass Varnhagen's von Ense, Tagebücher*, ed. Ludmilla Assing, 15 vols. (Leipzig, 1861–70, Berlin, 1905), xi. 300, 301.

35. GE Jour., 'Recollections of Berlin', *GE*, 175. For the relative freedoms in England and Germany during the 1850s in matters of religion, politics, and society see Ashton, *Little Germany*, 25 ff.

36. See *GE*, 177.

37. Agreement between Nutt and GHL, June 1855, MS Yale.

38. GE to Bray, 1 May 1855, *GEL*, ii. 199.

39. GE to Bray, 16 July 1855, ibid. 210.

40. *GE*, 177.

41. GE, 'Life and Opinions of Milton' (4 Aug. 1855), *Essays of George Eliot*, 156, 157.

42. For Carlyle's and GHL's importance in introducing Goethe to Britain see Ashton, *The German Idea*.

43. Carlyle to GHL, 7 Aug. 1855, *GEL*, viii. 141–2.

44. Doremus calculated that the German translation alone had gone through 18 editions by 1903, see 'G. H. Lewes: A Descriptive Biography', ii. 552.

45. Havelock Ellis, introduction to GHL, *Life and Works of Goethe* (London, 1908), vii–viii.

46. GHL, 'Carlyle's *Frederick the Great*', *Fraser's Magazine*, 58 (Dec. 1858), 644.

47. GHL, *Life of Goethe*, i. 144.

48. GHL to John Stuart Blackie, 19 Dec. 1855, *GEL*, viii. 147; GHL, *Life of Goethe*, ii. 34.

49. Ibid. 85–8, 356.

50. Ibid. 91.

51. Ibid. i. 194, 220.

52. Ibid. ii. 206, 207–8, 210–11.

53. GE, 'The Morality of *Wilhelm Meister*', *Leader*, 21 July 1855, 703, repr. in *Essays of GE*, 144–7.

54. GHL, *Life of Goethe*, ii. 375, 379.

55. Ibid. i. 106.

56. Espinasse, *Literary Recollections*, 285.

57. GHL, *Life of Goethe*, ii. 201.

58. Robert Vaughan, 'The Life and Works of Goethe', *British Quarterly Review*, 23 (Apr. 1856), 468–9.

59. *Edinburgh Review*, 106 (July 1857), 203; *Athenaeum*, 10 Nov. 1855, 1304 (reviewer identified as John Oxenford from marked file in the City University, London). For an extended account of English and German criticism of the *Life of Goethe* see Ashton, *The German Idea*, 142 ff.

60. Varnhagen Jour., 1 Dec. 1855 and 24 June 1858, *Tagebücher*, xii. 326–7, xiv. 297–8; Schöll in *Weimarer Sonntagsblatt* (Dec. 1857), copy at Yale.

61. GHL to Franz Duncker, 4 Feb. 1858, MS Kestner-Museum.

62. Carlyle to GHL, 3 Nov. 1855, *GEL*, viii. 145.

63. GE to Bray, 21 Nov. 1855, ibid. ii. 221.

CHAPTER 9

1. GE to Bray, 13 Sept. 1855, *GEL*, ii. 216.

2. What little we know of Edward Lewes is as follows: the Census of 30 Mar. 1851 describes him as aged 37, born in London, a medical student, living at 13 St Ann's Terrace, St John's Wood, with his wife Susanna, aged 23, and his mother-in-law Susanna Pittock, aged 46. Post Office Directories show him living at Southwood Lane, Highgate, in 1855. Efforts to trace him in the capacity of registered naval surgeon have failed, but we know from the one letter of his which survives (see n. 4 below) that he served in a medical capacity on long voyages. His only surviving child, Vivian Byam Lewes (1852–1915), became a professor of chemistry at the Royal Naval College, Greenwich, and was the author of a number of books on chemistry.

3. Undated MS (probably 1849) in Holyoake Collection, Co-operative Union.

4. F. O. Ward to Edwin Chadwick, 20 Apr. 1854, enclosing Edward C. Lewes to Ward, 18 Apr. 1854, MSS Chadwick Papers, UCL.

5. GE to Bray, 31 Mar. and 1 Apr. 1856, *GEL*, ii. 234, 235, 236 n.

6. GHL to John Sibree, 2 Apr. 1856, ibid. viii. 152.

7. Thornton Arnott Lewes to GHL and Agnes Lewes, 6 Dec. 1855, MS Yale.

8. GE to Sara Hennell, 6 Apr. 1856, *GEL*, ii. 236–7.

9. GE to Sara Hennell, 25 Feb. 1856, ibid. 230.

10. GHL to Spencer, 9 Mar. 1856, ibid. viii. 150–1.

11. Bessie Rayner Parkes was the worst offender at asking for 'Miss Evans', see GE to her, 24 Sept. 1857, ibid. ii. 384.

12. GHL to J. W. Parker, Jun., 12 Jan. 1856, and to J. W. Parker, 19 Jan. 1856, ibid. viii. 148, 149.

13. GE to Bray, 6 June 1856, ibid. ii. 253; GHL to Revd George Tugwell [Sept. or Oct. 1856], MS Yale.

14. GHL to John Blackwood, 17 Mar. [1856], MS Blackwood Papers, NLS; Blackwood to GHL, 19 Mar. 1856 (copy), MS NLS. See also GHL's reply, 7 May 1856, *GEL*, viii. 153.

15. GE Jour., 8 May–26 June 1856, ibid. ii. 242; 'The Natural History of German Life', *Essays of George Eliot*, 287. See also Rosemary Ashton, *The Mill on the Floss: A Natural History*, Twayne Masterwork series (Boston, Mass., 1990).

16. GHL, 'Sea-side Studies, Part I', *Blackwood's Magazine*, 80 (Aug. 1856), 190.

17. GE to Barbara Leigh Smith, 13 June 1856, *GEL*, ii. 225; see also *GE*, 204–5.

18. GHL to Bohn, 8 June 1856 (draft), Bohn to GHL, 13 June 1856, and GHL to Bohn, 15 June 1856, *GEL*, viii. 158, 159, 160 n. GE's translation of Spinoza's *Ethics* was finally published recently, ed. Thomas Deegan (Salzburg, 1981).

19. Charlotte Brontë to Ellen Nussey, 19 Jan. 1850, *The Brontës*, iii. 69; GE to Bray, 6 Aug. 1856, *GEL*, ii. 260.

20. GE, 'How I Came to Write Fiction', Jour., 6 Dec. 1857, ibid. 406–7.

21. GHL Jour., 25 and 26 Aug. 1856, MS Yale.

22. GHL Jour., 28 Aug.–4 Sept. 1856, MS Yale; GE to Bray, 5 Sept. 1856, *GEL*, ii. 262.

23. GE to Sara Hennell, 22 Sept. 1856, ibid. 264.

24. Cross, *George Eliot's Life*, i. 384–5.

25. GE, 'Silly Novels by Lady Novelists' (Oct. 1856), *Essays of George Eliot*, 301 ff.

26. GHL to Blackwood, 6 Nov. 1856, and Blackwood to GHL, 12 Nov. 1856, *GEL*, ii. 269, 272.

27. GHL to Blackwood, 22 Nov. 1856, ibid. 276–7.

28. GHL to Tugwell, [Nov. 1856], MS Yale.

29. Blackwood to GE, 30 Jan. 1857, and GE to Blackwood, 4 Feb. 1857, *GEL*, ii. 291, 292.

30. GE, 'How I Came to Write Fiction', Jour., 6 Dec 1857, ibid. 408.

31. Albert Smith to Blackwood and Blackwood to GE, 10 Feb. 1857, ibid. 293 and n. Smith was the author of a poem written on the founding of the Fielding Club in 1852, in which GHL appears as 'Vivian of the flowing locks', see Edmund Yates, *Recollections and Experiences*, i. 236–41.

32. GHL to Blackwood, 11 Feb. 1857, *GEL*, ii. 295.

33. Blackwood to GHL, 13 Feb. 1857, and GHL to Blackwood, 15 Feb. 1857, ibid. 296.

34. See GE, 'Literary Receipts', ibid. vii. 358 ff.

35. GHL Jour., 5 Dec. 1856, MS Yale.

36. Thornton Hunt to Royal Literary Fund, 21 Dec. 1855, MS Royal Literary Fund, BL. This is one of several letters from Hunt and his supporters in Dec. 1855 and Jan. 1856.

37. GHL Jour., 16 and 21 Dec. 1856, *GE*, 218.

38. GHL Jour., Mar. 1858, ibid. 255.

39. Agnes Lewes to Lizzie Gendle, [1862], MS Yale.

40. Mary Huddy to Elinor Ouvry, 30 June 1926, MS Yale.

41. Mrs Willim to GHL [Dec. 1860], MS Yale.

42. See *GE*, 228–33.

43. Ethel Welsh (née Lewes) to Blanche Colton Williams, 2 Dec. 1938, copy in the possession of the late Gordon S. Haight.

44. GHL to Blackwood, 4 Sept. 1857, *GEL*, ii. 380; GE to Sara Hennell, 21 Sept. 1857, ibid. 383.

45. Charles Lee Lewes to Agnes Lewes, 1 Mar. 1857, ibid. viii. 165–6.

46. Thornton Arnott Lewes to GHL, 1 Mar. 1857, ibid. 166.

47. GHL Jour., 7 Jan. 1857, MS Yale.

48. GHL Jour., 27 Mar. 1857, MS Yale.

49. GHL to Elizabeth Gaskell, 15 Apr. 1857, *GEL*, ii. 316.

50. Elizabeth Gaskell to George Smith, Sept. 1856, 2 Oct. 1856, and 2 Nov. 1857, *Letters of Mrs Gaskell*, 414, 418, 587.

51. GHL Jour., 15 and 18 May 1857, MS Yale.

52. See *GE*, 228–33.

53. GE to Sara Hennell, 16 Apr. 1857, *GEL*, ii. 319.

54. GHL to Blackwood, 27 July 1857, ibid. viii. 173; GHL Jour., 1 Jan. 1858, MS Yale.

55. GHL, *Sea-Side Studies*, 271, 4, 5.

56. Ibid. 13.

57. Charles Darwin, *On the Origin of Species by Means of Natural Selection, or the Preservation of Favoured Races in the Struggle for Life* (London, 1859, repr. Harmondsworth, 1984), 124–5.

58. Ibid. 127; GHL, *Sea-Side Studies*, 55.

59. Ibid. 46–7, 48, 51.

60. Darwin, *Origin of Species*, 457.

61. GHL, *Sea-Side Studies*, 30–1.

62. Ibid. 286 ff.

63. Ibid. 255–6, 341.

64. I am indebted to my colleague Sarah Wintle for noting the references to *Sea-Side Studies* in the entries 'anthropomorphic' and 'anthropomorphism' in the OED.

65. GE Jour., 16 Feb. 1858, *GEL*, ii. 434.

66. GE to Bessie Rayner Parkes, 19 Aug. 1859, and GHL to Alexander Main, 1 Mar. 1876, ibid. iii. 134, vi. 226.

67. GHL Jour., 19 Feb. 1858, MS Yale, and GHL to Huxley, 19 Feb. 1858, *GEL*, viii. 196.

68. See GHL to Arthur Helps, 17 Feb. 1858, ibid. 196; GHL to Charles and Thornie, 24 Mar. 1858, MS Yale.

69. Dickens to GE, 18 Jan. 1858, and Jane Welsh Carlyle to GE, 21 Jan. 1858, *GEL*, ii. 423–4, 426.

70. John Blackwood to his wife, 1 Mar. 1858, ibid. 436.

71. For the relationship with Blackwood see *GE, passim*, and J. A. Sutherland, *Victorian Novelists and Publishers* (London, 1976), 188 ff.

72. See *GEL*, iii. 48. The amazingly protracted Liggins affair is documented in detail in *GEL*, ii, iii, and viii.

73. GHL to Charles Lee Lewes, 28 Apr. 1858, MS Yale.

74. GE to Sara Hennell, 13 May 1858, *GEL*, ii. 454; GHL to J. W. Parker, 28 May 1858, MS Bayerische Staatsbibliothek.

75. GE to Sara Hennell, 10–13 May 1858, *GEL*, ii. 453.

76. GHL Jour., 5 May 1858, MS Yale.

77. GHL to Blackwood, 28 June 1858, *GEL*, ii. 467.

78. GHL Jour., 12 and 29 July 1857, 2 Apr. 1859, MS Yale.

79. See D. L. Ross, 'A Survey of Some Aspects of the Life and Work of Sir Richard Owen, K.C.B.', PhD thesis (London University 1972), 45; Cyril Bibby, *Scientist Extraordinary: The Life and Scientific Work of T. H. Huxley (1825–1895)* (Oxford, 1972). John Tyndall's letters show him also struggling on a poor salary at the Royal Institution in the 1850s, see Tyndall Correspondence, xii, MS Royal Institution.

80. See GE to Sara Hennell, 14 June 1858, *GEL*, ii. 465; GHL Jour., 13 and 14 June 1858, MS Yale.

81. For details of Dickens's separation from his wife, and his announcement of it in *Household Words*, 12 June 1858, see Edgar Johnson, *Charles Dickens: His Tragedy and Triumph*, 2 vols. (London, 1953), ii. 920 ff.

82. GHL Jour., 23 June 1858, MS Yale.

83. GHL to his sons, 20 July 1858, MS Yale.

84. GHL, 'Realism in Art: Recent German Fiction', *Westminster Review*, 70 (Oct. 1858), 493, 499.

85. GHL to Blackwood, 5 Sept. 1858, *GEL*, ii. 479.

86. GHL to Blackwood, 8 Oct. 1858, ibid. 487–8. Horne had acted Shylock, following GHL's sympathetic interpretation of the role, at a benefit performance in May 1850. See Dickens to Horne, *Letters*, Pilgrim Edn. vi. 101–2 and n.

87. John Blackwood to GHL, 30 June 1857, MS Blackwood Letter Books, NLS.

88. Blackwood to GHL, 5 May 1859, ibid.

89. Charles Kingsley to GHL, 8 Jan. 1859, MS Yale.

90. GHL, *The Physiology of Common Life*, 2 vols. (London, 1859–60), i. pp. vi–vii.

91. I. P. Pavlov, *Lectures on Conditioned Reflexes*, i. 13, ii. 170 and n. See also *GE*, 255 n.

92. GHL to Blackwood, 30 Jan. 1859, MS Blackwood Papers, NLS.

93. See J. M. Forrester, 'Who Put the George in George Eliot?' *British Medical Journal*, 17 Jan. 1970, 165–7.

94. GHL to his sons, 10 Nov. 1859, *GEL*, iii. 195–6. For GHL's three short papers see *Report of the 29th Meeting of the British Association for the Advancement of Science, held at Aberdeen in September 1859* (London, 1860), 166–70; for replies to GHL's papers see *Athenaeum*, 24 Sept. and 8 Oct. 1859, 407, 471.

95. GHL Jour., 28 Jan. 1859, *GE*, 272.

CHAPTER 10

1. Elizabeth Gaskell to GE, 3 June 1859, *GEL*, iii. 74.

2. Blackwood to GE, 27 Oct. 1859, ibid. 190.

3. Margaret Oliphant, who wrote novels to keep her family, was jolted into writing her autobiography in 1885 by reading Cross's biography of GE, and was half-envious of the 'mental greenhouse' in which GHL kept GE, see *Autobiography and Letters*, 5.

4. See *GEL*, iii. 40 n.; GE to D'Albert-Durade, 18 Oct. 1859, ibid. 186.

5. *GE*, 242, 291–2, 298–301.

6. For the complicated history of the rumours about authorship see ibid. 268–94.

7. GHL to Chapman, 12 Feb. 1859, *GEL*, iii. 13.

8. Barbara Bodichon to GE, 15 Apr. 1859 and 26 Apr. 1859, ibid. viii. 231, iii. 56.

9. GHL Jour., 5 May 1859, MS Yale; GHL to Barbara Bodichon, 5 May 1859, *GEL*, iii. 65.

10. Barbara Bodichon to GE, 28 June 1859, ibid. 103.

11. GE to Charles Lee Lewes, 7 Oct. 1859, ibid. 177.

12. GHL Jour., 10 and 20 Feb. 1859, MS Yale.

13. GHL Jour., 2 Mar. 1859, ibid.

14. GHL Jour., 27 May 1859, *GEL*, iii. 73.

15. Trollope to GHL, 13 Aug. 1869, *The Letters of Anthony Trollope*, ed. N. John Hall, 2 vols. (Stanford, Calif., 1983), i. 479.

16. Charles Lee Lewes to GHL, 3 July 1859, MS Yale.

17. GHL Jour., 13 July 1859, and GHL to Blackwood, 22 July 1859, *GEL*, iii. 116, 117.

18. Charles to GE, 24 July 1859, MS Yale; Thornie to GE, 18 Aug. 1859, *GEL*, viii. 242.

19. Thornie to GE, 9 Sept. 1859, MS Yale.

20. Bertie to GHL and GE, 21 Nov. 1859, *GEL*, viii. 253.

21. GE to Blackwood, 30 July 1859, ibid. iii. 124.

22. Sara Hennell to GE, 26 June 1859, ibid. 98, and 18 Sept. 1859, MS Yale.

23. George Simpson to Joseph Langford, 16 Nov. 1859, *GEL*, iii. 204–5. See also *GE*, 305–18. Blackwood's brother William, and later his nephew, also William, were less patient than Blackwood with what they took to be sharp practice on GE's and GHL's part, see R. F. Anderson, 'Negotiating for *The Mill on the Floss*', *Publishing History*, 2 (1977), 27–39, and '"Things Wisely Ordered": John Blackwood, George Eliot, and the Publication of *Romola*', ibid. 11 (1982), 5–39.

24. Blackwood to GE, 2 Dec. 1859, *GEL*, iii. 222.

25. GHL Jour., 10 Nov. 1859, and GHL to his sons, 10 Nov. 1859, ibid. 197, 195–6.

26. GHL's will, made 1 Nov. 1859, proved 16 Dec. 1878, Somerset House.

27. See Jennifer Glynn, *Prince of Publishers: A Biography of the Great Victorian Publisher George Smith* (London, 1986), 123.

28. GHL Jour., 27 Oct. 1859, *GEL*, iii. 189; GHL to George Smith, 31 Oct. 1859, MS John Murray Archives.

29. GHL, *Studies in Animal Life* (London, 1862), 1–2, 126–7, 136–40.

30. See J. R. Green to Boyd Dawkins, in *The Life and Letters of Charles Darwin*, ed. Francis Darwin, 3 vols. (London, 1888), ii. 322.

31. GHL to George Smith, n.d. (Jan. 1860), MS John Murray Archives.

32. GHL Jour., 14 Jan. 1860, MS Yale.

33. GHL to Blackwood, 5 Mar. 1860, and GHL Jour., 1 Mar. 1860, *GEL*, iii. 269, 267–8.

34. Thornie to GE, 23 Jan. 1860, MS Yale.

35. Thornie to GE and GHL, 20 Feb. 1860, MS Yale; GHL to Charles, 17 Mar. 1860, *GEL*, iii. 274.

36. Thornie to GHL, 20 Mar. 1860, ibid. viii. 259.

37. Thornie to GE and GHL, 16 May 1860, ibid. 267–8.

38. GHL Jour., 3 and 6 Apr. 1860, MS Yale.

39. GHL Jour., 18 Apr. 1860, ibid.

40. GHL Jour., 4 May 1860, *GEL*, iii. 291.

41. GHL Jour., 26 May 1860, MS Yale.

42. GHL Jour., 23 and 24 June 1860, MS Yale.

43. GE to D'Albert-Durade, 6 Dec. 1859, *GEL*, iii. 231.

44. GHL Jour., 23 July 1860, ibid. 326.

45. Trollope to GHL, 9 Aug. 1860, *Letters of Anthony Trollope*, i. 117–18.

46. GE Jour., 17 Dec. 1860, *GE*, 334.

47. Thornie to GHL, 11 Sept. 1860, *GEL*, viii. 270–1.

48. GHL to Blackwood, 6 and 10 Aug. 1860, ibid. iii. 327, 330.

49. GHL Jour., 6 Oct. 1860, ibid. 352.

50. Thornie to GE, 2 Oct. 1860, MS Yale.

51. GHL Jour., 20 Nov. 1860, MS Yale; GHL to Trollope, 15 Dec. 1860, *Letters of Anthony Trollope*, i. 134–5.

52. GHL Jour., 15 Feb. 1861, *GEL*, iii. 378.

53. GHL, 'The Novels of Jane Austen', *Blackwood's Magazine*, 86 (July 1859), 104.

54. *GEL*, iii. 240 n.

55. Blackwood to Langford, 10 Sept. 1860, ibid. 343. The painting is lost, but a chalk drawing for it hangs in Girton College.

56. GE to Barbara Bodichon, 26 Dec. 1860, *GEL*, iii. 366–7.

57. George Smith, 'Recollections', TS NLS, 216, 217; Elizabeth Gaskell to Smith, 30 Nov. 1859, *Letters of Mrs Gaskell*, 594.

58. GE to Blackwood, 12 Jan. 1861, *GEL*, iii. 371.

59. GHL to Blackwood, 25 Aug. 1860, ibid. 335; 'Seeing is Believing', *Blackwood's Magazine*, 88 (Oct. 1860), 381–95.

60. GHL to Blackwood, 6 and 31 Oct. and 13 Nov. 1860, MSS Blackwood Papers, NLS.

61. Blackwood to GHL, 5 Dec. 1860, MS NLS; GHL Jour., 6 Dec. 1860, MS Yale.

62. GHL to Blackwood, 7 Dec. 1860, MS NLS.

63. GE to Frau von Siebold, 26 Aug. 1861, and to Sara Hennell, 27 Mar. 1862, *GEL*, iii. 449, iv. 23.

64. GHL Jour., 16 Apr. 1861, MS Yale.

65. GE to Barbara Bodichon, 30 Sept. 1861, *GEL*, iii. 455 and n.

66. GHL to Tom Trollope, 5 July 1861, ibid. viii. 287.

67. See Cyril Bibby, *Scientist Extraordinary*, 32–3.

68. GHL Jour., 18 Apr. 1861, MS Yale.

69. *A Report of a Sad Case, Recently tried before the Lord Mayor, Owen versus Huxley, in which will be found fully given the Merits of the Great Recent Bone Case* (London, 1863), pamphlet in Huxley Collection, Imperial College, London.

70. GHL Jour. 1 Jan. 1862, MS Yale.

71. GHL Jour. 23 Jan. 1862, MS Yale.

72. See *GE*, 355.

73. Blackwood to Langford, 25 May 1862, and to GE, 20 May 1862, *GEL*, iv. 38, 35.

74. George Smith, 'Recollections', TS NLS, 200.

75. Thackeray to Smith, n.d. (Jan. 1860), MS NLS.

76. GHL Jour., 8 May 1862, *GEL*, iv. 29.

77. GHL to Smith, 6 Aug. 1864, MS John Murray Archives.

78. GHL Jour., 17 May 1862, MS Yale.

79. GHL to Smith, [July–Aug. 1862], MS John Murray Archives.

80. GHL to Blackwood, 31 May 1861, and GE to Sara Hennell, 23 Nov. 1864, *GEL*, iii. 421, iv. 168.

81. Trollope to GHL, 15 May 1862, ibid. viii. 300; GHL Jour., 17 May 1862, MS Yale.

82. GE to Blackwood, 25 Sept. 1861, *GEL*, viii. 290; John Blackwood to William Blackwood, 23 Dec. 1861, ibid. iii. 474; Thornie to GHL, 22 Dec. 1861, ibid. viii. 294–5.

83. GHL Jour., 21 Aug. 1863, *GEL*, iv. 102.

84. GE to Sara Hennell, 16 Oct. 1863, and GHL Jour., 1 Nov. 1863, ibid. 109, 111–12.

85. Bessie Rayner Parkes to Barbara Bodichon, 18 Nov. 1863, MS Girton.

86. GHL Jour., 8 Nov. 1862, MS Yale; GE Jour., 16 Mar. 1863, GHL Jour., 18 Apr. 1863, and GE to Vivian Lewes, 25 Dec. 1863, *GEL*, iv. 79, 83, 122.

87. GHL Jour., 1 Jan. 1864, ibid. 126.

88. GHL Jour., 11 Feb. 1864. Captain Willim's will is in Somerset House.

89. GHL to Blackwood, 8 Mar. 1864, MS NLS.

90. GHL Jour., 25 Feb. and 22 Apr. 1864, *GEL*, iv. 154 n.

CHAPTER 11

1. GE to D'Albert-Durade, 24 June 1864, and GHL Jour., 23 June 1864, *GEL*, iv. 154 and n.

2. GE to Sara Hennell, 28 Aug. 1864, ibid. 161.

3. Thornie to GE and GHL, 14 Nov. 1863 and 28 Jan. 1864, MSS Yale.

4. GHL Jour., 4 Apr. 1864, MS Yale.

5. Thornie to GHL, 7 Oct. 1864, *GEL*, viii. 323–4.

6. Arnold to his mother, 16 June 1863, *Letters of Matthew Arnold 1848–1888*, ed. George W. E. Russell, 2 vols. (London, 1895), i. 196.

7. GHL Jour., 23 and 29 June 1864, MS Yale.

8. J. W. Herschel to George Smith, 24 Dec. 1863, MS John Murray Archives; Huxley to GHL, 21 Mar. 1864, MS Yale.

9. Trollope to GHL, 21 Mar. 1864, *GEL*, viii. 317.

10. GHL to Smith, n.d. (late 1864 or early 1865), MS John Murray Archives.

11. GHL Jour., 25 Dec. 1864, *GEL*, iv. 172.

12. Trollope to GHL, 24 Dec. 1864, ibid. viii. 327.

13. GHL Jour., 30 Dec. 1864, ibid. iv. 173.

14. GHL to Henry Danby Seymour, 13 Jan. 1865, ibid. viii. 330–2; Tennyson's lines are from his poem of 1842, 'You ask me why, though ill at ease'.

15. GE Jour., 25 Mar. 1865, *GEL*, iv. 184.

16. John, Viscount Morley, *Recollections*, 2 vols. (London, 1917), i. 85.

17. See J. W. Robertson Scott, *The Story of the 'Pall Mall Gazette'* (London, 1950), 148.

18. Sir Edward Bulwer-Lytton to Robert Lytton, 21 Sept. 1865, Lady Emily Lutyens, *The Birth of Rowland: An Exchange of Letters in 1865 between Robert Lytton and his Wife* (London, 1956), 238.

19. Robert Lytton to GE, 22 Jan. 1879, and to Sir James Fitzjames Stephen, 2 Jan. 1879, *Personal and Literary Letters of Robert First Earl of Lytton*, ed. Betty Balfour, 2 vols. (London, 1906), ii. 138, 137.

20. Robert Lytton to GHL, 11 Feb. and 3 June 1866, *GEL*, viii. 363, 377–8.

21. GHL to Robert Lytton, 23 Feb. 1866, ibid. 365, 366.

22. GHL Jour., 12–14 May 1865, ibid. iv. 192.

23. GHL Jour., 13 June 1865, ibid. 195; GHL Jour., 1 Jan. 1866, MS Yale.

24. Notebook jottings from 1856, and a MS fragment 'Ariadne: or the Principles of Success and Failure in Literature' (1861), are at Yale.

25. See Doremus, 'G. H. Lewes: A Descriptive Biography', ii. 585.

26. Several of GHL's books have been reprinted: *The Biographical History of*

Philosophy (1857 edn., repr. Gregg International, 1970); *Ranthorpe* (Ohio University Press, 1974); *Rose, Blanche, and Violet* (AMS Press, 1984); *The Spanish Drama* (Gordon Press, 1980); *On Actors and the Art of Acting* (Greenwood Press, 1970); *Problems of Life and Mind* (AMS Press, n.d.). Two selections of GHL's essays are also in print: GHL, *The Literary Criticism of George Henry Lewes*, ed. Alice R. Kaminsky (University of Nebraska Press, 1964), and *Versatile Victorian: Selected Critical Writings of G. H. Lewes*, ed. Rosemary Ashton (Bristol Classical Press, 1991).

27. GHL, 'The Principles of Success in Literature', ch. 1, *Fortnightly Review*, 1 (15 May 1865), 86–7.

28. GHL, 'Principles', ch. 2, ibid. (1 June 1865), 186, 187.

29. GHL, 'Principles', ch. 3, ibid. (15 July 1865), 573, 579–82, 587, 589.

30. Trollope to GHL, 30 May 1865, *GEL*, viii. 341.

31. GHL, notice of Chapman, *Fortnightly Review*, 2 (15 Sept. 1865), 380.

32. GHL to Bray, Feb. 1866, *GEL*, viii. 361–2.

33. GHL, 'Victor Hugo's Latest Poems', *Fortnightly Review*, 3 (1 Dec. 1865), 183, 184, 185.

34. GHL, 'Varia', ibid. (1 Jan. 1866), 512, 514, and 'Causeries', ibid. (15 Jan. 1866), 646.

35. GHL, 'Auguste Comte', ibid. (1 Jan. 1866), 394–5, 400–1, 402.

36. GHL, 'Spinoza', ibid. 4 (1 Apr. 1866), 398.

37. GHL to Horne, 12 Feb. 1866, *GEL*, viii. 364–5.

38. GE to Barbara Bodichon, 12 Aug. 1864, ibid. 321.

39. GE to D'Albert-Durade, 17 Dec. 1865, ibid. iv. 211–12.

40. Thornie to GHL, 24 Feb. and 2 June 1866, ibid. viii. 367, 376.

41. GHL Jour., 10 Sept. and 25 Dec. 1866, MS Yale.

42. Leonard Huxley, *The House of Smith Elder*, 103.

43. GHL to Blackwood, 18 Apr. 1866, *GEL*, viii. 373.

44. Blackwood to GHL, 20 Apr. 1866, ibid. iv. 241.

45. Blackwood to GHL, 22 Apr. 1866, and GHL to Blackwood, 25 Apr. 1866, ibid. iv. 242, viii. 373–4.

46. Blackwood to GE, 26 Apr. 1866, ibid. iv. 246.

47. GHL Jour., 6 June 1866, ibid. 266–7.

48. GHL to Charles and Gertrude Lewes, 15 July 1866, ibid. 284.

49. Trollope to GE, 3 Aug. 1866, and GE to Trollope, 5 Aug. 1866, ibid. viii. 381–2, iv. 296.

50. Trollope to GHL, 9 Nov. 1866, ibid. viii. 388.

51. Trollope, *An Autobiography*, 2 vols. (Edinburgh and London, 1883), i. 256–7, 201.

52. GE to Sara Hennell, 22 Nov. 1866, *GEL*, iv. 314–15.

53. GHL, 'Farewell Causerie', *Fortnightly Review*, 6 (1 Dec. 1866), 890, 891–2, 895.

54. Carlyle to John Carlyle, 6 Jan. 1867, MS NLS.

55. Blackwood to GHL, 24 Dec. 1866, *GEL*, iv. 325.

CHAPTER 12

1. Nina Lehmann to Frederick Lehmann, 22 Jan. 1867, *GEL*, iv. 335.

2. GHL to Charles Lee Lewes, 18 Feb. 1867, ibid. 345.

3. GE to Frederic Harrison, 18 Feb. 1867, ibid. 344.

4. GE to Blackwood, 21 Feb. and 21 Mar. 1867, ibid. 347, 354.

5. GHL Jour., 31 Jan. 1867, MS Yale.

6. Jervis's will is at Somerset House.

7. GHL to Mrs Willim, 5 Feb. 1867, MS Yale.

8. GHL to Nikolaus Trübner, 29 May 1867, *GEL*, viii. 401.

9. GHL Jour., 5 and 7 May 1867, ibid. iv. 360, 361.

10. GHL to Lady Amberley, 8 May 1867, ibid. viii. 399–400 and n.

11. GHL Jour., 6 May 1867, ibid. iv. 361.

12. GHL, 'The Reign of Law', *Fortnightly Review*, 2 NS (July 1867), 100–1 (the *Fortnightly* had by this time become a monthly periodical, though retaining the original name).

13. GHL to Owen, 4 Oct. 1867, *GEL*, viii. 407.

14. GE to John Morley, 14 May 1867, ibid. iv. 364.

15. See Emily Davies to Barbara Bodichon, 20 Nov. 1867, ibid. viii. 409.

16. GHL Jour., 18 May 1867 , MS Yale.

17. GHL Jour., 19 Oct. 1867, *GEL*, iv. 392–3.

18. GE to Cara Bray, 7 Dec. 1867, ibid. 405.

19. GHL Jour., 25 Dec. 1867, MS Yale.

20. Alexander Bain to George Croom Robertson, 4 Nov. [1877], MS G. C. Robertson Papers, UCL.

21. GHL Jour., 10 Jan. 1868, MS Yale.

22. Blackwood to GHL, 22 Jan. 1868, *GEL*, iv. 417–18.

23. GE to Sara Hennell, 22 Mar. 1868, ibid. 424.

24. GHL, 'Darwin on Domestication and Variation', *Pall Mall Gazette*, 10, 15, 17 Feb. 1868.

25. Darwin to J. D. Hooker, 10 Feb. 1868, *Life and Letters of Charles Darwin*, iii. 76.

26. GHL to Darwin, 2 Mar. 1868, *GEL*, viii. 413–14.

27. Darwin to GHL, 18 Nov. 1868, ibid. 438.

28. GHL, 'Mr Darwin's Hypotheses I', *Fortnightly Review*, 3 NS (Apr. 1868), 353; GHL to Darwin, 26 July 1868, *GEL*, viii. 418.

29. GHL, 'Mr Darwin's Hypotheses II', *Fortnightly Review*, 3 NS (June 1868), 615 and n.

30. GHL, 'Mr Darwin's Hypotheses IV', ibid. 4 NS (Nov. 1868), 503.

31. GHL Jour., 18 Apr. and 25 Dec. 1868, MS Yale.

32. GHL to George Smith, 27 and 29 Oct. 1868, MSS John Murray Archives.

33. GHL to W. B. Scott, 12 May 1868, *GEL*, iv. 441; W. B. Scott, *Autobiographical Notes*, ii. 245.

34. GE to Cara Bray, 11 Oct. 1868, *GEL*, iv. 477. The last visit to Agnes which GHL records in his journal is 8 Nov. 1862. Thereafter his journals and diaries record his writing letters to her occasionally. He saw her again during Thornie's illness (1869) and after Thornton Hunt's death (1873).

35. See GE to Sara Hennell, 29 Sept. 1866, and to D'Albert-Durade, 30 Jan. 1868, ibid. 312, 419.

36. Thornie to GHL, 9 Mar. 1868, MS Yale.

37. Thornie to GHL, 12 Oct. 1868, *GEL*, viii. 431–4 and n.; GHL to Blackwood, 9 Jan. 1869, ibid, v. 4.

38. Blackwood to GE, 18 Feb. 1869, ibid. v. 15.

39. GHL Diary, 8 May and 1 June 1869, MS Yale.

40. Henry James, *Autobiography*, ed. Frederick W. Dupee (London, 1956), 575–7.

41. GHL Diary, 29 May and 4 June 1869, MS Yale.

42. GHL Diary, 27 Sept. and 11, 17, 18 and 19 Oct. 1869, MSS Yale.

43. GE Jour., 19 Oct. 1869, *GEL*, v. 60.

44. GHL Jour., 1 Jan. 1870, MS Yale.

45. GHL Diary, 17 Feb. 1870, and Jour., Mar. 1870, MSS Yale.

46. GHL Diary, 6 Mar. 1870, and GE to Blackwood, 7 Mar. 1870, *GEL*, v. 81–2 and n.

47. GHL to Mrs Willim, 28 Mar. 1870, ibid. 83–4.

48. GHL Jour., 25 Mar. 1870, MS Yale.

49. GE, 'Liszt, Wagner, and Weimar', *Fraser's Magazine* (July 1855), *Essays of GE*, 103.

50. GHL to Robert Lytton, 9 May 1870, *GEL*, viii. 475.

51. Examples from a very large number of such memoirs are: Robert Buchanan, *A Look Round Literature* (London, 1887), 218–28; Lucy Clifford, 'A Remembrance of George Eliot', *Nineteenth Century* , 74 (July 1913), 109–18; Sidney Colvin, *Memories and Notes of Persons and Places* (London, 1921), 90–2; P. G. Hamerton, *Autobiography and a Memoir* (London, 1897), 369–71; Rudolf Lehmann, *An Artist's Reminiscences* (London, 1894), 234–6; T. H. S. Escott, *Platform, Press, Politics and Play: Being Pen and Ink Sketches of Contemporary Celebrities* (Bristol, 1895), 259–60.

52. Norton to G. W. Curtis, 29 Jan. 1869, *Letters of Charles Eliot Norton*, ed. Sara Norton and M. A. De Wolfe Howe, 2 vols. (London, 1913), i. 317; George Meredith to Leslie Stephen, 18 Aug. 1902, *The Letters of George Meredith*, ed. C. L. Cline, 3 vols. (Oxford, 1970), iii. 1460.

53. GHL to Lord Houghton, 21 Feb. 1872, *GEL*, ix. 41. The quotation is from II *Henry IV*, I. ii. 190 (Falstaff: 'For my voice—I have lost it with hallooing and singing of anthems').

54. See John Blackwood to William Blackwood, 24 Oct. and 2 Nov. 1871, *GEL*, v. 205, 212.

55. Blackwood to GE, 20 July 1871, ibid. 167.

56. GHL to Blackwood, 7 May 1871, ibid. 146. For the marketing of *Middlemarch*, see J. A. Sutherland, *Victorian Novelists and Publishers*, 188–205.

57. GHL to Blackwood, 13 Feb. 1872, *GEL*, v. 246.

58. GE to Sara Hennell, 2 Jan. 1871, ibid. 131.

59. GHL to Alexander Main, 2 Jan. 1873, ibid. 360–1.

60. Bertie to GHL, 6 May, 14 June, and 15 Dec. 1871, ibid. ix. 16, 18, 34–5.

61. GHL to Charles Appleton, 6 Feb. 1871, ibid. 11.

62. GHL to Mrs Cross, 24 July 1871, ibid. 21.

63. GHL to Charles Lee Lewes, 26 Apr. 1871, and GHL to Blackwood, 21 Aug. 1871, ibid. v. 143–4, 179. See also v. 191 n.

64. Charles William Shirley Brooks, Diary, MS London Library, part published in George Somes Layard, *A Great 'Punch' Editor: Being the Life, Letters, and Diaries of Shirley Brooks* (London, 1907), 497–8; GHL to John Morley, Dec. 1871, *GEL*, ix. 32.

65. Trollope, 'George Henry Lewes', *Fortnightly Review*, 25 NS (Jan. 1879), 22. For an account of the controversy see Gordon S. Haight, 'Dickens and Lewes', *PMLA*, 71 (Mar. 1956), 166–79.

66. GHL, 'Dickens in Relation to Criticism', *Fortnightly Review*, 11 NS (Feb. 1872), 142, 151.

67. Ibid. 144, 145.

68. Ibid. 148–9.

69. John Forster, *The Life of Charles Dickens*, 3 vols. (London, 1872–4), iii. 302, 305.

70. GHL Diary, 9 and 10 Feb. 1874, MS Yale; Trollope, 'George Henry Lewes', *Fortnightly Review* , 25 NS (Jan. 1879), 23.

71. GHL to Herbert Spencer, n.d. (1874?), MS Spencer Papers, University of London Library; GHL to Blackwood, 13 July 1872, *GEL*, v. 291.

72. GE to Harriet Beecher Stowe, Oct. 1872, *GEL*, v. 322.

73. Blackwood to GE, 31 Dec. 1872, and GHL to Blackwood, 25 Nov. 1872, ibid. 352–3, 332; *Middlemarch*, ch. 48.

74. Blackwood to GHL, 17 Jan. 1873, *GEL*, v. 369.

75. GHL to Blackwood, 25 Mar. 1873, MS NLS; Peter Guthrie Tait to Blackwood, 17 Apr. 1873, *GEL*, ix. 89 n.

76. Blackwood to GHL, 24 May 1873, and GHL to Blackwood, 25 May 1873, *GEL*, v. 410–11, 413–14.

77. See GHL to John Cross, 19 Jan. 1873, ibid. ix. 71; GHL Diary, 21 Nov. 1873, ibid. v. 469 n.

78. Bertie to GHL, 29 Oct. 1873, ibid. ix. 106–7.

79. Carlyle to W. D. Christie, 2 June 1863, Sanders, *Carlyle's Friendships*, 188.

80. Administration, 20 Sept. 1873, Somerset House. There are three depressed letters of Thornton Hunt's, complaining of overwork, among the Miscellaneous MSS at Yale: one to John Chapman, 8 Mar. 1865, and two to William Hepworth Dixon, 10 Dec. 1863 and 26 Jan. 1869.

81. See *GE*, 460–1, 467.

82. GHL Diary, 8 Aug. 1875, MS Yale.

83. Bertie to GHL, 17 May and 24 June 1875, *GEL*, ix. 154, 157.

84. Marie Sanderson to GE, 3 July 1875, ibid. 162.

85. GE to Blackwood, 3 Nov. 1876, ibid. vi. 304.

86. GE to John Cross, 14 Aug. 1875, ibid. 165.

87. GE to Blackwood, 11 Nov. 1874, ibid. ix. 138 and n.

88. GE to Sara Hennell, 20 Nov. 1875, ibid. vi. 191.

89. GHL Diary, 18 May 1875, MS Yale; notes by the assistant librarian of the London Library, May 1875, MS London Library. I am indebted to John Wells for letting me see these notes.

90. GHL Diary, 14 Dec. 1875, MS Yale.

91. GHL to G. C. Robertson, 22 Jan. 1875, *GEL*, ix. 143.

CHAPTER 13

1. GE to Clifford Allbutt, 1 Nov. 1873, *GEL*, v. 450.

2. GE to Benjamin Jowett, 12 May 1873, ibid. 409.

3. See GHL's prefaces to successive editions, particularly *The History of Philosophy*, 2 vols. (London, 1871), v–vii.

4. Espinasse, *Literary Recollections*, 295–6.

5. GHL, *Problems of Life and Mind*, *The Foundations of a Creed* (London, 1874), i. 18, ii. 10; see OED for GHL's coining of the term 'metempirical'.

6. W. K. Clifford, *Academy*, 5 (7 Feb. 1874), 148–50; Douglas A. Spalding, *Nature*, 10 (7 May 1874), 1–2; James Sully, *Examiner*, 10 and 17 July 1875, 773, 803; Frederic Harrison, *Fortnightly Review*, 16 NS (July 1874), 89, 101. For modern discussions of *Problems* see Jack Kaminsky, 'The Empirical Metaphysics of George Henry Lewes', *Journal of the History of Ideas*, 13 (1952), 314–32, and K. K. Collins, 'G. H. Lewes Revised: George Eliot and the Moral Sense', *Victorian Studies*, 21 (1978), 463–92, an account of GE's revision of the unfinished portions, published in 1879, after GHL's death.

7. GHL to Main, 30 Nov. 1874 and 12 Feb. 1875, *GEL*, vi. 95–6, 125.

8. See GE to Cara Bray, 29 May 1874, ibid. 52.

9. GHL to Helps, 2 Mar. 1873, ibid. ix. 78; see also vi. 236 n.

10. See *Vivisection in Historical Perspective*, ed. Nicolaas Rupke (London, 1987).

11. GHL Diary, 31 Mar. and 5 Mar 1876, *GEL*, vi. 236–7 and MS Yale.

12. GHL to W. B. Scott, 1 May 1875, *GEL*, vi. 138.

13. *Dramatic Essays by John Forster and G. H. Lewes*, xiv.

14. GHL, *On Actors*, 125.

15. Blackwood to GE, 25 May 1875, *GEL*, vi. 145 and n.

16. GHL to Blackwood, 29 July 1875, ibid. 159.

17. Blackwood to GE, 17 Nov. 1875, ibid. 186.

18. GHL to Blackwood, 1 Dec. 1875, ibid. 196.

19. Blackwood to GHL, 2 Mar. 1876, ibid. 227; Blackwood to Langford, ibid. 262 n.

20. GHL to Mary Cross, 8 July 1875, ibid. 154–5.

21. GHL Diary, 9 and 10 Nov. 1875, ibid. 181.

22. GHL, 'Spiritualism and Materialism', *Fortnightly Review*, 19 NS (May 1876), 715.

23. GHL to G. C. Robertson, 1 Mar. 1877, and G. C. Robertson to GHL, 2 Mar. 1877, *GEL*, ix. 189, 190.

24. GHL, preface to *Problems*, iii, *The Physical Basis of Mind* (London, 1877), p. v.

25. G. C. Robertson, 'The Physical Basis of Mind', *Mind*, 3 (Jan. 1878), 24.

26. GHL to Robertson, 2 Jan. 1878, *GEL*, ix. 211.

27. GE Jour., 10 Nov. 1877, MS Yale.

28. GHL Diary, 30 Mar. and 20 Apr. 1877, *GEL*, vi. 360, 363.

29. GHL Diary, 9 Apr. 1875, MS Yale.

30. See *GE*, 501–2.

31. GHL Diary, 15 May 1877, *GEL*, vi. 373; see also ibid. 191 n.

32. GHL Diary, 6–8 Dec. 1876, ibid. 314.

33. GHL to Blackwood, 20 June 1877, and GE to Elma Stuart, 14 Sept. 1877, ibid. 389, 403.

34. GHL to Elinor and Mary Cross, 31 July 1877, ibid. 395–6.

35. GE to Sara Hennell, 23 Nov. 1877, ibid. 426.

36. GE to Sara Hennell, 22 Nov. 1876 and 20 Nov. 1868, ibid. vi. 310, 311 n., iv. 489.

37. GE Jour., 26 Nov. 1877, ibid. vi. 427 and n.

38. GHL to Barbara Bodichon, 31 Jan. 1878, ibid. vii. 12–13.

39. GHL, 'On the Dread and Dislike of Science', *Fortnightly Review*, 23 NS (June 1878), 805, 806, 815.

40. See GHL to Barbara Bodichon, 27 Feb. 1878, *GEL*, ix. 219.

41. GHL Diary, 15 Mar. 1878, MS in the possession of Gabriel Woolf, who kindly allowed me to consult it.

42. GHL Diary, 10 Apr. 1878, *GEL*, vii. 20; Henry James to his mother, 12 Apr. 1878, MS Houghton (part quoted in Leon Edel, *The Life of Henry James*, 5 vols. (London, 1853–72), iii. 370).

43. GE to Elma Stuart, 27 June 1878, *GEL*, vii. 34.

44. GHL to P. G. Hamerton, 18? July 1878, ibid. ix. 234.

45. GHL to Blackwood, 6 Aug. 1878, ibid. vii. 50.

46. GHL Diary, 30 and 31 Oct. 1878 and cash accounts, MS Gabriel Woolf.

47. GHL Diary, 16, 18, 19, 20 Nov. 1878, MS Gabriel Woolf.

48. GE to Barbara Bodichon, 25 Nov. 1878, *GEL*, vii. 84.

49. See Edith Simcox Autobiography, 5 Dec. 1878, ibid. ix. 248.

50. Holyoake to Spencer, 15 Dec. 1878, *GE*, 516 n.

EPILOGUE

1. Spencer to GE, 5 Dec. 1878, *GEL*, vii. 87.

2. Pigott to Charles Lee Lewes, 2 Dec. 1878, MS Yale.

3. Robert Browning to Lady Lindsay, 2 Dec. 1878, MS Armstrong Browning Library.

4. Blackwood to GE, 1 Dec. 1878, MS Yale. Blackwood died in Oct. 1879.

5. Robert Lytton to GE, 22 Jan. 1879, and to Fitzjames Stephen, 2 Jan. 1879, *Personal and Literary Letters*, ii. 138, 137.

6. *Nature*, 19 (5 Dec. 1878), 106; Frederic Harrison, *Academy*, 7 Dec. 1878, 543; Trollope, *Fortnightly Review*, 25 NS (Jan. 1879), 17–20.

7. Trollope, ibid. 15.

8. Michael Foster to GE, 1 Jan. 1879, MS Yale.

9. Clifford Allbutt to GE, 19 Jan. 1879, *GEL*, vii. 96, 97.

10. GE to Allbutt, 20 Feb. 1879, and to Barbara Bodichon, 8 Apr. 1879, ibid. 104, 128.

11. See GE to Barbara Bodichon, 2 July 1879, ibid. 176–7 and n. The correspondence about the Studentship, with drafts of its terms, is in Yale.

12. GE to Charles Lee Lewes, 18 Oct. 1879, *GEL*. vii. 213–14 and n.

13. Clifford Allbutt to GE, 6 Apr. 1879, MS Yale.

14. Isaac Evans to GE, 17 May 1880, *GEL*, vii. 280.

15. Cross to Elma Stuart, 11 May 1880, ibid. 276.

16. GE to Georgiana Burne-Jones, 5 May 1880, ibid. 269.

17. See Anne Thackeray Ritchie to her husband, 24 May 1880, ibid. 284.

18. Frederick Locker-Lampson, *My Confidences*, 316.

19. Anne Thackeray Ritchie to her husband, 24 May 1880, *GEL*, vii. 284.

20. George Smith, 'Recollections', TS NLS, 223; Edward Beesly to Herbert Spencer (quoting Ethel Harrison), 27 Dec. 1880, MS Beesly Papers, UCL; Henry James to Alice James, 30 Jan. 1881, *Henry James Letters*, ed. Leon Edel, 4 vols. (London, 1974–84), ii. 337.

21. Edith Simcox Autobiography, 26 May 1878 and 29 Apr. 1879, *GEL*, ix. 229, 266.

22. See GE Jour., 29 Nov. 1878, ibid. vii. 227.

23. Trollope, 'George Henry Lewes', *Fortnightly Review*, 25 NS (Jan. 1879), 24.

FAMILY TREE OF GEORGE HENRY LEWES

Charles Lee Lewes (1740 – 1803) m. Frances Wrigley (d. 1783)

James Wrigley Lewes (1781 – 1819)

John Lee Lewes (1776 – 1831) = Elizabeth Ashweek (1787 – 1870)

m. Elizabeth Pownall

m. John Gurens Willim [1823] (1777/8 – 1864) no children

John (b. 1803) Frances (b. 1804) Elizabeth (b. 1806) James (b. 1808)

Edgar James (?1809 – ?1836)

Edward Charles (1813/14 – 55) m. Susanna Pittock (b. 1827/8)

GEORGE HENRY LEWES (1817 – 78) m. Agnes Jervis (1822 – 1902)

Marian Evans (1819 – 80) no children

= m. John Cross [1880] (1840 – 1924)

= Thornton Hunt (1810 – 73)

Edmund (b. 1850) Rose (b. 1851) Ethel (1853 – 1939) Mildred (b. 1857)

Vivian Byam (1852 – 1915)

Daughter (died in infancy)

Daughter (d. aged 2 days 1841)

Charles Lee (1842 – 91) m. Gertrude Hill

Thornton Arnott (1844 – 69)

Herbert Arthur (1846 – 75) m. Eliza Harrison

St Vincent Arthy (1848 – 50)

Blanche Southwood (1872 – 1964) m. R. J. E. Hanson

Maud Southwood (1874 – 1942) m. J. R. Hopwood

Elinor Southwood (1877 – 1974) m. E. C. Ouvry

George Herbert (1875 – 1976)

Marian Evans (1872 – 1955) m. S. E. C. Williams (5 children)

The symbol m. is used for legal marriages, the symbol = for liaisons.

CHRONOLOGY

1776   GHL's father, John Lee Lewes, born 23 April in London, older son of the comic actor Charles Lee Lewes and his second wife Fanny Wrigley Lewes.

1787   GHL's mother, Elizabeth Ashweek, born 21 May in Devon.

1803   Charles Lee Lewes dies 23 June in London. John Lee Lewes lives in Liverpool with his wife Elizabeth Pownall Lewes. He is a Captain of the Third Lancashire Militia. Their first child, John Wild Lewes, born 13 May.

1804   John Lee Lewes's second child, Frances Wrigley Lewes, born 1 October in Liverpool.

1805   John Lee Lewes publishes *Memoirs of Charles Lee Lewes* in 4 vols.

1806   John Lee Lewes's third child, Elizabeth Allen Lewes, born 11 February in Liverpool.

1808   John Lee Lewes's fourth child, James Langmead Lewes, born 23 July in Liverpool.

1809?   John Lee Lewes leaves his wife and children to live with Elizabeth Ashweek. Their first son, Edgar James Lewes, born *c.* 1809, probably in Liverpool.

1811   John Lee Lewes publishes *Poems* in Liverpool.

1813?   Edward Charles Lewes, second son of John Lee Lewes and Elizabeth Ashweek, born between 31 March 1813 and 30 March 1814 in London.

1817   GHL, third son of John Lee Lewes and Elizabeth Ashweek, born 18 April in London. John Lee Lewes publishes *National Melodies* in London.

1819   James Wrigley Lewes, younger brother of John Lee Lewes, dies 19 August at St George's, Bermuda, where he was a Searcher in HM Customs.

1823   Elizabeth Ashweek [spinster] marries Captain John Gurens Willim [bachelor] 29 November at St Pancras Old Church, London. John Lee Lewes is by now a Searcher in HM Customs at Hamilton, Bermuda.

1825   GHL lives with his mother, stepfather, and brother Edward near Stroud in Gloucestershire. His eldest brother, Edgar, works for the wine firm Offley, Forrester, and Webber in Oporto.

1826   Edward Lewes and GHL attend boarding school in London.

1827   John Lee Lewes appointed Registrar of Slaves 28 March in Bermuda.

1828 GHL, Edward, and their mother (perhaps without Captain Willim) live at Kirby's Royal Hotel, St Helier's, Jersey. The boys attend a school in Jersey until 1830.

1829 John Lee Lewes leaves Bermuda with his daughter Fanny Wrigley Lewes, returning to Liverpool in poor health, May.

1830 Mrs Willim returns to Gloucestershire. GHL attends Dr Burney's school in Greenwich until 1832.

1831 John Lee Lewes dies 8 February in Liverpool. Administration of his estate (less than £100) granted to his daughter Frances Wrigley Lewes.

1832 GHL leaves Dr Burney's school at the end of the year. He probably works in a notary's office, then for a Russian merchant, before studying medicine briefly. His brother Edward is a medical student in London.

1832 First surviving GHL letter. Written to Leigh Hunt, asking him to publish a story.

1836? Edgar James Lewes dies abroad. GHL belongs to a debating club in Red Lion Square, Holborn.

1837 GHL lives with his mother at 7 Harrington St., Hampstead Rd. Plans to write a biography of Shelley, for which he seeks Leigh Hunt's help. Forms friendships with Hunt's eldest son Thornton and other young radicals and bohemians: William Bell Scott, Egerton Webbe, and the not-so-young Richard Henry (later Hengist) Horne. Begins to contribute to minor literary magazines, co-editing the short-lived *National Magazine and Monthly Critic*, in which he reviews Dickens's early work, December. Dickens writes inviting GHL to call on him.

1838 GHL goes to Berlin, August, with a letter of introduction to Varnhagen von Ense from Carlyle. Probably supports himself by giving English lessons. Works at the biography of Shelley; attends lectures at the University, where he meets Turgenev.

1839 GHL moves from Berlin to Vienna, April. Sees Liszt. Returns to London, June or July. Gives up the Shelley biography because of Mary Shelley's opposition.

1840 GHL writes articles in the *Monthly Chronicle*, and, through John Stuart Mill, publishes an article on the French drama in the *Westminster Review*, September. Plans to go to Germany again in the summer, but instead probably visits the house of Swynfen Jervis, MP, as a tutor to his children.

1841 GHL marries Agnes Jervis, eldest daughter of Swynfen Jervis, 18 February at St Margaret's Church, Westminster. She is 18 years old. They live with Mrs Willim at 3 Pembroke Square, Kensington. GHL writes an article on Shelley in the *Westminster Review*, April. Agnes gives birth to a daughter 22 December, who dies 24 December.

1842   GHL tries, and fails, to get plays accepted by Charles James Mathews at Covent Garden. Visits Paris in the spring with introductions from Mill to Comte, Cousin, and Michelet. Article on Hegel's *Aesthetics* in the *British and Foreign Review*, October. Charles Lee Lewes born 24 November.

1843   GHL publishes articles on Goethe in the *British and Foreign Review*, March, on Spinoza in the *Westminster Review*, May, on French philosophy and science in the *British and Foreign Review*, July and October. GHL and Agnes move from Pembroke Square to 2 Campden Hill Terrace, Kensington, 13 June. GHL visits Arthur Helps at Vernon Hill, Hampshire, at the end of the year.

1844   GHL publishes articles on French criticism in the *British and Foreign Review*, January, and on George Sand in the *Foreign Quarterly Review*, July. Thornton Arnott Lewes born 14 April.

1845   Vols. 1 and 2 of the *Biographical History of Philosophy* published by Charles Knight. GHL visits Berlin, May–June. Article on Lessing published in the *Edinburgh Review*, October.

1846   Vols. 3 and 4 of the *Biographical History of Philosophy* published. GHL visits Paris, February–April; meets George Sand. GHL and Agnes move to 26 Bedford Square, Kensington, June. Herbert Arthur Lewes born 10 July. GHL and Agnes contribute to *Fraser's Magazine*. *The Spanish Drama. Lope de Vega and Calderon* published by Knight.

1847   GHL is a founder-member of Douglas Jerrold's Museum Club. His first novel, *Ranthorpe*, published by Chapman and Hall, May. GHL joins Dickens's amateur acting company for *Every Man in his Humour* in Manchester and Liverpool, July. GHL and Thornton Hunt plan to buy the *Westminster Review*, but cannot raise the necessary money. GHL reviews *Jane Eyre* in *Fraser's Magazine*, December, and begins a correspondence with Charlotte Brontë.

1848   GHL reviews *Vanity Fair* in the *Morning Chronicle*, March. Thackeray writes in gratitude. *Rose, Blanche, and Violet* published by Smith, Elder, April. St Vincent Arthy Lewes born 11 May. GHL acts with Dickens again in London, Manchester, Liverpool, and Birmingham, May and June, and Edinburgh and Glasgow, July. GHL publishes articles on Alexandre Dumas and Charles Lamb in the *British Quarterly Review*, February, May, November.

1849   *The Life of Maximilien Robespierre* published by Chapman and Hall, February. GHL lectures on the history of philosophy at Manchester and Liverpool, February. Acts in his own tragedy, *The Noble Heart*, in Manchester and Liverpool, April and May. Plays Shylock with a professional company in these cities, and again in Edinburgh, November. Briefly considers becoming a professional actor. Jane Carlyle notices an estrangement between GHL and Agnes, April. GHL publishes articles on Macaulay and Disraeli in the *British Quarterly Review*, February and August. GHL and Thornton plan the *Leader*; GHL tours the country for subscriptions, November–December. Agnes is pregnant with her first child by Thornton Hunt.

1850　GHL reviews Charlotte Brontë's *Shirley* in the *Edinburgh Review*, January. Meets Herbert Spencer at John Chapman's house. *The Noble Heart* produced at the Olympic Theatre, London, running for 8 nights, February. The printed version, with a preface addressed to Arthur Helps, published by Chapman and Hall, March. St Vincent Arthy dies of measles 23 March, aged 22 months. First number of the *Leader* appears 30 March, with Thornton Hunt as political editor and GHL as literary editor. Edmund Lewes, Agnes's first child by Hunt, born 16 April. GHL begins his regular theatre reviewing for the *Leader* under the pseudonym 'Vivian'.

1851　GHL attends meetings of political refugees and supports reform at home. Edward Pigott buys the *Leader*. Marian Evans comes to London and lodges with Chapman at 142 Strand, January. GHL unhappy with Agnes, who is pregnant with her second child by Hunt. GHL ill during the summer; takes the water cure, and goes on walking tours with Spencer. GHL collaborates with Mathews in the adaptation of French plays for the Lyric Theatre, September. *The Game of Speculation*, their adaptation of Balzac's *Mercadet*, opens 2 October, is a great hit, and runs for 94 performances. Chapman introduces GHL to Marian Evans in a bookshop in Piccadilly, 6 October. Rose Lewes, daughter of Agnes and Thornton Hunt, born 21 October. Chapman takes over the *Westminster Review*, with Marian Evans as his assistant, December.

1852　First number of the *Westminster Review* under Chapman's nominal, and Marian Evans's actual, editorship appears, January. GHL is a founder-member of Thackeray's Fielding Club. 'Vivian' criticizes Charles Kean's acting, February. A feud ensues. GHL attends Chapman's meeting of authors and publishers to promote free trade in books; Dickens takes the chair, Marian Evans is the only woman present, May. Marian Evans in love with Spencer, June–July; but already fascinated by GHL, who probably leaves home after July, perhaps staying in F. O. Ward's rooms in Cork St., Piccadilly, while Ward is in Brussels from September. Article on Goethe as a man of science published in the *Westminster Review*, October. GHL criticizes the spontaneous combustion of Mr Krook in *Bleak House*, December.

1853　Dickens replies to GHL's criticism, January; argument continues in print until September. GHL and Marian Evans probably already intimate early in the year. GHL reviews *Villette* and Mrs Gaskell's *Ruth* in the *Westminster Review*, April. Plans to go to Germany to research his biography of Goethe. *Comte's Philosophy of the Sciences*, enlarged from his 1852 articles in the *Leader*, published by Bohn, October. Ethel Lewes, third child of Agnes and Thornton Hunt, born 9 October. GHL does not register the birth. Marian Evans moves from Chapman's house into lodgings in Cambridge St., Hyde Park Square, October. She translates Feuerbach's *Essence of Christianity* for Chapman.

1854   T. H. Huxley attacks GHL's *Comte* in the *Westminster Review*, January. GHL ill again, April; Marian does his *Leader* work while he goes to the country. GHL and Marian Evans go abroad together 20 July, arriving in Weimar 2 August. Friendship with Liszt. GHL writes explaining his position to Carlyle. Chapman and Charles Bray defend GHL and Marian, but literary London rings with the scandal. GHL and Marian leave Weimar for Berlin 3 November. Marian translates Spinoza's *Ethics* and helps GHL translate passages from Goethe's works for the *Life of Goethe*.

1855   GHL and Marian leave Berlin 11 March, arriving in Dover 14 March. GHL goes to London to find lodgings. Marian joins him 18 April in Bayswater. They take rooms at 7 Clarence Row, East Sheen, 2 May. Bessie Rayner Parkes is the only woman who visits at this time. Charles Bray comes, without his wife, July. GHL takes Charles, aged 12, Thornie, aged 11, and Bertie, aged 9, to Ramsgate on holiday, August. GHL hears of the death of his brother Edward at sea, leaving a young widow, Susanna, and two young children, September. GHL supports Susanna and pays for her one surviving child, Vivian, born 1852, to be educated. GHL and Marian move to 8 Park Shot, Richmond, October. *The Life and Works of Goethe*, dedicated to Carlyle, published by David Nutt, November. GHL borrows a microscope from Helps and begins his scientific studies.

1856   GHL and Marian go to Ilfracombe and Tenby, May–July. GHL studies marine life and writes 'Sea-side Studies' for *Blackwood's Magazine*. GHL rows with Bohn over the publication of the translation of Spinoza's *Ethics*, June. GHL takes Charles and Thornie to school at Hofwyl, near Berne, August. Marian begins her first story, 'The Sad Fortunes of the Reverend Amos Barton', at Richmond, September. GHL lends his letters from Charlotte Brontë to Mrs Gaskell for publication in her biography of Charlotte Brontë, September. GHL sends 'Amos Barton', by 'a friend', to John Blackwood, November. Blackwood accepts it. Thornton Hunt challenges GHL to a duel in a row over Agnes's support, December.

1857   J. W. Parker publishes a revised edition of the *Biographical History of Philosophy* in 2 vols. Marian's 'Scenes of Clerical Life' begin to appear in *Blackwood's Magazine*, alongside GHL's 'Sea-side Studies', January. She adopts the pseudonym George Eliot, February. GHL and GE go to the

Scilly Isles and Jersey for more 'Sea-side Studies', March–July. Mildred
Lewes, last child of Agnes and Thornton Hunt, born 21 May at 3
Campden Hill Terrace, Kensington, where Agnes is now living. GE
tells her brother Isaac of her relationship with GHL, May. He breaks
off relations with her, and induces their sister Chrissey to do so too.
GHL publishes 'New Sea-side Studies' in *Blackwood's Magazine*,
June–October. GHL takes Bertie to join Charles and Thornie at
Hofwyl, August. GE begins *Adam Bede*, October.

1858   *Scenes of Clerical Life* published by Blackwood, January. *Sea-Side Studies*
published, also by Blackwood, February. The identity of GE revealed
to Blackwood 28 February. GHL and GE go to Germany for GHL's
physiological research April–September. GHL visits his sons in Switzerland, June. GHL's papers on physiology read out at the Leeds meeting
of the British Association for the Advancement of Science, September.
GE finishes *Adam Bede*, November.

1859   *Adam Bede* published by Blackwood to great acclaim, February. Speculation about the authorship and claims for Joseph Liggins. GHL and
GE move to Holly Lodge, Southfields, near Wimbledon, February. *The
Physiology of Common Life* published by Blackwood in monthly parts,
then in 2 vols., 1859–60. GE's sister Chrissey dies 15 March. GE's
identity becomes generally known, June. GHL visits his sons at Hofwyl
and tells them about Agnes and Marian, July. They begin writing to
her as 'Mother'. GHL's papers on nerve physiology and the muscular
sense read out at the British Association for the Advancement of Science
meeting at Aberdeen, September; praised by Huxley. Dickens dines
with them to meet GE, November.

1860   First number of the *Cornhill Magazine*, published by George Smith and
edited by Thackeray, appears, January. GHL contributes 'Studies in
Animal Life', January–June. GE finishes *The Mill on the Floss* and they
go to Italy, March. *The Mill on the Floss* published, April. GHL and GE
visit the boys in Switzerland; they meet GE for the first time 24 June.
GHL and GE take Charles home to prepare for the Post Office exams;
he is appointed to a clerkship, August. Thornie goes to school in
Edinburgh to prepare for the Indian Civil Service exams, September.
GHL and GE move to 10 Harewood Square, September, then to 16
Blandford Square, December. The possibility of a divorce for GHL
looked into, to no avail, December. GE interrupts research for *Romola*
to write *Silas Marner*.

1861   GHL asked to lecture on biology at the Post Office by Trollope,
February. Becomes a Fellow of the Zoological Gardens, February. *Silas
Marner* published by Blackwood, April. GHL in poor health; visits
Italy, Malvern, and other places in search of a cure for headaches and
indigestion. GE begins the writing of *Romola*, October.

1862   *Studies in Animal Life*, reprinted from the *Cornhill Magazine*, published by Smith, Elder. Smith offers GE £10,000 for her next novel, *Romola*; she accepts, February, but in May insists on taking only £7,000. Thackeray resigns as editor of the *Cornhill Magazine*, March. GHL agrees to act as Smith's chief adviser on the magazine for £600 per annum, May. *Romola* begins to appear, to muted praise, in the *Cornhill Magazine*, July.

1863   *Romola* published by Smith, Elder, July. Bertie comes home from Hofwyl, July. Thornie hears he has failed the second set of Indian Civil Service exams, August; goes to Natal to farm, October. Bertie goes to learn farming in Scotland. GHL and GE buy The Priory, Regent's Park; move in, November. Charles's 21st birthday 24 November. Thackeray dies 24 December; GHL attends the funeral.

1864   Revised edition of the *Life of Goethe* published by Smith, Elder, January. Captain Willim dies 9 February, aged 86. *Aristotle, A Chapter from the History of Science* published by Smith, Elder, April. Charles Lewes gets engaged to Gertrude Hill, June. GHL gives up as consulting editor of the *Cornhill Magazine*, October, but agrees to advise Smith on his new evening paper, the *Pall Mall Gazette*, edited by Federick Greenwood. Trollope asks GHL to edit the new *Fortnightly Review*; GHL refuses on grounds of ill health.

1865   GHL does theatre criticism for the *Pall Mall Gazette*. Agrees to edit the *Fortnightly Review* after all, January. Charles marries Gertrude 20 March. First number of the *Fortnightly* appears, with contributions by Trollope, Bagehot, Herschel, GHL, and GE, May. GHL begins his series 'The Principles of Success in Literature' in the *Fortnightly*.

1866   GHL writes 'Auguste Comte' and 'Spinoza' in the *Fortnightly*, January and April. *Felix Holt* published by Blackwood, June. Bertie goes to join Thornie in Natal, September. GHL gives up the editorship of the *Fortnightly* through ill health, December. GHL and GE go to Spain, December.

1867   Swynfen Jervis dies 15 January; Agnes not included in his will. GHL elected to the Committee of the London Library, May. Revises the *Biological History of Philosophy*, published by Longmans in 2 vols., with the new title *The History of Philosophy*, August. GHL visits Bonn and Heidelberg to consult scientists about his work on the physical basis of mind, December.

1868   GHL reviews Darwin's *Variation of Animals and Plants under Domestication* in the *Pall Mall Gazette*, February. Darwin delighted with his praise. They correspond, and GHL writes four longer appreciations of Darwin's work in the *Fortnightly Review*, April–November. GHL attends the Oxford meeting of the British Medical Association, August. Darwin proposes GHL for the Linnaean Society, November.

1869   GHL receives a letter from Thornie telling of his spinal illness and great weakness; sends money for Thornie to come to England for treatment, January. GE begins *Middlemarch*, February. Thornie arrives home 8 May. Henry James visits 9 May. Agnes comes to see Thornie 18 May. GHL and GE nurse him until he dies of spinal tuberculosis 19 October, aged 25. GHL ill and depressed.

1870   Dickens visits, March. GHL and GE go to Germany, March–May. Dickens dies 10 June. Bertie becomes engaged in Natal, August. GHL writes a few scientific letters to the new periodical *Nature*. Mrs Willim dies 10 December, aged 83.

1871   New revised edition of the *History of Philosophy* published by Longmans. GHL and GE entertain Turgenev, April. Bertie marries Eliza Harrison in Natal 25 May. First part of *Middlemarch* published by Blackwood, December. GHL has suggested publication in 8 two-monthly parts.

1872   GHL writes 'Dickens in Relation to Criticism' in the *Fortnightly Review*, February. John Forster later attacks him for it in the third volume of his *Life of Dickens* (1874). Blanche Southwood Lewes, daughter of Charles and Gertrude, born 19 July. Marian Evans Lewes, daughter of Bertie and Eliza, born 2 November. GHL and GE visit the Cross family in Weybridge, December. Last part of *Middlemarch* published, December. Blackwood tells GE it will be remembered as one of the great events of 1872. John Cross invests the proceeds for them in American railway stock.

1873   GHL sends *The Foundations of a Creed*, vol. 1 of *Problems of Life and Mind*, to Blackwood, who dislikes it, March. GHL offers it to Trübner instead, May. *The Story of Goethe's Life*, an abridged edition of the *Life of Goethe*, published by Smith, Elder. Thornton Hunt dies 25 June, aged 63. GHL meets Agnes to arrange for her to receive money from an insurance policy on Hunt's life, August. GHL and GE set up their own carriage, December.

1874   *The Foundations of a Creed* published by Trübner, January. Maud Southwood Lewes, daughter of Charles and Gertrude, born 30 March. GE's *Legend of Jubal* published, May.

1875   G. C. Robertson of University College London consults GHL about the founding of a new periodical of psychology, *Mind*, January. Vol. 2 of *Problems of Life and Mind* published by Trübner, February. Bryan Hunt, son of Thornton, commits suicide at the London Library after returning vol. 1 of GHL's *Problems* 11 May. George Herbert Lewes, son of Bertie and Eliza, born 16 May. Third edition of the *Life of Goethe* published by Smith, Elder. Bertie dies of a glandular disease 29 June, aged 29. *On Actors and the Art of Acting*, based on GHL's *Pall Mall Gazette* theatre criticisms, published by Smith, Elder, July. GHL ill, December. Testifies to the Royal Commission on Vivisection 15 December.

1876   First number of *Mind* appears, January. GHL contributes gratis. *Daniel Deronda* published by Blackwood in 8 monthly parts, February–September. GHL a founder-member of the Physiological Society, March. Writes on 'Spiritualism and Materialism' in the *Fortnightly Review*, April and May. Visits the physiologist Michael Foster at Cambridge, November. GHL and GE buy The Heights at Witley as their summer home, near the Crosses in Weybridge, December.

1877   Wagner's London concerts, May. GHL and GE meet him and his wife Cosima, and also Princess Louise, Queen Victoria's daughter, at one of Wagner's rehearsals. GHL and GE at Witley, June–October. Elinor Southwood Lewes, third daughter of Charles and Gertrude, born 24 June. *The Physical Basis of Mind*, vol. 3 of *Problems*, published, July. GHL a candidate for the rectorship of St Andrew's University, November.

1878   GHL sits next to Henry James at a dinner given by John Cross, April. GHL's last article, 'On the Dread and Dislike of Science', published in the *Fortnightly Review*, June. GHL and GE at Witley, June–November. GHL too ill to work. GE writing *The Impressions of Theophrastus Such*. Return to The Priory 11 November. GHL's condition worsens rapidly. Dies of enteritis 30 November, aged 61. Buried in Highgate Cemetery after a Unitarian service 4 December.

1879   Trollope's appreciation of GHL published in the *Fortnightly Review*, January. GE gets help from Michael Foster and other scientists, including Huxley, in setting up a George Henry Lewes Studentship in physiology at Cambridge University, March–September. She changes her name legally to Marian Evans Lewes at this time. Eliza Lewes arrives with her two children from Natal, April. John Blackwood dies 29 October. GE sees *The Study of Psychology* and *Mind as a Function of the Organism*, the last two vols. of *Problems of Life and Mind*, through the press.

1880   GE marries John Cross, aged 40, 6 May. They return from their Italian honeymoon, July. Move to 4 Cheyne Walk, Chelsea, 3 December. GE dies suddenly of kidney failure 22 December, aged 61. Buried next to GHL in Highgate Cemetery 29 December.

1885   GHL's *Principles of Success in Literature* published for students of the University of California.

1889   Charles Lewes becomes a member of the first London County Council.

1891   Charles Lewes dies at Luxor 26 February, aged 48.

1896   GHL's 'Vivian' reviews reprinted from the *Leader* in *Dramatic Essays by John Forster and George Henry Lewes*, ed. William Archer and Robert Lowe.

1902   Agnes Lewes dies 22 December, aged 80.

BIBLIOGRAPHY

I. MANUSCRIPT SOURCES

The largest collection of GHL manuscripts is in the Beinecke Rare Book and Manuscript Library of Yale University. It includes originals or copies of all the surviving GHL and GE journals and diaries, a large number of letters from, to, and about GHL and GE, and a collection of GHL's articles and proofs together with reviews of his works.

The next largest collection of materials relating to GHL is in the National Library of Scotland, Edinburgh. GHL's letters to and from John Blackwood and his colleagues are in the Blackwood Papers; other GHL materials are to be found among the George Combe Papers, the W. & R. Chambers Papers, and the George Smith Papers.

Other libraries holding GHL manuscript material or material relating to GHL are

Armstrong Browning Library, Baylor University, Texas (Robert Browning MSS).
Bayerische Staatsbibliothek, Munich (MS GHL to J. W. Parker).
Bishopsgate Institute, London (Holyoake Papers).
Bodleian Library, Oxford (Bulwer-Lytton MSS).
Boston Public Library (MS GHL to Blackwood).
British Library (Charlotte Brontë MSS, Leigh Hunt MSS, Macvey Napier MSS, Plays from the Lord Chamberlain's Office, Royal Literary Fund MSS).
Brotherton Library, Leeds (Douglas Jerrold MSS).
Co-operative Union, Manchester (Holyoake Collection).
Folger Shakespeare Library, Washington (GHL's annotated collection of his early articles).
Girton College, Cambridge (Bessie Rayner Parkes Papers).
Harry Ransom Humanities Research Center, University of Texas at Austin (MSS GHL to R. H. Horne and F. O. Ward).
Henry E. Huntington Library, San Marino, California (GHL and GE MSS).
Hertford County Record Office (Lytton Collection).
Houghton Library, Harvard University (GHL and Henry James MSS).
Imperial College, London (Huxley Collection).
Iowa University Library (MSS GHL to R. H. Horne).
Jagiellonian University Library, Cracow (Varnhagen Collection).
John Murray Archives, London (George Smith Papers).
Keats Memorial House, Hampstead, London (MS GHL to Leigh Hunt).

Kestner-Museum, Hanover (MS GHL to Duncker).

London Library (Shirley Brooks Diary, London Library ledger).

London University Library (Herbert Spencer Papers).

New York Public Library (MSS GHL to Hickson, Berg Collection; MSS Thornton Hunt and Egerton Webbe, Carl H. Pforzheimer Collection).

Pierpont Morgan Library, New York (MSS George Sand to GHL, GHL to John Kemble).

Princeton University Library (MSS GHL to W. B. Scott; Mathews Family Papers in William Seymour Theater Collection).

Punch Library, London (Henry Silver Diary).

Royal Institution of Great Britain, London (Tyndall Collection).

University of California at Los Angeles Library (MSS Lady Blessington to GHL and GHL to Benjamin Webster).

University College London Library (Chadwick Papers, G. C. Robertson Papers, Sully Collection, SDUK Papers).

Victoria and Albert Museum, London (Forster Collection).

Wellcome Institute for the History of Medicine, London (Arnott MSS).

Dr Williams's Library, London (GHL's library).

Yale Medical Library, Yale University (MS Douglas Jerrold).

2. BOOKS AND ARTICLES

ABBOTT, E. and CAMPBELL, L., *The Life and Letters of Benjamin Jowett*, 2 vols. (London, 1897).

ACTON, LORD, 'George Eliot's "Life"', *Nineteenth Century*, 17 (Mar. 1885).

ALLOTT, MIRIAM, *The Brontës: The Critical Heritage* (London, 1974).

ANDERSON, R. F., 'Negotiating for *The Mill on the Floss*', *Publishing History*, 2 (1977).

—— '"Things Wisely Ordered": John Blackwood, George Eliot, and the Publication of *Romola*', *Publishing History*, 11 (1982).

APPLETON, WILLIAM W., *Madame Vestris and the London Stage* (New York, 1974).

ARCHER, WILLIAM and LOWE, ROBERT W. (eds.), *Dramatic Essays by John Forster and George Henry Lewes* (London, 1896).

ARNOLD, MATTHEW, *Letters of Matthew Arnold 1848–1888*, ed. George W. E. Russell, 2 vols. (London, 1895).

ASHTON, ROSEMARY, *The German Idea: Four English Writers and the Reception of German Thought 1800–1860* (Cambridge, 1980).

—— *Little Germany: Exile and Asylum in Victorian England* (Oxford, 1986).

—— *The Mill on the Floss: A Natural History* (Boston, Mass., 1990).

—— (ed.) *Versatile Victorian: Selected Critical Writings of G. H. Lewes* (Bristol, 1991).

BAKER, WILLIAM, *The George Eliot–George Henry Lewes Library: An Annotated Catalogue of their Books at Dr William's Library, London* (London, 1977).

BAKER, WILLIAM, 'G. H. Lewes and the *Penny Cyclopaedia*: 27 Unattributed Articles', *Victorian Periodicals Newsletter*, 7 (Sept. 1974).

BAYNES, THOMAS, 'An Evening with Carlyle', *Athenaeum* (2 Apr. 1887).

BELLOC, BESSIE RAYNER PARKES, *In a Walled Garden* (London, 1895, repr. 1900).

BEST, GEOFFREY, *Mid-Victorian Britain 1851–75* (London, 1971, repr. 1989).

BIBBY, CYRIL, *Scientist Extraordinary: The Life and Scientific Work of T. H. Huxley (1825–1895)* (Oxford, 1972).

A Biographical Dictionary of Actors, Actresses, Musicians, Dancers, Managers and Other Stage Personnel in London, 1660–1800, ed. P. H. Highfill Jun., Kalman A. Burnim, and Edward A. Langhans, 12 vols. so far (Carbondale, Ill., 1973–).

BLAINEY, ANN, *The Farthing Poet: A Biography of Richard Hengist Horne 1802–84* (London, 1968).

BLOUNT, TREVOR, 'Dickens and Mr Krook's Spontaneous Combustion', *Dickens Studies Annual*, 1 (1970).

BOUCICAULT, DION, *London Assurance*, ed. James L. Smith (London, 1984).

BRICK, ALAN R., '*The Leader*: Organ of Radicalism', PhD thesis (Yale University, 1958).

The Brontës: Their Lives, Friendships and Correspondence, ed. T. J. Wise and J. A. Symington, 4 vols. (Oxford, 1932).

BROWNING, OSCAR, *The Life of George Eliot* (London, 1890).

CARLYLE, JANE WELSH, *Letters to her Family, 1839–1863*, ed. Leonard Huxley (London, 1924).

—— *Letters and Memorials of Jane Welsh Carlyle*, ed. J. A. Froude, 3 vols. (London, 1883).

—— *New Letters and Memorials of Jane Welsh Carlyle*, ed. Alexander Carlyle, 2 vols. (London, 1903).

CARLYLE, THOMAS, *Latter-Day Pamphlets* (London, 1850, repr. with an introd. by M. K. Goldberg and J. P. Seigel, Canadian Federation for the Humanities, 1983).

—— *The Collected Letters of Thomas and Jane Welsh Carlyle*, ed. C. R. Sanders and K. J. Fielding, 18 vols. so far (Durham, NC, 1970–).

—— *The French Revolution*, 2 vols. (London, 1837, repr. 1888).

—— *New Letters of Thomas Carlyle*, ed. Alexander Carlyle, 2 vols. (London, 1904).

—— *Past and Present* (London, 1843).

COLEMAN, JOHN, *Players and Playwrights I Have Known*, 2 vols. (London, 1888).

COLLINS, K. K., 'G. H. Lewes Revised: George Eliot and the Moral Sense', *Victorian Studies*, 21 (1978).

COMTE, AUGUSTE, *Correspondance générale et confessions*, ed. Paulo E. Berrêdo Carneiro and Pierre Arnaud, 7 vols. so far (Paris, 1973–).

CROSS, J. W., *George Eliot's Life as Related in her Letters and Journals*, 3 vols. (Edinburgh and London, 1885).

DARWIN, CHARLES, *The Life and Letters of Charles Darwin*, ed. Francis Darwin, 3 vols. (London, 1888).

—— *On the Origin of Species by Means of Natural Selection, or the Preservation of Favoured Races in the Struggle for Life* (London, 1859, repr. Harmondsworth, 1984).

DAVIES, JAMES A., *John Forster: A Literary Life* (Leicester, 1983).

DENMAN, PETER, 'Krook's Death and Dickens's Authorities', *The Dickensian*, 83 (1987).

DESMOND, ADRIAN, *Archetypes and Ancestors: Palaeontology in Victorian London 1850–1875* (London, 1982).

DEXTER, WALTER, 'For One Night Only: Dickens's Appearances as an Amateur Actor', *The Dickensian*, 36 (1940).

DICKENS, CHARLES, *Bleak House* (London, 1853, repr. Harmondsworth, 1987).

—— *The Letters of Charles Dickens*, ed. Walter Dexter, 3 vols. (London, 1938).

—— *Letters of Charles Dickens*, Pilgrim Edition, ed. Madeleine House, Graham Storey *et al.*, 6 vols. so far (Oxford, 1965–).

—— *A Tale of Two Cities* (London, 1859, repr. Harmondsworth, 1970).

DOREMUS, ROBERT B., 'George Henry Lewes: A Descriptive Biography, with Especial Attention to his Interest in the Theatre', 2 vols., PhD thesis (Harvard University, 1940).

DUFFY, SIR CHARLES GAVAN, *Conversations with Carlyle* (London, 1892).

DUNN, WALDO HILARY, *James Anthony Froude: A Biography*, 2 vols. (Oxford, 1961, 1963).

EDEL, LEON, *The Life of Henry James*, 5 vols. (London, 1953–72).

ELIOT, GEORGE, *Essays of George Eliot*, ed. Thomas Pinney (London, 1963).

—— *The George Eliot Letters*, ed. Gordon S. Haight, 9 vols. (New Haven, Conn., 1954–6, 1978).

—— (trans.) Spinoza's *Ethics*, ed. Thomas Deegan (Salzburg, 1981).

ESPINASSE, FRANCIS, *Literary Recollections and Sketches* (London, 1893).

FORRESTER, J. M., 'Who Put the George in George Eliot?' *British Medical Journal* (17 Jan. 1970).

FORSTER, JOHN, *The Life of Charles Dickens*, 3 vols. (London, 1872–4).

FROUDE, JAMES ANTHONY, *The Nemesis of Faith* (London, 1849, repr. 1988).

GARY, FRANKLIN, 'Charlotte Brontë and George Henry Lewes', *PMLA*, 51 (1936).

GASKELL, E., 'More About Spontaneous Combustion', *The Dickensian*, 69 (1973).

GASKELL, ELIZABETH, *The Letters of Mrs Gaskell*, ed. J. A. V. Chapple and Arthur Pollard (Manchester, 1966).

—— *The Life of Charlotte Brontë* (London, 1857, repr. 1984).

GLOVER, HALCOTT, *Both Sides of the Blanket* (London, 1945).

GLYNN, JENNIFER, *Prince of Publishers: A Biography of the Great Victorian Publisher George Smith* (London, 1986).

GOODWAY, DAVID, *London Chartism 1838–1848* (Cambridge, 1982).

GREGORIO, MARIO A. DI, *T. H. Huxley's Place in Natural Science* (New Haven, Conn., 1984).

HAIGHT, GORDON S., 'Dickens and Lewes on Spontaneous Combustion', *Nineteenth Century Fiction*, 10 (1955–6).

—— 'Dickens and Lewes', *PMLA*, *71 (1956)*.

—— *George Eliot: A Biography* (Oxford 1968, repr. 1969).

—— *George Eliot and John Chapman* (New Haven, Conn., 1940, repr. 1969).

HELPS, ARTHUR, *The Correspondence of Sir Arthur Helps*, ed. E. A. Helps (London, 1917).

HOLLINGSHEAD, JOHN, *My Lifetime*, 2 vols. (London, 1895).

HOLYOAKE, GEORGE JACOB, *Bygones Worth Remembering*, 2 vols. (London, 1905).

—— *Sixty Years of an Agitator's Life*, 2 vols. (London, 1892).

HOPKIN, JOHN, 'George Henry Lewes as Playwright: A Register of Pieces', in *Essays on Nineteenth Century British Theatre*, ed. Kenneth Richards and Peter Thomson (London, 1971).

HOWE, SUSANNE, *Geraldine Jewsbury: Her Life and Errors* (London, 1935).

HUNT, LEIGH, *Autobiography*, 3 vols. (London, 1850).

[HUXLEY, LEONARD], *The House of Smith Elder* (privately printed, London, 1923).

IRVINE, WILLIAM, *Apes, Angels and Victorians: A Joint Biography of Darwin and Huxley* (London, 1955).

JAMES, HENRY, *Autobiography*, ed. Frederick W. Dupee (London, 1956).

—— *Henry James Letters*, ed. Leon Edel, 4 vols. (London, 1974–84).

JERROLD, BLANCHARD, *The Life and Remains of Douglas Jerrold* (London, 1859).

JEWSBURY, GERALDINE, *Selections from the Letters of G. E. Jewsbury to Jane Welsh Carlyle*, ed. Mrs Alexander Ireland (London, 1892).

JOHNSON, EDGAR, *Charles Dickens: His Tragedy and Triumph*, 2 vols. (London, 1953).

KAMINSKY, ALICE R. (ed.), *The Literary Criticism of George Henry Lewes* (University of Nebraska, 1964).

—— *George Henry Lewes as Literary Critic* (New York, 1968).

KAMINSKY, JACK, 'The Empirical Metaphysics of George Henry Lewes', *Journal of the History of Ideas*, 13 (1952).

KAPLAN, FRED, 'Carlyle's Marginalia and George Henry Lewes's Fiction', *Carlyle Newsletter*, 5 (1984).

—— '"Phallus-Worship" (1848): Unpublished Manuscripts III—A Response to the Revolution of 1848', *Carlyle Newsletter*, 2 (1980).

—— *Thomas Carlyle: A Biography* (Ithaca, NY, 1983).

KENNEDY, SISTER JEAN DE CHANTAL, *Frith of Bermuda: Gentleman Privateer; a Biography of Hezekiah Frith 1763–1848* (Hamilton, Bermuda, 1964).

KILHAM, ALEXANDER, *The Hypocrite detected and exposed; and the True Christian vindicated and supported* (Aberdeen, 1794).

KITCHEL, ANNA T., *George Lewes and George Eliot: A Review of Records* (New York, 1933).

LAWRENCE, W. J., *Barry Sullivan: A Biographical Sketch* (London, 1893).

LEWES, CHARLES LEE (senior), *Comic Sketches; or, the Comedian his Own Manager* (London, 1804).

—— *Memoirs of Charles Lee Lewes*, ed. John Lee Lewes, 4 vols. (London, 1805).

LEWES, GEORGE HENRY, *On Actors and the Art of Acting* (London, 1875, repr. 1970).

—— *A Biographical History of Philosophy*, 4 vols. in 2 (London, 1845–6, rev. and repr. 1857, 1867, 1871. Edn. of 1857 repr. 1970).

—— *The Life and Works of Goethe*, 2 vols. (London, 1855).

—— *The Noble Heart*, a tragedy in 3 acts, as performed at the Royal Olympic Theatre (London, 1850).

—— *The Physiology of Common Life*, 2 vols. (London, 1859–60).

—— *Problems of Life and Mind*, 5 vols. (London, 1874–9).

—— *Ranthorpe* (London, 1847, repr. with introd. by Barbara Smalley, Athens, Ohio, 1974).

—— *Rose, Blanche, and Violet*, 3 vols. in 1 (London, 1848).

—— *Sea-Side Studies at Ilfracombe, Tenby, the Scilly Isles, and Jersey* (London, 1858).

—— *The Spanish Drama. Lope de Vega and Calderon* (London, 1846).

—— *Studies in Animal Life* (London, 1862).

LEWES, JOHN LEE, *National Melodies, and Other Poems* (London, 1817).

—— *Poems* (Liverpool, 1811).

LOCKER-LAMPSON, FREDERICK, *My Confidences* (London, 1896).

LOWNDES, MARIE BELLOC, *I, Too, Have Lived in Arcadia* (London, 1941).

—— *Diaries and Letters of Marie Belloc Lowndes 1911–1947*, ed. Susan Lowndes (London, 1971).

LUTYENS, LADY EMILY, *The Birth of Rowland: An Exchange of Letters in 1865 between Robert Lytton and his Wife* (London, 1956).

LYNN, ELIZA (later Linton), *The Autobiography of Christopher Kirkland*, 3 vols. (London, 1885)

—— *Realities, a Tale*, 3 vols. in 1 (London, 1851).

LYTTON, ROBERT, *Personal and Literary Letters of Robert First Earl of Lytton*, ed. Betty Balfour, 2 vols. (London, 1906).

LYTTON, VICTOR A. G. R., *The Life of Edward Bulwer, First Lord Lytton*, 2 vols. (London, 1913).

MARSTON, JOHN WESTLAND, *Our Recent Actors: Being Recollections Critical, and, in Many Cases, Personal, of Late Distinguished Performers of Both Sexes*, 2 vols. (London, 1888).

MARTINEAU, HARRIET, *Autobiography*, 2 vols. (London, 1877, repr. 1983).

MAZZINI, GIUSEPPE, *Mazzini's Letters to an English Family*, ed. E. F. Richards, 3 vols. (London, 1920–2).

MEREDITH, GEORGE, *The Letters of George Meredith*, ed. C. L. Clive, 3 vols. (Oxford, 1970).

MICHELET, JULES, *Journal*, ed. Paul Viallaneix, 2 vols. (Paris, 1959, 1962).

MILL, JOHN STUART, *The Collected Works of John Stuart Mill*, ed. F. E. L. Priestley *et al.*, 25 vols. (Toronto, 1963–86).

MORAN, BENJAMIN, *The Journal of Benjamin Moran*, ed. S. A. Wallace and F. E. Gillespie, 2 vols. (Chicago, Ill., 1948).

MORLEY, JOHN, VISCOUNT, *Recollections*, 2 vols. (London, 1917).

NAPIER, MACVEY, *Selection from the Correspondence of the Late Macvey Napier*, ed. (his son) Macvey Napier (London, 1879).

NORTON, CHARLES ELIOT, *Letters of Charles Eliot Norton*, ed. Sara Norton and M. A. De Wolfe Howe, 2 vols. (London, 1913).

OLIPHANT, MARGARET, *The Autobiography and Letters of Mrs M. O. W. Oliphant*, ed. Mrs Harry Coghill (Edinburgh and London, 1899).

OSSOLI, MARGARET FULLER, *Memoirs of Margaret Fuller Ossoli*, ed. R. W. Emerson and W. E. Channing, 3 vols. (London, 1852).

PARTRIDGE, ERIC, *A Dictionary of Slang and Unconventional English*, 8th Edn. (London, 1984).

PAVLOV, IVAN PETROVITCH, *Lectures on Conditioned Reflexes*, trans. and ed. W. Horsley Gantt, 2 vols. (London, 1928, 1941, repr. 1963).

PICKETT, T. H., 'George Henry Lewes's Letters to K. A. Varnhagen von Ense', *Modern Language Review*, 80 (July 1985).

PORTER, BERNARD, *The Refugee Question in Mid-Victorian Politics* (Cambridge, 1979).

POSTLETHWAITE, DIANA, *Making It Whole: A Victorian Circle and the Shape of Their World* (Columbus, Ohio, 1984).

ROSS, D. L., 'A Survey of Some Aspects of the Life and Work of Sir Richard Owen, K.C.B. (1825–1895)', PhD thesis (London University, 1972).

ROSSETTI, CHRISTINA, *The Family Letters of C. G. Rossetti*, ed. W. M. Rossetti (London, 1908).

ROSSETTI, DANTE GABRIEL, *Letters of Dante Gabriel Rossetti*, ed. Oswald Doughty and John Robert Wahl, 4 vols. (Oxford, 1965–7).

—— *Dante Gabriel Rossetti and Jane Morris: Their Correspondence*, ed. John Bryson and Janet Camp Troxell (Oxford, 1976).

SADLEIR, MICHAEL, *Bulwer: A Panorama* (London, 1931).

SAND, GEORGE, *Correspondance*, ed. Georges Lubin, 19 vols. so far (Paris, 1964–   ).

SANDERS, C. R., *Carlyle's Friendships and other Studies* (Durham, NC, 1977).

SCOTT, J. W. ROBERTSON, *The Story of the 'Pall Mall Gazette'* (London, 1950).

SCOTT, WILLIAM BELL, *Autobiographical Notes*, ed. W. Minto, 2 vols. (London, 1892).

SHAW, GEORGE BERNARD, *Our Theatres in the Nineties*, 3 vols. (London, 1932).

SHELLEY, MARY, *The Letters of Mary Wollstonecraft Shelley*, ed. Betty T. Bennett, 2 vols. so far (Baltimore, Md., 1980–   ).

—— *Letters of Mary W. Shelley*, ed. Frederick L. Jones, 2 vols. (Norman, Okla., 1944).

SIMON, W. M., *European Positivism in the 19th Century: An Essay in Intellectual History* (Ithaca, NY, 1963).

SMITH, F. B., *Radical Artisan: W. J. Linton 1812–1897* (Manchester, 1973).

SPENCER, HERBERT, *An Autobiography*, 2 vols. (London, 1904).

STEPHENS, JOHN RUSSELL, *The Censorship of English Drama 1824–1901* (Cambridge, 1980).

SULLY, JAMES, 'George Henry Lewes', *New Quarterly Magazine*, 2 NS (Oct. 1879).

SUTHERLAND, J. A., *Victorian Novelists and Publishers* (London, 1976).

TATCHELL, MOLLY, *Leigh Hunt and his Family in Hammersmith* (London, 1969).

THACKERAY, W. M., *Letters and Private Papers of W. M. Thackeray*, ed. Gordon N. Ray, 4 vols. (London, 1945–6).

—— *Vanity Fair* (London, 1848, repr. Harmondsworth, 1968).

THOMAS, WILLIAM, *The Philosophical Radicals* (Oxford, 1979).

THOMPSON, E. P., and YEO, EILEEN (eds.) *The Unknown Mayhew: Selections from the Morning Chronicle 1849–1850* (London, 1984).

THOMSON, PATRICIA, *George Sand and the Victorians: Her Influence and Reputation in Nineteenth-century England* (London, 1977).

TJOA, HOCK GUAN, *George Henry Lewes: A Victorian Mind* (Cambridge, Mass., 1977).

TROLLOPE, ANTHONY, *An Autobiography*, 2 vols. (Edinburgh and London, 1883).

—— 'George Henry Lewes', *Fortnightly Review*, 25 NS (January 1879).

—— *The Letters of Anthony Trollope*, ed. N. John Hall, 2 vols. (Stanford, Calif, 1983).

TROLLOPE, THOMAS ADOLPHUS, *What I Remember*, 2 vols. (London, 1887).

VARNHAGEN VON ENSE, KARL AUGUST, *Aus dem Nachlass Varnhagen's von Ense, Tagebücher*, ed. Ludmilla Assing, 15 vols. (Leipzig, 1861–70, Berlin, 1905).

Vivisection in Historical Perspective, ed. Nicholaas A. Rupke (London, 1987).

VIZETELLY, HENRY, *Glances Back through Seventy Years*, 2 vols. (London, 1893).

WEBB, R. K., *Harriet Martineau: A Radical Victorian* (London, 1960).

WEISS, BARBARA, *The Hell of the English: Bankruptcy and the Victorian Novel* (London and Toronto, 1986).

[WHITE, WILLIAM HALE], *The Autobiography of Mark Rutherford* (London, 1881, repr. Leicester, 1969).

WHITTY, E. M., *Friends of Bohemia: or, Phases of London Life*, 2 vols. (London, 1857).

Who's Who of British Members of Parliament, ed. M. Stenton and S. Lees, 4 vols. (Hassocks, Sussex, 1976–81).

WILKINSON, HENRY C., *Bermuda from Sail to Steam: The History of the Island from 1784 to 1901*, 2 vols. (London, 1973).

WILLIAMS, DAVID, *Mr George Eliot: A Biography of George Henry Lewes* (London, 1983).

WRIGHT, T. R., *The Religion of Humanity: The Impact of Comtean Positivism on Victorian Britain* (Cambridge, 1986).

YATES, EDMUND, *Recollections and Experiences*, 2 vols. (London, 1884).

INDEX